THE 3rd UNDERGROUND SHOPPER®

THE **3**rd UNDERGROUND SHOPPER®

New Guide to
Discount Mail-Order Shopping

Sue Goldstein

Andrews, McMeel & Parker
A Universal Press Syndicate Affiliate
Kansas City • New York

Library of Congress Cataloging-in-Publication Data

Goldstein, Sue, 1941–
    The 3rd underground shopper.

    Includes indexes.
    1. Mail-order business—United States—Directories.
2. Mail-order business—Directories.   3. Discount
houses (Retail trade)—United States—Directories.
4. Discount houses (Retail trade)—Directories.
I. Title
HF5466.G6   1986   381'.1   86-28758
ISBN 0-8362-7937-9

To Josh, who didn't have to go shopping to find
his greatest gift of all . . . courage.

ACKNOWLEDGMENTS

Three strikes and we're *never* out of resources. In fact, we've just begun.

Bargains supposedly exist only in the eye of the beholder. Someone's trash inevitably becomes someone else's treasure. Bargains—*and* treasure hunting—always seem to balance out, like the $2.00 Anne Klein slacks that I was so proud of until I realized I just *had* to have the $38 matching blouse one frantic Saturday night . . . and paid retail!

So you see that even the best of shoppers go astray when time is of the essence.

If you've got the time and the money, you have my permission to buy your whole wardrobe, home, and office at retail. Pay! But if you'd rather take a few days to luxuriate your way through some of the best merchandise in the world at the *very* best prices, then, as they say, have I got a deal for you! No need to leave home the Shopper's way. After all, we offer 24-hour-a-day, seven-day-a-week convenience. Charge it all and have it delivered to your front door. *And* save 50% off in the bargain! That's what this book is all about.

And as our third edition strikes new terror in the hearts of many full-price retailers (as well as taking a healthy bite out of their bottom lines . . .), shed no tears. You'd never believe how many of them appear in the audiences at my speeches, notebooks in hand! Readers of *The Underground Shopper* never need to take notes, thank you. We go back a long way and I'll always share my best-buy secrets with you.

This year brought major changes to our lives. First and foremost, we moved our offices—and my home—to the lake. Creative juices now flow as we sit at typewriters overlooking a forest of trees and take morning runs and aerobic exercise breaks along the shore. My cats and Silkie Terrier, Nosh, nestle into every nook and cranny not occupied by letters from happy readers of the first two editions. All things considered, with the chaos of moving finally out of the way, it's the best decision I ever made.

Wendy Dunn returned home at last. Her mouth moves mountains and she is responsible for bringing her publicity prowess back where it belongs. She's the best in the business and, besides, I love her. Tina and Adam, too.

Special thanks are due to Barbara, who cleans all the messes and never misses a beat; to Rebel, who helps me avoid messes in the first place, thanks from the bottom of my heart; to Rebecca Huffstetler, who finely tuned the tons of new information, facts, figures, and phone numbers for this latest edition. And to Susan Von Flatern, Joy Eckertson, and Paula Berklund who called, culled, and colored many of the mail-order write-ups, my appreciation; to my dad, who sculpts out his love for life with finely tuned words of wisdom, and in whose heart it's good to know I'm etched forever; to Karen, who's in a class by herself, my thanks for her talent, her words, and her dedication to excellence. . . .

. . . And to the first man in my life who has proved to me that unswerving loyalty and love really exist, and never once told me to change in spite of the imperfections: this book is dedicated to Klaus, the first-quality, four-star European import I promise to love with an unconditional guarantee forever.

SUE GOLDSTEIN

CONTENTS

INTRODUCTION 1
TWELVE QUESTIONS ABOUT MAIL-ORDER 5
SYMBOLS KEY 13
Apparel:
      Children's 17
      Family 20
      Men's 34
      Women's 45
Appliances and TVs 59
Art and Collectibles 68
Art Supplies 77
Bed and Bath 83
Boating Supplies 90
Cameras, Opticals, and Photographic Equipment 95
Carpets and Rugs 107
Cars and Auto Supplies 109
Catalog Showrooms 117
China, Crystal, and Silver 119
Computers and Electronics 135
Cosmetics and Beauty Aids 141
Fabrics 152
Fitness and Health 167
Food 184
Freebies 199
Furniture and Accessories 210
Handbags and Luggage 231
Hard-to-Find and Unique Items 237

Hardware and Tools   245
Hobbies and Crafts   255
Housewares   270
Investments   280
Jewelry   288
Kits and Kaboodle (Do-It-Yourself)   299
Medical Products and Supplies   317
Musical Instruments   325
Novelties   334
Office Supplies   344
Pet and Ranch Animals   358
Plants, Flowers, Gardens, and Farming   364
Records and Tapes   378
Shoes   384
Sporting Goods   392
Stereo and Video   412
Surplus and Volume Sales   419
Telephone Services   427
Tobacco   431
Toys   435
Travel   439
Windows and Walls   452
NATIONAL CHAINS:
        YOUR HOMETOWN LINK TO SAVINGS   461
SALES-BY-MAIL   499
CONSUMER "TOLL FREE" NUMBERS   501
COMPANY INDEX   503
CATEGORY INDEX   517
READER'S FEEDBACK   531

INTRODUCTION

Remember the fun you had reading *Through the Looking Glass* when you were a kid? It's probably been a long time since you imagined yourself walking through a wonderland—unless you're a mail-order shopper!

Today's mail-order catalogs with their glossy pages, stunning photography, and alluring copy are contemporary looking glasses into a wonderland of modern living. You'll find thousands of things to add sparkle and zest to your life. Thumbing through a modern-day wishbook brings out the child in all of us; it's our boarding pass to a flight of fantasy. A well-designed catalog is like a springboard that lets you dive into a pool of possibilities and splash into a newer, brighter world of imagination.

Speaking of another world, price-quote firms, while not as glamorous or well-known as catalog companies, have some out-of-this-world discounts. Cost-conscious consumers with the shopping smarts to check out *all* the alternatives, including price-quote firms, can find savings of several hundred dollars on a major purchase. Savings like that are no idle fantasy; they're real and really fantastic! Price-quote firms often offer unsurpassed savings on large, functional items like appliances, furniture, and stereos, among other things. These companies don't provide you with a classy catalog—at best you'll get a flier listing the lines they carry. It's up to you to decide what you want—learn the manufacturer, model number, and other descriptive details—write or call to get a price quoted to you. If you like the price quoted, go ahead and order. It's that simple.

Direct marketing makes a lot of sense for today's consumers. It's cost-efficient and *convenient*. There are savings in time and gas, no wear and tear on your car, and best of all, no wear and tear on your nerves from battling crowds or locking horns with pushy sales-people. Some of the larger direct marketing companies even have 24-hour toll-free hot lines so you can order anytime, day or night. And don't forget, you don't pay sales tax when you buy out-of-state.

Many mail-order firms have excellent prices. Direct marketing companies avoid the overhead expense of maintaining retail store-fronts and they usually don't have a large number of employees, so payroll expenses are kept down. The bottom line is that it usually costs less to sell by mail, so even by charging lower prices they still make a profit. That's good for consumers who come out ahead.

When you stop to think that the corresponding disadvantages are only a small shipping charge, a delay of from one to a few weeks (except in the case of some larger items like furniture which can have much longer delays), and occasionally the price of a phone call (if you phone in your order rather than write), shopping direct offers big benefits. You get more than just convenience, you get savings. It's no wonder the popularity of mail-order shopping is at an all-time high and that direct marketing is being hailed as the wave of the future.

If there was ever any doubt about the popularity of mail-order shopping, it was dispelled by the first edition of this book. First pub-lished in April 1983, by July 1983 it was in its third printing and by the end of the summer *The Underground Shopper: A Guide to Discount Mail-Order Shopping* had sold over 100,000 copies. That meant our lowly book on discount mail-order shopping had sales placing it in the top 1½% of all books published!

There clearly was a market: people wanted to know about mail-order companies with superior buys. To readers, our book was an investment that paid off in savings (handsomely, we might add!); to the companies we listed, our book brought well-deserved recognition and increased sales; and to us, our book brought both psychic and monetary rewards. In short, there were no losers, only winners.

You might wonder how we went about deciding which companies to include and which to exclude. What criteria did we use and how did we research our book? Because this is a third edition, things were a little easier for us. We telephoned all the companies listed in our previous edition (with the exception of foreign firms) during Sep-tember and October of 1986 to reverify all information (particularly addresses and telephone numbers) and to get whatever new informa-tion we could. We collected new catalogs, new fliers, and new bro-chures, and even checked prices for comparison. We carefully reviewed our Reader Response files and companies that were the object of complaints were red-flagged; some new companies recom-mended to us by our readers or that we uncovered on our own were added.

(For all of you who are skeptical about mail-order shopping, out of the over 750 companies listed in our first edition and tested both by our staff and by our readers, we received only a handful of serious complaints. Even better news is that these problems were quickly resolved when we intervened. The most common complaint was a delay in getting a catalog.)

When we finished our data gathering, we added this new research to the information we already had on file (such as questionnaires filled out by company personnel; newspaper and magazine articles; and catalogs, brochures, and fliers). We then revised our earlier write-ups to include all the new information we thought would be useful to our readers.

Overall, we've expanded and revised our earlier edition, and made a number of changes suggested by readers, from reorganizing the Contents to noting the different types of payment accepted by each company. We've dropped about 100 listings and we've added almost 200. The vast majority of our listings were dropped not because they went out of business, but because they asked not to be listed; they could not or would not respond to our request for information; or because we simply uncovered other, *better* companies with lower prices. Very, very few of the companies listed in our first or second edition went out of business, a tribute both to the viability of mail-order shopping and to our own strict standards for evaluating companies.

To sum it all up, in this, our third edition, we've tried to make meaningful rather than cosmetic changes and to incorporate as many reader suggestions as possible. We've tried not just to put out another book, but a *better* book. This is it—we hope you like it.

Happy shopping!

TWELVE QUESTIONS ABOUT MAIL-ORDER

1. When ordering apparel, how can I be sure I get the right size?

You may be a perfect "10" in most clothing, but each manufacturer cuts its garments differently. There's always the chance the clothes you order might not fit. That's why it is smart to send your measurements. Then, if there is any variation in clothing size due to fabric, style, or cut, whoever is filling your order can double-check your measurements with their clothing sizes. It's a way of reducing the chance you'll get something that doesn't fit.

Here are some tips about taking your own measurements that we found in the Land's End catalog:

- Shirts—Neck: Pick a shirt with a collar that fits well. Lay the collar flat and measure from the center of the button to the far end of the button hole. The number of inches is your neck size. Sleeve: Bend elbow, measure from center of neck to elbow and down to wrist. The number of inches is your sleeve length.
- Chest or bust—Measure around the fullest part of chest, keeping tape up under arms and around (not below) your shoulder blades. Size equals the number of inches.
- Waist—Measure around waist and over shirt, but not over slacks or skirt. Measure at the height you normally wear your slacks or skirt. Keep one finger between your body and the tape. The number of inches equals your size.
- Seat and hips—Stand with your heels together and measure yourself around the area of greatest circumference.
- Inseam—Choose a pair of pants that fits you well. Measure from the crotch seam to the bottom of the pants. The number of inches (to the nearest half-inch) gives you the inseam length.

2. I've never shopped by mail. How do I get started?

A good place to start is with this book. Read through the sections that interest you and mark the companies that sound good to you. You'll be able to tell from the write-up how the company is set up to do business. For example, we've coded the listings in this book so you'll know if a company has a catalog (C), a brochure (B), a flier (F), or whether they just give price quotes (PQ). When you write or call a company for the first time, either to ask a question or to request a catalog, be sure to mention that you read about it in *The Underground Shopper*.

The next step is to read the literature you receive very carefully. Make sure everything is clear to you. Read product descriptions like size, weight, color, and contents very carefully; check the order form closely. Understanding the return policy is particularly important, since you'll want to know what your rights are if a problem develops. Type or print (legibly) all the relevant information like code numbers, etc., on the order form, and (optional) specify substitutions or second choices (if you're flexible). Observe minimum order requirements—many companies can only offer a discount on quantity purchases.

In filling out the order form and adding up the total, don't forget to include the shipping or other charges indicated on the order blank. Always request insurance if it's not already provided. Include sales tax when applicable. (You only have to pay sales tax if you live in the state where the mail-order company is located or where they have retail outlets, as the order form should explain.)

When ordering, either use a credit card number or enclose a check. Many companies won't ship your order until after your personal check has cleared the bank (meaning a delay of two to three weeks), so credit card orders are faster. Money orders and cashier's checks are readily accepted and will speed the processing of your order. *Never send cash!* If you send cash and your money "disappears" and you don't receive your order, you have no proof that you paid.

Whether you order by phone or by mail, be sure to keep complete, accurate records. Note the date the order was placed and the name of the order-taker, keep your receipts, etc. When you ask for a price quote, send a business-size SASE (self-addressed, stamped envelope), and you'll get your order faster.

3. What's a price quote, and how do I get one?

Many of the companies listed in our book have access to thousands of products from electric toothbrushes to talking bathroom scales. If one of these companies created a catalog, it would be the size of the Yellow Pages. Rather than try to publish a series of massive volumes and then continually update them, these companies have chosen a less expensive way to operate: quoting prices to people who call or write.

The price quote system is an extremely cost-efficient way to let you know: a) that the item is available and b) what the current (discounted) price is. Don't be afraid of price quotes—the system is simple. Just write or call and give the specifics of the item you're interested in (model number, style number, etc.), and wait to see if they have what you want, and how much they're selling it for.

Here's an example of how the price quote system works. Suppose you want to buy some Christian Dior panties that normally cost $7 a pair in a department store. After finding the stores in our book that sell lingerie, you'd write each one a letter. The letter might sound something like this: "Dear Sir, Do you have CHRISTIAN DIOR (manufacturer) INTIMATES (model) #82500 (style) size 6 (size) panties (item) in beige (color)? If so, what's the cost per pair, per six, and per dozen?" (Because clerks in these businesses are usually pressed for time, we suggest you ask about no more than three items.) Also ask: "How much is the shipping cost and how fast will they be shipped?" Remember to include a large, self-addressed, stamped envelope with your letter. You'll get an answer sooner and you'll know the letter they send back to you is properly addressed.

4. My porcelain heart is broken. Can I return it?

Maybe. The first thing to remember is *never* send anything back without first writing the company and okaying a return with them. Wait for their answer before you do anything. It's all right to telephone, but if you do, write down the name of the person who authorized the return and record his instructions to you. Some companies will pay the return postage; most won't.

It's always wise to ask for the return policies if they aren't spelled out in the catalog. (They should be.) Save the original packaging if you think there's a chance you'll return something.

5. Can you tell me what a restocking charge is? I've seen this mentioned in some catalogs I have.

Glad you asked. Restocking charges are definitely worth knowing about: they can be as much as 25% of an order in some cases. A restocking charge is a labor fee charged by a company when it has to take back an item it's shipped to you. Restocking fees aren't charged in the case of items that have been damaged in transit, but if you decide to send back something you've ordered because you've changed your mind or your purchase just wasn't right after all, you may have to pay. That increases your risk because there's a penalty involved if you don't like the merchandise you've ordered. If, for instance, you buy a $1,000 sofa from a furniture company that has a 25% restocking charge and then you decide to send the sofa back, you'll be out $250. That's why, when it comes to companies with restocking charges, you'd better be sure what you buy is what you want. Mistakes can be expensive.

Restocking fees are usually charged only by companies selling larger and more expensive items such as furniture and stereos.

6. I want to get a price quote. Where do I find the manufacturer, model, and style number of the item I want?

Catalogs usually include this information in their write-ups, but you may not have a catalog with the item you want. If you can find the item in a store, check the price tag. Price tags often have the model number (although sometimes it's coded). Some people just ask the salesperson for this information, but if you're going to turn around and order the item from somewhere else, that's a pretty shabby way to treat a store. Another alternative is to send an ad or photograph clipped from a magazine and hope someone can figure out what you want.

7. Can you explain the 30-day mail-order rule to me? I've heard about it but I don't know what it is.

Six to eight weeks is as long as you should have to wait to receive your order under normal conditions and many companies deliver your order much faster than that. According to the FTC 30-day mail-order rule, companies are required by law to either a) ship your goods within 30 days after receipt of your order or b) advise you there'll be a delay. They must do this unless their catalog specifically notes shipment will take longer. In the event that the company can't ship your order within 30 days, they must offer to refund your money and give you a cost-free way of canceling (either an 800 number or collect call).

8. My order never arrived, the company's phone is disconnected, and my check's been cashed. Help!

One trade organization that will intervene on your behalf or put you in touch with the proper agencies is the Direct Marketing Association (DMA), 6 E. 43rd St., New York, NY 10017, phone (212) 689-4977. Calling the Better Business Bureau or the Postmaster General to alert them is also a good idea, and you can alert the FTC and your state attorney general's office if you think you've been ripped off. We at *The Underground Shopper* will intervene and do what we can if you have a problem with a company listed in our book. We'll keep your written complaint on file and eliminate a listing if it proves necessary. (See the Reader Response page in the back of this book.)

9. After I pay shipping charges, am I really saving money?

If the item you want is available at a local discount store or will go on sale soon, it might be better to buy it locally, but not always. Some companies have charts in their catalogs to figure shipping charges according to weight and distance; other companies charge depending on the dollar amount of your order. Figure the shipping costs, calculate the savings in sales tax if you're ordering out-of-state, and *then* compare prices. That way you'll be comparing final cost to final cost.

There are three ways an order can be shipped. Parcel Post (PP) is one way. The United States Postal Service charges from 50 cents to $4.40 to insure parcels valued up to $500. Packages valued over $500 must be registered and sent First Class. These can also be insured. *The only way goods can be sent to a post office box is by Parcel Post.* To use this method, mark both your order and check "Deliver by Parcel Post Only" if you want delivery to your post office box. COD orders are more expensive since the carrier collects a money order fee of $1.50 and more, depending upon the value of the package.

United Parcel Service (UPS) automatically insures each package for $100 in value and charges 25 cents for each additional $100 in value on the same package. UPS charges should not include insurance unless the cost is greater than $100. The cost of using UPS is determined by the package's weight and measurement, the package's point of origin, and its destination. The price is usually worth it: Most people agree that UPS is the most efficient and reliable carrier.

A third means of shipping an item is by truck. Truckers are used for non-mailable orders (goods over 50 pounds) and combined orders (non-mailable goods with those under 50 pounds in weight). The weight of the goods and the distance they will be shipped determine the amount of the charges. The shipper specifies on the bill of lading the amount due (if any) and the form of payment the trucker should collect when he delivers the merchandise. On COD orders, for example, the shipper must specify that a personal check is acceptable. This may not include the freight company's charges, in which case an additional check may be required. You'll often see the abbreviation FOB meaning "freight on board." "FOB factory" means you pay the shipping charges from the factory to you.

10. Will the trucker's charges on a large purchase like furniture be so big that they eat up all the money I saved?

It's highly unlikely. If they did, no one would mail-order furniture! Often the price of having a piece of furniture shipped offsets the savings in sales tax, but doesn't significantly reduce the amount you saved off the retail purchase price. This depends, though, on the distance a piece of furniture must be shipped (whether it must cross the Mississippi River or the Rockies), the sales tax charged in your state (and the amount of your sales tax savings), and the price charged by the carrier used.

Deregulation of the trucking industry has caused freight companies to lower their rates for both long and short hauls. The price of shipping a single item has dropped a lot, too.

On the topic of savings, you'll save about 50% on freight charges on items like bookcases if you ship them "knocked down" or disassembled. The reason disassembled merchandise costs less is that it takes up less room on the truck.

Another money-saving tip is that residents of the east and southeast who are buying from the North Carolina furniture district should look for companies with their own trucks and crew. Their rates are generally lower than those of common carriers.

11. The idea of ordering from a foreign country scares me. What if I order a kaftan but get back an afghan?

Getting catalogs with exotic stamps, quaint idiomatic letters, and unusual products is like taking a small trip to a foreign country. It's fun! Just like taking a trip, though, there are some precautions.

Read the catalogs closely and look for such things as insurance, duty (each item is taxed at a different rate), the return policy, and delivery information. You'll pay a premium for air mail delivery, but the alternative is delivery via surface mail on a "slow boat."

The method of payment should be explained in the catalog. If not, write to the company before sending any money. Because of fluctuating currency markets, Deak International, a currency broker with offices in most major cities, suggests that a foreign company bill you in their own currency and you then pay in that currency. Currency brokers and most banks will issue a check based on the current rate of exchange. You can obtain a currency conversion table for approximate values from Deak International, 29 Broadway, New York, NY 10006. Paying by credit card when possible is another way to avoid exchange rate hassles.

Another tip you should follow in the U.S., but *especially* when you do business with a foreign company, is that if you must return your purchase for any reason because of damage, write for instructions first. If you don't take this step and get clearance, you may end up paying duty twice.

12. Please explain customs duties. How much extra will I have to pay?

Any purchase made outside the U.S. is subject to customs examination. That's the law. The U.S. Postal Service sends all incoming packages to customs to be examined and each dutiable item is charged a percent of its appraised value. The different percentages for individual items are obtained from the exhaustive *Tariff Schedules of the United States*. The duty on a silk blouse might be 18% while that on a cotton blouse may be 25%. It's hard to estimate what the duties will be beforehand: duties on different products are often based on political, rather than economic, considerations. It's a complicated process. Call your local customs office for details.

After customs has written the duty bill, the parcel is returned to the Post Office. The Post Office handles the delivery and the collection of the duty along with a $1.75 postal handling fee.

In Canada, the procedure for paying duty is roughly the same, except you will be notified by Canadian customs that your package is ready for pickup. Canadians pay slightly higher duties than U.S. citizens, plus a 9% federal sales tax.

While everything you buy out of the country must be inspected, not everything is subject to duty charges. Items classified as "duty-free" under the Generalized System of Preferences (GSP) come from over 140 under-developed nations, and include about 2,800 items that range from cameras to wood carvings. In order to take advantage of the GSP, you must buy an eligible article in the same beneficiary country as it was grown, manufactured, or produced. Bona fide "unsolicited" gifts aren't exempted under the laws for returning travelers.

SYMBOLS KEY

I. Types of payment accepted

CK   Personal checks. A few firms don't accept personal checks. They think that the inconvenience of waiting until the checks clear, and the resulting impatience of customers due to the delay in receiving their order, make checks more trouble than they're worth. Firms that *do* take personal checks have a "CK" symbol in the line beneath the address where types of payment are listed. When you pay by check, expect a delay in receiving your order of two to three weeks since most firms will wait until your check clears the bank before processing your order. Certified checks, cashier's checks, and money orders are all commonly accepted as payment by mail-order companies and won't mean a delay in processing your order.

MC   MasterCard. Using a credit card is advisable for orders you want to get quickly, since there is not the delay there is with a check that first must clear the bank. Using credit for orders that don't total large sums of money also makes some sense because you'll get your order faster and the credit charges won't be large in absolute terms. Credit card orders aren't advisable when purchasing large or expensive items since delivery of large merchandise usually takes a long time and because credit charges (in absolute terms) on expensive items will be high. It almost goes without saying that credit orders are mandatory when you order by phone. As a final word of warning, when you use credit, it's still a good idea to write down the model and style number, etc., of the merchandise you ordered, as well as the name of the person you spoke with if you ordered by phone. If a problem arises, this information may prove useful.

V   Visa.

AE   American Express.

DC   Diner's Club.

CB   Carte Blanche.

D   Discover.

C   Choice.

COD   Cash on Delivery. Firms that accept COD payments usually qualify that with some type of restriction, such as a 25% deposit which serves to protect them in case you change your mind and decide not to accept your order. When you order COD, know that COD means *cash* on delivery. If you expect to receive your order and pay by check, you'll probably be disappointed. You'll have to pay by cash or by some other form of payment that's "safe" for the seller.

MO   Money Order.

IMO   International Money Order.

II. Information about the supplier

C   Catalog. When it costs something to get a catalog, we've noted the amount immediately after the entry, as in "C $2." The charge for a catalog is generally small (if anything), only enough to cover postage and handling, and to discourage catalog requests from people who wouldn't actually order. We have indicated when the catalog price is refundable with your first order.

B   Brochure. A brochure is smaller than a catalog and often folds out. For our purposes, a brochure is eight pages or fewer.

F   Flier or price sheet.

PQ   Price quote. Companies with a "PQ" following their write-up will answer telephone queries or letters requesting information about specific merchandise. To get a price quote, you must know the manufacturer's name, the item's stock number, etc.

SASE   Send a self-addressed stamped envelope size 10.

III. Address information

Dept. US   You'll notice that many listings contain Dept. US in their addresses. "US" stands for *Underground Shopper*. We've included this as a convenience to the companies listed, since many companies like to know where their new customers heard of them. It also helps us, since our book becomes more important to the companies listed and they have a greater incentive to provide us with the information we ask for as we try to update our files. It gives us more clout. Ultimately, our clout helps you because if there is ever a problem and you contact us, there's a greater chance the company will listen to us when we intervene on your behalf.

Apparel: Children's

Baby your baby by buying diapers at wholesale prices. Rack up the savings on suits for your little prince, pinafores for your princess, and hand-knit clothing for toddlers and tykes at way below retail prices. Natural fibers imported from Europe are an alternative. If you're planning on more than one child, choose better quality clothing—it will last longer. Also, consider stocking up on items like sleepers and diapers. You'll have them when you need them next time, and you'll save money.

COTTON DREAMS
Dept. US
P.O. Box 99
Sebastian, FL 32958
(305) 589-0172
CK, MC, V, COD

End those polyester nightmares! Cotton Dreams means sweet dreams for the whole family with their 100% natural fiber clothing. Discounts are 10% to 20% off retail on hard-to-find items like 100% cotton knee socks, panties, slips, baby clothing, underwear, turtlenecks, and tights in different colors. OSHKOSH overalls came in a variety of colors and were priced at just $14.85. They have a variety of women's underwear like full and half-slips, cotton and nursing bras, briefs, camisoles, blouses, skirts, shorts, nightgowns, and socks. For men, terry robes, pajamas, shorts, and socks are offered. Shipping is $3 for the first $40 or less; customers usually get their order in about four or five days. Everything is unconditionally guaranteed: there's a 30-day limit on exchanges and a six-month limit on damaged goods. **C**

NATAN BORLAM CO., INC.
157 Havemeyer
Brooklyn, NY 11211
(718) 387-2983
(718) 782-0108
CK

Natan Borlam carries boys' clothing in sizes infants to 20; girls' clothing, infants to juniors, preteen sizes 4 to 14; and women's clothing. Everything sports tags and fabrics from the finest domestic and European manufacturers and is made expressly for Borlam. Savings run 25% to 50%. Borlam's offers a 14-day refund policy and tacks on $2 for shipping. There is a $2 minimum order. They're open Sunday through Thursday from 10 to 6, and Friday from 10 to 2. **PQ**

7TH HEAVEN
1800–L Rockville Pike
Rockville, MD 20852
(301) 231-5160 (orders)
(301) 231-5891 (customer service)
CK, MC, V, MO

Thank heaven for 7th Heaven—"The kids' fashion discounter." Their spring color catalog boasts 24 pages of heavenly stars including such stellar names as OSHKOSH, JETSET, PICCOLO, P.C.A., WONDERKNIT, and APPLAUSE. Save 20% to 40% on all kids' fashions and accessories. B'gosh, a solid cord overall by OSHKOSH from 12 months to size 7 was $14.99 to $15.99. Their warm 'n wonderful OSHKOSH girls' baggy denim overalls were priced from $14.99 (regularly $19) to $19.99 (regularly $25). Print turtlenecks by PICCOLO for boys and girls were $5.99 to $7.99 (regularly $8 to $10). Great-looking novelty gift items, warm-ups, underwear, sleepwear, and playwear complete the collection. Nobody beats their catalog prices. If you can find an item in their catalog advertised for less somewhere else, send them the ad and they will beat the price by 10%. $4 shipping fee is added to all orders. C

THE YOUNG IDEA LTD.
Aylesbury
HP 202JA England
phone: Despatch 88068
CK, MC, V, ACCESS, POSTAL ORDER

We don't know if this is where Lady Di buys the royal Di-apers, but busy mums can select reasonably priced children's wear from Young Idea's own or LADYBIRD label. From pinafores, schoolwear, cord jeans, pj's, and nightgowns to baby rompers and crawler sets, they've got 'em. Their free catalog is delightful reading, but blimey, all the prices are listed in pounds and pence! If you've been panting for a pair of pants, be sure to get the right size or else the London britches will be falling down. C

Apparel: Family

What's your pleasure? Chances are you'll find it here. From fashion to function, professional to playful, we'll bet you'll find the look you like. The Finals catalog, for instance, was a real find for us. It's devoted entirely to eye-catching swimming and jogging attire for men and women who aren't too tired to look their best after working out. In this section, you'll find a variety of bargains ranging from authentic military surplus to warm winter woolens to the preppie, durable clothing by Land's End. It's all here for you, and it's fit to be tried.

BABOURIS HANDICRAFTS
56 Adrianou Str.
105 55 Athens
Greece
01-32-47-561
CK, IMO

For those interested in telling a fantastic yarn story for entertaining after-dinner guests, why not tell the story of Babouris. Since 1958, they've been home-spinning woolen yarns and fancy cotton yarns in a variety of natural and fast-dyed colors, hand-knit sweaters, and knitted wear made from the above yarns at prices 70% off comparable U.S. products. Minimum order is five kilos of yarn or one sweater and your order is processed immediately. **B $3**

BEMIDJI WOOLEN MILLS
P.O. Box 277
Bemidji, MN 56601
(218) 751-5166
MC, V, COD

Play ragtime with a ragg knit cap or grab some woolens for your next ski trip to the wild and wooly, wintry West. Founded in 1921, this family-owned business specializes in men's, women's, and children's outerwear; yarns; LADY SLIPPER design products (decorative stuffed animals); plus they manufacture 100% wool and polyester batting. They'll also go to bat for you by reprocessing your old wool batting. They're most famous for their jackets and coats—they've made jackets for 15 northern governors in recent years. Yarns are another good buy: four ounce four-ply skeins of yarn that they manufacture were only $1.95, so they won't try to "skein" you alive. Prices are about 15% lower than you'd find in a department store and you'll find the same brands: WOOLRICH and DUOFOLD, for example. There's a 100% satisfaction guarantee, with exchanges or refunds made on request. Goods that must be back-ordered take two to three weeks; normal orders are shipped the same day. Check out their 32-page catalog. **C**

CHOCK CATALOG CORP.
Dept. US
74 Orchard St.
New York, NY 10002
(800) 222-0020
(212) 473-1929: NY residents
MC, V

This business is chock full of nuts who love Louis's heavenly bargains on undergarments. We found savings of 25% off hosiery and underwear for the whole family—a fitting discount for well-fitting unmentionables fit for newborns to grandparents. They've got CARTER's pj's, undies, and blankets; HANES briefs and boxer shorts; BURLINGTON socks; HANES and MAYER panty hose and much more. We're told their most popular brand-name items are their two-layer (cotton/wool) DUOFOLD underwear for men and women, VASSARETTE briefs and slips, CALVIN KLEINS for men and women, and the legendary BVDS. Tall men will find "T" shirts in their size (up to XXXX) for just three for $11.75 (retail, three for $15.50). Women's panty hose, however, are their real claim-to-fame. Shipping is $3 per order anywhere in the U.S.; 30-day exchange or refund period. **C $1**

CLOTHKITS
24 High St., LEWES
E. Sussex BN7 2LB
England
(0273) 477111
MC, V, Sterling Cheques, Sterling Postal/Money Orders, Euro-Cheques made out in Sterling, Access, Eurocard

Talk about a success story. For 18 years, this luscious 58-page color catalog has covered many satisfied shoppers from top to bottom with designer outfits that you make from a CLOTHKIT. This original screen-printed kit form allows you to save with your creative input. Those unwilling to do it "their way" also can choose from pages of ready-made clothes for adults and kids. Their kits are especially designed for nimble-fingered folks who have found dressmaking tough. Paper patterns are eliminated either by printing the cutting lines directly on the fabric or are offered already cut out and ready to sew. Instruction sheets are a snap. To coordinate with each kit, you can choose ready-made knitwear, hosiery, accessories along with original toys and household items. Perfect gifts for your entire family. Full refunds or exchanges if not completely satisfied. **C**

CUSTOM COAT COMPANY, INC.
227 N. Washington St.
Berlin, WI 54923
(414) 361-0900
MC, V

Custom Coat can transform raw hides into jackets, coats, vests, gloves, purses, hats, moccasins, and many other leather accessories. They tan deer, elk, and moose hides (yours or theirs). All garments (ladies' and men's) can be made with rayon, satin fleece, or pile lining. Their free 21-page catalog provides excellent information concerning care and shipping of your raw hides and tells you how to measure for your custom coat. Prices are at least 25% below retail costs for similar products. If you bag a small one and need some extra leather to complete your order, they can supply it at $3.50 per square foot. **C**

D & A MERCHANDISE CO.
Dept. US
22 Orchard St.
New York, NY 10002
(212) 925-4766
MC, V, COD

Elliot Kivell calls himself The Underwear King, and with a business in business since 1946, he's had more than a brief reign. D & A treats their customers royally with 25% savings on men's and women's robes, underwear, and lingerie. Ninety percent of their merchandise is branded and famous names aren't exactly feudal and far between. You'll see HANES and BERKSHIRE panty hose; panties and bras by LILY OF FRANCE, OLGA, WARNER'S, MAIDENFORM, CARNIVAL CREATIONS, LILYETTE, BALI, VASSARETTE, and FORMFIT ROGERS; DANSKIN tights; LORRAINE camisoles; MUNSINGWEAR, JOCKEY, and BVD T-shirts and briefs; and BURLINGTON, INTERWOVEN, CHRISTIAN DIOR, and WIGWAM socks. Bra sizes run to 48 and panties to size 12. Most orders are received within two weeks. (An exception was a $2,000 underwear order mailed to an Arab sheik in Europe: not surprisingly, that took a little longer!) No time limit on returns; cash refunds are given. Be specific when requesting a price quote; ask for the line and style number, size, and color. Shipping costs $2.50, except to Alaska and Hawaii. As Elliot asks, "Why pay more?"
C $1.50 (one time fee), **PQ**

DEVA COTTAGE INDUSTRY
Box US 7
303 E. Main St.
Burkittsville, MD 21718
(301) 663-4900
CK, MC, V

According to their catalog, "Deva is an attempt to humanize work and integrate it with home life." That's a worthy goal, and manufacturing natural fiber clothing for men and women is the means they've selected. Deva's drawstring pants at $21 postpaid are close kin to the surgical team look, and are very comfortable. The pants come in many colors and are perfect for running, lounging, or meditating. They also make drawstring shorts ($14 postpaid), wrap skirts ($24 postpaid), a wonderful "Spring Moon" kimono for $39, and many other products. They sell direct, so you can expect to save around 20%. Clothing comes in sizes small, medium, large, extra-large, and extra-extra large. Everything carries an unconditional guarantee, entitling you to exchange or claim a refund. They also sell books for devotees of Eastern philosophy and culture. Fabric samples are enclosed with their catalog. C $1

DOWN GENERATION/SYLVIA & SONS
Dept. US
725 Columbus
New York, NY 10025
(212) 663-3112
CK, MC, V, AE, DC, COD

Get down, get down! More than 35,000 down-filled garments including jackets, vests, and full-length coats are discounted 15% off retail. We found enough skiwear to outfit Jean-Claude Killy and his whole family for 10 seasons, and that's no snow job. Some of their most popular brands include WOOLRICH, CB, HEAD, OBERMEYER, TRAILWISE, and THE NORTH FACE. No shipping charges unless order is over 10 pounds (and that would take a *lot* of down). Exchanges or refunds offered for a 60-day period.

EDINBURGH WOOLLEN MILL, LTD.
Langholm, Dumfriesshire
Dept. 58
Scotland DG130BR
Phone: 0541 80092
MC, V, AE

Are you on a kilt trip about spending too much money? Don't skirt the issue, address it—and send it off to Scotland! (You'll be coming back for moor.) Tweed and tartan skirts and suits for men and women are priced well below those found in comparable stores in the United States. Sweaters by PRINGLE and their own brand cost from $20 to $75 ($35 to $125 retail). There's a 100% satisfaction guarantee and they'll gladly accept exchanges on items purchased through the mail or at one of their 80 retail shops in Britain. Since all prices are in pounds, it's easier to use your credit cards. They will honor prices for the duration marked in the catalog. A £6 (surface) or £12 (air mail) postage fee is required on any size order. **C**

THE FINALS
21 Minisink Ave.—UG
Port Jervis, NY 12771
(800) 431-9111
(800) 452-0452: NY residents
CK, MC, V, AE

When you're serious about swimming, don't forget to take The Finals. Make a splash for less cash in their own brand of factory direct swimsuits priced at just $13.25 for women and $8 to $12 for men. Lycra suits for men and women are the most popular. Discounts are given on quantity purchases—they'll knock $1 off the price for 13 or more swimsuits in the same style number. (Besides their discounted swimsuits, we were impressed with something else. The scantily clad models in their 51-page catalog would get on swimmingly at our pool anytime.) We tracked down running gear made from brightly colored nylon: lined shorts were $8 and the matching tank top was $8. Warm-ups in 12 attractive colors were $56. The 50% polyester/50% cotton long-sleeved polo shirts helped beat "la cost" of living at $12.50 apiece, or three for $36. Goggles, bags, swim caps, and other accessories, too. 10% team discount; $25 credit card minimum; seven- to 10-day delivery time on most items. **C**

HARVARD TROUSER COMPANY
Dept. US
P.O. Box 217
2191 S. Main St.
Pittsford, MI 49271
(517) 523-2167
COD

Park your car in the Harvard yard because they carry that classic from the fifties, the car coat. H.T.C. is the manufacturer of top quality insulated, washable nylon outerwear. Ladies' jackets, car coats, and long coats are all lightweight in a fantastic selection of colors. They also carry men's jackets, hunting jackets and bibs, duck work clothes, and snowmobile suits. Women's sizes ranged from 8 to 34 and men's sizes ranged from small to XXXXX-large. All American-made at the H.T.C. Factory and sold at factory prices. This company's been around since 1926—the time of the Model A Ford. No wonder their prices are so affordable! **B**

HOWRON SPORTSWEAR
295 Grand St.
New York, NY 10002
(212) 226-4307
CK, MC, V, AE, COD

How, Ron! We spent heap big pile of wampum at this place. (And we didn't need a reservation!) Chief labels like STANLEY BLACKER, DAMON, and OSCAR DE LA RENTA really Sioux-ted our tribe. (Squaw won't squawk when she can Chippewa-y for OSCAR DE LA RENTA, STANLEY BLACKER, DAMON, MEMBERS ONLY, SANSABELT, GIVENCHY, and many others!) Ladies' dressy and sportswear styles (sizes 4 to 18 or 38 to 48) by ACT III, VILLAGER, BRECKENRIDGE, PRESTIGE, STUART LANG, and LEE would catch any brave's eye. (Give 'em the old pow-wow!) Ladies HANES panty hose and underwear are discounted 25%; men's JOCKEY shorts carry the same discount. Most merchandise is 25% to 50% off retail. Orders take about a week. Indian givers get store credit only on returns. **PQ**

I. TUSCHMAN & SONS, INC.
61 Orchard St.
New York, NY 10002
(212) 226-4318
CK, MC, V

Tuschman has clothing for your tush, as well as for the rest of you.
This Lower East Side merchant has men's, women's, and children's
brand-name underwear, sleepwear, shirts, jeans, socks, sweaters,
and more, and all at a 25% to 35% discount. Children's pajamas
include brands such as DR. DENTON'S and CARTER'S, among others;
men's underwear brands include BVD, HANES, and FRUIT OF THE
LOOM; men's and women's jeans carry the VIOLA brand; and men's
pajamas bear such labels as YVES ST. LAURENT, BVD, and BOTANY 500.
Men's MARTEX terry cloth robes are also available, as are socks by
INTERWOVEN. Ladies will like LOLLIPOP and POOFI underwear, and
BURLINGTON panty hose. BILLY THE KID, GEOFFREY BEENE,
CAMBRIDGE, HANG TEN, and many other brands are available. This is
one of the few places to get original Grand Slam golf shirts by
MUNSINGWEAR (penguin logo) at a discount; another unusual store
feature is their full range of large size underwear, up to size 60 on
some items and XL to XXXX on others. There's a 30-day exchange or
refund policy; standard $4.50 shipping charges; two-week delay
before you'll receive your order. **PQ**

LAND'S END
Land's End Lane
Dodgeville, WI 53595
(800) 356-4444
(608) 935-2788: WI residents
CK, MC, V, AE

Land's End is a landmark with their line of clothing; just trekking
through their catalog makes you want to take a Tibetan hike or go
white water rafting in Wisconsin. Their clothing is sturdy, comfortable, classy, and fun. We saw beautiful cotton sweaters for men and
women, colorful polo and rugby shirts, twill pants, Madras shirts,
women's tops, and shorts and shoes along with belts, shoulder bags,
and nautical gifts fit for even land-locked sailors. Even boomerangs
are available for those one-step-above-the-average Frisbee freaks.
While not technically an "off-price" merchant, they do offer particularly high-quality clothing at quite reasonable prices. Satisfaction

guaranteed or complete refund; shipping charges at a flat rate of $3; free full-color 92-page catalog (a trip by itself). **C**

MELNIKOFF'S DEPARTMENT STORE
Dept. US
1594 York Ave.
New York, NY 10028
(212) 288-2419
(212) 288-3644
CK, MC, V, AE

Melnikoff's calls itself a department store, even though "neighborhood emporium" might be a better description. They've got an incredible amount of stuff crammed between their four walls and savvy New Yorkers have long made financial pilgrimages to this money-saving mecca. Quality clothing for men, women, and children is available at prices discounted anywhere from 10% to 25% below retail. ADIDAS and NIKE label sweat suits for men and boys are occasionally discounted as much as 40%; ladies can find MAIDENFORM bras; and there's clothing bearing the CARTER'S label for the kids. Occasionally RALPH LAUREN Polos gallop into Melnikoff's. Melnikoff's inventory fluctuates so you take your chances. Labels like IZOD and LEE, as well as others, are also available. Write or call with a description of what you want. $25 minimum with charge card orders. **PQ**

PAGANO GLOVES, INC.
3-5 Church St.
Johnstown, NY 12095
(518) 762-8425
CK, MC, V, COD

When it's spring, a young man's fancy turns to thoughts of gloves . . . Pagano Gloves, Inc., sells men's, women's, and children's deerskin gloves, coats, and jackets, accessories, leather attaché cases, novelties, and knit hats at 50% to 75% off retail store prices. Sound good? They've also got a Texas-size selection of ladies' handbags priced from $26.50 to $75, and for the rough and rednecks, cowhide jackets and vests beginning at $52. You can slip into a pair of feather-light slippers or moccasins to wear around the house for as little as $8.50. There are no refunds, but you can exchange for any item. Shipping is $3 per order; orders arrive in two to three weeks usually. Don't forget to mention you're an *Underground Shopper*—readers get an additional 10% off on purchases of $50 and more. **C $2.00** (refundable with your first order)

PRINCE FASHIONS LTD.
GPO Box 2868
Hong Kong
5-742938
5-744106
CK, IMO

You don't have to kiss a frog to find a prince among the high cost of clothing. Just look to the east—the Far East. Prince Fashions Ltd. offers high-quality clothing at royal savings. They are the biggest mail-order company in Hong Kong and have been in business for 25 years. Princess-pleasing prices abound in their full-color catalog. We discovered a kingdom of royal bargains. An angora wool cardigan was $20.80; a men's custom-made wool suit, $108; and a jade bangle bracelet was only $27.80. We couldn't possibly list all the items this Prince of fashion carried, but we can name a few: jewelry, watches, sportsuits, dresses, suits, jackets, and fans. *Underground Shoppers* receive an additional 10% off. If not pleased, you won't lose your crown. The Prince takes returns without a frown. **C $1** (refundable)

RAMMAGERDIN OF REYKJAVIK
Hafnarstraeti 19
P.O. Box 751-121
Reykjavik, Iceland

Question: What's the favorite comic strip of an Icelandic sheep shearer? Answer: Mutton Jeff! This company sells wool and fur clothing for the whole family, plus ceramics, souvenir gifts, and knitting products. Prices on their woolen sweaters, ponchos, coats, caps, mittens, shawls, and vests are about 50% less than U.S. retail for comparable quality (around $35 to $40 usually, versus $70 to $80). If you've been hankering to weave your own bargain, they also sell Icelandic yarn made from the mountain sheep fleece. It is well-known for being warm, yet very light and soft. There's a minimum yarn order of eight skeins. **C, B** with samples, **$1.**

RED FLANNEL FACTORY
P.O. Box 370
73 S. Main St.
Cedar Springs, MI 49319
(616) 696-9240
CK, MC, V

In response to a futile attempt by a New York writer to find red flan-
nels to cope with the blizzard of 1936, the town of Cedar Springs
piped up and became a specialist for the bright undergarments. In
1949, a shop opened and later became the Red Flannel Factory,
which now manufactures pajamas, undergarments, robes, and shirts
in white and red flannel for the entire family—even the dog. Fabric
can be either 100% sanforized cotton flannel, 50% polyester/50% cotton, or muslin. Long-sleeve three-button shirt, $18.97; knit bottoms,
$14.97; long johns, $29.25; long flannel gown, $28.97; nightcaps,
$4.97. Prices at this factory outlet are a good 20% to 30% lower than
retail. **C**

SOCK SHOP
Sweetwater Hosiery Mills
P.O. Box 390
Dept. US
Sweetwater, TN 37874
(615) 337-9203
CK, MO, COD

This place should help knock your socks off—at least as much as 30%.
Made in the USA, women's and girls' panty hose from as low as $1.39
including support irregulars at that price; queen sizes at $1.59; con-
trol top sandalfoot at $1.85; and support panty hose, first-quality at
$3.39. Knee-highs for 69 cents, bobby socks, 49 cents; cuff sport
socks, 70 cents; irregular pom poms for 59 cents. Other items include
panties, men's socks, FRUIT OF THE LOOM underwear (briefs, boxers,
T-shirts, etc.), boys' and girls' socks and anklets, and boys' FRUIT OF
THE LOOM underwear ($4.59 for the three-pair package). For orders
under $10, please add $2.50 postage. With orders over $10, postage is
free. **B**

STRAND SURPLUS SENTER
2202 Strand
Galveston, TX 77550
(800) 231-6005: charge orders only
(409) 762-7397: TX residents
CK, MC, V

"The world's only surviving general government surplus store" is
what the owners call it and they're right. We've been there: just
blocks away from the beach, surrounded by the beautifully restored
buildings downtown, and always full of enthusiastic shopping tour-
ists. They've got everything from pith helmets (and appropriate
machetes) to camouflage cotton pants and Italian army pullover
sweaters (both $39.95). Mess kits, tools, medals, hiking accessories,
and just plain campy things occupy the stuffed racks and packed bins
while shoppers maneuver their way through the crowded aisles.
Everybody buys something. Don't miss it if you're in Galveston.
Send $1.00 (refundable) for brochure and price list. Minimum order
$10.00. B $1

WACO THRIFT STORE INC.
Dept. US
P.O. Box 143
Waco, GA 30182
(404) 537-2702
COD

I dream of jeanies with the light brown wrappers. For men's and
women's first-quality jeans (including LEE) for just $18.95, you're
wacko if you pass up Waco. Goose down jackets for kids cost just
$49.95 and are ideal for school or play in colder climes. They've got
family clothing gently worn by gentle people. Men's clothing, including slacks and suits, are their best buys. They'll exchange on new
merchandise; you can expect your order in about a week. Write for
their brochure and price list with labels and styles for a prompt reply.
B

WEAR-GUARD CORPORATION
P.O. Box 400
Hingham, MA 02043
(800) 343-4406 (24 hours)
(617) 871-4100
CK, MC, V, AE, COD

If you're worn out wearing boring casual work clothes or uniforms, why not spruce up your wardrobe here with personalized uniforms, work clothing, rugged casual apparel along with silk-screened and embroidered hats, T's, and jackets. Weekend Editions (56 pages) are specialized mini-versions of their big catalog (96 pages) and would fit into anyone's outdoor wardrobe needs. New England-type separates and footwear, flannel shirts and chinos for the football games—all factory-direct priced at 10% to 30% off. Brands include HERMAN'S, TIMBERLAND, HANES, WRANGLER, and ADIDAS. Customer satisfaction is guaranteed 100% of the time—or your money back. Expect a response in one or two days. In addition to their mail-order division, WEAR-GUARD has 50 retail locations throughout the Northeast. Call their toll-free number above for the location nearest you. C $1

WORKMEN'S GARMENT CO.
15205 Wyoming
Detroit, MI 48238
(313) 834-7236
CK, MC, V, MO

You work hard for your money. At Workmen's Garment Company, they work hard to see that you keep it. They carry a variety of new work clothes: shirts, pants, coveralls, shop coats, jackets, insulated outerwear, shoes, and rainwear and you'll find huge savings on reconditioned work clothes. Though they've taken a licking, they still keep on kicking. Bring home the bacon and put it back in the piggy. Toil over this: Workmen's Garment Company has been laboring for the working man for over 30 years. They're quite a performer when it comes to keeping you warmer. There is no refund on reconditioned merchandise, but you can get your cash back on new items if returned within ten days. So exert some muscle and hustle. This will give you a raise: shipping and handling is paid. There is a $15 minimum order for checks or money orders; $20 with charges. If you are tired of the everyday grind of finding affordable work clothes, don't go on strike, go to the workmen's company. They work for you.
C $1 (refundable)

W.S. ROBERTSON (OUTFITTERS) LTD
40/41 Bank St.
Galashiels, Scotland
0896-2152
CK, MC, V, IMO

If you're a chip off the ole' block, you'll really love these PRINGLES—
probably the finest name in knitwear for men and women since 1815.
We won't pull the wool over your eyes—you'll save about one-third off
the specialty store prices in the U.S. Choose from cardigans and
pullovers in cashmere, lambswool, shetland, camel hair—all natural
fibers. Other names noted BALLANTYNE, BRAEMAR, and LYLE &
SCOTT LTD knitwear. All prices are quoted in pounds; be sure to
deduct the value added tax not charged on exported goods (15%)
after you've figured the conversion to dollars. Minimum order—one
garment. **C $5**

Apparel: Men's

For investment dressing without cashing in your cache of blue chips, you've come to the right spot. Check out the stock marketed here and get everything from ADOLFO to ZEROS at bargain margins. Classic clothing is never out of fashion. Natural fabrics feel better, wear better, and last longer, so indulge yourself—your clothing is an investment, remember? When you dress for success, good taste pays big dividends. If you're looking for ARROW shirts, BASS shoes, BROOKS BROTHERS suits, DIOR robes, SANSABELT slacks, or HANES underwear, we've got you covered at over-the-counter prices.

A. RUBINSTEIN AND SON
63 E. Broadway
New York, NY 10002
(212) 226-9696
CK, MC, V, AE, DC, CB, COD

Unlike the great musician, this A. Rubinstein's no pianist, although his prices on men's clothing definitely struck a responsive chord with us. This family's been playing our song for 64 years; three generations of Rubinsteins work in the store! Everything is first-quality. Suit sizes range from 34 short to 52 long. There are dozens of brands, including ADOLFO, CARDIN, CHARLES JOURDAN, STANLEY BLACKER, YVES ST. LAURENT, GUESS, GIORGIO ARMANI, and OLEG CASSINI—not to mention SAN REMO, MARZOTTA, DAMON, and LONDON FOG. Shirts, ties, sportswear, rainwear, and outerwear were also available at 20% to 30% discounts. There's a $25 minimum order: no restocking charge. They'll make refunds or exchanges up to two weeks after delivery. Alterations are free for New York City residents. No wonder note-able New Yorkers have kept in tune with the times by making this store their fashion forte. **B, PQ**

DAMART
1811 Woodbury Ave.
Portsmouth, NH 03805
(800) 258-7300
(603) 431-4700: NH residents
CK, V, MC, AE
($15 minimum for cards)

We've talking underwear folks! Who's going to know . . . Thermolactyl underwear, exclusive to Damart, will keep the north wind out. A 48-page catalog makes no mention of their factory seconds, but call the toll-free number and ask if an item from the catalog is currently in stock in seconds. The only possible drawback from this toasty underwear is that thermolactyl material cannot be thrown in a dryer. Even so, it is touted as fast drying, and there is no retail equivalent available anywhere. Besides offering an assortment of colors and styles (button-down, long-sleeved, vest, etc.), Damart also stocks an assortment of heavy duty socks. **C**

DAMON FACTORY OUTLET
Dept. US
7601 River Road
North Bergen, NJ 07047
(201) 861-1115
CK, MC, V, AE

For out-of-pocket savings that are completely out-of-hand, try this outlet. No more will you be roamin' the stores looking for clothing by DAMON, or paying prices only a king can afford. You can leave your chariot at home and get first-quality sportswear at close to wholesale. This store is owned by DAMON and (predictably) carries their own brands: DAMON CREATIONS and BILL BLASS (knitwear). Prices are a whopping 40% to 60% off retail. They now have four locations in New Jersey and one in Pennsylvania. They have a five-day refund and a 30-day exchange policy. Shipping's a flat $3 rate. **PQ**

THE DEERSKIN PLACE
283 Akron Road
Ephrata, PA 17522
(717) 733-7624
CK, MC, V, COD

"Deer-ly beloved, we are gathered here . . ." Those who don't run with the herd can let their fingers do the stalking through this brochure. You can fawn over jackets, coats, handbags, shoes, moccasins, sheepskin coats and jackets, gloves, and wallets for men and women at 30% to 50% off retail. (Talk about saving some bucks! Bargains like that belong on our trophy rack—our interest is mounting!) A woman's belted leather jacket was $225; men's fringed or unfringed moccasins were $28.95 ($39 elsewhere). We set our sights on a pair of women's unlined gloves for $19.98, and bagged a coonskin cap ($7.95) for the Bambi-no. Baby moccasin boots in sizes 1 to 6 were $12.95, while suede knee-high moccasins in sizes 4 to 10 with hard or soft soles were $35.95. Men's sizes typically run 6 to 13. There's no minimum order and no restocking charge on returns, although there *is* an exchange-only policy (no refunds). If you haven't gotten your order in two to four weeks, start hunting. Now that you don't have stiff leather prices to dis-suede you from buying, you won't have to lock horns with these guys. Satisfaction guaranteed. **B, PQ**

DORSETT DISTRIBUTING CO.
11866 Dorsett Road
Maryland Heights, MO 63043
(314) 291-8565
CK, MC, V

Another sports Cinderella story . . . Tony's toes were twinkling at the Foot Ball in celebration of Dorsett's contemporary designer men's clothing (which was free from offensive price hikes). Twenty-five to 50 top-name designer superstars were suited up on Dorsett's roster with prices huddling at 30% to 50% lower than retail. A line-up of fabrics included only the finest first-quality pinstripes, herringbones, tweeds, solids, plaids, and sharkskin (but no pigskin). Famous designer shoe lines are discounted 25% to 30%, AAAA to EEE widths in sizes 5 to 16. (Custom shirtings also available.) With a money-back guarantee if you're dissatisfied, no restocking charge, a free catalog, and a 100% warranty from both Dorsett and the manufacturer, we had to award a Tony to this Dorsett team. In fact, the only person not smiling at this gala event was Tom Landry. (He'd heard that at the stroke of midnight the coach would turn into a pumpkin.) **PQ**

FACTORY WHOLESALERS
Dept. US
United Ramex Division
P.O. Box 938
Litchfield, MN 55355
(612) 693-3413
Money Orders only

Their name tells you what you need to know. This is no place for cads and dandies, but if you're a working man, their duds are no duds. Used men's work clothes including pants, shirts, coveralls, jackets, socks, white shirts, and pants. Ladies' smocks made from washable linen are available. A bundle of five pants and five shirts was $16.50 plus $4.50 handling which works out to be just $4 per pair of pants. You can't beat that no matter how many times you strike! Shop coats were three for $8 plus $4 shipping, another nice bargain. Ladies two-piece slack uniforms were nearly new and just $2, while white house painter coveralls (unpainted) were only $1.50 (the same price as their lab coats and belt-length lab jackets). They tell us their clothes are made in America for American-sized bodies. This company says they'll save working men a minimum of 90% over a year. 100% satisfaction or your money refunded. **B, PQ**

GELBER'S MENS STORE
630 Convention Plaza at 7th Ave.
St. Louis, MO 63101
(314) 421-6698
MC, V, AE, COD

The St. Louis Cardinals may make us see red, but Gelber's is far from our Arch enemy. The inventory of discounted men's clothing changes weekly at this 94-year-old, St. Louis-based company. Everything's first-quality and discounted 20% to 70% off regular prices. Current styles are available in names such as ADOLFO, OLEG CASSINI, HAMMONTON PARK, RAFFINATTI, and PHILLIPE GABRIEL. RAFFINATTI'S double-breasted suits are their most popular bargains, although two-piece JOHN ALEXANDER suits ($149, $189 retail) are also good sellers. Factory overruns and salesmen's samples are available at very low prices: suits ranged from $109 to $199, sport coats from $69 to $109. They do alterations at little or no charge. Customers usually receive their orders in about 10 days. Send them a style description for prices and tell 'em you're an *Underground Shopper*—you'll get a free tie with every suit you order. **PQ**

G & G PROJECTIONS
62 Orchard St.
New York, NY 10002
(212) 431-4531
CK, MC, V, AE, DC, CB, COD

Gosh, golly, and gee whiz! They'll take the shirt right off their racks and mail it to you! For another option, order your name-brand and designer shirts and sweaters in names such as HATHAWAY and CHRISTIAN DIOR from their affiliated stores called Penn Garden and Liberty Menswear, phone (212) 966-5600. Shirts range in size from 14½ to 18; suits and jackets bear labels by GEOFFREY BEENE, STANLEY BLACKER, YVES ST. LAURENT, ADOLFO, PIERRE CARDIN, and CALVIN KLEIN. Virtually everything they carry is a name-brand. You'll save 20% to 35% and they pay the shipping (with no G-strings attached!). Alterations are free on suits, jackets, and raincoats. Orders are delivered in about two weeks; full refund or exchange policy should also put you at ease. Order by phone Sunday to Friday with credit cards. **PQ**

HARRY ROTHMAN, INC.
200 Park Ave. South
New York, NY 10003
(212) 777-7400
CK, MC, V, COD

Rothman is to the discount men's clothing business what Loehmann's is to women's. Suits, jackets, shirts, ties, rainwear, and haberdashery in a wide variety of styles hang out on the racks here. Sizes run from 36 to 56; there are extra-longs and extra-shorts, too. Many top men's manufacturers are represented, always in season, and always in large quantities; prices are from 25% to 50% off. (Though they wouldn't reveal labels to us over the phone, we know that many a Hick has become a Free Man after leaving his shop.) Write to their mail-order department describing your size, weight, height, waist measurements, and preference of patterns and fabric. They'll provide you with top-of-the-line menswear. Returns are accepted (if not worn or altered). **PQ**

HUNTINGTON CLOTHIERS
1285 Alum Creek Drive
Columbus, OH 43209
(800) 848-6203
(614) 252-4422: OH residents
CK, MC, V, DC, CB, AE

The Huntington Clothiers' catalog proves once and for all that "good things come in small packages." The 50-page booklet is a *must* for devotees of the classic prepped-out look. Shirts come in striped and solid Oxford, straight collar, button-downs, long and short sleeves, pinpoint Oxfords, "graph check," tattersall Madras, broadcloth, tartan plaids, and gingham. Cotton ties are $10 and are available in classic styles and colors. Suitable savings were found on poplin, worsted wool, khaki twill, pincord, hopsacking, and silk suits and sport coats. Dress trousers, shorts (sans alligator), rugby shirts, belts, and underwear should round out any man's wardrobe. A few pages of women's clothes are also featured. Stop hunting and start shopping this clothier. **C**

JOHN MABRY MENSWEAR
9780 LBJ Freeway
Dallas, TX 75243
(214) 340-1210
CK, MC, V, COD

Look your best without blowing your budget when you shop here. Fine clothing at up to 50% below retail lets you dress for success without paying high prices. Men's two-piece suits start at under $100 and include private label suits, sport coats, dress shirts, sport shirts, and slacks. Top quality accessories include ties, belts, socks, and underwear, also available at a discount. Clothing includes big and tall men's sizes. All clothing is guaranteed for one year given reasonable wear, and there's a 30-day exchange or refund on items (or by January 15 on clothing purchased for Christmas). Texans pay applicable sales tax, and all orders are responded to within 24 hours. **PQ**

JOS. A. BANK CLOTHIERS
109 Market Place
Baltimore, MD 21202
(301) 837-8838
CK, MC, V, AE

For investment dressing, this is a manufacturer you can Bank on. Savings of 25% to 30% on fine-quality traditionally styled men's, women's, and preppie clothing and accessories were tastefully tailored to fit our budget. Bank's holdings included good buys on silk ties (at $12.50 each, these are the ties that *won't* bind); men's Oxford cloth shirts (for just $18.50, they put us in high cotton, but left a little "lettuce" in our pockets); men's 100% wool worsted suits (for $210 they bested their competition in worsted suits); women's khaki slacks ($26.50); and ragg wool sweaters (for $20.50 they wouldn't leave even the Pillsbury doughboy looking like a ragg-a-muffin). Other Bank assets include shoes, belts, rain gear, handbags, hats, and caps. Returns are accepted within 30 days for exchange or refund (if the garment hasn't been worn or altered). If you write a personal check, your order will be held until your check clears. If you would like to put a finger on the supple fabrics they use, ask for samples. **C**

THE KING SIZE COMPANY
24 Forest St.
Brockton, MA 02402
(800) 343-9678
(617) 580-0500: MA residents
MC, V, AE

The kingpin of King Size, James Kelley, stands tall when he professes his motto: "A 6'8" man should not have to pay a penalty for being tall." They try to position their prices within 10% of what a 5'8" man would pay for the same clothing. They also have clothing to outfit large men (pants sized from 44 to 60; shirts from 17 to 22). They have their own label as well as JOCKEY, HAGGAR, BOTANY 500, PALM BEACH, HUSH PUPPIES, and LONDON FOG. Shipping via UPS costs 10% of the order up to $3.75 maximum; there's an unconditional guarantee. Their free catalog comes out 10 times a year; January and June are sale issues. **C**

LEE-McCLAIN CO.
U.S. Highway 60 West
Shelbyville, KY 40065
(502) 633-3823
CK, MC, V

Tired of jockeying for clothing at retail? (You bet!) Well, you can't get a Kentucky derby here, just suits, sport coats, and slacks at 40% to 60% off. This 50-year-old company manufactures its own line of STRATHMORE suits—other suits are given private labels and are sold in fine retail stores under the store's name. Summer-blend suits were 55% Dacron and 45% wool, while winter suits were 100% wool. Only one suit style is available—every suit has a two-button front with a center vent in the back. Prices on STRATHMORE suits ranged from $175 to $185 (suits comparable in quality run $295 and up), so discounts are about 40% to 60%. Navy blazers and navy suits with pinstripes are their most popular offerings, although a 100% camel's hair sport jacket for $175 is also a good seller. Suits are stocked in sizes 36 to 50 in extra-long, long, regular, and short. About 90% of their inventory is for men, but they do have some tailored suits and blazers for women, too. If you send them your suit size, they'll send you fabric samples (since not all fabrics are available in all sizes). Make your decision, and you'll be off to the races (looking like a thoroughbred) with their finished lines. **PQ**

MASTER FASHIONS
5318 Normandy Blvd.
P.O. Box 37559
Jacksonville, FL 32205
(904) 786-8121
CK, MC, V, AE

Heee-ey, men! Master Fashion's been the savior for many a man of the cloth: they're called to serve preachers, pastors, and Christian groups. Bless their heart, they have basic black, brown, and navy suits in two basic styles. Many brands are carried, and savings of 40% to 60% will leave you a lot of bread to be thankful for. Sizes run all the way from 36 to 70. At the risk of sounding judgmental, we noted their offering also included a simply styled two-button blazer in electric blue, orange, red, green, or gold. They tithe one free suit for every ten religiously ordered. Shipping charges are $3 or 5% of the total order, whichever is greater; most orders are received in two to three weeks; satisfaction is guaranteed. **B**

SAINT LAURIE LTD.
Dept. US
Mail-Order Dept.
897 Broadway at 20th St.
New York, NY 10003
(800) 221-8660
(212) 473-0100: NY residents
CK, MC, V, AE

Halo out there! This Sainted discounter can save you pennies from heaven on classic business suits. Sharp-looking men's and women's suits are discounted, as can be seen in their semi-annual combination swatch brochure. At Saint Laurie, men's suits range from $295 to $350; women's suits are $295 to $350. Fabric swatches of tweed, silks, mid-weight wools, linens, cashmeres, worsted wool, and camel's hair give you a feel for what you're buying. There's a two-week refund or exchange period; orders normally are delivered in about a week, although back-ordered items can take two to three weeks to arrive. If you're in the neighborhood, take a factory tour from 9 to 4 Monday through Friday. We don't want to make a suitcase out of this, but here is where the worst-ed can be the best. **C** (Swatch Club Membership: **$10**/year, 2 seasons, Fall and Spring)

STANLEY M. MIRSKY
2600 Stemmons, Suite 204
Dallas, TX 75207
(214) 634-1757
(214) 634-7249
CK

Stan's the man to see since "I can get it for you wholesale" is his standard operating procedure. Behind the sleek black blinds of this jobber's elegant shop are classically styled, private label, natural fiber suits and sports coats selling for 50% less than in retail boutiques. Quality's superb on his finely tailored clothes, as are his prices. A 100% camel's hair or gray hair sport coat retailing for $350 to $395 would wholesale at Stan's for $175. Another bargain: wool worsted suits retailing for $450 would wholesale here for under $200. Besides suits, there's another room crammed full of coats, including distressed leather jackets, down parkas, sheepskin coats, raincoats, and even leather pants. Silk ties were just $10, cotton shirts were $17. Although his private label stock makes up most of his inventory, he carries some designer merchandise, too. For instance, we had to give in to a GIVENCHY tuxedo that was on sale for $135 in any size. Want to know what happened to personalized service? Stan's still got it—he'll pick up folks with airport layovers and bring them to his shop, give advice on hotels and transportation, etc. He even meets people for Sunday shopping appointments. If you see something you like in a magazine, clip the page, send it to Stanley, and see what he can come up with. Chances are good he'll "get it for you wholesale." **PQ**

SUSSEX CLOTHES LTD.
302 Fifth Ave.
New York, NY 10001
(212) 279-4610
CK, MC, V, AE

Dress for Sussex means "power dressing" for the man who's upwardly mobile. This prestigious manufacturer's outlet "sells retail to the public at wholesale prices." They carry suits from $205 to $260 and sports jackets starting from $175. We saw a blue wool blazer for just $159 and a 100% camel's hair sports jacket for just $200. All fall and winter suits are 100% wool. Regularly stocked fabrics include camel's hair, herringbone, flannel, pinstripe, plaid, tweed, and solid wool . . . all imported fabrics. You'll also find 100% silk sport jackets;

trousers in sizes 30 to 40; two- and three-piece suits; tuxedos for $250. All bear the SUSSEX label; they're about 50% less than their usual retail price. Shipping costs $5 for the first suit and $1 for each additional garment. Return policies are very flexible: they'll swap sizes, or refund on anything within 10 days as long as the garment hasn't been altered or the tags removed. **B $2**

Apparel: Women's

Sport an international look without leaving your living room. With the right catalogs, you can snag souvenirs from around the globe and become a cosmopolitan lady with wearables from around the world. Go international with Danish or Irish hand-knit sweaters, or fine woolen clothing from the famous looms of Iceland. And here's a tip: if you're on the smallish side, save $$ on your IZODS by shopping in the boys' department. The conversions are: boys' 20 = women's large (38 to 40); boys' 18 = women's medium (34 to 36); boys' 14 to 16 = women's small (30 to 32). No matter what you're looking for, use your ingenuity. With a little shopping savvy, you can get your upstairs wardrobe at a bargain basement price.

ARTHUR M. REIN
Dept. US3
32 New York Ave.
Freeport, NY 11520-2017
(516) 379-6421
CK (CERTIFIED or CASHIER), MO

Arthur has put a Rein on high prices. No, not Dudley Moore, but Arthur M. Rein. He plays the title role in the hit, *Keeping Down the Cost of Beautiful, Luxurious Furs.* Sound like a movie you would like to see? We thought so, too. His prices of 10% to 50% below retail should win an Academy Award. The leading lady is always in top fashion with BLACKGLAMA, EMBA, BLACK WILLOW, SAGA, and more. If it's a brand, it's on hand, as well as unbranded generics which were also available at a lesser price. Arthur produces fur garments and any item capable of being made of fur. For example, review these box office hits: 99% custom-made fur coats, jackets, capes, boas, wraps, earrings, teddy bears—the list continues for several scenes. Custom-made garments are guaranteed to fit properly. If you would like an autograph from Arthur and a tour of his factory and showroom, you only have to make an appointment. "I deal on a personal one-to-one basis," the star was recently quoted. Want a quoted price? Send an SASE with your height, weight, bust or chest size, sleeve length, color, kind of fur, and estimated budget. About 90% of his inquiries are answered the same day. Here are some previews of his next movie: sometimes older style, used fur garments are available in excellent condition at about one-third the cost of new ones. Are you in the market for a hide but don't want to lose yours paying for one? Then don't forget Arthur's—Liza wouldn't. *Underground Shoppers* will receive a special discount on Rein mink fur teddy bears. Brown mink bears are $125 each, postpaid (suggested retail price $195), and white mink bears are $145 each, postpaid (suggested retail price $230). **PQ**

CAREER GUILD
Dept. US
6412 Vapor Lane
Niles, IL 60648
(800) 538-5380: member orders and new memberships
(800) 972-9999: IL residents
CK, MC, V, AE

We won't g(u)ild the lily when it comes to the Career Guild, 'cause we don't want to feel guild-ty later on. This is their firm offer: for $5 you can join the Guild and become eligible for discounts of 25% and more on coordinated fashions for working women. Members are under no obligation to buy. Examples of savings include $40 blouses that Guild members can buy for $30; wool blazers that cost $120 retail, $79 to Guild members; and even $180 wool suits are just $119. (As any apprentice will tell you, it pays to pay your dues!) Members also receive a Hertz rental discount, bimonthly newsletters, and credit plan eligibility. There's a 30-day exchange or refund policy, and the membership fee is refundable if you ever become dissatisfied. Two weeks is the usual delivery time for orders. There are eight free catalogs yearly. C

CHADWICK'S OF BOSTON, LTD.
One Chadwick Place
P.O. Box 1600
Brockton, MA 02403
(617) 341-2000

We were impressed with the mail-order division of Hit or Miss, a Boston-based off-price chain, featuring brand names direct to your doorstep. You'll recognize the models in the Chadwick's catalog from the pages of *Vogue* and *Harper's Bazaar,* but the prices won't be familiar. They are 20% to 50% below retail. We found a variety of fashion formats from casual khakis and polo shirts to elegant evening wear. Gabardine suits, silk blouses, shirtwaist dresses, and many other garments are featured. For a discounter, Chadwick's spared no expense in presenting a well-organized layout of merchandise. Much of the selection is classic but trendy themes are also represented. We highly recommend this catalog but watch out: Reading May Be Hazardous to Your Wealth. C

F.R. KNITTING MILLS, INC.
69 Alden St.
Fall River, MA 02723
(800) 446-1089
(617) 679-5227: MA residents
CK, MC, V

Are your yarns getting a little worn from the adventures you've been having (not to mention the stories you've been weaving)? If your warm woollies have seen better days, latch onto the Fall River Knitting Mill for discounted sweaters. Prices here are usually 30% to 50%

lower than retail and there are FALL RIVER sweaters for the whole family. Machine washable and dryable Shetland crew neck sweaters were $11.95 for women and boys, and $12.95 for men. They also stitch monograms or full names in various styles and different colors. There's a rainbow of colors available for cardigans, V-necks, and crew neck sweaters in cottons, acrylics, and woolens. Please call or write for your free mail-order catalog. C

GOHN BROS.
P.O. Box 111
Middlebury, IN 46540
(219) 825-2400
CK

Going, going, Gohn to the Brothers from Middlebury! This 85-year-old company sells Amish men's and women's clothing, plain clothing, underwear, hosiery, yard goods for quilting, and supplies and notions. (Their Amish Country Cookbook is $7.50 and features 600 old-fashioned Amish farm cooking recipes. That's one notion that really whetted our appetites.) Their line of 100% cotton underwear, socks, and bedding is their most popular offering. Clothing brands include HANES, HEALTH KNIT, GERBER, CHATHAM, RED WING (shoes), CANNON (towels), and V.I.P. SPRINGMILLS (fabrics). Prices were about 30% off retail. Gohn carries a good line of sewing supplies, too, in their eight-page newspaper brochure that lists their merchandise. This company exchanges and will give refunds upon request. **B, PQ**

GOLDMAN & COHEN
54 Orchard St.
New York, NY 10002
(212) 966-0737
CK, MC, V, AE

Oy-vey! This dynamic duo carries over 50 of the finest names in lingerie and loungewear, at savings ranging from 20% to 70%! (The usual discount is probably more like 40% to 50%.) Their inventory is mostly first-quality, with an occasional select irregular. You'll also find bras and lingerie by EVE STILLMAN, VASSARETTE, KAYSER, BALI, LILY OF FRANCE, and others. WARNER bras and daywear were also available from 20% to 70% off. Sizes in bras ranged from 32A to 44D; in lingerie from petite to extra-large. Exchanges are made, but the item must be clean, the tickets must still be attached, and you must have the receipt. There's a $15 minimum on credit cards. Shipping's $2.50 on orders under $50, $3 on orders up to $100. In-stock merchandise usually arrives in about a week; three to four weeks for things not on hand. **PQ**

THE ICEMART
P.O. Box 23
Keflavik Airport
235 Iceland
(800) 431-9003 (U.S. representative)
CK, MC, V, AE, DC, ACCESS, EUROCARD

Dyed-in-the wool sweater freaks yearning for undyed yarn will find their fancy looming on the horizon. Coats, caps, jackets, mittens, socks, scarves, and sweaters are made of wool shorn from descendants of sheep brought to Iceland in the ninth century. The hair has evolved to produce softer, glossier, lightweight wool. Picture natural wool in muted earth tones of creamy white, pale brown, and charcoal gray. You won't get fleeced either—prices are not baa-d! Blankets of 100% wool were $37 to $43; ladies' knitted fully lined jackets and coats from $84 to $92. Ladies' hand-knit pullovers in one-of-a-kind designs were made from hand-twisted yarn and cost from $54. Warning: if ewe miss this, you just might feel sheepish! **C ($1** for air mail; free by surface mail)

IRISH COTTAGE INDUSTRIES
44 Dawson St.
Dublin 2, Ireland

You can't earn a living churning cottage cheese, so the crafty Irish turned to making fine quality sweaters. It o'curd to them that the cottage industry could churn out homemade wool-you-be-mine's faster than granny could say "I feel a draft." Best of all, their prices on hand-knit Aran sweaters, scarves, and mittens won't get your Ire up. Not with savings of about 25%! With luck and a buck, you can get a charming catalog by air mail (free by surface mail). **C $1**

KENNEDY'S OF ARDARA
Ardara County
Donegal, Ireland

Shawl be comin' round the island when she comes! This is the place for savin' up to 50% on world famous hand-knit Aran Isle sweaters.

Kennedy's also carries shawls, scarves, mitts, and other items at 30% to 40% off. (Put *that* in your potato and boil it!) **C $3**

LADY ANNABELLE
541 Haverhill St.
Rowley, MA 01969
(617) 948-2105
CK, MC, V, AE

Ladies in weight-ing will find their teddies, camisoles, slips, bras, and nightgowns in hard-to-find sizes 38 to 56. While not a discount store, they do offer savings over custom clothing with their own LADY ANNABELLE label. (LADY ANNABELLE, incidentally, is now the country's best-selling label for fuller sized lingerie.) There's no minimum order, and they have a full money-back guarantee—all exchanges and refund requests are honored. The catalog price is refundable with the first order. **C $2 (refundable)**

LANE BRYANT
2300 Southeastern Ave.
Indianapolis, IN 46201
(317) 266-3311
CK, MC, V, DC, AE

This isn't Anita's company, but orange you glad you discovered them? We won't tell any tall tales: they carry "taller miss" sizes 16 to 24. If you're 5'7" and over, they have you covered in sizes 10 to 24. Big deal, you're a little larger now—sizes 36 to 60 and half-sizes 12½ to 34½ are also carried by Lane Bryant. Brands include LEVI'S, RUSS, SASSON, KORET OF CALIFORNIA, FIRE ISLAND, and LADY MANHATTAN. Prices are reasonable, and the selection is very good. Shoes in sizes 5 to 13 are also available. **C**

L'EGGS SHOWCASE OF SAVINGS
P.O. Box 1010
Rural Hall, NC 27098-1010
(919) 744-3434: orders and customer service
(919) 744-3435: catalog requests
CK, MC, V

Try this place on for thighs! Slightly imperfect L'EGGS panty hose, HANES underwear and socks for men and boys, UNDERALLS and

SLENDERALLS panty hose, and other brands are available at up to 50% off. We also found many discounted first-quality panties, bras, and slips with names such as BALI busting out. There's a large selection including discounted lingerie and activewear, but the best buys are still on panty hose. (Regular sheer-toe panty hose that retail for $1.69 are just 81 cents each when you buy 12 pairs.) Most items have a three-pair minimum. Their colorful 40-page catalog featured style and size charts for easy ordering; pages were tagged to indicate first-quality or imperfect merchandise. Postage varies depending on the amount you purchase: for under $10, you'll pay $1.10; for under $20, you'll pay $1.55, etc. L'eggs is a L'egg-acy from the Consolidated Foods Company. C

LINDA'S HOSIERY OUTLET, INC.
3407-A Archdale Road
Archdale, NC 27263
(919) 431-2568: call collect when ordering
CK, MC, V, COD

Got everything under control? If your undisciplined eating habits have made your tummy fat and lazy, Linda's Hosiery can help. Control top panty hose will put the squeeze on your stomach without putting the squeeze on your pocketbook. There's no need to drop names: you'll find the highest quality brands in a variety of colors at discount prices. The low prices on socks won't sock it to you and the ladies' panties will leave you panting for more. Ladies' dancewear will fit your bod and your bud(get). Discounts of 30% to 40% are the rule. There's a $10 minimum; a one-week shipping time; a refund-or-exchange policy. If you're ready for seconds, "repaired" socks are also available. PQ

THE LOFT DESIGNER SPORTSWEAR
Dept. US
491 Seventh Ave.
New York, NY 10018
(212) 736-3358
CK

When we saw the Loft's less-than-lofty prices on designer sportswear, we didn't hit the roof. With 38% to 60% discounts, we found prices much less steep-le than we expected; and even though we had a ceiling on our budget, we could put a designer on our back. Nothing comes between us and our CALVINS (KLEIN's that is), except high price tags. We found the latest PERRY ELLIS, and even ANNE KLEIN-ing the walls here. No price quotes by phone. Write in describing item requested. Include a $20 deposit per garment, refundable if they cannot locate requested item. Then, a balance due invoice will be mailed. After your check clears, item will be shipped.

MAYFIELD CO. INC.
303 Grand St.
New York, NY 10002
(212) 226-6627
CK, MC, V

Mayfield knows hose, and theirs go for 20% to 25% off retail. They carry a full line of lingerie, hosiery, and underwear in brands such as BERKSHIRE, BONNIE DOON, BALI, BARBIZON, CHRISTIAN DIOR, VASSARETTE, OLGA, WARNER, MAIDENFORM, FORMFIT, and HANES. Bras range in size from teen to size 48DD, and hosiery comes in all sizes. Merchandise is guaranteed to be first-quality; exchanges and refunds are made as long as the item is still intact; it's usually about a week before you receive your order. There's a $25 minimum order, so you may have to do some stocking up. **PQ**

MENDEL WEISS
91 Orchard St.
New York, NY 10002
(212) 925-6815
CK, MC, V, COD (when over $50)

Weiss up and become bosom buddies with Mendel Weiss. His 25% discounts will keep you abreast of inflation. A treasure chest of lingerie lines included LILY OF FRANCE, CHRISTIAN DIOR, OLGA, MAIDENFORM, BALI, PLAYTEX, WARNER, FORMFIT ROGERS, and others in bras, girdles, panties, garter belts, slips, camisoles, caftans, robes, bodysuits, swimsuits, cruise wear, car coats and raincoats, hostess gowns, and peignoirs. Bras are their claim-to-fame and to go with them, they also carry mastectomy forms. Special orders take about two weeks; you should receive standard orders in about 10 days. No minimum orders; refunds and exchanges are made within 30 days; handling and insurance is $2. **PQ**

MOTHERS WORK
Dept UGS1
P.O. Box 40121
Philadelphia, PA 19106
(215) 625-9259
MC, V

Are you one of the many working mothers of the '80s? Then let Mothers Work work for you. Exclusive maternity and afterwards business suits help you look stunning before, during, and after. We discovered jackets, dresses, and skirts, made of 100% worsted wool, developed to perfection for that tailored look. You won't find this quality under just any cabbage leaf. Many of the dresses and blouses coordinate with the suits for a complete look. Their full-color 32-page catalog arrives with a wardrobe design aid and a swatch card to help you mix and match so you can put together the perfect working wardrobe. You won't have to work hard at looking professional. Mothers Work will deliver a 100% refund or exchange within 10 days of receipt, and they offer next day shipping so your precious bundles won't be overdue. **C $3** (refundable)

MS., MISS, AND MRS.
Eighth Floor
462 Seventh Ave. at 35th St.
New York, NY 10018
(800) 223-6101
(212) 736-0557
CK, MO

Whether you're a Ms., Miss, or Mrs., you'll find what you're looking for here. They carry over 450 designer labels in sportswear, dresses, coats, and suits. There's a style to fit your way of life and budget. Everything is at least a third off retail, and some items are marked off 50% or more. Call to tell them what you're interested in and if they don't have it in stock (with 25,000 items in stock, this can be rare), they'll order it for you. This unique combination of quality, personal service, great selection, and the right price keeps their customers satisfied. Take care choosing your purchase: all sales are final.
PQ

NATIONAL WHOLESALE CO., INC.
Dept. US
Hosiery Division
Lexington, NC 27292
(704) 249-0211
CK, MC, V, AE

Does thigh-priced lingerie leave you feeling crotchety? Now all your dollars don't have to go to waist! Brief-ly summarizing, National Wholesale carries ladies' bras, panties, girdles, gowns, robes, hosiery, and socks, ranging from tummy tamers, body slimmers, and surgical hose, to ankle, thigh-, and knee-high hose. (Their thigh-thinner panty hose for slimming thighs, squeezing bulges, and diminishing saddlebags are particularly popular, but don't let the camisoles and slips slip by, either.) We found sheer savings from heel to toe (and on up!) with queen-sized control top panty hose. Regular panty hose are available at good prices, too: order a half-dozen at a time. Even pugnacious men won't fight their prices on boxers, T-shirts, or socks. Most orders are received in about five days; everything has a money-back guarantee. Don't forget to say you're an *Underground Shopper*—they'll give you a free pair of panty hose. C

O'CONNOR'S YANKEE PEDDLER WAREHOUSE SALE
116 Newman St.
East Tawas, MI 48730
(517) 362-3437
CK, MC, V, AE, COD (cash only)

Wanna be the tog of the town? The answer's just around the O'Connor. These Yankees peddle last season's stock along with first run closeouts from over 100 manufacturers including PENDLETON, WHITE STAG, JANTZEN, COLLEGE TOWN, CALVIN KLEIN, LEVI'S, HAGGAR, ARROW, GANT, MISTY HARBOR, and others at 30% to 70% discounts. They also have men's clothing, gifts, and furniture. There's an exchange policy on returns less a 10% restocking charge— they'll honor justifiable returns only. Call for a price quote. PQ

RAYMOND SULTAN & SONS, LTD.
47 Orchard St.
New York, NY 10002
(212) 966-3488
CK, COD

Bravo! Bravo! We did an understudy of undergarments and decided this was a class act for brassy brassieres in broad(way) sizes (32A to

50DD). Current and discontinued styles get favorable reviews. Sultan's the sheik of cheap chic, and if you know your lines, you'll score 20% savings on lingerie by BALI, POIREET, MAIDENFORM, and a crowd of others. Their supporting cast of characters includes a large selection of black bras and girdles. Shipping's a flat $2.50 charge; there's no minimum order; your tickets to comfort should arrive in a week or two. No wonder folks keep coming back for an encore! Send them a postcard giving the manufacturer, style number, size, and color to get a price quote. **PQ**

REBORN MATERNITY
1449 Third Ave.
New York, NY 10028
(212) 737-8817
CK, MC, V, AE

For a pregnant pause that refreshes, flip through Reborn Maternity's color catalog. Revive your maternity wardrobe with moderate to better sportswear and evening wear: you'll find born-again bargains in sizes 4 to 20. It won't be long before you'll be singing praises, either, when you see the 10% to 40% savings on name-brands like SASSON, DENNIS GOLDSMITH, BELLE FRANCE, and FINE SPORT. The minimum order's just $20 and you won't have to wait nine months to get your order, either—most orders are delivered in two and a half weeks, or well before the stork makes *his* delivery. Be sure to mention *The Underground Shopper* and get an additional 5% across-the-board discount. **C $2**

ROBY'S INTIMATES
1905 Sansom
Philadelphia, PA 19103
(800) 631-1610
(215) 751-1730; PA residents
CK, MC, V

The daughter of A. Rosenthal of New York, Robin Langert, is following in her father's footsteps in offering the finest bargains in women's lingerie. Roby's is definitely one of our favorites when it comes to underwear, bras, girdles, lingerie, robes, nightgowns, and panty hose discounted 20% to 50%. Roby's is a firm supporter of over 50 brands of lingerie, including MAIDENFORM, LILY OF FRANCE, VASSARETTE, LADY MARLENE, FORMFIT, KAYSER, EVE STILLMAN, DANSKIN, and many imports. Sizes range from 28AA to 46F, and everything is first-quality. HANES and BERKSHIRE hosiery lines represent a new addition to their product line. No returns on special order merchandise, on worn, torn, or soiled items, or on items that have had the tags removed. There is a $2.50 shipping and handling fee on all orders. Write and send an SASE for their brochure or send them the manufacturer and style number for a price quote. **C $1, B, PQ (SASE)**

ROYAL SILK
Royal Silk Plaza
45 E. Madison Ave.
Clifton, NJ 07011
(201) 772-1800
CK, MC, V, AE, DC, CB

Although Royal Silk isn't a bona fide discount company (they sell their own wares rather than discounting those made by other people), you can still find excellent values on silk blouses, dresses, and menswear. Prices are usually at least 40% lower than those on retail lines of comparable quality. The *Royal Man* collection exhibited a shantung silk tuxedo shirt for $45, silk shorts for $18, and several styles of silk and cotton shirts. Men's basic silk shirts made from Calcutta silk in a 40-gram weight were only $24. Batiste shirts for men and women (60% silk, 40% cotton) ranged from $22 to $27. The women's Royal Silk catalog featured a colorful array of tastefully elegant silk blouses, most from $15 to $60. A women's silk safari jump suit was just $60. The Royal Silk Dress Collection displayed a dozen brightly colored dresses priced from $58 to $75. Royal Silk has a 100% guarantee, so if you're unhappy for any reason, they'll refund, exchange, or give credit. Shipping's $1 per accessory; $2 per garment. Check out Royal Silk's catalog ensemble. Their basic, 40-page, full-color catalog displays over 70 items. **C $2**

RSL
3200 S. 76th St.
Dept. 785
Philadelphia, PA 19153
(215) 492-9619

We really don't know what RSL stands for, maybe Razor Sharp. Who knows? We do know, though, that we found some razor sharp fashions in their full-color catalog. You'll be sharp in a chic chemise

PROTECT
Your Treasured Dining Table Top
With CUSTOM FIT
TABLE PADS
ASK ABOUT
FREE LEAF SPECIAL
SAVE UP TO 70%
Call Factory now & order
direct before prices increase
UNBELIEVABLY PRICED FROM
$29.95 Quality Pad
Any Normal Size
COMPARE AT 99.95
Min. 5 year guarantee—MC/VISA
Look under table
for numbers & tell us
what they are.
FACTORY DIRECT TABLE PAD COMPANY
TOLL FREE 1(800) 428-4567

BUYING GUIDE

Most products featured in *1,001 Home Ideas* are available in leading stores nationwide. Or write sources listed below for information on where to get their products. Antique, custom-made or privately owned items are not always listed. Prices, where given, are approximate retail. **Sources are manufacturers unless otherwise noted. Key (R)Retailer; (D)Through decorators or to trade only.**

TABLE OF CONTENTS PAGE 4

Background—100% cotton fabric from the "Book Binders" collection by Ameritex for United Merchants, 1407 Broadway, NYC 10018.

HOTLINE PAGE 8-10

Napkins—Den Permanente Export, Inc., Dept. TH, 2920-3000 Wolff St., Racine, WI

signs, 225 Canyon Rd., Santa Fe, NM 87501. **All antique furniture, accessories, pillows**—Spider Woman Designs (address above).

KITCHEN

Sink—Elkay Mfg. Co., 2222 Camden Court, Oak Brook, IL 60521. **Faucets**—Kohler Co., Kohler, WI 53044. **Dishwasher**—KitchenAid, 701 Main St., St. Joseph, MI 49085. **Oven**—Thermador/Waste King, 5119 District Blvd., Los Angeles, CA 90040. **Cooktop**—Chambers, by KitchenAid (address above). **Microwave**—Thermatronic II, Thermador/Waste King (address above). **Refrigerator**—Sub Zero Freezer Co., P.O. Box 4130, Madison, WI 53711. **Cabinets**—MasterCraft, 6300 S. Syracuse, Suite 700, Englewood, CO 80111. **Saltillo floor tiles**—Artes_____ ports, Inc., 222 Galisteo St., Santa F_____

66207. **Curtain fabric**—P_____
Box 956, Fairfax, CA 9493_____
crest, 60 W. 40 St., NYC_____
wicker chair—Robert Alle_____
Fabrics (address above). **Pa_____
ney Wallcoverings, 23645 M_____
Cleveland, OH 44122, or call_____
Wallpaper—Marimekko, 7 We_____
10019. **Fabric**—Westgate, 10_____
Parkway, Grand Prairie, TX 7505_____

MASTER BEDROOM

**Window treatment : Curta_____
lance**—Paper White (addres_____
table skirt, stripe—R and M_____
2355 Rusman, Cape Girard_____
Bed table skirt, moire—Ro_____
Contract Fabrics (addre_____
handmade_____

which costs only $35.95. Slice the cost of buying a new winter coat, their Grand Illusion coat had us mystified with its low cost of $99. A paisley, pleated dress had us com-pleat-ly delighted with a low price of $34.99. We found the latest looks at affordable prices. You can pull one over; a velour oversized pullover was a low $27.99. RSL slashes the high cost of looking great by as much as 30%. They guarantee you the best prices on every item, every day. If you find it cheaper in another catalog, they will refund you the difference. They carry fashions in every category (lingerie, sportswear, dresses, suits, and shoes), and their sizes (misses 6 to 16, large 38 to 52) have everyone covered. Whatever your passion, RSL has the fashion. **C**

SWEETWATER HOSIERY MILLS
Dept. US
P.O. Box 390
Sweetwater, TN 37874
(615) 337-9203
CK, MC, V

Sock it to me, baby! (We've got to put our foot down on these wornout phrases.) The deal with this merchant is sweet indeed: the manufacturing plant next door produces brand names, but the store gets the leftovers, which, unlike mashed potatoes, are as good as the original. At this 88-year-old sock shop, you'll be out of the woods with 40% off men's over-the-calf zephyr wool/nylon socks for $2.25 a pair. Ladies' support panty hose irregulars were $1.10 a pair; girls' and boys' cotton/nylon crew socks, three pair for $1.25. Men's athletic shirts were three pair for $4.99. My, what big T-shirts they have! 'Tis better (heh, heh) to save you money, my dear. **C, PQ**

THE SWISS KONNECTION
Suite 300
5330 Alpha Road
Dallas, TX 75240
(214) 233-0627
CK, MC, V, AE, COD

A cut above any other furrier, it may seem ludicrous to stuff a 40% to 50% off sable coat in your mailbox, but trust me, no matter what size you are, it'll fit. Primarily a source for mink, dahhling, but connections can also be made on blue, white, red or silver fox, Canadian lynx, beaver, coyote, and sable. Although this retailer is also a full-

service discount jeweler, we couldn't resist highlighting their fur collection, too. All brand-name and fine jewelry offered, including
watches and accessories (lighters, pens, clocks, and crystal), custom-
made creations (just send them a picture), and loose stones, their
specialty. Save one-third to one-half on items made to retail from
$300 to $50,000. Merchandise returned for exchange or credit
(except special orders) and no refunds unless returned within 72
hours. Minimum order, $100. C

V. JUUL CHRISTENSEN & SON
96 Strandboulevarden
DK-2100 Copenhagen
Denmark
26 60 00: dial 01 for operator assistance
CK, AE, DC, MONEY ORDER

Knit one of these pearls and you'll receive one of their beautiful
Danish hand-knitted sweaters for men, women, or children. Over 36
years in the business of keeping the family warm, these hand-knit
garments take 30 to 40 hours to knit. Made of 100% pure new wool,
light, soft to the touch, this Juul of a manufacturer is but a catalog
away. C

W.S. ROBERTSON OUTFITTERS LTD
40/41 Bank St.
Galashiels, Scotland
0896-2152
CK, MC, V, IMO

See entry on page 33.

Appliances and TVs

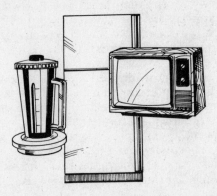

What do you do if your mail-order appliance starts getting a little balky? If your video game is on the blink or your vacuum cleaner is upchucking more than it's sucking in, don't despair. First, write the manufacturer and give them the opportunity to respond. If your problems aren't ironed out that way and you're still dissatisfied, write the Major Appliance Consumer Action Panel (MACAP), 20 N. Wacker Drive, Chicago, IL 60606 or call their toll-free recording (800) 621-0477 or their office (312) 984-5858 during working hours. The recording gives a step-by-step plan of action when your major appliance problem isn't resolved by the dealer. Supply them with the manufacturer's name, the type of appliance, the model number, the date the appliance was purchased, a description of the problem, copies of correspondence, and all receipts. They'll take it from there.

AAA ALL FACTORY VACUUMS, FLOOR CARE, & CEILING FANS
Dept. US
241 Cedar
Abilene, TX 79601
(915) 677-1311
CK, MC, V, COD, D, LAYAWAY

Vaccinate yourself against high-pressure salespersons selling high-priced vacuums—the prices here are innocuous enough! First-quality brand-name dirtbusters like KIRBY, RAINBOW, FILTER QUEEN, HOOVER, EUREKA, PANASONIC, COMPACT, as well as MASTER CRAFT (a line of commercial vacs and floor care products), are discounted up to 50% and 75% on some makes! AAA is the oldest and largest mail-order vacuum and floor care discount store in the country. Your satisfaction is 100% guaranteed or your money back. AAA issues their own product protection guarantee for up to three years on "door-to-door" makes, and provides factory-authorized warranties in your own locality for most other makes. Quality ceiling fans are another money-saving opportunity and a proven means of lowering energy bills during both summer and winter. Don't forget to mention you read about AAA in *The Underground Shopper.* **B** $2 (refundable with first order)

ABC VACUUM WAREHOUSE
Dept. US
6720 Burnet Road
Austin, TX 78757
(512) 459-7643
CK, MC, V, AE, COD

There's a sucker born every minute. That's why ABC doesn't want you to be taken in or get left holding the bag. Although science tells us there is no such thing as a perfect vacuum, we found some of the best brands (RAINBOW, KIRBY, FILTER QUEEN, PANASONIC, ROYAL, and ORECK) discounted up to 40%. That's probably why business has been picking up since 1977 for owner Ralph Baccus. KIRBY cleaners are warranted for parts and service for two years. All others have a one-year warranty for parts and service. Merchandise is shipped within 24 hours; 90% of their customers receive their orders within 10 working days. They give full refunds within 15 days (excluding shipping charges). Before you buy a vacuum from a door-to-door salesman, check out the prices here. **B, PQ**

BONDY EXPORT CORP.
40 Canal St.
New York, NY 10002
(212) 925-7785
CK, MC, V, AE

Small, name-brand appliances discounted 30% to 50% pay big dividends for Bondy's. The last time we shopped Bondy's, they had the best price anywhere on KRUPS coffee grinders, $17 compared to a normal $32 retail price. In fact, they've got irons, toasters, hair dryers, coffee makers, can openers . . . it looks like a Smithsonian exhibit on "Modern Savings and Loan Gift Giveaways for People Opening New Accounts." Bondy's portfolio includes stock from hundreds of companies, including GE, OSTER, HAMILTON BEACH, CLAIROL, HOOVER, SANYO, SONY, ZENITH, CORNING, FARBERWARE, SMITH-CORONA, and SAMSONITE. RAY BAN and PORSCHE CARRERA sunglasses and BUSHNELL binoculars were also discounted, along with PANASONIC answering machines and cordless phones, SEIKO and CASIO watches, and ITT telephones. Bondy's specializes in products for use overseas (220 volts). Cameras by CANON, MINOLTA, YASHICA, POLAROID, plus all kinds of film, make getting a price quote first from Bondy's a wise investment. Bondy also carries microwave ovens by GE, SHARP, and TOSHIBA; radar detectors by FOX, BELL, and COBRA; and "Walkmans" by SONY, SANSUI, and AIWA. Orders are shipped UPS and can arrive anywhere between two and seven days. Buy carefully: there are no returns. **B, PQ**

C.O.M.B.
1405 Xenium Lane North
Plymouth, MN 55441-4494
(800) 328-0609
MC, V, AE

You could scour the country with a fine-tooth comb and still not uncover a better deal than here. For the past 13 years, this over-the-counter public company has come up with savings of 50% off suggested retail on all the major brands in phones, stereos, TVs, housewares, appliances, computer hardware and software, radios, exercise equipment, and automobiles. Yes, savings of $4,000 on your bigger ticket items is commonplace. Offering both the manufacturer's warranties and C.O.M.B.'s assurance that you be completely satisfied, you can start the ball rolling; call toll-free and receive your order in less than two weeks. Their 48- to 64-page monthly catalog is free including a biweekly insider's hotline. **C**

COMP-U-CARD
777 Summer St.
Stamford, CT 06901
(800) 835-7467
(800) 252-4100
(203) 324-9261
CK, MC, V

She'll be Comp-in' round the mountain when she comes! She'll be savin' time and money, she'll be shoppin' for her honey, she'll be Comp-in' round the mountain when she comes! For $30 a year, subscribers to this "electronic shopping service" can get all the price quotes they want on over 250,000 items of major brands of appliances, furniture, jewelry, wallpaper, electronics, computers, china, crystal, exotic teas and coffees, luggage, audio equipment, etc. Subscribers also get "Best Buys," Comp-U-Card's monthly publication which lists current bargains (including special, immediate deals like closeouts and sales). If you've been waiting for a "big brake" on buying a new car, Comp-U-Card claims they can get it for you from their dealers or yours for $125 over dealer cost (plus destination charges from Detroit to your door). **B, PQ** ($30 membership)

DIAL-A-BRAND
110 Bedford Ave.
Bellmore, NY 11710
(718) 978-4400
(516) 783-8220
(201) 653-6727
CK, MC, V

One ringy-dingy, two ringy-dingies . . . well, you won't get Ernestine, but you can get the low price lowdown on TVs, air conditioners, major appliances, videotape recorders, or microwaves. Major airlines, universities, and banks all have patronized this company in an effort to save money. Recommended by national consumer groups, Dial-A-Brand's easy to do business with. Just call and give the model number of the item you want, and lo and behold, it's whisked COD to your door in its factory-sealed carton (complete with full warranty and service). They'll exchange at no cost if your purchase is damaged or is defective on delivery. No membership fees required. **PQ**

EBA WHOLESALE
Dept. US
2361 Nostrand Ave.
Brooklyn, NY 11210
(718) 252-3400
CK, MC, V

At last, at last! There'll be no more suffering by savings suffragettes! This company voted to pass this EBA (Equal Bargains Amendment) and give up to 60% discounts on all major and small appliances, TVs, and video equipment. Become un-FEDDEREd and liberate yourself from the economic heat of high-priced air conditioners. (In other words, stay cool, fool!) It's a g-ratifying experience to find dozens of products from over 50 top-name manufacturers like ADMIRAL, PANASONIC, LITTON, KITCHENAID, WESTINGHOUSE, GENERAL ELECTRIC, and many others. Send a description of the item to EBA (including the model number) and they'll quote a price. If you decide you want to exchange for another model, they'll be glad to make amends, but there's a 20% restocking charge on returned merchandise. Expect your order to arrive in about two weeks. **PQ**

FOCUS ELECTRONICS
4523 13th Ave.
Brooklyn, NY 11219
(800) 223-3411: Electronics orders only
(800) 221-0828: Camera orders only
(718) 871-7600: NY residents, electronic inquiries
(718) 436-6262: NY residents, camera inquiries
CK, MC, V, AE

See entry page 99.

HUNTER AUDIO-PHOTO LTD.
Dept. US
507 Fifth Ave.
New York, NY 10017
(212) 986-1540
CK, MC, V, AE, DC, CB

Watch out for these a-wrist-ocrats: SEIKO, BULOVA, and CASIO watches at savings up to 50%. Or take a few cheap shots at their complete line of cameras by MINOLTA, MAXXUM, CANON, PENTAX, YASHICA, FUJICA, and NIKON. Feeling adventurous? Take a walk on the wild side with SONY, SANYO, PANASONIC, and TOSHIBA persona stereos, all at discount prices. (SONY Walkmans were a particularly good buy.) You can write your own ticket with pens by MONT BLANC, PARKER, and CROSS, up to 50% off. Write for flyers that list the prices. Getting tired? Your days are numbered with adding machines by CANON, SANYO, TEXAS INSTRUMENTS, and HEWLETT-PACKARD. Run that by us one more time: they have over 2,000 movie videos in stock, along with videos of operas and ballets, all at 10% to 25% below their list price. Send for their free "Video Yesteryear" catalog. There's no minimum order; no refunds. Orders usually arrive in about two weeks. There's a free video catalog for *Underground Shopper* readers. Tally ho, this Hunter's a fox! **PQ**

INTERNATIONAL SOLGO, INC.
1745 Hempstead Turnpike
Elmont, NY 11003
(800) 645-8162
(718) 675-3555 or 895-6996
(516) 354-8815
CK, COD

This company marks down their merchandise Solgo faster. Both major and minor appliances, washers/dryers, air conditioners, televisions, camera equipment, jewelry, dishes, silverware, clocks, radios, luggage, and other 20th century essentials are solidly discounted up to 40%. (Actually they price 7% above their cost.) Leading brands include: GE, ZENITH, MAGNAVOX, RCA, SANYO, SONY, POLAROID, TOSHIBA, and KODAK. It's hard to say no to SEIKO watches discounted 40%. (Over 500 brands are carried.) This firm is firmly established and carries a lot of buying clout in the industry: they've been around since 1933, or for over half a century. A large selection of all voltage merchandise is available for export. They can also arrange shipments to include prepaid charges for preparing the proper documentation, insurance, etc., for shipments either to pier or airport. Caveat emptor—they don't accept returns. **C $5** (refundable with $100 first purchase)

LVT PRICE QUOTE HOTLINE
Dept. US-87
P.O. Box 444
Commack, NY 11725-0444
(800) 645-5010
CK, MO

No, LVT is not E.T.'s big brother, even though a lot of people do phone, and even though some prices they quote are "out of this world." Given the model number of any item carried by one of the 75 big-name manufacturers they do business with, LVT will quote a price to you, often as much as 40% lower than retail. Major appliances, televisions, microwave ovens, typewriters, video recorders, radar detectors, telephone answering machines, computers, calculators, scanners, office equipment, food processors, vacuum cleaners, and air conditioners are all items they regularly handle. Videocassette recorders, telephone answering machines, CUISINARTS, and vacuum cleaners remain their most popular bargains. All merchandise is covered by manufacturer's warranties, but be sure of your selection—all sales are final; there are no returns. Orders are processed within 24 hours of receipt of your cashier's check, certified check, or money order. LVT pays all surface UPS shipping charges nationwide. A nice personal touch: if your order is out-of-stock, LVT will telephone you to inform you of the delay, rather than just send you a postcard like most firms. Write for their brands list, find out the model numbers of the items you want (cheap!) and phone home to LVT. They'll give you the spiel, no matter your burg. **B, PQ**

McALISTERS, INC.
926E Fremont
Sunnyvale, CA 94087
(408) 739-2605
CK, MC, V, AE, COD

See entry page 416.

THE PINE CONE
Dept. US
P.O. Box 1378
Blake Building
Gilroy, CA 95021
(408) 842-7597
(408) 842-4797
CK, MO

You might have to suck in your stomach for this one, but it'll be worth it. This miracle Mini-Vac is a revolutionary new tool for cleaning minute particles of dust and debris from hidden and hard-to-reach places. Unlike compressed air which simply disperses the pollutants, Mini-Vac vacuums them away FOREVER! Mini-Vac is the tool for all reasons and seasons. Perfect for computers, camera equipment, typewriters, stereo equipment, automobiles, and a myriad of household uses. Regular retail is $29.95 plus $2 shipping; *Underground Shoppers'* price is $24.95 plus $2 shipping. Allow three to four weeks for delivery. Your satisfaction is guaranteed. Product: $26.95

SEWIN' IN VERMONT
84 Concord Ave.
St. Johnsbury, VT 05819
(800) 451-5124
(802) 748-3803: VT residents
MC, V, COD plus $2.50

"Why pay through the nose when you can save through the mail?" Sewin' in Vermont has sewn up the market on mail-order sewing machines with low, low prices that will keep you in stitches. We found a common thread of excellent values running between both domestic and foreign brand sewing machines. Their most popular brand is SINGER, as you'd expect, but PFAFF, a European model, is also in demand. Prices of about 30% below retail on most models won't leave you hemming and hawing. Inventory is maintained on the premises: credit card orders are shipped the same day; orders paid by check are delayed until the check clears. (A stitch in time saves—period.) Merchandise is returnable for 30 days; refunds or exchanges are made depending on the problem. Write for manufacturer's brochures and price lists; soon you'll be bob, bob, bobbin' along. **B, PQ**

S & S DISCOUNT SERVICE
P.O. Box 76
Bedford Hills, NY 10507
(914) 666-4641: collect
CK, MC, V, COD

Survey the discounts at S & S and you'll be singing your way to your savings account. This company sells SINGER, VIKING, and NEW HOME brands at 25% to 35% below retail. The most expensive SINGER they carry costs $889; bought in a store at suggested list price it would cost $1,500. (They are most famous for their buys on SINGER machines.) A-hem, we don't want to needle you, but write or call for a price quote on the model you want. Delivery should take about a week, maybe longer. **PQ**

Art and Collectibles

Are you basically a pack rat—but one with good taste? Maybe you're someone who just loves collecting. You live for the thrill of discovery and the pleasure of creating a nest for yourself with interesting "found" objects. On the other hand, maybe you're someone who knows exactly what you want, and you're motivated by the excitement of the chase. You've been on the trail of a particular ivory netsuke statue ever since you brought one back from Japan last year. Finally, maybe you just have a taste for the unusual. You're struggling with that room in your house that needs to be jazzed up and a hand-loomed rug from Tibet would be just perfect. Whatever you want, your search is over. You'll find it (whatever "it" is) here.

A. GOTO
Shibuya, P.O. Box 261
Tokyo, Japan 150
BANK DRAFT, MO

Goto this dealer if you want a deal in Japanese antiques! A. Goto specializes in netsuke, (pronounced NUTSKE—and you'll go nutsky over their prices), Inro, snuff bottles, wood block prints, and cloisonné. You'll find these antiques up to snuff for they are all in good to excellent condition, dating from the 1850s to the 1900s. Prices average 30% to 90% less than retail. Here are some examples from their price list. Netsuke range from $10 to $200 each, compared with $90 to $2000 retail; woodblock prints were $60 to $300, compared with $100 to $450 retail. Prices vary for several reasons; quality, age, the artist, etc. Many of these items are rare collectibles not available in retail stores. We must bow to the variety of Netsuke; ivory, black coral, amber, stag horn, hornbill, ivory nut, porcelain, and Manju. Stock is subject to change, so alternates must be indicated on the order. Be warned that items may not be returned. We found the price list and photos which were sent somewhat incomplete, so be sure to ask for complete shipping information. Orders will be processed within five days. Items are shipped by sea mail or there is a surcharge of 15% for air mail. Insurance is not automatic, so be sure to request it. (There is also an extra charge for it.) The good news is that there is no shipping or handling charge except postage and a $1 mail charge. No sales tax or duty on items over 100 years old. F

ANTIQUE IMPORTS UNLIMITED
P.O. Box 2978-US
Covington, LA 70434
(504) 892-0014
CK, MC, V, MO

This company's made some inter-continental moves in their day, beginning in Ireland and crossing the Atlantic ultimately to land in Louisiana. What you lose by eliminating browsing through the antique shops is about 40% to 60% off the retail prices. If you know your stuff, period, you'll love to order their sample lists in a variety of categories; either for $2 or on a yearly subscription basis. From their antiquities (ancient items of Egypt, Greece, Rome, Persia, etc.), with a minimum order of $30, you could choose from the fifth century A.D., a semi-circular stamp seal of mottle quartz in orange, red, and white for $60, the face (intaglio) engraved with the figure of a stag's head, and pierced for suspension. Listed in good condition. That's just one detailed listing from one of the categories available. Others include: Antique & Collectible Jewelry; Antiques & Collectibles; Antique Maps, Prints, and Paintings. Readers placing an order will receive free of charge the next two issues of the catalog from which they ordered. Orders over $500 receive all catalogs free. **C** $2 single issue/also available for yearly subscription, rates vary.

THE FRIAR'S HOUSE
Bene't Street
Cambridge, England CB2 2QN
(0223) 60275
CK, MC, V, AE, DC

The elegance of merry old England can be yours at a low cost. From traditional to modern, this company carries a selection of china, crystal, and enamel collectibles to start or complete a special look in your particular decorating taste. Values include modern glass paperweights in British and European styling, enamel decorator boxes in true BILSTON, and BATTESEA style, DAVID WINTER COTTAGES, and all the crystal and china collectibles you're looking for. Names include almost all British companies, with special added discounts offered at certain times throughout the year. Money refunded if not completely satisfied with purchase, and immediate delivery is provided by air mail. From The Friar's House to your house, this worldwide service is sure to please. **C**

GALLERY GRAPHICS, INC.
Dept. US
Box 502
227 Main St.
Noel, MO 64854
(417) 475-6367
CK, COD

Stop waiting for your Prints Charming! Gallery Graphics carries over 250 art prints and reproductions of antique classics at savings of up to 50% off. Everything is in stock, including Christmas cards, note and greeting cards reproduced from old antique prints, and framed and matted prints. Orders normally go out the same day; none take longer than 72 hours. Customer satisfaction is guaranteed, and in all their years of business, there's never been a single request for a refund. Their price list is wholesale prices. Shipping charges are 5% of the invoice price of the merchandise. Smile with the *Mona Lisa*, turn green with envy at *Blue Boy*, or kick up your heels with a Degas for as little as $2. This place has the largest selection of antique reproductions in the world! Minimum order is $50. **C $5** (refundable)

**GEORGE CHANNING ENTERPRISES/
INCREDIBLE ARTS**
P.O. Box 342
Carmel, CA 93921
(408) 372-0873
CK, MC, V, AE

Imitation is the sincerest form of flattering one's pocketbook, and these reproductions of rare art prints from beautiful hand engravings are no exception. Each print has been faithfully duplicated in the finest of detail as it appeared in *Harper's Weekly* more than a 100 years ago. What's so incredible, though, are the prices—at least 50% less than other comparable prints. Notables: Frederic Remington, Thomas Nast, M. Vely, Kollwitz, and John Singer Sargent. Shipping and handling $1.25 per print, $3.50 for three or more. No artful dodger here—an absolute 100% satisfaction guarantee. Phone orders can be delivered in three to seven working days. Visit their retail shop called Incredible Arts at 711 Cannery Row, Monterey, CA 93940 when in the area. **C $4**

GOOD SHEPHERD'S STORE
P.O. Box 96
Manger St.
Bethlehem, Israel

Holy mother of pearl! While Good Shepherd's Store watches their stock by night, wise men won't have to travel to get good buys on religious icons. You won't have to dip into your cache of cash to get a crèche you like. We'd have walked a mile for one of their camels, starting at $6, or a Bible, $14 ($21 at U.S. flea markets) both in olive wood. Chess sets, candlesticks, religious figures, and jewelry boxes are all available. An inlaid mother-of-pearl cross was $4. The minimum order is $30. **C $2**

GREEN RIVER TRADING CO.
Boston Corners Road
R.D. 2
Box 130
Millerton, NY 12546
(518) 789-3311
CK, COD

Have a barn-building party (or put up a garage for a noble steel steed) with kits from Green River. Their specialty is rustic looking log cabin kits, and they'll sell you blueprints or help you design your own. Prices are 20% to 40% less than conventional prices. There's no minimum order, no restocking charge on returns, and exchanges or refunds are honored up to 60 days after delivery. All materials are warranted for one year. For those who want to avoid slivers from timbers, Green River sells novelty log siding—for the log look without the log. Green River also publishes and sells Western art, originals and limited editions, and—get this!—they raise and breed Texas Longhorn cattle. **C $6**

HOOVEY'S BOOK SERVICE
10 Claremont
Hastings, Sussex
England
(0424) 430398
MC

Looking for an obscure title or an out-of-print book? Greetings, bibliophiles, your search is ended. Hoovey's book search has been heralded for the speed of locating mint condition books and selling them for reasonable prices. Hoovey's has connections with a vast majority of secondhand book dealers in the United Kingdom and United States. They also deal with private collectors. Novels, children's books, text books, reference works, and more have been located. The cost of a search is 50 pence (roughly $1, we suggest you check the current rates) per title per week; you are under no obligation to order when you use the service. Overseas customers are asked to remit by sterling payment only and to add one pound to the total cost of their book search to cover the fast air mail service report system. An order form is available on request. **B**

MISCELLANEOUS MAN
Box 1770
New Freedom, PA 17349
(717) 235-4766
CK, MC, V

Who is the Miscellaneous Man behind the scenes? He travels the globe searching for items some would consider trash: old stamps, handbills, labels, guides, and other memorabilia. One man's trash is another man's treasure should be his motto. All his items are original and some are antiques. Who is he? George Theofiles, ephemerologist (is that fancy for pack rat?). Among his huge collection you'll find circus posters, cigar labels, war posters, and so on. Prices are 30% to 50% below retail, and that should be posted. He claims every one of his items represents history. This diversified man looks twice at things the rest of us walk on. He has accumulated enough miscellaneous items to fill the Taj Mahal. If you are adding to your valuable collection or just adding pizzaz to your bedroom wall, give this man a call. Twelve hundred posters, books, etc., are offered in his semi-annual catalog. Every item is shipped in gorilla-proof tubes and is insured. No monkeying around. The next time you clean your attic, think twice about what you throw away. **C $3**

MURRAY'S POTTERY, INC.
802 Kings Highway
Brooklyn, NY 11223
(718) 376-6002
CK, Money Orders

Remember that rock promoter, Murray the Clay? (He had to go underground after the mass kiln.) Well, this Murray offers a 170-page catalog filled with sculptured replicas of famous as well as contemporary works, from ancient Chinese pieces to cowboys and horses at very reasonable prices. In addition to the familiar (Rodin, Michelangelo, etc.), he carries many lesser known works by even lesser known artists. Glassware, barware, crystal, and coffee mugs are also available, but only for walk-in customers (they are not shippable). Murray's glassware and crystal are "misprints" from famous name manufacturers (whom Murray prefers to keep quiet about). Decorated barware retailing for $18 for four pieces is priced as low as $3.95 in some cases. Catalog prices are about 20% to 25% less than retail, but if you visit, you'll find even bigger discounts: up to 80% in some cases. Shipping is done by UPS, and refunds are made at your request. **C $3** (deductible from your first order)

MUSEUM EDITIONS NEW YORK, LTD.
105 Hudson St.
New York, NY 10013
(800) 221-9576
(212) 431-1913: NY residents
MC, V

This international publishing and distributing company is one of the best sources for fine art posters. Poster styles range from abstract to classic; photographic to silk screen prints. You can find something for every room of the house: posters of herbs and spices for the kitchen, Monet's *Waterlilies* for the bedroom, and maybe Cleworth's *Double Ferrari* or Cota's *Lilies* for the living room or dining room. They'll keep you posted through their 32-page catalog, and special quarterly fliers that announce sales. The shipping fee is just $5 for up to 20 posters; your order should come within 10 days to two weeks. Museum Editions supplies posters from the Guggenheim Museum, the New York Philharmonic, the Phoenix Art Museum, the Corcoran Gallery, the Boston Symphony Orchestra, and independent artists among other sources. Mention that you're an *Underground Shopper* reader—they'll enclose a coupon in their catalog entitling you to 20% off gallery prices. **C $5** (refundable)

NEPAL CRAFT EMPORIUM
G.P.O. Box 1443
Katmandu, Nepal
12500-21220

Nepal Craft Emporium's handsome handicrafts should be featured in "Home Buddha-ful." Thirty Buddha gods and goddesses ranging in price from $2 (for children of a lesser god) to $99 (Oh, God) are cast by the ancient "lost wax process" which apparently has been found again. As a result, these pieces are sought-after collector's items. Turquoise-and-coral-studded filigree boxes, birds, animals, and jewelry make unique, inexpensive gifts priced from $1 to $8. The minimum order is $300 (FOB Katmandu). **C $3**

TIBETAN REFUGEE SELF-HELP CENTRE
Havelock Villa 65
Gandhi Road
Darjeeling-734101
India
2346-DE: office (dial "01" for operator assistance in making this call)
CK

Learn about "the courageous plight of the Tibetan people driven from their homeland by invaders in 1959." What price knowledge? Just $2.50, and for your money you can also learn about the many wonderful crafts made at this Centre. The Centre was created to help the Tibetan refugees not only earn a living, but also to preserve their craftsmanship and cultural heritage. Using vegetable dyes and wools imported from Nepal, the refugees make a beautiful assortment of rugs. Complicated designs sell for about $10.70 per square foot. Add 10% for carpets larger than 50 square feet, and 5% if it's a custom-made carpet. Sweaters, woolen half-boots, Tibetan soldier's hats, greeting cards, and stationery may also interest you. Either bank transfers to the Grindlays Bank P.L.C., Darjeeling, or checks are acceptable payment. **C $2.50**

WORKS OF MAX LEVINE
Dept. US
19-18 Saddle River Road
Fair Lawn, NJ 07410
(201) 797-7216
MC, V

Max Levine's three-dimensional, original wall sculptures are made from heavy gauge steel finished with a patina of gold leaf and solid brass accents. Many of these "limited edition" contemporary works are specially designed to blend artistically in homes or offices. Prices range from $65 to $325. Since this is the only outlet for Max Levine's work, it's impossible to compare prices. There's a 10-day full refund policy: orders are typically delivered in four to six weeks. **B $1**

WURTSBORO WHOLESALE ANTIQUES
Dept. US
P.O. Box 386
Wurtsboro, NY 12790
(914) 888-4411
CK, MC, V, COD

These folks aren't afraid to peddle their wares (accessories and smaller items only) through the mail, Wurts and all. (Do you suppose Wurtsboro got its name when somebody toad the county line?) This company sells European primitive antiques that are at least 100 years old. (American primitive pieces are sold in the store only.) Their hottest selling items are spinning wheels for $95 and carousel horses; butter churns ranging from $40 to $65 and wooden hay forks are also popular and fit in well with the "country look." Although they are mainly wholesalers (Bloomingdale's buys from them for resale), if you buy, you can buy-pass the middle man. Orders are usually shipped by UPS; there are five-day return privileges. Their catalog is 16 pages. **C $2;** Antique and Estate Jewelry **C $1**

Art Supplies

Art for art's sake, without the art ache? Free expression often isn't; at least, not when you're an artist. Art supplies are expensive. But now starving artists can put food on the table, by buying their art supplies at a discount. It's as easy as setting up your easel. Just draft a letter from your drafting table, and quality products like LIQUITEX acrylics, WINSOR & NEWTON Designer's Gouache, GRUMBACHER oils, and REMBRANDT pastels will come to you—by mail. Discounts can be up to 50% off the prices in an art supply store. And if you're a member of an artist's guild or a student in a class, you can buy in larger quantities and save even more. Van Gogh for it!

A. I. FRIEDMAN
44 W. 18th St.
New York, NY 10011
(212) 243-9000
CK, MC, V, AE, COD

Supplying the fashion industry with markers, paints, and drafting supplies contributes to this man's Fried-dom. Their other clients include publishers, Fortune 500 companies, and even the Muppets. This 56-year-old company features a complete, state-of-the-art inventory from airbrushes to zipatone in their thick 345-page catalog, $3. Over 10,000 brands are carried and many items are discounted 20% or more. A special list of items included LIQUITEX acrylics and oils, WINSOR & NEWTON watercolors, REMBRANDT and BOCOUR BELLINI oils, and a large selection of brushes discounted up to 40%. Canvas panels, watercolor papers, stretchers, canvas, and turpentine are also discounted. The minimum order is $35. You'll have to add 10% to your purchase for shipping, handling, and insurance. Exchanges or refunds are made up to seven days after purchase. C, B

DICK BLICK COMPANY
P.O. Box 1267
Galesburg, IL 61401
(800) 447-8192
(800) 322-8183
MC, V, COD

Use your Bic to write Dick Blick and get their 370-page, full-color catalog of creative materials. A leading supplier of high school and university art departments, your best bet for savings are quantity buys of Blick's brand of paints and papers. "Blick City" tempera paints were 20% lower than a comparable brand (a six-gallon pump kit was $62.90.) CRAYOLA crayons were just 87 cents (list $1.23) if you bought in bulk (72 boxes.) Discounted posterboards by Blick in six-, eight-, and 14-ply were a good sign at 30% below retail. Most discounts are between 10% and 20%; temperas and acrylics are the most popular purchases. Most orders arrive at their destination in about two weeks. Their catalog is free if you say you're an *Underground Shopper* reader. C

FRANK MITTERMEIER INC.
Dept. US
3577 E. Tremont Ave.
New York, NY 10465
(212) 828-3843
CK, COD

Whenever Mister Chips goes to the Bronx, he always calls on Frank. Frank's no chiseler, but his collection of tools will steel your heart away. He carries over 40,000 tools for wood-carvers, sculptors, engravers, ceramists, and potters, plus many how-to books for the knot-so inclined. Discounts of 10% and a "no charge for shipping" policy when you buy six or more tools will whittle down your bill. DASTRA woodcarving tools, finely crafted by DAVID STRASMANN & COMPANY of Germany, were 10% lower than retail including shipping. A set of five tools (chip carver, skew chisel, parting tool, and two gouges) was just $34.90. Send for the free 32-page illustrated catalog—"every whittle bit helps." **C**

GREAT TRACERS
3 N. Schoenbeck Road
Prospect Heights, IL 60070
(312) 255-0436

This family of Great Tracers will trace a trail to your hearts but not your wallets. They offer *great* savings of up to 50%. You won't be tracing these low prices to other firms, and that's nothing to shake a pencil at! They provide made-to-order letter stencils in a variety of sizes. There is a $1 shipping and handling fee and a $5 minimum order. Satisfaction is guaranteed. "Our reward is in serving our customers and learning from each other as we work together." Mention the *Underground Shopper* and receive an additional 20% discount. So, follow the line to great savings— — —Great Tracers.
B 50 cents (SASE)

JERRY'S ARTRAMA, INC.
Dept. US
P.O. Box 1105 (inquiries and orders)
117 S. Second St.
New Hyde Park, NY 11040
(800) 221-2323
(516) 328-6633: NY residents
CK, MC, V

A trial by Jerry probably means you'll get hung in some art gallery. Brands like WINSOR & NEWTON, 3M, D'ARCHES, GRUMBACHER, and STRATHMORE are witnesses for the state (of the art, that is). Character witnesses give testimonials to Jerry's discounts of "20% to 40% off" (a charge to which he pleads "guilty.") One of Jerry's best-selling items is the GRUMBACHER #286 French easel (genuine) which is $159.95, $259.95 retail. (With savings of $100, it's no surprise why it sells so well!) The minimum order is $25; phone order minimum is $50. Refunds and exchanges are accepted for 90 days. Check out Artrama's annual 160-page catalog, which is free with mention of *The Underground Shopper.* C $2 (refundable)

NEW YORK CENTRAL SUPPLY CO.
Dept. US
62 Third Ave.
New York, NY 10003
(800) 242-2408
(212) 473-7705
CK, MC, V, AE

"We cater to our mail-order customers," says Steven Steinberg, third generation owner of one of New York's oldest fine art supply stores. Discounts of 20% do nothing to discount his claim. They claim to have "the most complete artist's supply inventory in the world," so even hard-to-find items are no problem. Every major brand in every type of artist supplies is available. Their paper department covers the entire second floor of their three-story building: it includes over 2,000 papers from 17 countries. New York Central really showed their true colors with 250 lines of paints by WINSOR & NEWTON, LIQUITEX, REMBRANDT, GRUMBACHER, and BELLINI. Besides their general catalog, there are special catalogs for paints, $2; paper, $2; calligraphy, $1; and airbrushes, $2. The price of their catalogs is refundable with your first order. C $ varies

PEARL PAINT
Dept. US
308 Canal St.
New York, NY 10013
(800) 221-6845: orders only
(212) 431-7932: NY residents
CK (certified), MC, V, MO

Now there's a string of Pearls (Long Island, New York; Paramus, New Jersey; and Fort Lauderdale, Florida) to help you paint the town red, white, or cobalt blue. Pearl is a huge supplier of art and craft materials with "more artist's paints than anybody else in the world." Their 48-page "fine art" catalog displays only 2% of their inventory. Over $50,000 dollars worth of merchandise is carried with brands such as WINSOR & NEWTON, GRUMBACHER, MORILLA, STACOR, LIQUITEX, MARTIN, and HUNT. Discounts are 20% to 50% off. Look what Tex got in the LIQUITEX line of acrylics: 20% off two-ounce tubes of color. The ROBERT SIMMONS red sable hair watercolor brushes we saw here let us "sable" little money at 15% below normal retail, too. If you send them a product description, they can usually fill it (as they've done for folks like Peter Max, Andy Warhol, and Helen Frankenthaler). Customers get their orders in about two weeks; the minimum order's $50; there's a 10% restocking charge on returns. C $1 (refundable), PQ

POLYART PRODUCTS CO.
1199 E. 12th St.
Oakland, CA 94606
(415) 451-1048
CK, MC, V, COD (with minimum of $100)

If you paint the town red you'll save, but if you paint your red wagon you'll pay close to retail. Savings come with volume orders. (We almost lost our tempera because we had to order $40 of their acrylic artist paint to get an extra 10% discount.) Polyart manufactures their own high-quality paints. Prices are discounted, but not a great deal; paint costs $5.50 a pint including shipping. Additional discounts are given, however, depending on the size of your order. They have 12 colors plus gloss clear, gel clear, modeling paste, and gesso. There's a $20 minimum order (with no additional discount); orders of $400 and more get up to 30% off. B

STU-ART SUPPLIES
2045 Grand Ave.
Baldwin, NY 11510
(800) 645-2855
(516) 546-5151: NY residents
CK, MC, V

Artichoke you up? Get your framing and presentation supplies cheaper (approximately 50%) and wind up on the Dick Cabbage show. We'll be art-iculate about their discounted NIELSON metal frame sections, wood and tenite, sectionals, five varieties of mats, shrink wrap, D'ARCHES watercolor paper, and all-media art boards. Minimum orders of $15 on frame sections and $25 on mats, but if you combine the two, there's just a $25 minimum. Orders over $250 are shipped free in UPS delivery areas only. Refunds are given to dissatisfied customers. **C**

UTRECHT ART & DRAFTING SUPPLY
33 35th St.
Brooklyn, NY 11232
(718) 768-2528
CK, COD (with 50% down and the rest on delivery)

To etch his own. With over 100 brands here, there's a big enough selection for everyone to draw from their extensive inventory. Discounts are 20% to 75% off on art and drafting supplies. They carry Utrecht and other major-brand supplies ranging from acrylics, brushes, canvas, and drafting machines to frames, watercolors, and zipper cases. We found a complete line of D'ARCHES, K&E, and DESIGN ART MARKER. Their complete line of PANTONE products is discounted 30%, and STRATHMORE, BIENFANG, and CHARTPAK are discounted 50%. Quantity discounts on UTRECHT products (up to 20% off orders over $450) rounded out their portfolio. There's a $40 minimum order and a two-week delivery time. Returns are accepted only with prior authorization. Before u trek all over town, u try Utrecht. **C**

Bed and Bath

Bed and bath bargains abound between the sheets of this section. Take comfort in outfitting your bed and bathrooms at half the price. You'll salute the four-star savings on brass beds, and march to the beat of decorated deals on MARTEX towels, NETTLE CREEK bedspreads, or SPRINGMAID sheets. With the great savings you'll be getting on sheets, pillowcases, towels, etc., you may even be too excited to sleep!

CAMEO, INC.
Dept. US
503 Grandville Ave. S.W.
Grand Rapids, MI 49503
(616) 451-2759
CK, COD

When we gazed at this Cameo, our faces were etched with relief. This 27-year-old company pillow-ries high retail prices with 25% to 30% savings on piles of bed pillows, decorative pillows, down comforters, and rocker and chair pads. Names like DUPONT, SONTIQUE, ADORATION, and CAMEO give you quality you can re-lie on. Orders usually come in about two weeks. There's a $15 minimum on custom orders, no restocking charge, and a guarantee against defective workmanship. When you sleep on this decision, you'll know you've made the right choice. **PQ**

THE COMPANY STORE™
500 Company Store Road
P.O. Box 2167
La Crosse, WI 54601
(800) 356-9367
(608) 785-1400: WI residents
CK, MC, V, AE

Get down, get down! Save up to 50% at the same time. A simple but elegant selection of pure down products is available from the factory outlet of Gillette Industries. Some of The Company Store's fine-feathered friends include designers BILL BLASS and GLORIA VANDER-BILT, whose quilted coats and robes are made by The Company Store. We warmed up to high-quality, crafted and styled down pillows, comforters, crib comforters, and booties available in classic colors (beige or blue). Rest assured that you will have these products for many years to come. **C**

ELDRIDGE TEXTILE CO.
Dept. US
277 Grand St.
New York, NY 10002
(212) 925-1523
CK, MC, V

If you're looking for a big selection for the boutique bed, bath, or boudoir, at discounts of 30% to 40%, this is the place for you! They've got four floors and over 10,000 square feet blanketed with first-quality merchandise. The inventory's enough to floor you. But the buck doesn't stop there, not in *this* 46-year-old business. You'll find ground floor opportunities for name-brand and designer towels, sheets, area rugs, blankets, pillows, and closet accessories. Move on to the main attraction: kitchen curtains, tablecloths, bed and bath boutique items, and place mats (including lots of imports, even linen from China). Give free reign to your immodest ambitions and climb the ladder of success to the second floor. It's laden with bedspreads, draperies, and vertical blinds. Their hundreds of brand names read like a "Who's Who" in home decorating: MARTEX, WAMSUTTA, DAKOTAH, FIELDCREST, and LAURA ASHLEY are just a sampling. Shipped UPS by weight; they go out within 48 hours. Returns are accepted if the item is unused and still salable. **PQ**

ELECTROPEDIC ADJUSTABLE BEDS
Dept. US
1534 E. McDowell Road
Phoenix, AZ 85006
(800) 423-2725
(602) 253-6600
CK, MC, V, AE, DC, CB

Open your own chiropractice by ordering direct from this manufacturer. For over 20 years, this company has been selling "America's best-built electric adjustable bed." According to their literature, there's a five-year guarantee on lift motors (which can be replaced easily, even by an all-thumbs teenager), and a one-year guarantee on heat. A 39-by-74 twin regular bed was $899 (comparable retail price: $1,498), while a twin long was $800 (typically $949 in a store). You can rest assured that shipping's not outrageously expensive either; about $75. Other products include an at-home massage unit that kneads out the competition. Usually, orders are received in seven to 10 days. We'd say more, but we don't want to rub it in. (We have a hands off policy here.) **C**

EZRA COHEN CORP.
307 Grand St.
New York, NY 10002
(212) 925-7800
CK, MC, V

It's E-Z to save with Ezra Cohen of New York. A veritable institution for bargains in towels and bed linens, this famous discounter's been around since 1912. Name-brand, top-of-the-line linens we encountered included WAMSUTTA, UTICA BY J.P. STEVENS, BILL BLASS BY SPRINGMAID, MARTEX, MARIMEKKO BY DAN RIVER, VERA, CANNON, LAURA ASHLEY by BURLINGTON, and many others. Ezra Cohen features a wide variety of products, from neck rolls and pillow shams to duvets and down comforters and bedspreads by DAKOTAH, NETTLE CREEK, CROSCILL, and BATES. Coordinated linens are presented in bedroom settings reminiscent of *Architectural Digest*. Ezra Cohen specializes in custom designs. A team of professionals will design "almost anything" using material from regular sheets. **C**

THE FACTORY STORE
585 Baltimore St.
Hanover, PA 17331
(717) 632-8691
MC, V, CK

Since July of '63, the Acme Quilting Co. has been turning out the textiles. Over 5,000 bedspreads alone are available for the great American cover-up. Inventory also includes bedspreads, towels, draperies, pillows, sheets, comforters, quilts, and blankets from NETTLE CREEK, BEAU IDEAL, BATES, ACME, CANNON, DAKOTAH, SPRINGMAID, and others. About 20 to 25 brands are carried. The Factory Store is probably best known for its NETTLE CREEK bedspreads, but mattress pads may be their best buy. Save 30% to 50% on first-quality merchandise and 50% to 60% on irregulars. (Who cares if your bottom sheet's a little faded at the corner!) There's a liberal exchange and refund policy with shipment by UPS. (Tack on an additional 50 cents for the carton and handling.) Tightwads like us sleep tighter on bed linens without the (retail) bedbug bite. **B**

HARRIS LEVY, INC.
Dept. HL
278 Grand St.
New York, NY 10002
(212) 226-3102
CK, MC, V, AE

With only two complaints (both resolved) in 90 years, we'll Levy this Grand Street granddaddy our finest honor. Harris Levy throws in the towel, as well as the sheets, comforters, and other bed and bath items at 25% to 50% off. They carry every major brand in the business, including WAMSUTTA, J.P. STEVENS, MARTEX, SPRINGMAID, FIELDCREST, DAN RIVER, and CANNON. They carry over 60 different styles of sheets with an especially big selection of country-style sheets and towels, so be specific when ordering by mail or by phone. Their custom order department can fill special requests for table linens, draperies, and shower curtains including monogramming. Returns are handled on an individual basis within 30 days as long as the item is returned in its original condition; store credit is usually given. Expect your order in two to three weeks. **PQ**

J. SCHACHTER CORP.
115 Allen St.
New York, NY 10002
(212) 533-1150
CK, MC, V, AE, COD (with 50% deposit)

Is there a Schachter in the house? You're darn right! Since way back in 1919, they've been hiding out in the bedroom buried beneath the largest fabric selection for comforters in the country. There are over 200 to choose from as well as other accessories to complete the ensemble: shams, ruffles, table covers, draperies—even a decorator, if you're color-blind. They also carry both custom and stock comforters, and pillows and linens by WAMSUTTA, MARTEX, CANNON, and DAN RIVER. Imported bathrobes listing for $200 were priced at just $160; merino wool blankets from New Zealand were another good buy. Savings run 25% to 40% usually, but up to 60% on closeouts. Recovering old down comforters and pillows is a store specialty. Odd-sized sheets for boats and water beds are another store novelty. No returns are accepted on custom or special orders, but full credit is issued on unopened, stock merchandise. In-stock items are shipped within 48 hours and are usually received in about a week. Custom orders generally come in three to five weeks. Take two bedspreads and call them in the morning. **C $1, PQ**

PENNY WISE WAREHOUSE STORES
2025-A Midway Road
Carrollton, TX 75006
(214) 458-2337
CK, MC, V

Brass will last where money is concerned; a penny saved *is* a penny earned. Penny Wise carries brass beds, mattress sets, and uphol-

stered furniture at excellent prices. Owlishly wise shoppers who give
a hoot about preserving their nest egg can save 35% to 60% on items
by name-brand manufacturers like DRESHER, SWAN, ARTISAN,
SEALY, SERTA, MAYO, RIVERSIDE, BASSETT, NORWALK, and others.
Penny Wise has an enormous selection of trundle, iron, and brass
beds by DRESHER and CORSICAN, too. They'll send a bed anywhere in
the continental U.S. and Canada, and tuck in a one-year full replacement guarantee or a two-year guarantee on DRESHER products for
defective materials or workmanship. There's a $40 delivery price
within Texas; other delivery charges are quoted upon order. Customer satisfaction's guaranteed. Orders are usually received in
about 10 days. Check their full-color brochure for more details.
B $3, PQ

QUILTS UNLIMITED
Dept. US
203 E. Washington St.
P.O. Box 1210
Lewisburg, WV 24901
(304) 647-4208
CK, MC, V

This company believes that where there's a quilt there's a way to buy
it for less. So if you appreciate the fine crafting and fascinating colors found in American antique quilts, send for this 16-page catalog.
In addition to describing each quilt's colors, fabric, and design elements, the catalog lists prices, sizes, and any flaws the quilt might
have. A packet of 12 to 20 photographs, each showing eight quilts, is
sent with every catalog. Quilts Unlimited is "America's largest
antique quilt shop" selling to over 1,000 mail-order customers each
year. Bette Midler, Lauren Bacall, and many overseas customers
have bought from this shop. Avid collectors Joan and Albie Fenton
issue a new catalog "once per month, generally" as new quilts are
acquired. Prices are about 20% to 30% less than antique dealers for
quilts; animals made from quilts and crib quilts are discounted 10%
and 30%, respectively. The Fentons guarantee authenticity and if
you're not satisfied, return the purchase within three days and your
$5 will be applied to your first order. **C $5** (refundable to readers);
$20 for annual monthly subscription.

RAFAEL
291 Grand St.
New York, NY 10002
(212) 966-1928
CK, MC, V

Put your money worries to bed! Rafael means pleasant dreams. They offer seductive savings of 25% to 40% off the nightmarish cost of bed and bath creations. You can take comfort in comforters, or softly sink into sheets, pillowcases, towels, table linens, and more from the houses of BILL BLASS, DAN RIVER, VERA, BURLINGTON, MARTEX, and SPRINGMAID. In all, over 50 brands are carried. Imported tablecloths in a variety of sizes are particularly popular. Most orders arrive in about three to four weeks: there are no refunds. Write or call for your particular passion. **PQ**

RUBIN & GREEN INTERIOR DESIGN STUDIO
290 Grand St.
New York, NY 10002
(212) 226-0313
CK, MC, V, AE, COD

Rubin & Green has made a few changes over the past few years— they're a custom design company now. They carry an extensive line of 20 to 30 name-brand fabrics including SCHUMACHER, DAVID DASH, ROBERT ALLEN, STROHEIM, and ROMANN. From these materials they create custom design draperies, fully upholstered furniture, and custom designed window treatments. (They'll build furniture from the frame up, to your specifications.) They still make designer bedspreads (and comforters of goose down, lamb's wool, or Dacron) from your plans: they'll take your sample, picture, or diagram and quote prices and custom design according to your specifications. Prices are 50% off what you'd pay retail and sometimes more (depending on the fabric and design you choose). Interior designers are on staff at all times. The delivery time usually is four to six weeks for most work; eight to 10 weeks for furniture. Request specific information and a price quote. **PQ**

Boating Supplies

Are you the seafaring type? When the sails of your boat are billowing, the wind's at your back, and you're slicing through the spume and waves with a thin cool mist spraying your face, then do you feel truly alive? If you're a boat owner, or soon will be, this section is for you. Whether you're getting ready for the America's Cup race, preparing for a weekend of waterskiing, or just planning a strategic assault on the local black bass population at an area lake, these companies can regale you with regalia. From a tiny rubber raft to equipment for the biggest yacht, when it comes to mail-order marine supplies, selection and (watered-down) savings are the name of the game. And it's a game well worth playing.

DEFENDER INDUSTRIES
Dept. US
255 Main St.
P.O. Box 820
New Rochelle, NY 10801
(914) 632-3001
CK

Up periscope to sight in on savings! Defender torpedoes the competition with sub-marine prices—in fact, the lowest prices (35% to 65% off) we've seen on a complete line of nautical gear. Discounted items ranged from SETH THOMAS clocks to dinghies, to marine stoves, to electronics instruments, to engines, to sailboat hardware, all the way to heads. Defender also will match any competitor's advertised price. The depth of their fiberglass inventory (the largest in the U.S.) gave us a real charge. ACHILLES inflatable rafts weren't made for heels; and TIMBERLAND shoes were a good buy, as was foul weather gear imported from Taiwan and Korea. Before you Destroyer finances paying retail, bow down to their stern 40% discounts on boat and sailing supplies. There's a $15 minimum order and a 10-day refund policy. Orders are shipped out within 24 hours: most are received in about 10 days, while those during the peak boating season take about 14 days. Boat-owning *Underground Shoppers* who identify themselves get Defender's (hefty!) 200-page catalog free. C $1.25 (refundable)

E & B MARINE SUPPLY
980 Gladys Court
P.O. Box 747—(US 3049)
Edison, NJ 08818
(201) 287-3900
CK, MC, V, AE, DC, CB

No nautical disasters here: landlubbers and boaters will discover that the prices here won't rock the boat. Their 140-page catalog is swamped with thousands of boating accessory items. Savings billow upwards from 20% to 60% on marine marvels such as depth sounders, marine radios, electronic navigational aids, cushions, furniture, toilets, pumps, water skis, etc. Other discounted items include fair and foul weather clothing, boat shoes, nautical ties, inflatable boats, teak galley ware, clocks and barometers, and much more. Nineteen convenient East Coast discount stores all stocked up with the catalog items and then some. E & B's most popular item is their "All

Weather" suit. The polypropylene-lined pants and jacket set lists for $380 but E & B is offering it for only $139.88. Completely *waterproof,* yet machine washable and made in the U.S.A. The minimum order is $10; orders are shipped UPS within 48 hours. All rates include postage, packaging, handling, and insurance. **C**

GOLDBERG'S MARINE
202 Market St.
Philadelphia, PA 19106
(800) B-O-A-T-I-N-G
(215) 829-2214: PA residents
CK, MC, V, AE

Buoy, oh buoy, this company's been afloat for 42 years! Goldberg's has really gone overboard on pleasure boating equipment and nautical clothing at seaworthy savings averaging about 20% below retail. We piered at items like life vests, boat covers, pumps, fishing equipment, marine radios, and depth finders in their massive 200-page catalog of cargo. DANFORTH anchors held fast at 15% to 30% off manufacturer's list which gives us anchors a way we want'em—at a discount. With discount stores in New York City and Philadelphia, there's a boatload of savings to be found in their prices. There's a $25 minimum order and a 30-day money back guarantee. **C $2**

JAMES BLISS MARINE CO., INC.
Dep. US-3067
P.O. Box 3139
Edison, NJ 08818
(201) 287-3900
CK, MC, V, AE, DC, CB

If you've set your sails to saving, then this Bliss-ful 128-page catalog full of nautical accessories for the boater and landlubber is just what the sailor ordered. A 155-year veteran of the discount business (since 1832), this company also has nine discount retail locations in the Northeast (MA, RI, NY, CT). Included in their water-logged inventory are compasses, clothing, foul weather gear, boots, galleyware, sailboat hardware, cleaners, life vests, boat covers, ladders, paint, teak, lights—all at 20% off; many as much as 50%. Names on board were APELCO, AQUA METER, SEA RANGE, SCHAEFFER, TAYLOR, STEARNS, and PAR. Expect 10 days to two weeks for delivery. **C**

M & E MARINE SUPPLY CO.
Dept. US
P.O. Box 601
Camden, NJ 08101
(609) 858-1010
CK, MC, V, COD

Think you've seen everything in the way of marine accessories? Think again, bilge breath! Everything you've ever wanted to buy for your boat (over 24,000 items and over 1,400 brands) is contained in this two-pound, 350-page catalog—and at discount prices! As if this massive catalog weren't enough, they even come out with special sale supplements four times annually. You'll find power and sail equipment, marine electronics, hardware, paint, sport fishing equipment, furniture, clothing, and gifts. They even sell marine toilet paper. Everything is offered at 20% to 40% discounts. There's a $15 minimum order; orders are shipped within 24 to 48 hours. Full refunds are given within 30 days. **C $2**

WEST MARINE PRODUCTS
Dept. US
2450 17th Ave.
Santa Cruz, CA 95062
(800) 538-0775
(408) 476-1905: CA residents
CK, MC, V

Set sale! There's a breeze blowing 30% to 50% discounts off full retail here, and the trade winds are even more fair during seasonal catalog offerings. West Marine sells marine equipment, supplies, clothing, accessories, and electronics. Some 600 major brands are stocked in their more than 60,000-square-foot warehouse, including lines like PETTIT, INTERLUX, WOOLSEY, JAB, and PAR. There are over 22,000 different items for sale, ranging from rope to paint. Customer satisfaction's guaranteed. Most orders are shipped within 24 hours. You don't have to be into new wave to appreciate their tide-y, 200-page thick catalog. **B, C**

YACHTMAIL CO., LTD.
The Quay
Lymington, Hants. So49E
England
0590-72784
CK, MO, BANK CHECK

The sea of cruiser yacht equipment available from this company is all-encompassing. Flares and foghorns, heads and hatches, pumps and pulleys, lights and logs, and on and on it goes. (You name it, they've got it!) We're not dinghy, just a little dizzy with discounts of 20% to 30% off U.S. prices. (They're about 10% to 20% lower than UK prices.) That's a lifesaver in today's economy. We found seaworthy savings on AVON, SEAFARER, AUTOHELM, and ZEISS sextants. The only albatross not-so-ancient mariners must contend with is freight charges on the AVON life rafts. We were buoyed by the tax-free export price of $1,400, but shipping by air freight nearly sank our spirits at $320. **C**

Cameras, Opticals, and Photographic Equipment

Don't look to the stars for a good buy on cameras, telescopes, and binoculars. Focus your attention on our tips. Before deciding to order a camera, telescope, or binoculars by mail, visit several shops to look over the selection and get some professional assistance. When you've narrowed your choices down to a few, contact some mail-order sources to see if they stock the equipment you want. Resist the impulse to order over the phone. Always send in your order and keep copies of your correspondence. That way, if anything goes wrong, you'll have records. When your equipment arrives, unpack it carefully and save all the packing materials, in case you need to return your purchase. Don't fill in the warranty cards until you're sure everything is working perfectly. If you follow these tips, with the money you save, you can buy an extra lens!

AAA CAMERA EXCHANGE
43 Seventh Ave.
New York, NY 10011
(800) 221-9521: orders only
(212) 242-5800: NY residents
MC, V

Strictly a mail-order house, AAA features triple-good discounts on optics, many from famous makers. Discounted zoom lenses were a particularly good deal. A NIKON 80mm to 200mm f/4.5 zoom usually retails for $540. AAA has a comparable range and speed CAMBRON 70mm to 210mm f/3.8 macro for only $180 and an unnamed 75mm to 205mm f/4.5 for only $140. That's a lot of money saved—and that's only one of the many bargains! Between 30 and 50 brands are carried, and 90% of the merchandise pertains to 35mm cameras. Discounts are about 50%, so expect low, low prices. Orders are shipped out in 24 to 48 hours: shipping charges are a minimum of $3.75. Merchandise is fully guaranteed and is exchangeable within 14 days. There's a 15% restocking charge on returns. If you know what you LEICA, but you're not a name snob, you'll get the picture fast. **PQ**

ABC PHOTO SERVICE
9016 Prince William St.
Manassas, VA 22110
(703) 369-2566
CK, MC, V, AE, COD

Learning the art of photo finishing is as easy as learning your ABC's if you know where to start. Beginning at this service lab offering the finest color and black-and-white processing and printing, you can shop where the pros do. Trained Kodak technicians use the best equipment and materials. Payment must accompany all mail orders. Free mail-in envelopes. **C $2.50**

AD-LIBS ASTRONOMICS
Suite 106
2401 Tee Circle
Norman, OK 73069
(800) 422-7876
(405) 364-0858
CK, MC, V, AE, DC, COD

Heaven help us if there's a better source than this eight-year-old company specializing in telescopes, telescope accessories, spotting scopes, telephoto lenses, binoculars, books, and star charts. Chart your course with savings typically between 25% to 50% on name brands such as MEADE, CELESTRON, EDMUND, BAUSCH & LOMB. We were star-struck with their manufacturer's warranties (typically five years to lifetime). Service charge assessed on all orders under $25. You'll receive a free *Star Atlas* with a telescope purchase just by saying *The Underground Shopper* sent you. Their price list is free but there is a $1 charge for the 52-page catalog listing and describing over 70 telescopes and 500 accessories with helpful information on picking the right telescope and accessories. **C $1, PQ (send SASE)**

B & H FOTO ELECTRONICS
119 W. 17th St.
New York, NY 10011
(800) 221-5662: orders
(212) 807-7474: inquiries
MC, V, COD

B & H has seen the light on photographic specialty equipment. They've got light meters by GOSSEN, CALCULIGHT, SEKONIC, and VIVITAR, tripods by BOGEN, GITZO, SLIK, and even the strangely exotic NOVOFLEX follow-focus system that lets you keep your subject in focus even when it's moving. NIKON, CANON, HASSELBLAD, SPEED-OTRON flash systems, not to mention COKIN, TOKINA, TAMERON, and KIRON, and a host of other unpronounceable brands. (They have about 20 brands in all.) Everything's discounted, and the prices are hard to beat (15% to 20% lower than conventional retail). Thirty-six exposure KODAK film with KODAK processing for just $7.69 is a favorite of bargain-minded photo buffs. There's a 14-day exchange or refund policy and no restocking charges. Most orders are delivered in about 10 days. **PQ**

CAMBRIDGE CAMERA EXCHANGE, INC.
Seventh Ave. and 13th St.
New York, NY 10011
(212) 675-8600
CK, MC, V, COD

You'll find some of the sharpest students of camera equipment at Cambridge. While Cambridge isn't in England, or even in a suburb of Boston, discounts are in the vicinity of 30% to 50% on cameras, lenses, and lights. We found thousands and thousands of cameras in every known brand present and accounted for. NIKON, PENTAX, and CANON were priced at far below retail; less expensive, less well-known equipment was also on a roll. Cambridge is one of the few stores handling European cameras like HANIMEX, PRAKTICA, and EXACTA—these brands offered the greatest savings. Some of their specials advertised in magazines and select mailings are available at truly mind-boggling prices. We saw the NIMSLO Three Dimensional (stereo) camera (which regularly lists for $199.50) for an unbelievable $26.95! Cambridge has a 20-day exchange or refund policy; no restocking charge on returns; and their merchandise is fully guaranteed. Shipping's at least $4.75. They don't quote prices, but they do quote Shakespeare (and sometimes Goethe, Schiller, Pushkin, and La Fontaine). To get a catalog and free mailings, you must tell them the name of the camera you own. They separate their mailings by different cameras. **C**

DANLEY'S
Dept. US
P.O. Box 1
Fort Johnson, NY 12070
(518) 842-7853

Stargazing lately? Or maybe the cost of telescopes is up there with Venus and Mars. Danley's has brought the price of optical products back down to Earth. You'll find the products in their assortment of brochures out of this world—and at up to 63% discount. OPTOLYTH twilight telescopes/spotting scopes are precision-made in Germany and retail for $410 but were $307.05 here. SWIFT binoculars in a variety of styles ranged in price from $38.88 to $240. A galaxy of other bargains are offered. Birdwatchers, hunters, and sports spectators will goggle over name-brand binoculars like BUSHNELL, CELESTRON, SWIFT, and a flock of others at prices that won't have you up a tree. No minimum order, but there is a $1 shipping charge for orders under $25. You can receive price quotes by phone or by sending a SASE. Orders are handled within 24 hours. Get this rare money-saving bird in your sights. **C $2** (refundable), **PQ**

EXECUTIVE PHOTO AND SUPPLY CORP.
120 W. 31st St.
New York, NY 10001
455 Central Ave.
Scarsdale, NY 10583
(800) 223-7323: orders only
(800) 882-2802: Computer Hot Line
(212) 947-5290: NY, AK, HI residents, inquiries
MC, V, AE, D, COD

We always thought executives were known more for flashing rolls of bills than rolls of film, but then again, how else can they see the Big Picture? Executive Photo's a midtown photo dealer with a less buttoned-down outlook. Besides cameras, lenses, film, paper, and photographic accessories with names like NIKON, HASSELBLAD, MINOLTA, and CANON, they sell computers, calculators, and electronic gadgetry. (Check out their 50-page catalog to get an idea of their wide inventory and the varied brands they carry.) Prices are 40% to 50% lower than their full retail competition (so there's no competition there!) and are on a par with other NYC photo mail-order companies. (Executive sells at dealer's net.) The minimum order's $45; orders are usually delivered in seven to 10 days; and full refunds are given within 10 days. Manufacturer's warranties apply. Whether you're the Big Cheese, or just someone who gets chewed out a lot, you'll like this place. **C, PQ**

FOCUS ELECTRONICS
4523 13th Ave.
Brooklyn, NY 11219
(800) 223-3411: Electronics orders only
(800) 221-0828: Camera orders only
(718) 871-7600: NY residents, electronic inquiries
(718) 436-6262: NY residents, camera inquiries
CK, MC, V, AE

Focus is no hocus-pocus place even though they juggle cameras, TVs, copiers, computers, audio, video and stereo equipment, large and small appliances, telephones, answering machines, typewriters, and even film. Focus carries a full line of 220 volt appliances and electronic gadgets. They've been in business for 20 years, so they won't do a disappearing act, either. They can pull most cameras, camcorders, and VCR's out of their hat at prices "lower" than full-price retail stores. It's still a mystery as to how they do it, but then again, maybe we just weren't focusing. They have prompt shipments anywhere in the USA and abroad. Returns accepted within 10 days if in original mint condition as shipped. **C $2** (refundable)

47TH ST. PHOTO
36 E. 19th St.
New York, NY 10003
(800) 221-7774
(800) 221-5858
(800) 221-3513: video hotline
(212) 260-4410: AK, HI, NY residents
(212) 398-1410
(212) 608-6934
CK, MC, V, AE, COD (down payment on credit card;
the rest cash)

Since 47th St. Photo's mail-order operation is at 36 E. 19th St., we can only conclude that either somebody's heavily into numerology or else they've got it in for the postman. We'll forgive them if they don't "address" this issue, because while these people may not know where they're at, they definitely know what they're doing. A broad selection of top brands, efficient service, a 15-day return/exchange policy, and discounts of 25% to 75% below retail on cameras, watches, audio video, computers, copy machines, microwaves, TV games, typewriters, shredders, dictation equipment, answering machines, fine jewelry, exercise equipment, health aids, home appliances, and cordless phones make this company a top name in mail-order. Their selection of electronics products is so extensive they've got a whole catalog devoted just to video products. (They've also got a separate division to fill corporate, industrial, and institutional requests.) You can follow their latest sale prices in the national edition of the *New York Times* on Sunday and during the week. Their minimum order is $35; they're open Sunday through Thursday, plus Friday till 2 P.M. If you tell 'em you're an *Underground Shopper,* they'll send you their catalog free of charge. **C $2, B, PQ**

GARDEN CAMERA
345 Seventh Ave.
New York, NY 10001
(800) 223-5830: orders
(212) 868-1420: NY residents, inquiries
MC, V, AE

Not long ago we heard about a man who accidentally locked himself in a darkroom. (He died of exposure. Needless to say, it was not a pretty picture.) But here's a story that won't make you shutter: good prices, good service, good selection, and ads that tell you exactly what you're getting. Garden Camera has a large darkroom equipment center that's abloom with such items as enlargers, meters, CIBACHROME paper and chemicals, color drums, and analyzers. In fact, you can find cameras, videos, calculators, electronic games, watches, computers, and telephones sprouting throughout their 48-page, color catalog. Brands included NIKON, MINOLTA, CANON, PENTAX, OLYMPUS, KODAK, POLAROID, HASSELBLAD, CIBACHROME, SEIKO, SONY, PANASONIC, RCA, PHONE-MATE, CODE-A-PHONE, and FREEDOM PHONE. Prices are 30% to 50% below retail; their NIKON and CANON lines are their biggest selling bargains. There's a $50 minimum order and a 10-day limit on returns. Ordering's a snap, so see what develops. **C**

HIRSCH PHOTO
Dept. US
699 Third Ave.
New York, NY 10017
(212) 557-1150
MC, V, AE

No "Judd-heads" need to Taxi to this Hirsch outlet. With a no-questions-asked service policy, years of reliable customer recommendations, and bargain prices, you'll cross the photo finish line without the meter running. There are no hidden surprises and over 100 leading brands of camera equipment, including NIKON, PENTAX, MINOLTA, and OLYMPUS. Audiovisual equipment such as projectors is also available. Prices are set at 10% above their cost, which translates to hard-to-beat savings. Orders are shipped within 48 hours, and carry a full factory warranty. Refunds are given within 10 days; there's no restocking charge. **PQ**

JERSEY CAMERA
540 Cedar Lane
Teaneck, NJ 07666
(201) 836-8863
MC, V

OK, everybody, let's all smile! And if you won't say "cheese," at least say "Jersey." Jersey's a good word to know if you're looking for camera equipment. In fact, if you live in Jersey, you might want to visit one of their four stores. They feature camera specials, where you not only get a camera, but a flash and some accessories, too. Besides cameras, they sell calculators, TVs, video recorders, and microwave ovens. Big name-brands they stock include CANON, MINOLTA, NIKON, PANASONIC, RCA, and SHARP. Discounts are over 30% on cameras, but their hottest selling items are PANASONIC VCRs. (Everybody loves a bargain! Even Dave Winfield, the mega paid baseball player, shops here!) Orders are shipped the same day; satisfaction is guaranteed; returns are accepted within seven to 10 days. Don't forget to mention you're an *Underground Shopper* reader when you call: good things might happen! **PQ**

MARDIRON OPTICS
37 Holloway St.
Malden, MA 021248
(617) 322-8733
CK, MO

Here's looking at you with this brochure that is bulging with bargain-priced binoculars, telescopes, astronomical telescopes, and night scopes to make certain you find the stars or any other faraway objects. Top-quality German craftmanship makes these brands reliable, with names such as STEINAR, OPTOLYTH, HERTELL & REUSS, SWIFT, and VARO. All binoculars and scopes are factory fresh and carry the manufacturers' guarantee . . . plus, they're 35% to 40% below retail. Price includes shipping and handling costs; Massachusetts residents add 5% sales tax. You won't want to look any further once you've looked at these prices! Company offers complete refund or exchange if customer is dissatisfied. Immediate response to inquiries. **B**

OLDEN CAMERA
Dept. US
1265 Broadway at 32nd St.
New York, NY 10001
(800) 223-6312: orders only
(212) 725-1234: NY residents, inquiries
CK, MC, V, AE, DC

Olden is one of the granddaddies of the mail-order camera business, and they've got ordering down to a science and selection down to an art. From new NIKONS to old MINOLTAS, if it's photographic, they've got it. Well-known and not-so-known meters and motors, stereo cameras, and slide projectors are displayed in their 200-page catalog, and a leasing plan's available for purchases of $3,000 or more. Video equipment, electronics, computers, business machines, copying equipment, and parts for cameras made from 1900 to the present are also available. There's no set discount, but they claim their prices are "the lowest prices found." Olden's buyer protection plan lets you return equipment in 30 days (in its original condition) with no questions asked. They even take trade-ins through the mail! Olden's a topnotch organization, so you won't expose yourself to any dangers dealing with them. **C $2.50** (refundable)

SAVERITE PHOTO & ELECTRONICS
46 Canal St.
New York, NY 10002
(800) 223-4212
(212) 966-6655
MC, V, AE

Remember the hunchback of Notre Dame, Quasi Photo? Quasi took pictures of the belfry with a camera bought from Saverite. (If the name of this company doesn't ring a bell, we have a hunch it soon will.) Besides cameras, Saverite also carries small appliances, silver, stereo and video equipment, TV screens, CASIO keyboards, calculators, and watches discounted 40% to 45%. Other brands include CANON, VIVITAR, and YASHICA. According to Martin Mittleman, the owner (don't cut out the Mittleman here!), "Everything's a bargain!" Orders are shipped the day they're received; they're guaranteed for 30 days; 10-day return privilege. There's a minimum of $25 for credit card orders; a 20% deposit's required on all orders (unless they're COD). **C, PQ**

SOLAR CINE PRODUCTS, INC.
Dept. US
4247 S. Kedzie Ave.
Chicago, IL 60632
(800) 621-8796: orders only
(312) 254-8310: inquiries
CK, MC, V, DC, CB, D

Get some variety in your mailbox and focus on the star performers! Solar Cine carries a full line of 35mm accessories including screens, tripods, camera bags, and over 2,000 other items. (Photo-finishing, accessories, processing, film, and video transfers are what they're most known for. Film for movies and cameras is probably their best buy.) Brands include KODAK, PENTAX, and POLAROID, as well as about 20 others, and discounts range up to 40%. Most customers receive their orders in about one week. Refunds are given only when the item proves defective. **C**

SPIRATONE
Dept. US
135-06 Northern Blvd.
Flushing, NY 11354
(800) 221-9695: orders only
(718) 886-2000: NY residents, inquiries

Also:
130 W. 31st St.
New York, NY 10001
(718) 886-2000
CK, MV, V, AE, DC

Spiratone is *the* camera specialty equipment store. They don't sell cameras, but they *do* sell a lot of camera accessory items. In fact, they pioneered the field of photographic accessories over 40 years ago. Their 44-page catalog displays items that will make your cameras (and you!) do creative things you never thought possible. Some of their special lenses (made especially for Spiratone) are unmatched in value. They have more special filters than a Japanese tour group has cameras. Spiratone does much of their own manufacturing, but they do carry SHARP, BENBO, MITSUBISHI, CLEARLIGHT, and FUJIMOTO. There's no minimum order; most orders are shipped within four to seven working days. Exchanges are accepted with prior authorization. **C $1**

T. M. CHAN & CO.
P.O. Box 33881
Sheung Wan Post Office
Hong Kong
CK (bank or certified), POSTAL ORDER

Ever wonder what happened to Charlie Chan's heirs? The great sleuth's namesakes have cracked the case of the overpriced piece of electronic equipment. We grew suspicious when we priced the Asahi

PENTAX ME camera with a 50mm f/1.7 lens and case at $277 (about what the catalog distributors offer on a regular basis without across-the-ocean anxiety). However, the watch selection clued us into a SEIKO Sports 100 watch for only $99 (retail $215) and ROLEX watches in the sub-$1,000 category We detected similar bargains (savings of 30% to 50%) on their high-quality clothing tailored from the finest British and Italian fabrics. Bank check, money order, certified check, or cashier check (no credit cards) must accompany every order before shipping. All goods come with a one-year warranty; insurance is extra. C

WALL STREET CAMERA EXCHANGE
82 Wall St.
New York, NY 10005-3699
(800) 221-4090
(212) 344-0011
CK, MC, V, AE, DC, COD

Go for broker at this Wall Street institution. Though they were named the largest LEICA camera dealer in the country last year, they also carry other name brands such as NIKON, ROLLEI, HASSELBLAD, MAMIYA, OLYMPUS, and ROLEX. This wall-to-wall collection in the 100-page catalog includes photo cameras, lenses, accessories, camcorders, video cameras, video recorders, personal copiers, typewriters, keyboards, scanners, radar detectors, and more and can save you up to 75% off retail. Exchanges accepted within 10 days of receipt of merchandise. Used photo equipment bought and sold. Repair department on the premises. Manufacturers' warranties where applicable and extended warranties available. Minimum order, $25. C $1

WESTSIDE CAMERA INC.
Dept. US
2400 Broadway
New York, NY 10024
(212) 877-8760
CK, MC, V, AE, COD

MAMIYA! I just bought a camera named MAMIYA. Cool your jets and stop fighting for the lowest prices. This gang's got it, man. There's a place for us, and it's here. Westside's story is selling all photographic equipment and supplies at 25% to 30% lower than retail. Brands include camera gang leaders like NIKON, CANON, MINOLTA, and OLYMPUS. Discounted darkroom supplies like chemicals and equipment will enlighten you to the savings possibilities and keep you in the dark. (Now you won't have to be out cruising the streets.) Oriental paper, SPRINT chemicals, and a full line of KODAK products all are discounted, too. A $15 minimum order will initiate you into the Westside brotherhood. (Are you man enough to handle it?) Be tough, write to Barry Glick and ask for a brochure or price quote. There's a 10-day return policy. That love affair with a NIKON doesn't have to be just a dream. Make it real, man. **B, PQ (SASE)**

Carpets and Rugs

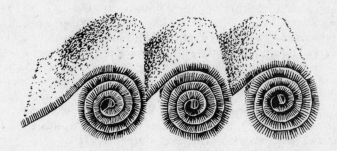

Does the price of wall-to-wall carpeting drive you *up* the wall? Going barefoot on the carpet is fun (unless it's because after buying carpet, you can't afford shoes!) Oriental rug prices can be a knotty problem, but not if you shop by mail. Beautiful, high-quality rugs can be shipped to you (by truck—there's no such thing as a flying carpet). Why not try it? Instead of just being bugged, you'll be snug as a bug in a rug.

ELKES CARPET OUTLET
2910 Archdale Road
High Point, NC 27263
(919) 434-4104
CK

You've heard of having an uncle in the business? Well, now you have an ant-ler in the business! Elkes can rack up 30% to 50% savings on first-quality items, and even more on top-choice irregulars, close-outs, discontinued colors, and promotional styles of name-brand contract carpet. With access to most major lines (including commercial, industrial, and institutional lines) with names like GALAXY, ALEXANDER SMITH, COLUMBUS, STEVENS CARPET (formerly GULISTAN), WORLD, CORNET, WUNDA WEAVE, and PHILADELPHIA, their selection is excellent. Ordinarily, orders are delivered in two to three weeks. If you've been hunting and hunting, trying to track down a good buy on carpet (i.e., you caribou-t savings on major brands), this just might be the place where you can bag your limit. And if you don't see what you want, call or write for a price quote. We floored a well-known Sacramento radio talk show host who is now walking on an entire houseful of parquet floors from this carpet resource. **B, PQ**

WAREHOUSE CARPETS
P.O. Box 3233
Dalton, GA 30721
(800) 526-2229: outside GA
(404) 226-2229: GA residents
CK

Roll out quality carpet at 30% to 50% off. Every carpet this company sells is first-quality, no off-goods or seconds. They handle such major lines as BIGELOW, MOHAWK, KARASTAN, GALAXY, LEES, CABIN CRAFT, and PHILADELPHIA. These generous discounts are made possible in part by their convenient location in Dalton, Georgia, where many large carpet manufacturers are established. In most cases, the shipping charges via common carrier run from $25 to $100. Even so, the shipping charge is often offset by the tax break (usually $50 to $125, or more) incurred from out-of-state purchases. Warehouse Carpets requires a 50% deposit upon placing your order and the balance before shipment. Simply specify the manufacturer's name and the carpet's style name, and Warehouse Carpets will invariably secure the same carpet at a substantial savings. **PQ**

Cars and Auto Supplies

Everybody has heard horror stories about auto mechanics. And it's true: some mechanics couldn't fix a martini, let alone a Mercury. So what can you do to protect yourself—short of enrolling in a series of do-it-yourself auto repair courses at the local community college? One alternative is to decrease your chances of getting an incompetent mechanic. For three minutes of your time and the price of a postage stamp, you can get a listing of local service mechanics who've been certified in specialized areas of training. Write to the National Institute for Automotive Service Excellence, 1825 K St. N.W., Washington, D.C. 20006 or call (202) 833-9646 for more information. The name of the company they work for, its address, and its telephone number are given.

AMERICAN AUTO BROKERS
Suite 110
24001 Southfield Road
Southfield, MI 48075
(313) 569-5900
CK (personal or cashier), MO

As a 17-year veteran in the business of managing car dealerships, Mel Palmer decided to open his own company, American Auto Brokers. Knowing the industry inside and out, Palmer made his move and was, in fact, instrumental in lifting the ban on auto brokering. Mel and his brokering crew negotiate deals nationwide. You can save anywhere from $150 to $4,000, depending, of course, on how much margin there is to play with and whether or not the car is in great demand. A firm quotation is issued in writing and costs $3. (*Underground Shoppers* get their first quote free). American Auto Brokers deal in all makes, domestic and foreign autos and in all styles as well—cars, trucks, and vans. If you have not arranged your own financing, GMAC, Ford Motor Credit, or AMC Credit is available on domestic automobiles. The order is placed upon receipt of deposit, which is refundable if the order is canceled within 72 hours. Delivery, which is made to any dealership in the country and includes manufacturer's warranty, takes approximately six weeks. When you ask for your price quote, be sure and have specific information on model and options desired. **PQ (SASE)**

BELLE TIRE DISTRIBUTORS, INC.
Performance Dept.
3500 Enterprise Drive
Allen Park, MI 48101
(313) 271-9400
CK, MC, V, COD

These belles are properly at-tired by such companies as MICHELIN, BF GOODRICH, GOODYEAR, FIRESTONE, UNIROYAL, PIRELLI, and KELLY SPRINGFIELD priced 15% lower than most full-priced stores. (Check local sources, however, before purchasing long distance to insure maximum savings.) This company's been in business for over 65 years and had performance tires long before other companies did. They're experts when it gets down to where the rubber meets the road. Shipping's by UPS and costs $5 to $20 per tire. Tires are shipped within 24 hours. Readers can get an extra 2% discount by mentioning *The Underground Shopper*. **PQ**

CAPITAL CYCLE CORP.
Dept. US
1508 Moran Road (Route 634)
Sterling, VA 22170
(703) 444-2500
CK, MC, V, COD

Too pooped to pop a wheelie? Here's a spokes-person for your mechanical cause! Capital Cycle got us charged up with the largest inventory of genuine and original BMW parts in the U.S.—and at 20% off the regular BMW list price. (They're the only BMW parts dealership in the U.S. with discounted prices.) Frankly, we aren't too exhausted to give a muffled roar of approval: Easy Riders like us don't need any price shocks to get us all choked up. You can rev up your classy chassis here with everything from a vacuum screw gasket to telescopic fork parts. They carry over 4,000 parts in stock and promise clutch performances on mail and telephone orders. The 80-page catalog we got was (what else?) encycle-opedic. There's a $20 minimum order ($20 with MC or V credit cards). Orders are shipped the same day. C

CHERRY AUTO PARTS
Dept. US
5650 N. Detroit Ave.
Toledo, OH 43612
(800) 537-8677
(419) 476-7222: OH residents
MC, V, COD (if under $50)

Say "cherry-o" to high-priced auto parts! Cherry has been in business for more than 35 years, both as a store and as a mail-order (price quote) business, so they're well worth a pit stop. Cherry's offers sweet deals on a large selection of quality used parts for foreign cars and trucks—there are no lemons here! Small electric parts are in particularly good supply. Discounts on most items are in the 50% to 80% range, since the parts are used. Most parts have been surgically removed from hapless autos that have met untimely deaths on the roadway; the parts are now available to be transplanted into other autos. They also carry a full line of rebuilt foreign starters and alternators. Used engines and transmissions are perhaps the best bargains: they're certainly the biggest. A carburetor that would retail for $150 (new) was $60. There's a $15 minimum order; orders are shipped the next day. Parts are guaranteed to be good. There's a 20% restocking charge on returns. **PQ**

CLARK'S CORVAIR PARTS, INC.
Route 2
Shelburne Falls, MA 01370
(413) 625-9776
CK, COD

Have you been racing all over the country to find parts for your Corvair? We have some great news for all of you die-hard Corvair owners. Take a pit stop and gas up on some great savings with the Clarks. Their Corvair parts company will keep you on the track and running smooth. They stock enough parts to fill Indianapolis. Over 4,500 different items: mechanical, trim, interior, suspension, emblems, and over 1,000 items that are not available anywhere else in the world. With a pit crew like the Clarks, you'll stay in the lead. Brands like DELCO, TRW, and MOOG will keep you in tune. The Clarks make hundreds of their parts themselves, including all upholstery. They've got you covered. The Clarks have made the collectible Corvair affordable. Their 400-page catalog with over 1,000 photos and sketches is worth its weight in gold. You can find anything you need at a savings of up to 30%. You may find a knock or two in their return policy though. All returned parts must be in perfect condition, and a 15% restocking fee is charged. No returns on electrical items or incorrectly ordered parts. Speed off to savings and the checkered flag. **C $4**

CLINTON CYCLE & SALVAGE, INC.
Dept. US
6709 Old Branch Ave.
Camp Springs, MD 20748
(800) 332-8264
(301) 449-3550: MD residents
CK, MC, V, AE, COD

Here's something that'll make you want to crack up! Clinton's a mail-order used motorcycle parts business that specializes in Japanese 250cc and larger street motorcycles. (KAWASAKI, SUZUKI, YAMAHA, and HONDA are the makes.) They offer 40% to 60% off retail parts; the prices vary with the condition of the particular part. Satisfaction's guaranteed or your money back when you return the item within two weeks of purchase: there's a restocking charge when a customer changes his mind. Most orders are received within seven to 10 days; there's no minimum order. If new (and very expensive) parts aren't needed for your bike's image, get it from Clinton and spend the savings elsewhere. **B, PQ**

EURO-TIRE INC.
P.O. Box 1198
Fairfield, NJ 07006
(800) 631-0080
(201) 575-0080: NJ residents
CK, MC, V, AE

Euro-Tire carries European-made wheels and tires as well as shocks and lights. All are discounted 25% to 40%. If you're in the market for tires, they have a toll-free number available for consultation. All tires are steel-belted radials and come with a warranty against defective workmanship. Brands include PIRELLI, MICHELIN, GOODYEAR, DUNLOP, VREDESTEIN, KONI, BILSTEIN, BBS, FIRESTONE, UNIROYAL, CONTINENTAL, KLEBER, and FULDA. If your tire is not in stock, the company will call you immediately to arrange an alternative selection or give you the option to go elsewhere. **C**

EXPLOSAFE GASOLINE CANS
44 County Line Road
Farmingdale, NY 11735
(516) 454-0880
CK, COD

We'd like to say business is booming here, but when you're selling explosion-proof gasoline cans, the fewer booms the better. "Most ordinary gas cans emit dangerous fumes and do not have anti-explosion systems," we learned from their flier. "Explosafe cans won't explode . . . the special vent prevents escape of dangerous explosive fumes." The gasoline cans are metal and have a plastic spout, and are manufactured by KIDDE. Star performers, the cans have been featured on "That's Incredible!" (which is more than can be said about your ordinary cans). Better yet, their prices are 50% off retail. Five-gallon gas cans cost $22 ($44 retail), while 2.5 gallon cans cost $18 ($36 retail). Shipping is $4 per can: expect delivery seven to 10 days after you place your order. "That's Incredible!" **F, PQ**

FREEDMAN SEATING COMPANY
4043 N. Ravenswood
Chicago, IL 60613
(312) 929-6100
CK, MC, V

Have a seat . . . or two! This company offers ready- and custom-made seating for all vehicles. A full range of styles makes it simple to find just the seating arrangements you're looking for. Manufactured by Freedman, color swatches are available upon request to match your color needs. Seats, sofa beds, benches, dinettes, and pedestals for vans, recreational vehicles, four-wheel drive vehicles, and trucks are all included in the selection. Choose elegant wood-trimmed velvet seats, plush pillow-back chairs and sofa beds, tweed and vinyl combinations, or durable vinyl seats and dinette sets. Fabric and vinyl to match all seats are available by the yard, and accessories let you adapt and adjust your vehicle's seating arrangements with swivels, pedestals, and more. Designer lighting, trays, and tables add the finishing touches. Illinois residents add 8% tax; prices include shipping and handling. Guarantees available upon request, orders filled within one week. C

J.C. WHITNEY & CO.
1917-19 Archer Ave.
P.O. Box 8410
Chicago, IL 60680
(312) 431-6102: orders only, 24 hours
MC, V

When your car budget's been totaled, and the sum is greater than the parts, call J.C. If you've got a car, RV, or motorcycle, J.C. Whitney has everything you've always wanted to put on, but didn't know where to get. You'll find all sorts of customizing items from hood ornaments to fuzzy dice in their 100-page catalog. Or maybe you'd like to fix up your older car with replacement parts like ball joints, convertible tops, seat covers, or new carpets—the company (established 1915) has perhaps the largest selection of automotive parts and accessories around. And don't forget they have all the special tools necessary for these jobs. J.C. Whitney is chock full of parts for all cars, foreign and domestic, going back to the Model T: there are hundreds of brands. Prices can range up to 60% off, although the average is probably more like 20% off. There's even an across-the-running-board discount if you order promptly. Orders are shipped within 48 hours of receipt; there's a full refund if you're not satisfied. Friendly order-takers take orders 24 hours a day, seven days a week. C

KARZUNDPARTZ
P.O. Box 19289
Greensboro, NC 27419
(800) 334-2749
(919) 299-4646: NC residents
MC, V, AE, COD (cash)

Ach tune-up? Is your Gesund t-heit enough? Nein? Das ist nicht gut! This mail-order company carries BMW parts exclusively. They have 'em all, ranging from engine to muffler to wheels to roof. Discounts of 10% to 30% will set your engine to purring like a kitten. There's a 15% restocking charge if you change your mind about an order shipped to you; most orders are shipped within 48 hours. Their 60-page catalog costs just $3, so mail for it, macht schnell! **C $3**

MANUFACTURER'S SUPPLY
Dept. US
P.O. Box 157
Dorchester, WI 54425
(800) 826-8563
(800) 472-2360: WI residents
MC, V

This party of the first part packs small engine parts, snowmobile parts, cycle parts, ATC parts, lawn mower parts, and chain saw parts to ship to parts unknown. Part of their appeal and what sets them apart are national brands like CHAMPION, NGK, WISECO, REMINGTON, GRAVELY-HAHN, ARCTIC CAT, HUSQVARNA, OREGON, and HELI-COIL. Their inventory's extensive: over 10,000 different parts to choose from, and they even have a service department. (Check out their 150-page, black-and-white catalog for the full story on parts.) Discounts are 30% to 40% off retail. Orders are shipped within 24 hours. Savings like these are in our department! **C**

NATIONWIDE AUTO BROKERS
17517 W. 10 Mile Road
Southfield, MI 48075
(800) 521-7257
(313) 559-6661: MI residents
MC, V

In business for 22 years, Nationwide is one of the largest and best known car brokerage firms. (They're even computerized!) For $9.95

(chargeable to MC or V), you'll receive a form showing all the available optional equipment for the car you want, so all you have to do is check what you'd like and return the form. You will get a personalized price quote for a car that's equipped the way you'd like it. Nationwide charges just $50 to $125 over factory invoice on American-made cars; $125 to $300 on most foreign makes. Certain cars produced in limited quantities aren't always available. Foreign and domestic cars, trucks, and vans are available, and all come with factory warranty. Domestic autos can be financed with GMAC or Ford Motor Credit. Most deposits are about $100, but sometimes are as high as $500. Prices are quoted FOB Detroit or delivery will be made to your local dealer. A telephone staff is available to answer your questions.

TELE-TIRE
17622 Armstrong
Irvine, CA 92714-5791
(800) 835-8473
(714) 250-9141: CA residents
CK, MC, V

This Tele isn't Kojak but if your tires are bald, they can probably come to the rescue and be pretty tough on the competition. Hey baby, look at these brands: BRIDGESTONE, PIRELLI, MICHELIN, CONTINENTAL, QUANTUM, ENGLEBERT, and SEMPERIT. Shop around and find out what tire you need, then let them throw the book at you—a comprehensive catalog of tires and prices. **C**

Catalog Showrooms

What's a catalog showroom? Think of it as a giant smorgasbord of merchandise—everything you could ever need or want. Now, before you start getting depressed because you can't *have* everything, remember everything's discounted. (Catalog showrooms are like a low-calorie buffet where you can pig out on products, but still not blow your financial diet.) If there's not a showroom near you, you can still flip through their catalog and stock up on savings while you stockpile the bargains. If you can imagine a small Yellow Pages telephone directory with glossy pages and pictures of products instead of ads (let your fingers do the shopping!), you've got the right idea. And as long as you've got the right idea, why not get the right goods at the right price—by mail, of course!

BEST PRODUCTS CO.
P.O. Box 25031
Richmond, VA 23260
(800) 221-BEST
CK, MC, V

You don't have to be modest when you're Best. This company has over 200 stores nationwide, and they sell by mail, too. Their 400-page catalog displays over 8,000 different branded items including GE, SUNBEAM, NORELCO, COLEMAN, COLECO, SONY, RCA, ZENITH, PANASONIC, COMMODORE, and ATARI. Watches are a specialty—they're the fifth largest watch dealer in the U.S.—and they carry watches ranging from TIMEX to JULES JURGENSEN and SEIKO. Discounts range from 10% off on electronics items to 40% off on jewelry. The minimum order is $20; orders usually come in seven to 10 days; refund and exchange policies are liberal. **C $1**

SERVICE MERCHANDISE CATALOG SHOWROOMS
P.O. Box 24600
Nashville, TN 37202
(800) 251-1212
(800) 342-8398: TN residents
(615) 366-3900
CK, MC, V

Dare to compare! If you're a comparison shopper, keep this catalog handy to check out those locally advertised retail "bargains." Service Merchandise has the *real* bargains. Whether you're ruminating over a ruby or contemplating a computer, the low prices, top brands, popular models, and informative product descriptions in this bulging catalog will make your decision easier. Folks who live close to one of Service Merchandise's 166 stores in 32 states probably already know about them and snap up their bargains on a regular basis. We found many great buys on toys, electronics, housewares, and jewelry. One bargain we especially liked was their towel rack/valet BORG bathroom scale with four memory modes, automatic zero set, LCD readout, and quartz clock. It was priced at just $69.97—we've seen it elsewhere for as much as $100. That's savings! **C**

China, Crystal, and Silver

Are your cupboards down to the bare essentials? Bone up with china! From GORHAM to WEDGWOOD, antique English to patterns that have gone by the wayside, there are matching services that will track down your long-lost china and silver patterns. Other companies offer super deals on current patterns. Most carry name-brand silver, china, and stemware. If you're looking for something special, be specific and tell them *exactly* what you want. And whenever you write with a request, it's always smart to enclose an SASE (unless you're writing someone outside the U.S.). Replies from Europe can take a while, so be patient.

A. BENJAMIN & CO.
80-82 Bowery
New York, NY 10013
(212) 226-6013
CK, COD

Been looking for discounted china? Don't throw in the TOWLE! When we found this place, we went on a buying "Benj" with top-name makers like GORHAM, INTERNATIONAL, REED & BARTON, WALLACE, WEDGWOOD, HEIRLOOM, and LUNT. Savings were 25% to 50% off on 40 to 50 brands of silverware, china, and crystal. (Only established brands are carried.) Sterling flatware's probably their biggest value and strongest claim to fame. Store policies are: minimum order of $100, no restocking charge on returns, and no refunds on special orders. If what you order is in stock, you'll get your merchandise in about a week; if not, count on a three- to four-week wait. If you're writing to request a price quote, be sure to specify the model or style number, the pattern, the pieces you want, and the color. **PQ (with SASE)**

A.B. SCHOU
4 NY Ostergade
1101 Copenhagen
Denmark
CK, MONEY ORDER, BANK CHECK

Schou, fly Schou! The prices here definitely didn't bug us or bore into our savings. Savings were 30% off U.S. retail on porcelain by ROYAL COPENHAGEN, LLADRO, HEREND, and crystal by WATERFORD, LALIQUE, and ORREFORS. This company sells more than a dozen WATERFORD stemware patterns, as well as miscellaneous serving pieces, too. Seconds of figurines by makers like ROYAL COPENHAGEN that have minimal flaws are reduced an additional 20%. Schou's policies include: full satisfaction or your money back; no restocking charges on returns; and no minimum order. The price for the main catalog or the stemware catalog is refundable with your order. All prices include surface postage and insurance costs. **PQ, B, C $4 (refundable)**

ALBERT S. SMYTH CO., INC.
Dept. US03
29 Greenmeadow Drive
Timonium, MD 21093
(800) 638-3333
CK, MC, V, AE, CB

When it comes to plates and china these folks can dish it out, but when it comes to money, it's another story. They can't take it (or at least they won't take much of it!). We dug through their world of catalogs and came up in china. Since 1914, Albert S. Smyth's been in china, and in crystal and gifts, too. They carry famous makers like LENOX, MINTON, ROYAL DOULTON, WEDGWOOD, and others at 20% to 60% off retail. Fine jewelry discounted 25% to 50% is a recent addition to their product line. Their 24-page color catalog displayed some beautiful items at excellent discounts off the suggested list price. There's a written 30-day full refund policy; no restocking charge on returns; and no minimum order. Orders are usually shipped within 24 hours and received within 10 days. Albert S. Smyth is a member of the National Bridal Service. If you're in the area, visit their showroom store at 29 Greenmeadow Drive, Timonium, MD. C

AMERICAN ARCHIVES
5535 N. Long Ave.
Chicago, IL 60630
(312) 774-2020
CK, MC, V, AE, DC, CB

When you polish up on silver, you soon tarnish the myth that all that glitters is merely gold. Sterling silver, tabletop, and giftware items at 15% to 75% lower than suggested retail definitely puts a gleam in our eye. This 82-year-old company certainly is a cloud with a silver lining. We dug deep into their catalog and dreamed of getting mother loded with a punch bowl at $299.95 ($350 retail). A stunning silver candelabrum was a "miner" miracle at $39.95 ($55 retail). Delivery of orders usually takes about 10 days. B, F, PQ

BEN MORRIS JEWELRY CO.
P.O. Box 7305
4417 Lovers Lane
Dallas, TX 75209
(214) 526-7565
CK, MC, V

Morris isn't the Cat-alog man but he will put more money in your purrs. This company carries fine lines of sterling silver, stainless flatware, silverplate holloware, china, crystal, diamonds, and watches. We saw brands like GORHAM, REED & BARTON, WALLACE, TOWLE, KIRK-STIEFF, INTERNATIONAL, LENOX, ROYAL DOULTON, AYNSLEY, MINTON, and OXFORD. China and crystal were about 20% off, SEIKOS and jewelry about 30% off (some are up to 50% off), and prices on sterling silver, flatware, holloware, and stainless were discounted about 30%. There's no minimum order and no restocking charge: they only make exchanges with the sales slip. Orders usually are delivered in about a week. Inquiries on specific brands, lines, or models are welcome. There's no literature, but they'll give out information on current sales to folks who call in. **PQ**

CHINACRAFT OF LONDON
Parke House
130 Barlby Road
London W10 6BW, England
phone 01-960-2121

We thought a China craft was like a Chris-craft, only without the motor. (Sort of a junk?) We were wrong, wrong, wrong! Yin-terested folks will find this company yan-ks their prices on china down substantially. And if you know china, we're willing Tibet you'll find a lot to yak about in their catalog. Got something particular in mind? Ask for price quotes on gorgeous china and hand-cut crystal from WEDGWOOD, SPODE, ROYAL WORCESTER, ROYAL DOULTON, BACCARAT, WATERFORD, and STUART. A price list is enclosed to give an indication of the approximate cost. **C $5, PQ**

THE CHINA MATCHERS
P.O. Box 11632
Milwaukee, WI 53211
No phone
CK

Matchmaker, matchmaker, make me a plate . . . catch me a cup . . . do me a dish. While this may never make Broadway, if you're singing the blues over a set of china missing a few supporting players, give The China Matchers a holler. They specialize in LENOX, HAVILAND, and WEDGWOOD patterns, and it's a buyer's and seller's market. For information, send the name of the pattern or a picture of a dinner plate to The China Matchers. On opening night, your table will get a standing ovation. **PQ (SASE)**

THE CHINA WAREHOUSE
P.O. Box 21797
Cleveland, OH 44121
(800) 321-3212
(216) 831-2557
CK, MC, V

Has the Kosta living got you Boda tears? Well honey, there's no need to fret. You can still have fine china on your table. Just shop the warehouse where 20% to 50% savings are given on brands like KOSTA BODA, ONEIDA, MINTON, ROYAL DOULTON, DENBY, MIKASA, FITZ & FLOYD, NORITAKE, and others. Your table will have a style all its own but you won't be paying top dollar for china, crystal, or stainless and sterling flatware—that's *not* your style. Supply manufacturer's name, pattern, and number of pieces for price quote. **PQ**

EMERALD MAIL ORDER
Ballingeary County
Cork, Ireland
or
290 Summer St.
Boston, MA 02210
(617) 423-7645: phone orders
CK, V, AE, ACCESS, MONEY ORDER, BANK CHECK

No sham, Sam, (and no blarney, Barney), Emerald's rock-bottom prices make them a gem on the Emerald Isle. Drink in the 40% savings on the full line of WATERFORD crystal and BELLEEK china, plus AYNSLEY, COALPORT, and LIMOGES. You won't get lepre-conned by these fine folks. Now you can thank your lucky stars and eat 'em too—from a BELLEEK bowl! Credit card charges are subject to a $20 minimum order. **C** [free by surface mail, but $2 (refundable) by air mail]

FORTUNOFF
681 Fifth Ave.
New York, NY 10022
(800) 223-2326
(212) 758-6660 ext. 242: NY residents
CK, MC, V, AE, DC, CB

Some folks swear by 'em, others swear at 'em, but when it comes to china, everybody's got an opinion about Fortunoff. Patterns from GORHAM, TOWLE, INTERNATIONAL, REED & BARTON, KIRK-STIEFF, LUNT, and ONEIDA are put out to pasture here at passionate prices. Other goodies go for full fare. (Discounts vary depending on the category of merchandise.) Four times annually, catalogs fortunately arrive to herald each major shopping season. Choose from over 500 patterns of flatware in sterling, silverplate, or stainless steel; or choose a gem from their beautiful collection of fine jewelry priced at less than you'd imagine. Their newest line of merchandise is clocks in brands like SEIKO, HARRIS & MALLO, and DERICHRON. Others will make a Fortunoff you, but when it comes to contemporary and antique silver, Fortunoff boldly proclaims, "No one sells sterling flatware for less." C $1

GERED
173/174 Piccadilly
London WIV OPD
England
01-629-2614
MC, V, AE, DC, IMO

SPODE from Gered, ROYAL DOULTON, MINTON, and ROYAL CROWN DERBY from Gered, WEDGWOOD from Gered—all the most sought-after names in bone china straight from these catalog pages. Though not a discounter by acclamation, the price savings between the U.K. price and U.S. price should net 50% after allowing for shipping, insurance, and U.S. duty. Strikingly beautiful examples with sumptuous detail jump out of each page. Since our old office address was on Fitzhugh in Dallas, I was understandably tempted by SPODE's Fitzhugh offerings. Several members of the English Fitzhugh family were officials in the East India Company in Canton, and it's probably from them that the name of this Chinese pattern introduced by SPODE in circa 1800 derives. A five-piece place setting was $47.05. C

GREATER NEW YORK TRADING CO.
Dept. US
81 Canal St.
New York, NY 10002
(212) 226-2808
CK, COD

If you don't want to let some full-price retailer take a bite out of your budget, nibble on the prices at this Big Apple business. (You won't find seeds of destruction here!) What could be tastier than tableware by: GORHAM, INTERNATIONAL, LENOX, LUNT, MIKASA, MINTON, NORI-TAKE, ONEIDA, ORREFORS, ROYAL DOULTON, REED & BARTON, ROSEN-THAL, ROYAL WORCESTER, KIRK-STIEFF, TOWLE, WATERFORD, and WEDGWOOD? Discounts of 40% to 60% off are oh-so-sweet and are always in season. A 91-piece setting of NORITAKE china in the Vienna pattern would normally be about $1,500, but it was just $730 here. A 91-piece setting of MIKASA china in the Charisma pattern (normally $600) was just $275.

JEAN'S SILVERSMITHS
16 W. 45th St.
New York, NY 10036
(212) 575-0723
CK, MC, V, COD

Jean blows the others to smith-ereens with over 1,000 current and discontinued patterns in sterling silver flatware, new and used silver, and antique jewelry. They've been tracking down discontinued patterns and hard-to-find items since 1932. We inquired about INTERNATIONAL's discontinued Silver Rhythm pattern and were quoted a price of $34 each for place spoons and salad forks. (Elsewhere we were quoted prices of $52 and $48, respectively, for the same items.) Probably Jean's most popular item is sterling silver liquor labels in five different styles. Their price?—$16 each. To order, send an outline of the items you want to match, noting the type of knife blade, whether it has a bright or dull finish, and whether it's stainless or silver plated. Most orders are received in two weeks; shipping charges are only $3.50. PQ

THE KIPPEN GROUP
Dept. US
2401 Springcreek Parkway #2801
Plano, TX 75023
(214) 964-0829
CK, MC, V, AE

With prices going so high, it's nice to know someone is "Kippen" them down. That's what Frances Kippen is doing. She can help you purchase famous-brand china and crystal at up to 50% savings from Great Britain, and that's after shipping and insurance! For example, a ROYAL DOULTON "Carlyle" place setting costs $96.90 including shipping from The Kippen Group. It retails for $195 plus 6% tax so you save $84.10. WEDGWOOD, AYNSLEY, SPODE, MINTON, BACCARAT, and WATERFORD were just a few names we noticed. Just write Frances with your pattern, and she will quote prices immediately. Your order will be shipped from Great Britian and received by you within eight to 12 weeks. All merchandise is first-quality and guaranteed against breakage. The Kippen Group also carries fine perfumes such as CHLOE, BAL A VERSAILLES, JOY, CHANEL, and LAUREN. These perfumes are 50% below retail and subject to availability. **PQ**

LOCATOR'S, INCORPORATED
908 Rock St.
Little Rock, AK 72202
(501) 371-0858
CK

Once lost, now found . . . Locator's Incorporated sells, buys, and brokers discontinued patterns of china, crystal, and sterling silver flatware. What a scope! Their shop boasts 50,000 pieces of china and crystal in discontinued patterns and eight times that is in their matching registry. This registry holds over 40,000 cards linking buyer to seller and vice versa. They handle all major china manufacturers in the United States, England, France, Germany, and Japan. If they don't have a particular piece available, they will keep your name on file until they locate a match and contact you. If you have a pattern to match, simply write or call giving manufacturer, pattern and, if necessary, a description or photo of distinguishing marks. **PQ (SASE)**

MESSINA GLASS & CHINA CO.
Route 30
Elwood, NJ 08217
(609) 561-1474
CK, MC, V, AE, DC, CB

The tables will turn and so will heads when you serve your guests from famous-name china and crystal you bought for 30% to 70% less than retail. Entertaining brands we found: ROYAL DOULTON, MINTON, WEDGWOOD, NORITAKE, GORHAM, AYNSLEY, and many others. The selection of patterns ranged from formal to casual. Just write Messina with the manufacturer and style you desire and they will send you a price quote. **PQ**

MICHAEL C. FINA
580 Fifth Ave.
New York, NY 10036
(800) 223-6589: orders only
(212) 869-5050
CK, MC, V, AE, DC, CB

Fina-lize your wedding plans at this bridal registry and jewelry emporium. You'll find all kinds of glittering goodies in this distributor's catalog: sterling silver tea services, crystal stemware, bone china, even a set of pewter goblets. Low prices, a large selection (hundreds of brands are available) and the special Personal Gift Catalog Service frees you from the mental straitjacket of your gift-giving fears. It's a super idea for those folks with hard-to-buy-for picky friends and relatives. Prices on their sterling silver flatware fluctuate with the silver market. Catalogs are available in the states of Maryland, Virginia, Texas, Illinois, New York, and the District of Columbia. **C**

NAT SCHWARTZ CO., INC.
549 Broadway
Bayonne, NJ 07002
(800) 526-1440
(201) 437-4443: NJ residents
CK, MC, V

Champagne, anyone? Or would you prefer a glass of WATERFORD? Make a toast in WEDGWOOD, GORHAM, LENOX, or many other brand names to savings of up to 45%. You won't be LAUFFER-ing at these low prices. You'll find all your ONEIDA and much, much more. In their 36-page full-color catalog, you will ogle at gifts ranging from $10 to $500. We found adorable sterling rattles just $49, or how about an exquisite LLADRO figurine? There were several to choose from. Let Nat go to bat with a GORHAM, WALLACE, TUTTLE, and several others, enough to fill a GEORGIAN HOUSE. Eat like a king on ROYAL CROWN DERBY, ROYAL WORCESTER, or WEDGWOOD QUEENSWARE. Take your PICKARD if you can. If ever in the metropolitan New York area, stop by and see Nat. The showroom is filled with thousands of magnificent pieces, but Nat would never dream of making you feel like a bull in a china shop. There is a shipping and handling fee of $3 on sterling and $4 on all other merchandise. The company offers full refunds and exchanges on your unused purchase, if returned within a reasonable time. "High Ho Silver," don't delay! **C**

PATTERNS UNLIMITED
P.O. Box 15238—US/TX
Seattle, WA 98115
(206) 523-9710
CK

Tired of plastic Mickey Mouse forks or Michael Jackson cups completing your incomplete china and silverware patterns? Use a pattern matching service to replace those lost or broken items and restore symmetry to your table setting. With Patterns Unlimited *you* don't have to hunt to try to match discontinued patterns of china, crystal, silver, and earthenware from all makes and manufacturers. They do the legwork. Just write Patterns Unlimited and tell them exactly what you want (color photos or make and model numbers are good). If readily available, you will receive a reply within 30 days. If not, all requests go on file until they're filled. There's a 20% restocking charge if you return an item because of your mistake. Packing and shipping charges are included in the price. A service like this can keep you from being at odds over replacing odd china patterns. **PQ**

REJECT CHINA SHOP
33-34-35 Beauchamp Place
London SW3 1NU
England
phone 01-581-0733
MC, V, AE, DC, CB, INTERNATIONAL MONEY ORDER

If you think it's no fun being Reject-ed, you haven't shopped here. (When it comes to classic china patterns, most places you don't stand a chinaman's chance, pricewise.) In this shop, you'll find some of the best deals around on imports. Get on their mailing list and become pen pals internationally with renowned favorites like SPODE, AYNSLEY, COALPORT, ROYAL WORCESTER, LIMOGES, WEDGWOOD, and DENBY. Discounts are 15% to 50%. Prices vary depending on shipping, but according to our British correspondent, they're "jolly good." China settings and porcelain are their specialty. If the goods you get are not-so-good (chipped, cracked, etc.), you'll get a full refund. **C $3**

REPLACEMENTS, LTD.
1510 Holbrook St.
Greensboro, NC 27403-2785
(919) 275-7224
CK, MC, V, AE, COD

This company may be serving just what you need if you've got a cupboard full of mismatched crystal or china. More than 10,000 crystal and china patterns provide the promise of restoring complete place settings, even if the pattern has long since been discontinued. Among the crystal selections carried in the catalog are TEFFIN, LENOX, CAMBRIDGE, and GORHAM. China patterns include NORITAKE, WEDGWOOD, ROYAL WORCESTER, and MIKASA. Bone, fine, and earthenware discontinued china are all available from Replacements, Ltd. as are numerous non-major manufacturers. Savings here are crystal-clear, as patterns still in stock are sold one-third off retail prices, and prices on discontinued patterns are dependent on the age of the pattern. Orders over $1,000 receive a 10% discount upon request. Customers are offered a full refund if dissatisfied for any reason. Orders are shipped via UPS within two weeks, and charged UPS shipping charges. **C**

RICHARD YERXA JEWELRY AND SILVER
Suite 139
8411 Preston
Dallas, TX 75227
(800) 527-5913
(800) 442-5799: TX residents
(214) 386-6995
CK, MC, V

This company wrote the book when it comes to discounting name-brand silver like REED & BARTON, WALLACE, and GORHAM. Sterling silver and silverplate flatware was 32% to 35% off, and holloware was discounted 30%. Exchanges and refunds are made on merchandise that hasn't been unwrapped, although returns are subject to a 10% restocking charge. Immediate shipping on in stock items, four to six weeks on orders. **PQ**

ROBIN IMPORTERS
510 Madison Ave.
New York, NY 10022
(212) 753-6475
(212) 752-5605
CK, MC, V, AE, DC, CB

Robin Importers Sher-wood save both rich and poor from poverty; not by robbin' hoods but by offering 20% to 60% discounts on a large selection of stainless steel, china, cutlery, crystal, giftware and bakeware, and even tablecloths. They carry 50 brands of china and 25 different brands of flatware. Brands in this forest of imports include WALLACE, GORHAM, MIKASA, WEDGWOOD (Midwinter and Stonehenge), and ARABIA in patterns which have made marryin' so wonderful. Hard-to-find discounted ROSENTHAL, and FRENCH LIMOGE dinnerware, VAL ST. LAMBERT stemware, and giftware set us all a-quiver. In-stock merchandise is usually delivered within about two weeks. Write (including a stamped, self-addressed envelope) or call Robin with a description of what you want, and before you know it, his band of merry men (and women!) will help you. **B, PQ**

ROGERS & ROSENTHAL
105 Canal St.
New York, NY 10002
(212) 925-7557
CK

It took us a while to get oriented, but after padding through the paddies we took a slow boat down the Canal on our quest for china and silver discounted up to 40%. The bargains we found let us set an exquisite table even though there were so many hungry Maos to feed. The shop features every major advertised brand (GORHAM, WALLACE, LENOX, and WEDGWOOD). Send for their price list, but be specific about what you want. Orders are shipped UPS: allow from one to eight weeks for delivery. Rogers & Rosenthal has been in the same location for 44 years and has served three generations of satisfied customers. **F, PQ (SASE)**

ROSS-SIMONS OF WARWICK
Dept. US
136 Route 5
Warwick, RI 02886
(800) 556-7376
(401) 738-6700
CK, MC, V, AE, DC, CB

At Ross-Simons "the money-back policy is guaranteed even if the wedding isn't." We got a factory-sealed four-piece sterling place setting by GORHAM, Chantilly pattern, for $78.75 (retail $250) plus $3.50 for shipping and handling. Discounts on top-quality merchandise were about 25% to 45% below retail. Brands in fine china include WEDGWOOD, NORITAKE, LENOX, and ROYAL DOULTON; in crystal, brands include LENOX and GORHAM. They also carry CONCORDE gold watches and CORUM watches, too. Most orders are received in two to four weeks. A knowledgeable clerk told us about our selection and the free 90-day layaway. Check out their full-color 36-page catalog. **C $2**

SAXKJAERS
53 Kobmagergade
1150 Copenhagen K
Denmark
CK

Have a Danish. Trying to cut down? Try Saxkjaers for ROYAL COPENHAGEN (RC) and BING & GRONDAHL (BG) porcelain collector's plates at 40% below their U.S. retail price. RC Christmas plate was $32.50 (retail $52.50), while a BG Mother's Day plate was just $22 (retail $35). The creation of new designs every year and destroying the mold after each issue (i.e., planned obsolescence) makes these plates very valuable. Original hand-crafted Swedish lead crystal and LLADRO porcelain figurines were also pictured and described in the brochures we received. Prices include shipping, insurance, and door-to-door delivery. **C, B**

SGF
P.O. Box 620047
Dallas, TX 75262-0047
(214) 484-4095: credit card orders only
(214) 484-1517
CK, MC, V, AE

Our initial response to this catalog: A-OK to SGF! We've always been
big fans of The Horchow Collection's Grand Finale catalog. Now this
sibling savings book brings more of the same. What a selection!
WEDGWOOD china, MIKASA crystal, TOWLE silverplate . . . and that's
only page one. Plenty of linens, jewelry, floor coverings, plus seasonal closeout items. In the case of the spring '86 catalog we found
last season's coolers, umbrellas, and pool and patio furniture to be
greatly discounted and not noticeably out of style. Get on their mailing list and get on with saving money ASAP. **C**

SHANNON MAIL ORDER
Shannon Free Airport
Ireland
phone 011-35361-61444

The luck o' the Irish will have you Dublin your pleasure and saving
nearly 50% on handmade Irish lace, WATERFORD crystal, French perfumes, pure Irish linen, Irish and Norwegian pewter, mohair wool
blankets, GOEBEL and HUMMEL figurines, and German music boxes.
A single place setting, five pieces, of WEDGWOOD bone china in the
Wild Strawberry pattern was $50. Adding duty tax made it $69, but
at Neiman-Marcus in Dallas, it was $115. Follow your nose to a
quarter-ounce bottle of OPIUM perfume for $46.50, ORREFORS
perfume for $39.85, or one ounce of BAL A VERSAILLES for $97. **C**

STECHER'S
27 Frederick St.
Port of Spain
Trinidad, West Indies

Some of the best buys in the world can be found at the many duty-free
shops located in the West Indies. Stecher's is a good example with
branches at Hilton Hotel, Trinidad, W.I.; perfumes, tobacco, and gift
shop at Piarco International Airport; other branches in shopping
malls and in Tobago. They carry watches and clocks by PATEK PHIL-

LIPPE, AUDEMARS PIGUET, CARTIER, SEIKO, GIRARD PERREGAUX, HEUER, and others; China and porcelain by WEDGWOOD, ROYAL DOULTON, ROYAL CROWN DERBY, MINTON, ROYAL WORCESTER, SPODE, COALPORT, AYNSLEY, IRISH BELLEEK, ROYAL COPENHAGEN, BING & GRONDAHL, ROSENTHAL, HUTSCHENREUTHER, HUMMEL figurines, CAPODIMONTE, LLADRO from Spain, etc. Crystal by WATERFORD, BACCARAT, ST. LOUIS, LALIQUE, DAUM, ORREFORS, SWAROVSKI, VAL ST. LAMBERT, RIEDL, IITTALA, etc. Fine jewelry from the best design centers in the world. Pens and lighters by CARTIER, DUPONT, DUN-HILL, PIERRE CARDIN, PARKER, WATERMAN, CROSS, SCHAEFFER, LAMY, etc. Their cargo usually sells for 30% to 50% off. To get a price quote, write them with specific information about what you want. **PQ**

STEPHEN FALLER (EXPORTS) LTD.
Mervue
Galway, Ireland
Phone: 011-35391-61226
CK, MC, V, AE, BANK CHECK

Stylish Irish! We fell for Faller and his beautiful, four-color mail-order catalog packed with fine collectibles: WATERFORD crystal, BELLEEK china, LLADRO figurines, MINTON tableware, and WEDGWOOD, SPODE, and WORCESTER Beatrix Potter collectibles were all available. Traditional Irish linens, tweeds, Aran knits, and more were 30% to 40% off. Glory be, they've been in business for better than 100 years. **C $1**, surface mail; **$2**, air mail

STERLING & CHINA, LTD.
Dept. US
P.O. Box 1665
Mansfield, OH 44901
(800) 537-5783
(800) 472-5667: OH residents
CK, MC, V

If your name isn't Hunt, the next best way to buy silver is to go the refinished route. Heirloom silver, silver purchased at estate sales, or just tarnished silver from a wedding long ago can be restored or replated. This company had the best prices and most efficient service we found. Refinished versions of silver are from one-third to one-fourth the price of new silver. They also carry new silver: sterling flatware, silverplate, holloware; and stainless. Brands of new silver carried (at 25% to 50% savings!) include: INTERNATIONAL, KIRKSTEIFF, ONEIDA, REED & BARTON, GORHAM, TOWLE, WALLACE (any American manufacturer), and others. They also carry discounted off-brand lines like WHITING and ROYAL CREST that were previously sold door-to-door. We ordered a teaspoon, $20, from our discontinued pattern (current pattern price was $120), which was located minutes after we called and put on reserve. It arrived promptly and in perfect condition. Orders of new silver usually arrive in two to eight weeks; previously owned silver that looks like new usually arrives in about three weeks. You'll pay postage, handling, and insurance. There's no restocking charge on items returned within 30 days. **B**

WALTER DRAKE SILVER EXCHANGE
Drake Building
Colorado Springs, CO 80940
(800) 525-9291
(800) 332-3661: CO residents
CK, MC, V

So what if you weren't born with a silver spoon in your mouth? Few of us were. Somehow, over the years you have acquired a set of silver, but your set's no longer a set—you're missing a fork, spoon, knife, or other utensil. Let Walter Drake come to your rescue! Walter Drake specializes in pattern replacement and will help you identify, locate, and purchase the pattern you need. The Exchange also buys sterling flatware. When you tell them the pieces, pattern, and the manufacturer you're interested in, they'll feed the information into their computer and print out a complete itemized price list for your pattern. Prices fluctuate with the silver market, but savings on certain patterns can be substantially below suggested retail. All sterling purchased carries a 30-day money-back guarantee. **C, PQ**

Computers and Electronics

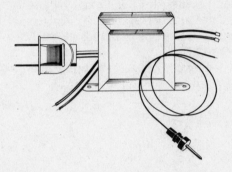

When it comes to computers and electronics, you may not know a transistor from a resistor, but there's one thing *everybody* should know: In this ever-changing world of electronics, technology updates itself almost daily. Month after month, year after year, prices on many items continue to drop. What is state-of-the-art today fades from sight faster than campaign promises after an election. That means if you can last a few more months without the item you want, doing so could save you some bucks. If you've just got to have some nickel cadmium batteries or the latest IBM computer, shop around and be sure to get some price quotes from mail-order companies. The savings will be worth it.

AEROCOMP INC.
2544 W. Commerce Ave.
P.O. Box 24829
Dallas, TX 75222
(800) 527-0347
(800) 442-1310: TX residents
(214) 634-3336
CK, MC, V, AE

Jettison your overloaded file cabinets and get into the computer age at a discount. You can order Aerocomp's 5¼-inch and 8-inch floppy disc drives or a complete line of IBM Clone hardware and software discounted 10% to 15%. TANDON and TEAC disc drives are available and the OKIDATA lines and CITIZEN printers are OK, too. There's a 14-day full refund period, and repair after that. **C**

ALL ELECTRONICS CORPORATION
905 S. Vermont Ave.
Los Angeles, CA 90006-0406
(800) 826-5432
(800) 258-6666: CA residents
(213) 380-8000
CK, MC, V

Could be one of the largest collections of surplus and new electronics parts anywhere. Quality merchandise, low prices (10% to 50% off depending on quantity) and fast service (except during holidays and busy seasons, all orders processed and shipped in 48 hours). Their merchandise comes from a variety of sources—OEMs (original equipment manufacturers), surplus dealers, importers, and distributors all over the world. Sometimes, sales are limited but run the full spectrum from battery chargers, bell/buzzers, chassis boxes, circuit breakers, connectors, semi-conductors, fasteners, fusers, switches, relays, speakers, transformers, lights, video accessories, and wire. Minimum order, $10 with usual manufacturer warranties as indicated in their black-and-white illustrated 48-page (mostly foreign in origin) merchandise catalog. **C**

COMPUTER PLUS
P.O. Box 1094
Littleton, MA 01460
(800) 343-8124
(617) 486-3193
CK, MC, V, AE, COD, MO

If it's computers and peripherals you're after, this company is a plus—plus they're an authorized Radio Shack dealer (but save you up to 25% off the retail). Brand name peripherals include EPSON, OKIDATA, PANASONIC, STAR MICRONICS, TOSHIBA, and HAYES MODEMS. Add 5% of merchandise shipped; 10-day return policy and 5% restocking charge for authorized returns on non-defective items. Software is not restockable and is replaced if defective, on an exact exchange basis only. **B**

ELEK-TEK
6557 N. Lincoln Ave.
Chicago, IL 60645
(800) 621-1269
(312) 677-7660
MC, V

As you might expect, Elek-Tek elects to offer high-tech consumer electronics direct to the customer. About 75 major manufacturers are carried, among them HEWLETT-PACKARD, SHARP, TEXAS INSTRUMENTS, CANON, and CASIO in calculators, and AT&T, TELEVIDEO, EPSON, HEWLETT-PACKARD, and SHARP in computers. Percentage discounts vary, but are often substantial, particularly on more expensive items. Discounts on their accessory lines are a minimum of 20% off. The HP-41CV calculator was just $126 ($225 retail), the HP-12C was $72 ($120 retail), and the HP-11C was $41 ($70 retail). (Elek-Tek carries a complete line of HP products.) EPSON 80 column printers were $235. All merchandise is covered by the manufacturer's warranty; Elek-Tek will replace defective merchandise within the first 30 days, but won't accept returns otherwise. Their minimum order's $15; orders are shipped within 48 hours. Write for their 52-page, black-and-white catalog. **C**

LYBEN COMPUTER SYSTEMS, INC.
1050 East Maple
Troy, MI 48083
(313) 589-3440
CK, MC, V, COD

When it says Lyben, Lyben, Lyben on the label, label, label you will
like it, like it, like it on your . . . budget! We discovered a cannery of
computer supplies: diskettes, ribbons, storage products, paper, calculators, phone copiers, and accessories. Lyben Computer Systems
offered hot brand-name products at savings that will take a byte out
of the cost of operating your computer. Computer paper cost only
$11.50 per 1000 sheets. Pressure sensitive labels were priced at $12.95
per 5000. HEAD cleaning kits will make your heads spin at a low cost
of $13.50. Jump for joy with a Joystick from APPLE only $25.95. This
stick retailed for $39.95. You save enough to buy that KOALA pad for
your APPLE, only $88.95, or for your IBM, only $109.95. This bulk
package deal would keep your computer pantry stocked for years.
Get 100 single side, double density disks with a five-year guarantee
for only $55. Some of the brands carried were MAXELL, CANON,
TEXAS INSTRUMENT, and MEMOREX. The minimum order is $15 and
should arrive within 10 days. You won't get stuck with a floppy deal.
Lyben guarantees all products and offers full refunds. C

MARYMAC INDUSTRIES INC.
22511 Katy Freeway
Katy, TX 77450
(800) 231-3680: orders only
(713) 392-0747
CK, MC, V, AE

Next time someone asks "where's the beef?" send them a "shack in
the box." That's what Marymac Industries just may be, the fast-food
equivalent of computer sales. If you're dead set on owning a TRS-80
computer by RADIO SHACK, simply call or write this Houston outlet
(conveniently located only hours from Fort Worth, home of Radio
Shack) for a price quote. "We will meet or beat any legitimate advertised competition that has brand-new merchandise in stock" is their
claim. They pay freight and insurance. So if you want the TRS-80
products, you better get shackin'. PQ

PAN AMERICAN ELECTRONICS, INC.
1605 East Expressway 83
Mission, TX 78572
(512) 581-2766
MC, V

Dallas Cowboys Coach Tom Landry was born in (and with a) Mission and Pan American has their goals, too. Pan handles 10 to 15 different brands of electronics, including RADIO SHACK. Discounts are about 10%, with bigger discounts on quantity orders. RADIO SHACK products, including the TRS-80 computers and software, were marked down 10% to 20%. Your prospecting will pan out and you'll also find TVs, radios, security systems, and calculators. There's no minimum order; orders are usually delivered in eight to 10 days. Shipping's free on orders of over $100. There's a three-month guarantee on purchases and a $10 restocking charge on returns.

PHONE CONTROL SYSTEMS
Dept. US
92 Marcus Ave.
New Hyde Park, NY 11040
(516) 248-3636
(212) 343-1215
CK, COD

Does your phone control you? Put a ring around the caller with Phone Control Systems. You can get wired by choosing from a large selection of answering machines from CODE-A-PHONE, PANASONIC, PHONE-MATE, RECORD-A-CALL, SANYO, and others. Portable phones by ELECTRA, EXTEND-A-PHONE, ITT, FANON, PHONE-MATE, TECH-NIDYNE, LA PHONE, and WEBCOR let you take it with you when you go. Long play recorders (24 hours!) by NORWOOD are a specialty. Dialers, diverters, dictaters, transcribers, and novelty telephones . . . it's one way to find out who's "phoney" among your friends. Phone Control also carries electronic games, calculators, and tape recorders. Prices are 15% to 20% above *wholesale*. There's a 10-day refund or exchange policy on defective merchandise. **B, PQ (SASE)**

TELEMART
2222 E. Indian School Road
Phoenix, AZ 85016
(800) 426-6659
(602) 224-9345
CK, MC, V, AE, COD

"Low prices are born here and raised elsewhere" screams their bold price list. Save from 30% to 60% on computer hardware, software, and peripherals; IBM compatibles, hardware, software, boards, printers, and peripherals. Input these brands: EPSON, TOSHIBA, BROTHER, HAYS, LOTUS, MICROSORT, and others. Add $6 under 10 pounds; $9 over 10 pounds for shipping and handling. All manufacturer's warranties apply and all orders shipped within 72 hours of request. They made our day with their price on the WORDSTAR 2000 2.0. and finally our checkbook balances with the help of the MULTIPLAN SPREADSHEET. **B, PQ**

WESTERN S & G
P.O. Box 12345
San Luis Obispo, CA 93406
(800) 233-9750
(800) 843-8181: CA residents
CK, MC, V, COD, MO

These days you could get lynched buying computer wares. At Western S & G, you won't have to rob a bank to afford software, floppy disks, and accessories for your computer. Just look at this roundup of major brands: SCOTCH, ALENBACH, DYSAN, CERTRON, FRYE, IBM, MEMOREX, and a whole herd of other famous breeds. Be careful, these low prices may cause a stampede. A Joystick with toggle switch that retailed for $39.95 cost only $26.83 here. The game, "Six Gun Shootout" which retailed for $39.95 was only $27.49. Savings of up to 40% can be corralled. Western also carried an entire canyon of books that would make you feel at home on the range with your computer. No minimum order, but there was a shipping and handling fee of $5. Their 71-page price list and catalog offered a prairie of savings. So, spur your steed to Western or face the posse. **C**

Cosmetics and Beauty Aids

If you've always wanted to shop for perfume on the rue de la Paix, now's your chance. Buy fragrances direct from Paris, the perfume capital of the world, and do it without leaving home! (Ooh-la-la—no "jet lag" est magnifique!) Savings are up to 50% so you can really parley the "parlez-vous Français?" route into a trip to the banque. Even with the small handling fee and duty (usually 8% on the wholesale value), by avoiding the thorny U.S. markups, you'll still come out smelling like a rose. Remember that most (but not all) perfumes are "restricted brands" by U.S. customs. That means there's a per-person limit of one or two bottles of each scent allowed for import. Closer to home, if you've never tried one of the various beauty-buy clubs we list, you should. Discounts of 50% and more on famous-name cosmetics are nothing to sneeze at.

ALEXANDER SALES ASSOCIATES, INC.
4137 S. Hannibal
Aurora, CO 80013
(303) 699-7786
CK

Put on a happy face because Alexander Sales sells high-quality cosmetic brushes and accessories direct to the public. We received an attractive retractable powder brush with gold case and tortoise-shell colored handle for $3.35. This brush is comparable to the finest brushes selling for $7 to $10 elsewhere. You'll lick your lips when you see the fancy retractable lip brushes for $2 (retail around $7). Alexander also carries eight- and 12-piece brush sets for $4.75 and $6.50 respectively. You'll pay $10 to $25 for these brushes elsewhere. Gorgeous Italian eye shadow kits were $6 to $12 (retail $10 to $20). Minimum order of $10; orders shipped within four days. **B, SASE**

BEAUTIFUL BEGINNINGS
Dept. US
Spencer Building
Atlantic City, NJ 08411
(609) 645-5450
CK, MC, V

A good beginning to beauty is saving money because it makes you feel good, and a lady who feels good is likely to look good. Save 50% to 75% on big name-brands: ELIZABETH ARDEN, REVLON, MAX FACTOR, FRANCES DENNEY, COTY, JOVAN, HELENA RUBENSTEIN, HALSTON, YVES ST. LAURENT, GERMAINE MONTEIL, PRINCE MACHIABELLI, LANVIN, POLLY BERGEN, and others. You'll also find perfumes, lipsticks, eye shadows, and even a ceramic bunny that dispenses cotton as you pull its tail. Perfume spray by YVES ST. LAURENT was $4.95 (retail $20) and RIVE GAUCHE was $4.50 (retail $13). Beautiful Beginnings can sell their wares for much less than retail stores because they're introducing manufacturer's products to the public. The idea is that you'll discover that special scent that suits your fragrance fancy and become a regular retail buyer. Orders are delivered in about two to three weeks. As an added incentive to buy, they offer periodic cash sweepstakes. **C**

BEAUTY BOUTIQUE
6864 Engle Road
Cleveland, OH 44130
(216) 826-1900
CK, MC, V

You've seen these products in your drugstore or discount chain but never at these wholesale prices. Direct from the manufacturer, this company's cache of cosmetics includes lipsticks, nail care products, shampoo, skin care products, and fragrances discounted 35% to 60%. So make it your strategy to send for their color catalog—start saving face and saving money at the same time. **C**

BEAUTY BY SPECTOR
Dept. USMA-4
McKeesport, PA 15134-0502
(412) 673-3259
MC, V

In-Spector Clousseau might say, "Hmmm, vot have ve hair?" Wigs, wiglets, cascades, falls, toupees at 50% below comparable retail are this 29-year-old company's crowning glory. Prices in the sales brochures and descriptive fliers didn't dis-tress us: a two-ounce human hair wiglet was $9.95 (retail $20); a "Blow Cut" wig was $24.50 (retail $49); and a man's toupee was $99.95 (retail $200). At these prices, you can wear someone else's hair (or a synthetic) without worrying about getting scalped. We won't split hairs over hair care items, fragrances, European skin-treatment products, fashion jewelry, or instructional books on beauty and self-improvement priced less than at retail clip joints, either. Special effort will be made to service *Underground Shopper* readers. Add $3 shipping with each order. **B**

BEAUTIFUL VISIONS
C.S. 4001
810 S. Hicksville Road
Hicksville, NY 11802
CK, MC, V, MO

Beauty is in the eyes of the beholder. Behold a vision of dazzling discounts. Beautiful Visions offers an eyeful of famous brand-name cosmetics that are truly a sight for sore eyes. Eyebrow and eyeliner pencils were 25 cents each. L'ERIN mascara which retails for $3.35 was only $1.25, an AZIZA eye accents, 16 powder shadow collection, a $32 value was an amazing $5.95. These low prices should have you seeing double. It was love at first bite when we discovered luscious lipsticks in a mouthful of brands. For instance, REVLON MOON DROPS lipsticks were priced right at $1.85 each. We also took time to smell the roses and a variety of other sensual scents. TATIANA Parfum spray was smelling fine for $5.95. That is a savings of over $35. CACHET by PRINCE MACHIABELLI was a sweet flower, available for the special price of $2.95. There was also a selection of jewelry to adorn the body without removing an arm and a leg. No minimum order, just beautiful, affordable visions. **C**

CAL-RICH LTD.
P.O. Box 707
78 Tenafly Road
Tenafly, NJ 07670
(201) 568-4735
CK

We hate to be nosey, but in this case it's our business. (Thankfully, nose news is good news). We sniffed out some odorable fragrances here, and at nose-talgic prices reminiscent of yesteryear. Cal-Rich sells copies of such famous perfumes as JOY, CHARLIE, BAL A VER-SAILLES, and many others at prices much lower than those of the originals. Men will like Cal-Rich's reproductions of ARAMIS, CANOE, and OSCAR DE LA RENTA, also priced considerably less than the originals. Ask for sample cards saturated with their fragrances and smell for yourself! There's a $15 minimum order, and a full money-back guarantee (no restocking charge) if you're not completely satisfied. Orders usually arrive in about three to four weeks. Perfume reproductions may be scorned by the snooty, but for our money, these are heaven-scent. **PQ**

CATHERINE
6, rue de Castiglione
Paris, France 75001
(011 331 4261 3227)
CK, V, AE

Parlez-vous Fran-savings? Catherine's "tax-free" shop afforded quite an "Eiffel" of perfumes, cosmetics, and gifts. Even better, prices were about 40% to 60% lower than retail in the States. For example, buying by mail from Catherine's one half ounce of CHANEL NO. 5 would cost $45 compared to $95 in most U.S. stores ($7 surface mail). Besides all the authentic famous French perfumes (except GUERLAIN), you can get cosmetics from CHANEL, DIOR, ORLANE, STENDHAL, LANCÔME, YSL, and CLARINS at the same low prices. Viva la differ-France! **B**

COSMETIQUE
P.O. Box 9001
North Surburban, IL 60197
(800) 621-8822
(312) 583-5410: IL residents
CK

Me and m-eye shadow searched for blemishes in this cosmetics offer to no avail. In fact, we were tickled firefrost pink to find such flawless fashion. Cosmetique will send you a special introductory coupon if you ask for it. Then, for just $1 you'll receive $100 worth of famous-name cosmetics, all by top name manufacturers like DIANE VON FURSTENBERG, ADRIAN ARPEL, and REVLON. If you decide to remain a member, you pay $10.95 (includes shipping) for each future kit. That adds up to 80% savings of retail—a pretty slick offer—leaving us at a g-loss for words. Even better, if you change your mind and don't want to keep your kit, it's returnable with no penalty charges. Orders come in about 30 days. Cosmetique is open Monday through Thursday 7:30 A.M. to 5:15 P.M. **B**

ESSENTIAL PRODUCTS CO., INC.
Dept. US
90 Water St.
New York, NY 10005
(212) 344-4288
CK

A scent-sational fragrance find! Now you can exude the aromas of affluence and get a snootful of savings to boot. Essential Products copies the most successful fragrances of name designers (just about any top-seller you could want). Since their products don't carry the burden of massive "image advertising" costs and the resultant astronomical markups, they sell the smell, not the mystique. A one-ounce bottle of a leading woman's fragrance costs $19, regardless of the brand copied: a half-ounce bottle costs $11. Men's fragrances come only in a four-ounce size and are $10. Savings off the real thing (GIORGIO, BAL A VERSAILLES, etc.) can be 90% and more. Their copy of BAL A VERSAILLES is their most requested reproduction. Shipping's by UPS and orders go out the same day. Charges are $3 for the first bottle and 50 cents for each additional bottle. The minimum order's $19 and merchandise returned within 30 days of purchase will receive an exchange or refund (your choice). Send a self-addressed stamped envelope for five free sample scent cards, fragrance list, and order form without any obligation. For fragrances at prices you won't get incensed over, this place is Essential. **B, PQ**

FREDDY
10 Rue Auber
75- Paris 9ᵉ France

We're ready, Freddy! Freddy was the least expensive Paris-based mail-order cosmetics supplier the last time we (price) checked. JOY from Freddy was significantly cheaper than JOY from their competitors—about 20% less than the price charged by their nearest rival. Overall, perfume extracts and toilet water matching the perfumes are about 20% to 25% less than you'd find in the U.S.; men's lotions, cosmetics, bags, and scarves are about 20% off. For an additional $6.50 they'll have your order to your door within five days. (With other companies, air mail can take six to eight weeks.) Freddy doesn't have a catalog (the fluctuating price of the dollar makes it impractical), but they do send customers a pro forma invoice with the prices quote net in U.S. dollars and available for two weeks. You have to write and ask the price of everything (definitely an inconvenience), and sometimes they're a little slow in answering, but the savings can make it all worthwhile. **PQ**

GRILLOT
10 rue Cambon
Paris 1ᵉʳ, France
CK

Grillot (pronounced Gree-o) sells at prices be-low retail. From France, the fragrance capital of the world, come tres chic savings on famous perfumes like CHANEL NO. 5, CHLOE, GUCCI, and many others. Men, don't just "promise her anything," give it to her, and save 50% over department store prices in the process. **B** (in English)

HOLZMAN & STEPHANIE PERFUMES INC.
P.O. Box 921
Lake Forest, IL 60045
(312) 234-7667
CK, MO

Welcome to the House of Holzman & Stephanie. Entering their fabulous home, you will discover a mansion of world-famous designer fragrances. In the kitchen you'll find Madame Holzman, who was educated in organic chemistry, and the French master perfumer, with his sophisticated smeller. They are cooking up their own versions of 53 sensuous perfumes, including OPIUM, COCO, CHANEL NO. 5, and GIORGIO. No scrimping on their ingredients. They use only top-quality oils and alcohols aged to perfection. "Excellence is a way of life with us" is their motto. How about a sniff? Just send $1 per sample (limit four) plus 50 cents shipping and handling. Next, off to the right, you will come to the den which is filled with colognes for him: ARAMIS, KOUROS, ROYAL COPENHAGEN to name a few. Down the hall is LAUREN, in the bath baring SHOCKING, WHITE SHOULDERS (pardon moi). Finally, you will come to the library with its PRIVATE COLLECTION of OSCAR DE LA RENTA and NORELL. On your way out, you'll pass a garden of florals and spice perfumes: TEAROSE, MIMOSA, and JASMINE, all kissed with YOUTH DEW. Oh, in the side court, don't miss LAGERFELD and HALSTON playing POLO in GREY FLANNEL. Original perfumes run as high as $250 per ounce. Their prices here average $25 per ounce (tres bien). *Underground Shoppers* receive an extra 10% off—what a JOY! Visit again and again, but at these prices, their house may become an OBSESSION. C $1

HOUSE OF INTERNATIONAL FRAGRANCES
4711 Blanco Road
San Antonio, TX 78212
(512) 341-2283
CK, MC, V

For scents that mean savings (and savings that make sense!), order copies of the most popular fragrances under the TOUCH & GO label. Women can save over 80% on reproductions of OPIUM, OSCAR DE LA RENTA, CHLOE, HALSTON, ANAIS ANAIS, GIORGIO, WHITE LINEN, COCO, OBSESSION, POISON, SHALIMAR, CHANEL NO. 5, and ESTEE LAUDER. Their men's lines are as strong as their lines for ladies, with savings of 50% on reproductions of PACO RABANNE, POLO, GREY FLANNEL, LAGERFELD, POUR LUI, VAN CLEEF & ARPELS, and ARAMIS.

Over 100 different fragrances are available: they reproduce almost every brand you can think of. These fragrances in essence last longer than the originals: one drop of 100% essence lasts eight hours; one bottle at $5.99 will last three months when used daily. In-stock items are shipped within 48 hours. **PQ**

J.W. CHUNN PERFUMES
43, Rue Richer
75009 Paris, France
4824.42.06

Atten-Chunn! This place is the pulse point of savings for famous perfumes and toilet waters like CHLOE, ARPEGE, JOY, OPIUM, COURREGES, BAL A VERSAILLES, CHUNGA (by Weil), and dozens more. Discounts are 50% and up. Skin care products from LANCÔME and ORLANE were also listed in their brochure. For example, a 6.8 ounce bottle of ORLANE cleansing milk was $12.80 (plus $5.75 shipping, plus duty). While some of the world's greatest beauties swear by this product, the department store retail price of $24 is prohibitive to most non-cents folk. If you sniff out the fragrance you want, write them with your request. They can usually fill it. **B**

KSA JOJOBA
Dept. US
19025 Parthenia St.
Northridge, CA 91324
(818) 701-1534
CK, COD

Here at the office, we like to watch the soaps. It's good clean fun and, from time to time, we find an interesting item—such as KSA's jojoba soap. Browsing through the literature we learned that jojoba is a plant that produces beans that contain an oil similar to sperm whale oil. The oil is used in shampoos, lubricants, cosmetics, machine and automotive oil, and even lotions. If enough jojoba plants were grown, there'd be no need to kill any whales, we also learned. The effects of this oil on healing and protecting skin are remarkable, says KSA, which sells jojoba products (including plants) wholesale to the public. A half-ounce bottle of pure jojoba oil costs $3.95; a bar of jojoba glycerin soap is $1.50; four bars are $5.75. Teddy bear and rabbit soaps-on-a-rope are $2.50; they've also got a glycerin snowman. Liquid soaps, creams, lotions, and lip balms are among their offerings.

They don't sell shampoo, since you can just add pure jojoba oil to a shampoo yourself. A "Save Our Whales" rubber stamp will make a big impression with Cleveland Amory as well as on your ecology-minded friends at $5.50 each. "We stand behind our products and will replace and/or refund any product found to be defective." All orders require $2 extra for postage and handling. **F (with SASE)**

MICHEL SWISS
16 rue de la Paix
Paris, France
phone: 261.68.84 or 261.69.44
CK

Ooh-la-la! You'll save enough at Michel Swiss to open your own Swiss bank account. OK, maybe we exaggerated a little bit on that one. Prices were terrific on palpably pungent Parisian perfumes. Franc-ly speaking, you don't knead to pay in French bread either, since prices are quoted in American dollars. Lagerfeld's CHLOE in a quarter-ounce size was $31.15; and Nina Ricci's L'AIR DU TEMPS was $27.75 for the quarter-ounce size. They have many new fragrances such as PALOMA PICASSO, GUCCI III, MISSONI, RALPH LAUREN FOR MEN, DIVA by Ungaro, and many more. Skin-tillating soaps, crystal limoges, bath oils, body creams, bubble baths, men's colognes, and after-shaves were also available at reasonable prices. On the down side, LACOSTE alligator shirt prices were no jaws celèbre for us. Prices swamped our budget. Michel Swiss's prices include full insurance and you get a gift with each order. You may go in-Seine, though, waiting two to three months for delivery via normal mail, or two to three weeks via air mail. **C**

TULI-LATUS PERFUMES LTD.
146-36 13th Ave.
P.O. Box 422
Whitestone, NY 11357
(718) 746-9337: charge orders only
MC, V, AE

We were fuming at the price of fine fragrances, but once we found Tuli, we were Tuli elated. Tuli-Latus (Latin for "after having been created or made") has sniffed out the costliest French and American designer perfumes, and has created its own reproductions of these aromatic blends at savings up to 90% (no doubt, using only the keenest ol' factory equipment). They sell reproductions of 29 perfumes, including BAL A VERSAILLES, LAUREN, L'AIR DU TEMPS, OPIUM,

OSCAR DE LA RENTA, CHANEL NO. 5, GIORGIO, NORELL, HALSTON, PRIVATE COLLECTION, CALANDRE, and SHALIMAR from $15 to $40 per ounce. A reproduction of 1000 BY PATOU (retailing for about $265 per ounce) was their most expensive duplicate at $40. (We won't turn our noses up at savings like that!) Perfumes come packaged in beautiful French glass stoppered bottles with French looking labels, or, for a slightly lower price, in regular bottles. Purse spray atomizers also sneeze at a squeeze. Shipping's $1 per item; there's a money back guarantee within 15 days of purchase; and most orders are delivered in about two weeks. New customers identifying themselves as *Underground Shoppers* get a $5 discount on their first order. **B**

VALRAY INTERNATIONAL, INC.
739 N.E. 40th Court
Fort Lauderdale, FL 33334-3034
(305) 563-8411
CK, MC, V, MO

Let's face it—it's all in the name. Here at Valray, since 1974, you've been able to save about 50% off comparable skin care products (scrubs, cleansers, masks, toners, eye and throat creams, wrinkle smoothers, bleaching creams, etc.) and makeup lines (foundations, powders, blush, eyebrow pencils, cover sticks, lipsticks, and mascara). Marketing similar products, without the million dollar ad campaigns, under the house name MAXIMILIAN®'S REJUVENATION®, and SCENTIQUE perfumes and colognes, you'll get the benefits and the "looks" without the hefty price tags. Returns accepted within 30 days for complete refund if not completely satisfied. Shipping charges are all $2 regardless of the number of products ordered. **B**

VICKIE-BEE PERFUMES
1285 Morrow Road
Pittsburgh, PA 15241
(412) 221-6174
CK

At Vickie-Bee, the buzz word is copy. And these folks aren't bumbling idiots when it comes to making first-rate copy perfumes of OPIUM, SHALIMAR, CHANEL NO. 5, WHITE SHOULDERS, JOY, OSCAR DE LA RENTA, L'ORIGIN, and PHEROMONE ("One of the most expensive perfumes in the world"). They take the sting out of pricing, too—only $12 per ounce. Send for a few bottles today and smell for yourself just how close a copy can come to "bee-ing" the real thing. **B**

WORLD OF BEAUTY
65 E. South Water St.
Chicago, IL 60601
(312) 977-3700
CK, MC, V, MO

Try before you buy. It's a fun and sensible way to experiment with a variety of cosmetics and toiletries. For $7 to $10, World of Beauty will send you a package every six weeks filled with product samples they've selected. You'll receive items from about 10 to 12 prominent manufacturers, among them REVLON, RITZ, HALSTON, and ADRIAN ARPEL. The HALSTON kit is their most popular offering. Savings are about 30%. Shipping's $2 (although there's no shipping charge on their enrollment offer). Expect your order to come in about three weeks. Write for their free brochure and enrollment forms. **B**

WYNNEWOOD PHARMACY
Wynnewood Shopping Center
Wynnewood, PA 19096
(800) 445-PERF
(215) 642-9091
(215) 878-4999
CK, V, MC, AE

This Philadelphia suburb has a real winner, the Wynnewood Pharmacy where famous name-brand perfumes and colognes such as NORELL, YVES ST. LAURENT, HALSTON, LAUREN, ARAMIS, and others are discounted up to 50% off retail. The pharmacy will mail-order your favorite fragrance if they have it in stock. We found our own scent, BAL A VERSAILLES, selling for $12.50, an incredible savings from $28 at the department store. Another shopper ordered NINA RICCI's L'Air du Temps spray for $14.50 and saved $6. The toilette spray for ANAIS ANAIS was $14.50 at Wynnewood Pharmacy, $19.50 elsewhere. If you don't have a large discount pharmacy in your area, this company can get you the best price on certain perfumes and colognes. But in many cases, the $3 handling and packaging in addition to the postage makes many of the discounts less of a bargain. Write for their *FREE* 32-page fragrance and cosmetic catalog for men and women called "Paris in Wynnewood!" **C, F, PQ**

Fabrics

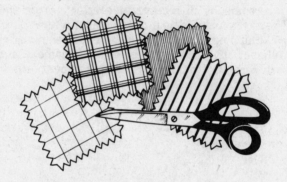

Shopping for designer fabrics like Oriental silk, camel's hair wool, natural cottons, or linens? How about drapery and wall fabrics? Whatever your pleasure, shop these pages first. Fabric clubs offer excellent bargains for seamstresses who have special interests such as "haute couture" fabrics. When ordering specific fabrics, be sure to include a recent sample so that colors and fabric details like width can be matched precisely. It's always a good idea to order a little more than you'll actually need especially when buying exotic fabrics from international sources. Mistakes can be costly if you don't. And remember, with your elegant leftovers, you can always make a quilt or a pillow.

ALBANY WOOLEN MILLS
Dept. US
2 Green St.
Rensselaer, NY 12144
(518) 465-2371
CK, MC, V

Been weaving through some heavy retail traffic lately? Straighten up and park here. Fort Crailo's an outpost that offers shelter from full-priced wooly bullies. Yarns for weavers sold by the pound are cheaper when bought in large volume. About 30 different colors (bright, pastel, and muted) manufactured by Albany Woolen Mills are available. All yarns are prepared and spun expressly for hand weavers and craftspeople using a variety of fine wools from Australia, New Zealand, and the United States. Wool is imported from all over, but everything carries its own brand. A set of four wool sample cards is $2, cotton cards are 80 cents, and a sample card of mill ends is free. Without spinning any tales, we found savings to be about 30% lower than other imported yarns of the same quality. Raw wool is also available on request. There is an 85 cents packing and handling charge. Credits are issued on returns; refunds if the problem results from their mistake. **SAMPLES, $** varies

ALL AMERICAN FABRICS
Dept. US
636 S. Lafayette St.
Shelby, NC 28150
(704) 482-3271
CK, MC, V

We bet Betsy Ross came away from this store with flying colors. They sent us a handful of tapestries, early American prints, and in-stock velvets in response to a brief letter we wrote in which we described the shape of the room we were working on, the color of the walls, carpet, and draperies, and the style of furniture we had. They had ab-salutely the best discounts we've seen (up to 75%) on close-outs, overruns, seconds, and millends. In fact, they have some jacquards that retail for $39.95 per yard, but their price was just $6.50 per yard. (Velvets, jacquards, and tapestries are their hottest items.) There are no refunds or exchanges. To get samples of this *upholstery* material, send them a SASE and specify the color and type of fabric you want. **PQ** (samples)

BEE LEE CO.
Dept. US
P.O. Box 36108
2714 Bomar Ave.
Dallas, TX 75235
(214) 351-2091
CK, MC, V, COD

Bee Lee-ve us when we say this is *the* source for "sewing supplies with a Western accent." With 191 different colors and styles of Western snap fasteners and trims, you'll have the C&W crowd sewn up in no time. You'll snap to attention, too, when you see their tremendous selection of snaps and their excellent prices! Trims, threads, buttons, interfacings, and zippers from the finest manufacturers are also displayed in their free 24-page, color catalog. Brands include WISS scissors, DRITZ notions, and WHITE sewing machine needles priced well below retail. Most merchandise is discounted between 10% to 50%. Shipping charges are staggered: on orders up to $5 they're $1.25; the maximum charge is $2.50 for orders over $20. Most orders are shipped in two to three working days maximum. **C**

BRITEX-BY-MAIL
Dept. US-87
146 Geary St.
San Francisco, CA 94108
(415) 392-2910
CK, MC, V, AE

This unique shop features top-quality domestic and imported fabrics, including many from American and European designer collections. Britex-by-Mail will bring the best of them to you, several times a year, with swatch samplers of 32 fabrics, chosen for their beauty, quality, and value to the consumer. Fabrics are seasonal and may include wools, silks, cottons, linens, knits, and synthetics, priced at a fraction of their ready-to-wear cost. Write today to receive an introductory packet of swatches and be placed on the mailing list.

BUFFALO BATT & FELT CORP.
Dept. US
3307 Walden Ave.
Depew, NY 14043
(716) 688-7100
CK, MC, V

These big leaguers have been in the batter's box since 1919 (when mighty Casey was at batt?). While we struck out on craft felt (which they don't sell), the batting averages about 30% to 40% off—definitely a hit with us. We dugout this source for home sewers and groups who need team-ing quantities of pillow inserts, quilt batts, and fiberfill. BB&F only sells by the case, with a minimum order of two cases. They also include a sample brochure of their own 100% polyester "Superfluff" products which, along with their other items, are in the same ballpark as other top-of-the-line retail products. There's 48-hour order processing. Make your pitch for a $1 brochure and samples, and then make out your batting order. Orders must be prepaid with a check or money order. Phone orders are accepted using Visa or MasterCard. **B** $1 (refundable), **PQ**

CAMBRIDGE WOOLS, LTD.
40 Anzac Ave.
Auckland 1, New Zealand
MONEY ORDER, POSTAL ORDER

What will you find here? Cheerful, bright knitting yarns, or knitting yarns in earthy, toasty tones sold by the ounce or by the pound. These yarns are hard to find in the U.S. and when they're available, are often very expensive. Cambridge also sells Aran sweaters and sheepskins, plus knitting, spinning, and weaving supplies. Satisfaction is guaranteed by this 32-year-old company. If you return the merchandise, they'll refund your money. **B** $1 (includes samples)

CAROLINA MILLS FACTORY OUTLET
Box V
Highway 76 West
Branson, MO 65616
(417) 334-2291
CK

What's a factory outlet in the Ozarks doing selling first-quality designer fabrics made in North and South Carolina? Who cares? All

we know is that their reputation is flawless and people come from hundreds of miles to shop at the Branson store. You can take advantage of tremendous savings (30% to 50%) on fabrics used to make the clothing of ACT III, JANTZEN, JONATHAN LOGAN, LESLIE FAY, LONDON FOG, KORET OF CALIFORNIA, and JACK WINTER among many others. Swatches are sent in coordinated colors and patterns with the designer's name shown. Now you can copy the clothing seen in your favorite boutique or department store. You'll pay for each set of approximately 100 fabrics until you place your first order. Specify whether you're interested in wovens or knits. Then you'll automatically receive two additional mailings. They send out four sets of swatches per year, so get one set for $2 or all four sets for $5.
B, swatches $2/$5

CLEARBROOK WOOLEN SHOP
P.O. Box 8
Clearbrook, VA 22624
(703) 662-3442
MC, V

Is the big bad wool-f of high fabric prices keeping you wide awake? Instead of counting sheep, dream of saving up to 25% on attractive solid, tweed, and plaid patterns in 100% wool. (Wool is the big item here, shorn 'nuf!) We received some stunning swatches in maroon, navy blue, charcoal, and cerulean blue, but with over 1,500 different fabrics, and all of them beautiful, we have to admit there's a lot we didn't see, too. Prices are excellent—they range from 15% to 35% off, and they'll take the risk out of ordering by sending you 12 to 30 sample color swatches to ensure there's a good match. Shipping charges are a standard 75 cents per square yard and exchanges and refunds will be made gladly, without any restocking charge. Paul revered his savings when he ordered, "One if by lamb, two if by sheep." **C, PQ**

D. MACGILLIVRAY & COY
Muir of Aird
Benbecula
Western Isles, Scotland, PA 88 5NA
phone: Benbecula 0870 2204
CK, V, AE, ACCESS, INTERNATIONAL MONEY ORDER, MONEY AND POSTAL ORDERS, BANK CHECK

Here's the Harris tweed and Shetland knitwear specialist "patronized by royalty and nobility." Even Her Majesty the Queen and Princess Margaret own one of their hand-knit Shetland shawls (54"-by-54", $56). For the materialistic, hand-woven Harris tweed was a good buy at $11.60 per yard ($19.98 in the U.S.), as well as Scotch tweed at $7.60 per yard. They have Scotch tweeds and Donegals, Scottish clan tartans, Shetland tweeds, mohair and camel's hair, sweaters, socks, bedspreads, caps, ties, rugs, and even hand-blended Hebridean perfume! We were intrigued by their "real grouse claw brooches" for $10. There's no minimum order, no restocking charge, and an unconditional exchange or refund policy if not satisfied. **C $1; $4** with swatches

HARRY ZARIN CO.
292 Grand St.
New York, NY 10002
(212) 925-6134 or 925-6112
CK, MC, V, AE

The Harry Zarin Co. has been a direct importer for 53 years and is famous for a huge, diverse selection of drapery and upholstery fabrics. This includes both imported and domestic goods at prices usually 25% to 33⅓% off department store *sale* prices. In addition to a long list of famous brands like SCHUMACHER, ROBERT ALLEN, RIVERDALE, and COVINGTON, they're one of the largest distributors of French embroidered tergal sheers. Heard enough? There's more: they're the largest mail-order business in the U.S.A. for LEVOLOR and KIRSCH blinds (including ready-mades), which they sell for at least 50% off. Shipping's *free* and that can mean savings of as much as $30 to $40. No mail orders to Hawaii, Alaska, or Canada (condolences to those far-flung folk!). Since Harry Zarin has such a large inventory of different fabrics, no samples can be sent without specific information. Write for price quote. **PQ**

HOME FABRIC MILLS, INC.
882 S. Main St. (Route 10)
P.O. Box 888
Cheshire, CT 06410
(203) 272-3529
MC, V, MO

Where there's a mill there's a way to save up to 50% on velvets, antique satins, sheer and textured patterns, and all sorts of "newly designed" fabrics. Accessories like drapery rods, trim, foam, upholstery supplies, thread, and pillows are also available. Although there's no catalog, they will "cheerfully send" swatches along with a pleasant note. They have literally thousands of bolts of fabric, so if you want samples, be sure to be specific about what you want. Send color samples or a swatch of fabric similar to what you want, plus a description of what you need it for—bedroom, bathroom, etc. The more information you provide (style, type of furniture, other colors), the greater the likelihood that they'll be able to send what you want. Most orders are processed in about 10 days; all sales are final. Visit their other stores in Belchertown, MA, and Scotia, NY, if you are in the area. **PQ**

INTERCOASTAL TEXTILE CORP.
Dept. M
480 Broadway
New York, NY 10013
(212) 925-9235
CK, COD (cash only)

Roll, roll, roll your bolts, gently down the seam! This company's products struck us like a bolt from the blue! Their 10,000-square-foot wholesale jobbers' warehouse and walk-in store has just about everything you could possibly tweed. There are first-quality slipcover, upholstery, drapery, and curtain fabrics (everything for home decorating), and prices are around 50% to 75% less than retail. Polyester sheers were just $1 to $1.50 per yard, and slipcover fabrics were just $2 to $3 per yard. With over 10,000 different sample fabrics, it's not surprising that they don't answer letters requestsing they send samples of upholstery fabric. To get them, you must send in a sample similar to the fabric you want, or else provide a color swatch and a description of the type of fabric you need. They will make exchanges, but only if the fabric was not cut. **PQ**

INTERTWINE YARN & FIBER SUPPLY
130 E. 900 South
Salt Lake City, UT 84105
(801) 363-9305
CK, MC, V

Confucius say, "Woman need her space, so give prenty of loom" and loom supplies from this discounter. Everything from temple stretchers to warping boards can be found in this catalog. Besides loom and spinning wheel supplies, they carry books on loom construction, weaving, designing patterns, and other related topics. The selection of yarns was impressive, emphasizing classic colors and textures. Country silk, for example, was $5.50 per skein. Alpaca was $3.95 for natural colors and $4.50 for colored skeins. Donegal tweed in fabulous colors for bulky sweaters was $5.95 per skein. C $2

JAY'S YARNS
Dept. US
969 Central Park Ave.
Scarsdale, NY 10583
(914) 472-3005
CK, MC, V, AE

Yarn nobody 'til somebody loves you and Jay's does! Old softies like BUCILLA are discounted at least 20% (up to 50% on closeouts). PINQUOIN sport yarn was $1.55 (retail $2). Jay's has a huge inventory of name-brand yarns, all of them discounted 15% to 30%. They carry the largest variety of kits and full lines of materials possible from PARAGON, BERNAT, SUNSET, DIMENSIONS, BUCILLA, and others. If you happen to find a kit that sounds interesting in a craft magazine, write Jay's and they can probably get it for you for less than you'd pay elsewhere. We saved 35% on a SUNSET Rainbow Balloon kit. They also mount needlepoint and crewel pillows from $26 to $40 which includes fabric, zipper, and blocking. When ordering, be safe and buy a little more than you'll probably need—just in case. Jay's will take back extra yarn for up to one year and give a full refund. Mailing charges usually run $1.60 to $2.00 for UPS and you'll probably receive your order in about two to three weeks. Need a further testimonial? Why not ask Nancy Sinatra or Roberta Peters—they've bought here. C

KNIGHT'S
Dept. US
100 Broadway
Albany, NY 12204
(518) 436-1822
CK, MC, V

Knight's into white satin, silk, and other designer fabrics, as well as BERNINA sewing machines and sewing machine repairs. Savings on sewing machines and service were between 5% and 20% (we're not jesting), but savings of 25% to 40% off retail on fabrics really jousted us into action. One of our ladies-in-waiting inquired about blue silk, and could hardly wait to receive her sample of 45 inches wide light blue palace silk for just $14.80 per yard; 36 inches wide navy blue fabric for $11.60 per yard; 45 inches wide medium blue fabric for $13.98 per yard; and silk jacquard in cornflower blue, 45 inches wide for $10.49 per yard. Most of their 36 inches wide silk that they sold for $25 per yard would cost $45 per yard in a store. Knight's not errant: they proved chivalry is not dead by slaying the dreaded Dragon of Retail and by keeping our office damsels from distress. All you Middle Ages types should pick up your phone and give Knight's a (heraldic) ring—we've tested the waters and "Serf's Up!" Shipping's $1.50 for four yards or less, but it's free for five yards or more. **PQ**

MARY JO'S CLOTH STORE, INC.
Dept. US
401 Cox Road
Gaston Mall
Gastonia, NC 28054
(800) 342-1229: NC residents
(704) 861-9100
CK, MC, V

By Jo, Mary's fabric-ating all kinds of cloth in first-quality dress goods, including calico, gingham, bridal, lace, eyelet, drapery, and upholstery fabric. (Their motto is "If you sew it with a needle, we have it.") Most name-brands are available: costume materials are a new addition to their lines. They also carry notions and accessories at shear savings—everything's marked up as little as possible (but enough to stay in business!). All brands of patterns are 20% off. Once fabric has been cut, it's yours: there are no exchanges or refunds unless the fabric was defective. Inquire about their inventory since there is no catalog. There's a small charge for samples. **PQ**

NEWARK DRESSMAKER SUPPLY
Dept. US
Box 2448
Lehigh Valley, PA 18001
(215) 837-7500
CK, MC, V, COD

Sew you say you're looking for oceans of notions, materials, and supplies? Find needles, hand and sewing machine thread in bulk, displayed in this company's 56-page catalog. They carry basic fabrics like muslin, crinoline, and buckram. The LILY line of crochet cottons and weaving supplies is a recent addition to their product line. Elastic, zippers, ribbons, bindings, bobbins, and much more are also available. Discounts range from 10% to 50% off, with bigger discounts with bigger orders. (They'll give a $2 gift on orders of $18 and more.) The best buys are probably on appliqués; they're 50% off. Shipping is $1.25 for orders under $10, $2 for orders more than $10. Delivery is within seven working days. C

ROMNI WOOLS AND FIBRES
3779 W. 10th Ave.
Vancouver, B.C. Canada
V6R 2G5
(604) 224-7416
V, MO

If starting from scratch is your style, look into this company. Raw wools, natural and synthetic fibers, silks, cottons, and linens let you create your own sewing and knitting goods. Dyes let you add the color that suits you best, and all the equipment you need is available all under one roof. Famous brands such as LECLERC, LEMIEUX, SUPERBA, BEKA, LOVET, and their own ROMNI brand plus a complete selection of knitting machines, spinning wheels, carding machines, and shuttles. To dress up your designs, choose from exotic wood buttons, abalone buttons, yew buttons, and more. Instruments for measuring, cutting, and framing are also available at low prices. For both beginning and experienced spinners, knitters, and weavers, this catalog holds everything to get you started or keep you going. Equipment carries manufacturer's warranties. C $1.50

SHAMA IMPORTS, INC.
P.O. Box 2900
Farmington Hills, MI 48018
(313) 553-0261
CK, MC, V, COD

Hey Christopher, we really discovered India when we hit upon Shama Imports. They offer such a variety of Kashmir Indian craftsmanship that you'll think you're in India. Columbus couldn't have been more thrilled discovering America. You might jump the boat when you catch sight of savings up to 50%. We discovered a bold new land of colorful crewel embroidery in their brochure, which comes with a price list, swatch, and helpful hints. You can explore wonderful savings on multicolored hand-embroidered fabrics to cover your favorite chair, walls, or couch. You can also buy ready-made bedspreads, tablecloths, cushion covers, and other items. Queen-pleasing prices can be conquered: a full-size bedspread cost $90, cushion covers cost only $8 to $10 a piece, and unique tote bags were $10. You can return uncut, undamaged merchandise within 30 days. **B**

STAVROS KOUYOUMOUTZAKIS
Iraklion, Crete
Greece

You'll ab-Zorba the Greek bargains here. Don't go up and down the Isles—just flip through the Greek pages. We'll be dis-Crete in saying their beautiful, unusual weaving and knitting yarns from Crete and Australia would cost twice as much in the States. **C**

TESTFABRICS INC.
Attn: Finley Klaas
P.O. Drawer O
200 Blackford Ave.
Middlesex, NJ 08846
(201) 469-6446
CK, MC, V

The luxury of a pure silk blouse or dress can be yours if you know how to sew. Silk crepe de chine was just $12.75 a yard (retail $22); silk shantung was $9.75 a yard (retail $20); and silk voile was $9.25 a yard (retail $13). Save up to 50% on 44-inch widths; with large orders, save even more. Wools, linens, and poly/cottons available also. All fabric is in its natural state (not printed or dyed) making Testfabrics a lifesaver for folks allergic to fabric dyes. The samples we ordered were not only lower in price, but higher in quality than most full retail material. This 52-year-old company requires a $25 minimum order, accepts exchanges or refunds with proper approval, and has a 15% restocking charge if your dissatisfaction is not their fault. Occasionally, they will have seconds on cottons available at your own risk.
C, B, PQ (SASE)

THAI SILKS
Dept. US
252 State St.
Los Altos, CA 94022
(800) 722-SILK
(800) 221-SILK: CA residents
(415) 948-8611
CK, MC, V, AE, COD

Marco didn't trek to the Far East looking for Polo shirts—he wanted silk. Likewise, we were lured westward by *Vogue Patterns* ads for 60 kinds of silks. These "pillars" of the community "catered" to our expedition and wormed their way into our hearts with shantung silk in 15 colors priced at just $9.80 per yard. Natural and bleached raw silk ranged from $4 to $13, while scarves were just $4. They also sold cotton poplin for only $2.20 per yard and batik for $6.20. Ready-made silk blouses were on sale for $14.50 to $16.50; linen tablecloths and lambswool sweaters were also available. Savings average 25% off on their non-sale items, and discounts are even bigger when they sell to store owners or dressmakers. Raw silk voile is probably their biggest selling item. There's a 15-day exchange or refund policy; they don't guarantee colors, but they'll exchange if there's not a match. Send $2.50 for sample packet of closeout silks and see what they've been "cocoon" up for you. **B**

TRIBLEND MILLS
Dept. US
4004 Anaconda Road
Tarboro, NC 27886
(919) 823-1355
CK, MC, V, AE

Try buying direct from the mill at Triblend: they're tried and truly tremendous! We found a very satisfying blend of price, service, and quality here. You can get new insulating fabrics, decorator sheers, or fabrics to drape your windows and get the free booklet "How to Sew Draperies" with your order. Prices average at least 50% lower than retail since they make everything themselves, and you'll get free sample swatches and a variety of materials. Millie Grackin and her staff stand ready to send samples, tell what's on sale, and give advice to do-it-yourselfers. Ten days is the limit to return your purchase for a refund or replacement if you're not satisfied, but there's no restocking charge. Most folks get their order in about 10 days. Their brochure offers information about how to measure your windows, conserving heat with insulating fabrics, and items currently on sale. **B, PQ**

UTEX TRADING ENTERPRISES
710 Ninth St.
Niagara Falls, NY 14301
(416) 282-8211
CK, MC, V, COD

Getting tired of the "what to wear" syndrome? Be a little enterprising and trade your everyday blues for an exciting new look with accessories and fabrics from Utex. With a company that caters to designers, high couture, and even royalty, you'll find yourself looking like a princess without becoming a pauper. Utex offers the largest selections of silk fabrics in North America, including Chinese as well as European silks, at discounts of 30% to 50%. Utex also carries scarves, lace, and other accessories at discounted prices. Further discounts of 5% to 25% are available with volume purchases. No minimum order required though there is a shipping and handling fee plus sales tax. **C**

WAY STATION FABRIC SHOP
Dept. US
Oak Springs Road
Rutherfordton, NC 28139
(704) 287-3573
CK, MC, V

This outlet sells fabric for ladies clothing only, so this isn't the place to get drapery or upholstery fabric. It *is* a place to get good deals, though. Fabrics are sold at near wholesale prices, or about 30% to 50% less than most other places. Specify the type of fabric you want and they'll send you small samples, including information on width, price, and fiber content. From there, it's just a matter of returning the sample you like along with your check for payment (plus $2.50 to cover postage). Fabrics are leftovers from the Doncaster-Tanner manufacturer-retailer, so don't expect to find the same fabrics twice at this place. They ship promptly, but won't exchange or refund. **PQ**

THE WOOLRICH STORE
Dept. US
Woolrich, PA 17779
(717) 769-7401
CK, MC, V, COD

Sheep chic! From "the store for outdoor people" come the richest wools perfect for mountain life. Do what you wool—purists know to go for the golden fleece in outdoor clothing! The fabric of Woolrich's life is over 150 years old. Their woolens are sold at mill prices and remnants are sold by the pound. Chamois cloth and poplins are their biggest sellers. Less than a yard of wool is $1.50 per pound; more than a yard is $2.50 per pound. Get a pound of tartan, plaid, or solid wool by sending a SASE for samples and information. And if you're in the neighborhood (three miles off Route 220 between Lock Haven and Williamsport), you're invited to drop in for a nickel cup of coffee, a stroll through the park and their outdoor hall of fame, and a look at one of their two films about the manufacturing of woolens. **B**

WONDER CRAFT
1 Constitution St.
Bristol, RI 02809
(401) 253-2030
CK

Have no fear, Wonder Craft is here! A division of Robin Rug, Inc., this company offers an assortment of cotton, wool, and cotton/rayon blends, synthetics, and 2/24 acrylic yarns at very reasonable prices. The yarns are sold by the pound: for example, a pound of wool suitable for making a child's sweater is $6. Samples are sent attached to a flier with prices. If you spend over $150, an additional 35% is allowed. It's no Wonder they do such a large mail-order business. **B**

YARN BARN
P.O. Box 1191
Canton, GA 30114
(404) 479-5083
CK

Latch onto this barn for discounted yarn because the selection is incredible. Bouclé, chenille, flaked cotton, cable cotton . . . to name a few samples we received. Knitters won't knit pick the selection or prices. Most yarns are mill ends, so be sure to order enough to finish the job. Fibers are natural, synthetic, and blends in various weights from thread to rug yarn. **C $2** (puts you on a mailing list for continuous samples)

ZAMART INC.
11 W. 37th St.
New York, NY 10018
(212) 869-7606
CK, MC, V ($30 minimum)

On Zamart, get zet, sew—I mean knit! Zamart sells "wholesale to the public" yarns from Europe and South America which are used by manufacturers on Seventh Avenue to produce the high-fashion sweaters seen in *Vogue* and other fashion magazines. The selection of samples we were sent was truly unusual and beautiful. If you knit, you can fashion sweaters which would retail for hundreds of dollars from just a few cones of yarn you'll purchase for $10 to $15 (mohair, etc.) per pound. In many cases, the yarns are available exclusively through Zamart, which purchases them directly from designer sample rooms. Color cards can not be sent as stock changes rapidly. **B**

Fitness and Health

Now more than ever, it pays to stay fit! Throw out those baggy, gray sweats and jump into some super fitness deals! Save on items from home gyms and great looking fitness wear to natural, wholesome food. Having a fabulous body and a healthy lifestyle is not only fashionable but smart these days! Need some vitamins to give you energy for all this exercising? Visit your local natural foods store or contact a good nutritionist to learn how to combine vitamins for best absorption. Shop around to get the best deal. Oftentimes, the same product will be priced quite differently by various companies. So save more and look and feel better with style and grace—without paying a well-conditioned arm and a leg.

BARTH'S
Dept. US
865 Merrick Ave.
Westbury, NY 11590
(800) 645-2328
(800) 553-0353: NY residents
CK, MC, V ($15 minimum on credit orders)

Barth is a manufacturer and distributor of vitamins and health foods: you'll find their products in many natural food stores. Although they say they "stress quality rather than low price," their mailers announce frequent sales during which savings can range up to 70%. (Who says you can't have both quality and low price? Production costs affect quality, but marketing costs—which often account for most of the price—can be cut by savvy management without affecting quality.) Barth's stresses new ideas in nutrition and they use unique formulas of natural ingredients in their line of cosmetics. One hundred of Barth's extra-strength HI-C-PLEX 500 milligram tablets of vitamin C with wild rose hips, 100 milligrams of bioflavinoids, 50 milligrams of rutin, and 25 milligrams of hesperidin were reduced from $6.95 to just $3.13 in a mailer we saw. Natural selenium was reduced from $11.75 to $5.29 (for 100 tablets) and their timed-release All Day B-100 Complex tablets were reduced from $17.50 to $7.88 for 100. **C**

CALIFORNIA CARGO
P.O. Box 4178
Dept. 63
Carlsbad, CA 92008
(800) 223-2526
(800) 445-4343: CA residents
CK, MC, V, MO

California—the land of sunshine and bronzed, muscular bodies. California Cargo brings you the tools to help you look like you're a California baby, even if you're living in Kansas. They carry a variety of fitness tools such as soft weights and athletic shoes. In fact, they're the folks who specialize in shoes at mail-order prices. They often carry new models and colors of aerobics shoes before the local stores, so theirs is a good mailing list to be on. **C**

CREATIVE HEALTH PRODUCTS
5148 Saddle Ridge Road
Plymouth, MI 48170
(800) 742-4478
(313) 453-5309: MI residents
CK, MO

Creative Health Products has one of the best selections of high-tech ways to bring your performance into the 21st century. They offer heavily discounted medical scales and other medical supplies, such as a wide range of pulse monitors to monitor your heart rate accurately to maximize your workouts. There is a "pulmometer" for testing lung capacity, and if you're ready to invest in a bodyfat measuring device, look no further. They offer simple-to-use bodyfat measurers for $9.95, to digital, computerized ones for $349. There was also a 22-page guide called "How to Measure Your Percentage of Body Fat" for just $2. There are strength and flexibility testing tools, blood pressure kits from $14.95 to $209, a Pulsecoach-2 with alarms to tell you if you're under or over your target heart rate discounted from $129.95 to $99.50, sports watches, exercise bikes, and 200 different models of weight scales, all sold at discounts of 10% to 50%. They also sell a wide range of wrist, ankle, and specialty weights (like the kangaroo weights) at substantial discounts, along with stretch ropes. For high-tech fitness options, you can't beat the prices here. C

EFFECTIVE LEARNING SYSTEMS, INC.
5221 Edina Industrial Blvd.
Edina, MN 55435
(612) 893-1680
CK, MC, V

Effective Learning Systems offers tapes in both subliminal (messages only your subconscious can hear under soothing sounds of sea or music) and standard versions. One interesting program is Slim Image Weight Control and Slim Image II, which offers motivation, affirmations, and visualizations for those on a diet. As a daily support partner, audiotapes can be an effective adjunct to your diet and fitness routine (and who doesn't need that extra help to stay away from chocolate chip cookies). This catalog offers discounts on multiple purchases and accessories such as an inexpensive PANASONIC portable cassette recorder ($39.95), pillow speaker for listening to tapes in bed without forcing your mate to listen, too, ($5.95) and a combination sleep mask and earphone ($17.95). **C**

THE FINALS
21 Minisink Ave.
Port Jervis, NY 12771
(800) 431-9111
(800) 452-0452: NY residents
CK, MC, V, AE

The Finals is the final stop for fitness wear for swimmers. They offer high quality items, popular with athletes; such as the suits made of MIRACULON®, a "drag-free, non-absorbent, non-porous, and water-repellent" fabric for maximum speed. They were available for men and women for $14.95 and $29.95 respectively. The Finals sells their own hand paddles for strength building resistance in water workouts, a bargain at $4 each. SWIMIT is a webbed lycra glove that looks exactly like the Creature from the Black Lagoon's hand, $3.75 each. A training tube worn around the ankles to increase resistance was $9.50, kickboards were $7.25, and a paddle designed by Coach Dick Hannula is said to "maximize swimmer's sensitivity to water and awareness of tempo" for $4.50 each. They also carry a variety of sports stopwatches, a headband with a secret key/cash pocket for $2.50, very attractive running tights, singlets, and vests. All athletic gear is at factory-direct prices. Everything is fully refundable, with exchanges available up to 30 days of shipment. They also offer discounts for quantity, so teams can order their swimsuits at additional discounts for over 13 pieces. **C**

FOX RIVER NATURALS
33719 116th St.
Twin Lakes, WI 53181
(414) 862-2395
CK, MO

Fox River is the place to go to find just about everything in body care products as well as bulk herbs and spices that you might hope to find in the best-stocked whole foods store. Their natural body care products do not contain any animal by-products. They offer a wide variety of mineral bath products and bath soaps. While you're making your skin feel good, make the inside of your body feel better with the different herbal formulas and dietary supplements they carry. Herbs and spices can be bought in bulk, by the ounce or by the pound. They also carry Chinese ginseng products and remedies, along with other traditional folk remedies. Shipping cost is 15% up to $25, and 10% of the total after $25. **C**

FREEDA VITAMINS©
36 E. 41st St.
New York, NY 10017
(212) 685-4980
CK, MC, V, COD

Feel Freeda gulp these power-packed dietary wonders. Vitamins aren't hard to swallow when they're priced 30% to 50% below usual market prices. Mega-vitamins, multivitamins, B complex family, C family, children's vitamins, minerals, amino acids, nutrients . . . starch-free, vegetarian, and Kosher-approved. (They're on the Feingold Association of the U.S.A. approved food list!) We felt peppier just scanning the selection in their 36-page catalog. Just about every food supplement on the market today was offered under the Freeda label by this friendly, family-owned pharmacy. They've offered fast and efficient service since 1928. There is no minimum order, and if the item is unopened, you can exchange it for something of equal value. Shipping is $2. We got a charge out of discovering a remittance is required with first-time mail orders to establish credit. **C, PQ**

HEALTHTRAX INTERNATIONAL
P.O. Box 911
Newport, RI 02840
(401) 849-2400

If you're trying to stay on track, exercise-wise, we found no better source for home fitness equipment than Healthtrax International. Perhaps because these friendly folks manage health clubs themselves, they really know the ins and outs. Want to know which multi-station gym really holds up under family use? Or which exercise bike won't leave you limping? Ask Healthtrax. Healthtrax offers top-of-the-line, first-quality equipment at near wholesale prices, and prides itself in follow-through and customer service and even has an in-house credit plan for purchases up to $5,000. And when your fit new body requires an even more challenging piece of equipment,

Healthtrax has a trade-up option. Prices are too low to quote here, but discounts are substantial. **B, PQ**

HIGH MEADOW FARM
100 Davis Hill Road
New London, NH 03257
(603) 763-2535
CK, MC, V

You don't have to go to the farm to get wholesome, natural food. The farm will come to you. If you can imagine whole food *diet* meals delivered to your front door, you'll love High Meadow Farm. Precooked natural meals emphasize whole grains and include three main meals per day along with two snacks. Each day's package averages around 1,000 to 1,200 calories and includes wholesome broths, soups, brown rice, pilafs, soy milk, and other non-perishable yet wholesome foods. A seven-day package of 21 meals plus extras was just $49.95 (plus $4 shipping), and a 28-day package was available for $159.95 (plus $12 shipping). Mom couldn't keep you better fed. **C $3**

HUDSON VITAMINS
Dept. US
21 Henderson Drive
West Caldwell, NJ 07006
(800) 526-2262
(201) 575-5017: NJ residents
CK, MC, V, AE

Hudson has the healthy tonic that you and your wallet need. They offer wholesome savings of 40% to 50% on their HUDSON brand of vitamins and natural skin products. If you know your ABC's, you can pick out the best alfalfa sprouts as well as Korean ginseng, papaya ("the miracle digestive aid"), bee pollen, brewer's yeast, or a succulent granule of everyone's favorite flavor: desiccated liver. Their "geriatric formula" vitamin is very popular with sunset citizens. Shipping and handling not included. They offer gifts (we won't tell) according to the dollar amount of your order. **C**

L'EGGS SHOWCASE OF SAVINGS
P.O. Box 9983
Rural Hall, NC 27045
(919) 744-3434: orders and service
(919) 744-3435: catalog requests
CK, MC, V

In addition to irregular hosiery, first-quality activewear such as leotards and tights are available at discounted prices. Their colorful catalog featured style and size charts for easy ordering: pages were tagged to indicate first-quality or imperfect merchandise. Postage varies depending on the amount you purchase: for under $10, you'll pay $1.10; for under $20, you'll pay $1.55, etc. C

LEOTARDS BY LETICIA
P.O. Box 32201
San Jose, CA 95152
(408) 251-2345
CK, COD, MO

Leticia really knows her leotards. She began designing and creating her own exercise wear in self-defense. A dedicated exerciser, as her own workouts began paying off, she wanted to show it off. (Wouldn't you?) Bored with what she found on the shelf, Leticia turned her own sewing talents to create high-fashion exercise wear that was fun and exciting, not humdrum, without the high-fashion price tags! Now you, too, can have her luscious, custom-made, practically one-of-a-kind leotards for your own workout wardrobe. Her tights and leotards come in all sizes (from Petites, 4 to 6, to XXXXL, 20 to 22), so there's a size to fit YOUR body, not a mannequin's. For tights that fit right and leotards that are dyn-o-mite, Leticia's prices won't bite! Tights and leotards in heavy Lycra, with or without stirrups, were $14 to $16.50 (try that on for size!) retailing at $20 or more; briefs were $8 (retail, try $16). Leticia's creations come in solids, florals, abstracts, and stripes. Sample fabrics are available upon request. Get an additional 10% discount on orders of $50 or more! Shipping and handling costs not included. So, whether you're just starting out or you're a workout fanatic, stay in style for less with Leotards by Leticia. F (SASE)

L & H VITAMINS
37-10 Crescent St.
Long Island City, NY 11101
(800) 221-1152
(212) 937-7400: NY residents
CK, MC, V

At L&H, you'll find the ABC's of vitamins in such names as SCHIFF, PLUS, THOMPSON, STANDARD PROCESS LABS, NUTRI-DYN, as well as over 100 other national brands. Discounts are a standard 20%, plus there are several 40% off sales during the year. Their 56-page catalog features every conceivable nutritional supplement, including the kitchen zinc. There's no minimum order; returns are accepted within 30 days; orders are shipped out the same day they're received. The SCHIFF Acidophilus with Goat's Milk (100 capsules for $3.60; retail $4.50) caught our eye with alluring copy which said: "Natural aid for introducing friendly organisms to the lower intestines—20 million living lactobacilli in every capsule." Yumm! Hope none of those little fellows has claustrophobia. A new catalog published quarterly. **C**

L.L. BEAN
Fitness Catalog
Freeport, ME 04033
(207) 865-3111: phone orders
CK, MC, V, AE

L.L. Bean publishes a beautiful fitness specialty catalog; one came with a really valuable little Guide to Fitness that included information on starting a fitness program. Bean makes running shorts with reflective stripes integrated into a subtle design (coral and gray are especially appealing) for safe walking or running when the sun goes down. These sold for $16.50 postage paid. GORE-TEX running suits (the miracle material that is waterproof, windproof, and breathable) that fold into a briefcase for running on business trips or lunch hours ($86 postage paid), a pedometer for measuring your walking distance ($16), as well as other products with brand names such as NEW BALANCE, AVIA, and HEAVYHANDS®. These catalogs sell out quickly, so you must be on the list to be sure to receive yours. **C**

LIONEL ENTERPRISES
3017 Santa Monica Blvd.
Suite 304-222
Santa Monica, CA 90404
(213) 820-3632
CK, MC, V

One of the most common diet hints is to serve your little meals on littler plates. The idea is to make your diet-sized portion look bigger. The folks at Lionel Enterprises have come up with a solution that psyches dieters out to feel as though they are eating more. The DIET-HELPER PLATES are high-quality porcelain, microwave- and dishwasher-safe, with full-color photographs of mouth-watering food right on the plates. The "phood" is arranged at the top of the plate, so that when you place your own meal on the lower portion, it looks like a veritable feast! There are dinner and breakfast plates at 10¼ inches (the dinner plates add "one baked potato heaped with sour cream and chives, one serving of hot buttered golden sweet corn and lima beans, one freshly baked sesame seed dinner roll and butter, three ripe black olives"), while lunch and dessert plates are 8½ inches in diameter (dessert is an unbearable "scoop of cherry-walnut ice cream, one slice of devil's food cake with fudge frosting and cherry filling, generous bed of fudge sauce with chocolate leaves and three maraschino cherries"). What is especially clever is that these descriptions—plus the awesome calorie counts—appear on the back of the plates with the message to "Leave the Calories On the Plate!" You can order the DIET-HELPER PLATES factory direct. Dinner and breakfast plates were $10.95 each, lunch and dessert $9.95 each, and any four plates were $35.95. Add $2.75 shipping and handling.

THE MAIL RUNNER'S SHOP
Route 6
Scranton Carbondale Highway
Scranton, PA 18508
(800) 624-5786
MC, V, AE

Don't let Jack Frost keep you indoors this winter. The Mail Runner's Shop offers a full line of fitness wear to keep you comfortable outside during those long winter months. Hats, gloves, long underwear were among their items that will keep you snug. One of their most popular items is the GORE-TEX winter running suit. Its price should keep you warm—$119 (suggested retail price, $200). But winter isn't their only season. They offer a wide selection of discounted basics for runners like SPORTCO women's running tights (gray, violet, emerald, coral, and blue), discounted from $34.95 to $30, and the ALL SPORTS BRA for $6.95. Their full line of running shoes (NIKE, TIGER, BROOKS, and more) will keep you running on the right track. Shipping and handling fee is based on U.P.S. rates. Check their current catalog for current deals and prices. **C**

MEGA FOOD
Box 5036E
Manchester, NH 03108
(603) 434-6254
CK, MC, V

Mega Food exclusively offers the only brand of vitamins that are made out of food vitamins, they are not synthetic. Whether you want a once-daily multivitamin or the full spectrum of 100 different vitamins, minerals and food nutrient factors, Mega Food has it all. B-complex, vitamin C, stress formula, and mineral formulas are just a few of the 21 multivitamin products available. Their ONE-DAILY brand was available at $12.75 for 45 tablets. **C**

MOSS BROWN & COMPANY, INC.
P.O. Box 9992
Alexandria, VA 22304
(516) 794-6020
CK, MC, V, AE, DC, MO

Moss Brown & Co. caters to serious runners with their own popular shorts and singlets as well as brands like DOLFIN. Their T-shirts, duffel bags, and rugby wear are all beautifully designed. They also carry hard-to-find items and accessories like THE WEB. No, it's not for Halloween, but rather for water exercises. It is a half-fingered glove with webbing between the fingers to more than double the displacement of water by your bare hand. It's to add resistance to your water workout, not to catch flies. Moss Brown also carries a handsome racing swimsuit for women with high-cut legs and racer back for $33. A favorite in the current catalog was the orchid printed running tights—now that's style! If you're running around the Washington D.C. area, stop by their Georgetown store. **C**

NUTRITION HEADQUARTERS
104 W. Jackson St.
Carbondale, IL 62901
(618) 457-8103
CK, MC, V

Put your money where your mouth is and feel good about it. Nutrition Headquarters offers a healthy dose of vitamins, high potency formulas, minerals, and amino acids, as well as health and beauty aids, and weight loss products at substantial savings. We obtained 50 tablets of L-Glutamine 500 milligrams, for $3.75, $5.95 elsewhere. One hundred tablets of L-Tryptophane 100 milligrams were $3.75, $5.50 in a local health food store. They also carry a wide selection of pure natural herbs in capsule or tablet form. The catalog is enlightening for the uninitiated. Minimum order of $15 on credit card orders. C, F

RAINBOW HOT TUBS AND SPA INC.
5921 N. High St.
Worthington, OH 43085
(614) 888-8881
CK, MC, V, COD

When in Rome, do as the Romans. You might think you're in Rome when you see the selection of hot tubs and spas offered by Rainbow. We certainly found a pot of gold at the end of Rainbow Hot Tubs and Spas. They offer a bath house of spas, saunas, steamers, solariums, and tanning beds. You'll take a dip when you see their plunging prices of up to 60% off. They carry LANDIA, SKYTECH, CURTIS FRP, FOUNTAIN VALLEY, GALAXY, and enough others to satisfy any Roman bather—even Caesar. For all of the sun worshippers, KLAUS and others offer a selection of tanners. So, after riding in your chariot all day, come home to a hot tub or spa and relax. You'll feel like a Roman god, but you won't have to pay an empire at Rainbow. C $5

ROBY'S INTIMATES
1905 Samson St.
Philadelphia, PA 19103
(215) 751-1730

Whether it's leotards, tights, or sports bras, Roby's Intimates offers some of the best bargains in the business. Name brands like

MAIDENFORM, VASSARETTE, FORMFIT, and KAYSER are available at a discount of 20% to 50%, and DANSKINS can be ordered for 25% off their retail price. Dressing great while getting your body in shape doesn't have to be expensive. Send the name of the manufacturer and style number for a price quote. A fee of $2.50 is charged for postage and handling. **C $1, B, PQ (SASE)**

SAMPSON & DELILAH
Suite 208
7324 Reseda Blvd.
Reseda, CA 91335
CK, MO

Only an Olympian could have created the sexy, body-revealing leotards, swimsuits, and playwear featured in Corinna's Fitness Fashions. This catalog is inspiring enough to tape to your refrigerator, for "Corinna" is none other than Cory Everson, two-time Ms. Olympia body-building champ, and owner of the ultimate '80s physique. Once you see how she looks in these great fitness outfits, you'll want to head straight for the gym. Her free $10 gift with orders over $100 is just added motivation. Shipping and handling costs ranged from $1 to $4, depending upon the cost of your order. **C $1** (or free with order)

STAR PROFESSIONAL PHARMACEUTICALS, INC.
Dept. US
1500 New Horizons Blvd.
Amityville, NY 11701
(800) 262-STAR
(800) 645-7171: NY residents
CK, MC, V

Twinkle, twinkle, little Star,
Through the mail you're not so far.
If I gulp your vitamin weaponry,
Will my bod, too, become then, heavenly?

We checked out their 48-page catalog and liked what we saw, particularly their two-for-one specials on best-selling natural vitamins. Specials change as the catalogs change. Prices on their house brand (STAR) vitamins deserve a gold star for being up to 60% lower than comparable retail products, but their brand-name goods were priced comparably to retail. They also carry natural health and beauty aids and gifts. Premium gifts are offered with orders: you get *Mary Ellen's Helpful Hints* with all orders; Mary Ellen's book plus the *American Heart Association Cookbook* on orders of over $25; Mary Ellen's book, the Heart Association's cookbook, and *How to Flatten Your Stomach* on orders of over $50; and Mary Ellen's book, the Heart Association Cookbook, Flattening Your Stomach, and *The Consumers Guide to Prescription Drugs* on orders of over $100. (Orders over $1,000 get four calling birds, three French hens, two turtle doves and a . . . oh, never mind!) Star guarantees satisfaction: if after 30 days of use you aren't satisfied, you can return the unused portion for a complete refund. Shipping is free on orders over $10; there's a $2 assessment on credit card orders of under $10. *Underground Shoppers* get an additional 10% off on their first order, so tell 'em who you are. **C**

STUR-DEE HEALTH PRODUCTS
Dept. US
Austin Blvd.
Island Park, NY 11558
(800) 645-2638
(516) 889-6400
CK, MC, V, COD

Stur-Dee's carries their own brand of drugstore products like vitamins, minerals, cosmetics, etc., formulated to their specifications. Many of their products are natural and contain no sugar, artificial color, or starch. Prices on house vitamins, minerals, cosmetics, healing agents, and aloe vera products averaged a sturdy 15% to 30% lower than most national brands; they also offer gifts with orders. Orders are delivered ASAP. Folks on their mailing list periodically receive catalogs announcing sales. **C**

SUNBURST BIORGANICS
P.O. Box 607
Rockville Centre, NY 11571
(516) 623-8478
CK, MC, V, COD ($2.65)

"Combat dietary deficiencies with all-natural (no preservatives, no artificial flavorings or color) supplements!" says Millie Ross. Her family sells the preferred form of vitamin C, calcium ascorbate 550 milligrams, 100 tablets for $3.82, retail $6.95. Spirulina—a protein food praised by dieters and joggers, was $6.29 for 100 500-milligram tablets (a special introductory offer). You can also pep up pets by getting them to pop pet vitamins. Discounts are usually about 70% off; brands include SUNBURST, FUTURE BIOTICS, and HERBAL TEAS. For an added bonus, order over $25 and get a gift worth $25. (We don't want to B complex; check out their 48-page catalog and C for yourself.) All orders are processed within 24 hours and, except for a $1 handling charge, customers don't pay postage when orders are shipped within the continental US. Full refunds are given within 30 days. Folks identifying themselves as *Underground Shopper* readers can request a free vitamin and mineral wallchart with their first order. C

SUPER STRENGTH SYSTEMS
2218 86th St.
Brooklyn, NY 11214
(212) 372-1019
CK, MC, V

Jane Fonda getting to you? Last month's case of frostbite got you thinking about quitting jogging? Or has the nickname "Wimp" suddenly lost its appeal? Hey, just because you're a 97-pound weakling who couldn't fight his way out of a box of Vanilla Wafers doesn't mean you have to stay that way. Here's a Super idea: send for this catalog and check out the YORK and MANPOWER body-building systems. What are you weighting for except maybe the chance to be *some* body? C

SYBERVISION SYSTEMS
Fountain Square
6066 Civic Terrace Ave.
Newark, CA 94560
(800) 227-0600
CK, MC, V, AE, DC

SyberVision offers a variety of cassette programs that are comprehensive and thoughtful. "The Neuropsychology of Weight Control" is a 15-tape program that comes with a 144-page study guide that includes recipes and charts for keeping track of your progress. These tapes may provide the daily motivation needed to stick with a successful diet plan. The price was $69.95. Equally fascinating are the "master classes" on video. "Master classes" were offered in martial arts, tennis, bowling, baseball, racquetball, and golf. Each class is instructed by an expert in that particular field. Along with the video images of an expert at work, the videos include computer-enhanced sequences that may actually teach the brain to pattern your own body movements after the perfect form of the pro. It's an exciting concept. These video teaching programs were $89.95. There are sometimes discounts such as $10 off on two or more programs. Order the complete SyberVision catalog, which also includes programs on self-discipline and achievement. **C**

TAFFY'S-BY-MAIL
701 Beta Drive
Cleveland, OH 44143
(216) 461-3360
CK, MC, V, AE

Dancers get to wear the best clothes. Dancewear makes great, stylish streetwear as well as great fitness wear. Taffy's offers the best selection of fashion for dancers, aerobic athletes, gymnasts, and even cheerleaders. Just about everything comes in regular sizes and hard-to-find extra-large sizes (have you ever tried to find extra-large warm-up pants? Taffy's had them for $9.50). There are "gotta dance" shoelaces, the full line of Capezio dance shoes, from ballet to tap (the classic character pump with two-inch heel is one of the most comfortable dress shoes you can wear; at $70 in flesh or black, it's a foot-saving bargain), and great leg warmers (over 30 colors including electrics in lime, orange, pink, rose, and yellow for $8.95). Every possible style of leotard, unitard, and tight is available in a rainbow of colors, with kids' sizes as well. There are also resources for dancers and teachers: records, videos, magazines, and teaching tools. **C $3**

TRAMPOLKING SPORTING GOODS
P.O. Box 3828
Albany, GA 31708
(800) 841-4351
(912) 435-2101: GA resident
CK, MC, V

A mini-trampoline can be an excellent way to get a joint-sparing, soft aerobic workout. Trampolking sells factory direct so all their equipment can be ordered at substantial savings. Their Jogging Tramps retail at $69.95, but can be ordered for about $39.95. They also sell full-sized trampolines for backyard family fitness, as well as rowers, exercise bikes, and other home equipment. Call or write for their free brochure and price list. **B, PQ**

VIENNA HEALTH PRODUCTS
54 Phillips Way
Sharon, PA 16146
(412) 342-2525
CK, MC, V

Want to work out in the convenience and privacy of your own home? It's actually possible to build your own weight training benches and stations, at great savings. Vienna Health Products provide kits with pre-cut heavy wall two-inch square steel tubing, hardware, upholstery, detailed prints, and instructions. Welding and painting is required, however. There are more than 40 kits available, either assembled or unassembled pre-fab. The savings by doing it yourself can be substantial—up to 75%! An unassembled T-bar rowing kit sells for $60 while the same machine already put together runs $145. **C $1**

VITAMIN SPECIALTIES CO.
8200 Ogontz Ave.
Wyncote, PA 19095
(215) 885-3800
CK, MC, V

Here's a well-established, 40-year-old company you'll want to specialize in if you're prone to vitamin deficiencies. This company will have you back on your feet in no time, nourishing your bank account as well, with prices at 40% to 60% off retail on brands of vitamins, dietary supplements, over-the-counter drugs, and cosmetics. Compare actual prices by ordering their 96-page catalog. All products are manufactured under the Vitamin Specialties brand. We checked and found that approximately half of the products offered were 100% natural. Merchandise is guaranteed to meet all F.D.A. requirements. Unopened merchandise may be returned within 30 days for a full refund or credit. No shipping costs on orders over $15. **C**

WESTERN NATURAL PRODUCTS
Dept. US
Box 284
511 Mission St.
South Pasadena, CA 91030
(818) 441-3447
CK, MC, V

Whoa down there, podnuh, and don't get roped into paying retail! These Westerners have rounded up a corral full of house-brand natural vitamins, and hair and skin products. They've reined in on high prices, too. We were spurred to savings on multivitamins, megavitamins, and children's chewables, along with aloe vera, bee pollen, papaya enzymes, ginseng, and a whole herd of other items at 30% to 70% off. They've branded their own products (comparable to national brands in quality) so sage shoppers can feel at home on their price range. NATURE'S GATE in health and beauty products and ALOGEN cremes are also available. Popular new offerings included sugarless children's chewable vitamins, purse-sized packets of six vitamins, and amino acid and diet products. There's a $2-off coupon on any initial order. All products are unconditionally guaranteed and can be returned with no questions asked. There's no restocking charge and no minimum order—there *is* a 95-cent charge on orders under $12. You can lick the Christmas vitamin stamp-ede if you stock up on vitamins sooner. C

YEARS TO YOUR HEALTH
406 E. Irving Blvd.
Irving, TX 75060
(214) 579-7042
CK

Add years to your health and dollars to your wealth by shopping here. If you know gota kola from Coca-Cola, you'll find over 500 botanicals to choose from at prices 30% to 50% lower than most health food stores. This husband-and-wife team offers one of the largest selections in the country of bulk herbs, potpourris, spices, teas, and vegetarian vitamins. They carry their own line of over 50 different herbal extracts. Just write to Lonnie and Richard for their catalog and discover the exciting and wonderful world of herbs. C

Food

Who says there's no such thing as a free lunch? Happy hours at local bars feature tacos, cheeses, chicken wings, maybe even shrimp or oysters for the patrons. (Who's going to notice a few missing egg rolls?) Gallery and store openings are a dandy way to fill up on pâté, salmon, and imported cheeses washed down with a glass of wine. (Whoops, you left the invitation at home!) Show up for any demonstration of food processors, blenders, etc. (Always something cooking here.) Watch for those nice ladies giving out samples of the latest pizza flavors in the supermarket. (Get extras—for mother.) There's a bowl of caviar dip over in the deli. Go for it. If you're a teacher, confiscate all the gum and candy before class. (Ummmm, a Cadbury bar!) Finally, if you find you must pay for your food, check the pages that follow for some fantastic deals. You'll be glad you did.

ACE PECAN CO.
Dept. US
9th and Harris Streets
P.O. Box 65
Cordele, GA 31015
(312) 364-3277
CK, MC, V, AE, DC

Education is a wonderful thing. Introduce your friends to the nice-
ties of nuts—they'll soon be walking the hallowed halls of
macademia. (Education correlates with success, too: maybe someday
the two of you can join in a chorus of "Almond the Money!") Besides
the obvious inventory of pecans and other nuts, their 22-page catalog
contains five pages of new items such as fruit butters, cannoli kits,
dried fruit, pecan barks, nugget bits and logs, chocolate hand-dipped
banana chips, and apricots. Selling direct and packing in bulk cuts
the costs of these tasty items. "AM Chicago" and "People Are Talking in Baltimore" go nuts every time we're on the program with our
Ace in the whole. Delivery of orders typically takes seven to 10 days
though their bleached plump pistachios are generally devoured in
record time of thirty minutes or less. Add $3.50 for APO and FPO
(delivery via military for points outside the US); $6 for delivery to
Alaska, Hawaii, the Virgin Islands, or Puerto Rico. **C**

THE AMISHMAN
P.O. Box 128
Mount Holly Springs, PA 17065
CK, MC, V

Anyone who's ever lived in Pennsylvania has probably had scrapple.
It's a nostalgic food like White Castle hamburgers. So, if you're living in Texas or Tuscaloosa, you'll be glad to know that The
Amishman sells scrapple by mail. A 15-ounce tin of pork scrapple
costs $3.25. Other Pennsylvania Dutch treats include horehound
drops, buttermints, coal scuttle (a licorice novelty), Brother George
apple butter, and chow chow. If you come from the city of brotherly
love, you'll feel right at home with The Amishman. Minimum order,
$10. **B**

ARIZONA CHAMPAGNE SAUCES
c/o Sugar's Kitchen
P.O. Box 41886
Tucson, AZ 85717
(602) 624-3360
CK

The craze for NO SALT in your diet wins praises in my kitchen, so stock up on these NO SALT sauces. Three cheers for the ARIZONA CHAMPAGNE SAUCES from Sugar's Kitchen, a 10-year-old gourmet aficionado resource. There are three famous mustard sauces: hot, cajun style, and regular. Great addition to your deli platters, spreads for chicken or ham or as a marinade. Also delicious are their vegetable dip, salsa preparation, and dry herbal spice dip. For a distinctly different taste sensation, try their mild or hot jalapeno jellies, only $3.89 an eight-ounce jar. Wonderful gift packs available. All prices include shipping. Usually one day turnaround depending on U.P.S. zone. **C**

CACHE VALLEY DAIRY ASSOCIATION
Dept. US
P.O. Box 155
Smithfield, UT 84335
(801) 563-6262
CK

No cheesey trap here, cheese lovers, just delicious, fresh quality cheese. Cache has nibbled away the ratty retail to sell at factory direct prices. They even make cheese for other folks who put their own label on it and jack up the price. Cheese flavors include common Swiss, cheddar, Monterey Jack, and mozzarella, as well as taco, green onion, smoky, Swiss 'n salami, hot pepper, and kuminost. If you're in the area, stop by—taste tours through the cheese factory, and samples are offered free. Sharp and medium cheddar sliced off at $10.50 to $10.75 for three pounds; Monterey Jack was $14.50 for five pounds. Swiss cheese, a favorite, was $14.50 for four pounds; $26.95 for eight pounds. That's a lot less expensive than you'll find at Hickory Farms. Send for your mail-order catalog. Orders arrive in about a week; shipping charges are included in the price. Anyway you slice it, your cash will go further at Cache. **C**

CAVIARTERIA
29 E. 60th St.
New York, NY 10022
(800) 4-CAVIAR
(800) 422-8427
(212) 759-7410: NY residents
CK, MC, V, AE

If you're fishing for compliments at your next cocktail party, send for this luscious catalog and serve caviar, Scotch salmon, and other delicacies to your guests. Founded by New York City ad-man Louis Sobol, this family-operated business has been discounting fine gourmet foods for over 35 years at the same location. Russian, Iranian, or new American caviar is shipped to your door within days of being received at the Caviarteria warehouses. This means you could have fresher caviar than if you bought it at your local gourmet shop. And the saving is about 50%! Besides caviar, the catalog features a wide assortment of unique gourmet specialty items such as truffles, pâtés, caviar servers, caviar spoons, and 25 varieties of "freezer pac" snacks. **C**

CHARLES LOEB
615 Palmer Road
Yonkers, NY 10701
(914) 961-7776
CK, MC, V

Charles Loeb might define the changing of the seasons as spices that lose flavor as thyme goes by. Mr. Spiceman, as he's called, offers 131 spices and seasonings to specialty stores, ethnic restaurants, and *now* to the public at wholesale prices. Everything is carefully sealed in airtight pouches to insure freshness. Sesame, saffron, charcoal salt, cinnamon, juniper berries, anise star, pignolia nuts, crab boil, kelp, shallots, instant herbal flash tea—it's all here, and prices are up to 90% off those in supermarkets. There's no minimum order, but there's a $1.50 charge on orders under $10. Shipping is free on orders over $75; if you're unhappy, they'll exchange or refund (your option) within 10 days. Do yourself a flavor, seasoned shoppers, curry up— order one of their black-and-white catalogs now! **C $1** (refundable)

CHEESELOVERS INTERNATIONAL
P.O. Box 1200
Westbury, NY 11590
(800) 645-3197; credit card orders only
(800) 228-2028
(516) 997-7045
CK, MC, V

To bric or not to brie? That is the (delectable) question. Whether 'tis nobler in the mind to suffer the slings and arrows of a $6 membership fee and receive a monthly color newsletter which features domestic and imported cheeses and $6 worth of gift certificates toward your first purchase, or whether you should just down a six-pack of Falstaff—who knows? Tasting authentic, nonmechanically aged cheddars, havarti, port salut, the scarce cheshire cheese, and new twists such as fromaggio d'amaretto makes us smile and say cheese. Monthly sales enable cheese aficionados to sample at lower prices (usually about 10 cents a pound above wholesale.) You're under no obligation to buy anything and president Gerard Paul guarantees that everything will taste "Gouda." **C**

CHEESES OF ALL NATIONS
153 Chambers St.
New York, NY 10007
(212) 964-0024
MC, V, AE

What a friend we have in cheeses! Since the summer of '42, this nationally acclaimed wholesale cheese source has been supplying New York restaurants with some of the finest deals in wheels. Now shoppers can take the bite out of both the Big Apple and 1,000 different cheeses. Wisconsin sharp, $2.75 a pound; French imported Swiss, $2.75 a pound; French brie, $2 a pound; Denmark Fontina, $2.98 a pound; and French goat cheese, $3.98 a pound. Minimum order, one pound. They guarantee products to arrive in Gouda condition. Muenster up one dollar for their catalog. **C $1** (refundable)

COLONEL BILL NEWSOM'S
127 N. Highland Ave.
Princeton, KY 42445
(502) 365-2482
(502) 365-6311
CK

If you're a ham and in a class by yourself, you'll feel right at home here. Over 100 food writers have saluted this 70-year-old colonel in their articles or columns, and this one is no exception. Bill's genuine green hickory smoked Kentucky hams are carefully selected, dry cured, slow-smoked, and aged many months by methods used for nearly 200 years. The weather in this particular area of Kentucky seems to aid in the natural enzymes that produce this melt-in-your-mouth delicacy. No chemicals and no quick-cure methods. Each ham is gift-wrapped, packed, and shipped in individual boxes. Gift cards can be included. Current price was $2.69/pound with each ham weighing 14 to 17 pounds. **B** (includes recipes)

GRACE TEA COMPANY, LTD.
50 W. 17th St.
New York, NY 10011
(212) 255-2935
CK

What price luxury tea? Though the cost of Grace Rare Teas on a per pound basis is among the highest of all teas in the U.S., the cost, in comparison to gourmet coffees, bottled water or soft drinks, for example, can be low—10 cents a cup. So sip the savings, Grace, and order from their selection of black loose teas: superb DARJEELING 6000; WINEY KEEMUN ENGLISH BREAKFAST; LAPSANG SOUCHONG SMOKY #1; EARL GREY SUPERIOR MIXTURE and POUCHONG tea: BEFORE THE RAIN JASMINE. Instant refund if not completely satisfied. One eight-ounce canister and shipping and handling would run about $10.90 to $14.90. Their brochure gives information on the quality of Grace Teas as well as some helpful tips on making tea, serving, storage, and gift ideas. **B**

IDEAL CHEESE SHOP
1205 Second Ave.
New York, NY 10021
(212) 688-7579
CK, MC, V, AE

You can smile when you say "Cheeses" at this Second Avenue emporium. Celebrating its 33rd anniversary, this is the haven for some of the finest cheeses in the country. This trend-setting shop was reviewed by famed Craig Claiborne in 1962 in an article in the *New York Times* and since that time, owner Edward Edelman continues to tempt the fanciers with some of the finest and freshest cheeses from all over the world. Find exotic double and triple creams, the perfect brie, French St. Andre and Boursault, Danish Saga, and Creama Donia or Italian Taleggio. Experts on hand to guide you through their extensive and mouth-watering catalog. **C**

JAFFE BROS.
Dept. US
P.O. Box 636
Valley Center, CA 92082-0636
(619) 749-1133
CK, MC, V, DC, COD

Jaffe's ranch puts a healthy squeeze on high-priced organic dried fruits, nuts, grains, and vegetarian food supplements. Picky people will go nuts over organic unsalted peanut butter priced at $4.15 a quart: unrefined olive oil made us Pop-eyes at $16.75 a gallon. Bee pollen, honey, brown rice, rolled oats, soy and mung beans were also available, although their dried fruits (unsweetened pineapple, mango, papaya, and 15 others) in five-pound bags are a real specialty. Prices are much lower than health food stores; there's a real incentive for bulk buying. (Down-to-earth prices would make Holden Caulfield a real "Catcher in the Organic Rye!") **B, PQ**

KOLB-LENA CHEESE COMPANY
P.O. Box 486
3990 N. Sunnyside Road
Lena, IL 61048
(815) 369-4577
CK, MC, V, AE

Craving cheese—go direct to the Big Cheese. Since 1900, Kolb-Lena has been the place to go for cheese. They even have the biggest mouse in Illinois—"Swiskers" who stands outside of their DELICO cheese plant. Kolb-Lena offers the finest in cheese gift packs. The cheese packs were stuffed with more than a dozen cheeses they produce. Brie, camembert, feta, Sno Belle, havarti, rexoli, and their own baby Swiss can keep "Swiskers" and you smiling. Buy your favorite cheese in bulk form, too! All products guaranteed. If you're ever in Illinois, visit their cheese factory to see their award-winning DELICO cheese being made. Our favorite part of the tour—free taste samples. Minimum order is $10. Only one week wait for your cheese order. **B**

LE GOURMAND
Box 433
Route 22
Peru, NY 12972
(518) 643-2499
CK, MC, V

Close your eyes and picture a fancy gourmet feast, featuring products from Le Gourmand at 30% to 200% below other gourmet mail-order companies. For example, we found a 17-ounce bottle of walnut oil by GUENARD which normally retails for $10.95 that Le Gourmand sells for $6.75, a savings of 38%. Herbs, spices, oils, vinegars, teas, coffee, LENOTRE chocolate coatings, pastry products and such are available under those names of: PAUL CORCELLET, TABLE LYONNAISE, DEAN & DELUCA, PAGES, GASTON LENOTRE, BARRAL, LA PERRUCHE, BARRY, LA BALEINE . . . They stock a wide assortment of miscellaneous foods ranging from brown cane sugar in irregularly cut cubes to hazelnut praline.

LYNN DAIRY FRESH FROM THE
HEART OF THE DAIRY STATE
Box 177, Route 1
Granton, WI 54436
(715) 238-7129
(715) 238-7120
CK, MC, V

Do you have a mouse in your house? Lynn Dairy would please any cheese lover. They manufacture 15 basic cheeses including mild, medium, and sharp cheddar, colby, Monterey Jack, caraway, mozzarella, and others to satisfy even the fattest rat. Even that famous mouse, Mickey, might be tempted. This family dairy has been sending cheese across the United States and Europe for over 35 years. They have a daily cheese production of 80,000 pounds! No cat-and-mouse games here. We licked our whiskers over the mouth-watering cheeses pictured in their full-color 12-page catalog. Tempting morsels of mild cheddar were only $2.55 per pound. Mozzarella was only $2.80 per pound. Several gift boxes are offered. Each order is quickly filled and shipped to arrive fresh within two weeks. You won't be trapped if you're not completely satisfied; Lynn Dairy guarantees all products. So if you have some mice in your house, fatten them up without getting a hole in your wallet. **C**

MANGANARO FOODS
488 Ninth Ave.
New York, NY 10018
(800) 4-SALAMI (472-5264)
(212) 563-5331
CK, AE, COD

Mama mia! Now that's Italian. Founded in 1893, in its present location, Manganaro continues in the same fine family tradition. Their rafters are hung with imported hams, cheeses, and provoletti. Now the taste of old Italy can be yours with their wide variety of cheeses (parmigiano, reggiano, Swiss gruyère, smoked mozzarella, fontina, and Bel Paese to name a few); vinegars and olive oils; pastas; Italian delicacies (pesto, baby clams, baby mushrooms in oil, Nutella, eggplant strips, and more); espresso and desserts (yum, cannolis!) and, of course, their famous Italian-style salamis. Their gift boxes and baskets are gifts no one would return. Make sure your next party is a hit with their famous six-foot sandwich filled with meats, cheeses, and garnishes. It feeds 30 to 35 people and it only costs $65. Minimum order, $15. Shipping and handling is included in their prices. Allow three to six weeks for your order. Rome wasn't built in a day, after all. **C**

MEXICAN CHILE SUPPLY
Dept. US
304 E. Belknap
Fort Worth, TX 76102
(817) 332-3871
CK

Rumor has it that this is the place that supplies J.R. Ewing with his peppers, and you know what a hothead he is. These folks have been in cahoots since 1891 (when cowboys were really tough). Custom-blended chile powders and many other spices are sold in bulk pack-ages, saving consumers 50% to 75% or more off those high-priced bottles in retail stores. All seasonings and spices are sold under the brand PENDERY'S. No returns on food products; no problem with refunds if request is reasonable. No matter if it's chile today or hot tamale, you'll get a taste for the flavor of the Southwest—the hottest part of the country! **B, PQ**

THE MEXICAN KITCHEN
P.O. Box 213
Brownsville, TX 78520
(512) 544-6028
CK

You don't have to cross the border to taste something from this Mex-ican Kitchen. Their menu offers various brands of foods, chiles, spices, sauces, cookware, and cookbooks. Write to them for anything you might want pertaining to Mexican foods. Send an SASE for a list of closeouts and discounted items. Taco-bout some great deals, you'll have a fiesta when you see these hot prices. Dried whole chile pods ranged in price from $3.50 to $22 depending on your selection. Fresh ground chile powder cost from 50 cents to $1.80 per ounce. They also stock a library of spicy cookbooks that will have you dancing around your hat. A few of the titles: *Cooking Texas Style, The Art of Mexican Cooking,* and *Our Cookbook, An Adventure From South of the Border.* Several samplers are provided to let you experience real Mexican seasoning. Better be near some water, though, these seasonings could start a fire! You might get a little hot under the collar waiting for your goodies; 30 days is the normal length of response time. **F**

MORAVIAN SUGAR CRISP CO., INC.
Route 2
Friedberg Road
Clemmons, NC 27012
(919) 764-1402
CK, MO

Cookies and milk will never be the same. Mrs. Travis F. Hanes bakes the finest cookies in the world from an old family recipe. Each cookie is rolled, cut, and packed by hand. "The flavor is literally rolled into the cookie." There were five delicious flavors to choose from: "Chocolate Crisps," "Lemon Crisps," "Butterscotch," "Ginger Crisps," and their original "Sugar Crisps." Wrapped in individual stacks in a tin container, the cookies are guaranteed to arrive fresh and in good condition. One-pound tins were priced at $11, two-pound tins were $18. Gift packs were also available. All prices included postage and handling, except cookie monsters in Alaska and Hawaii should add $4. **B**

PAPRIKAS WEISS IMPORTER
1546 Second Ave.
New York, NY 10028
(212) 288-6117
CK, MC, V, AE

From the wooden shelves of this 100-year-old gourmet food shop come some of the world's finest delectables. Owner Ed Weiss "has to be the greatest and fastest and most complete and thorough source of food information in the world," wrote Maida Heatter, the famous creator of the *New York Times* recipe series. The imported foods and cookware (hard to find on many local fronts) included many Hungarian specialties like double-smoked Hungarian bacon, paprika paste, fresh-baked Dobosh torte (seven-layer cake), even a dumpling machine. Plus cheeses, pâtès, coffees, teas, and candies. Corporate gifts available. **C $1**

SAN FRANCISCO HERB CO.
250 14th St.
San Francisco, CA 94103
(800) 227-4530
(800) 622-0768: CA residents
(415) 861-7174
CK, MC, V, MO

For the spice of life, slice off at least one-half the price for the same or similar products from the supermarket. Since they buy in bulk quantities and repackage in their own one-pound units, you can reap the benefits of wholesale prices on spices, teas, and natural foods. If you'd rather leave your heart in San Francisco but bring home botanicals (like Mexican chamomile), pine nuts, tapioca pearls, or tropicana orange pekoe blend teas, then we can't sing our praises loud enough for this mail-order resource. Additional discounts 5% on $200; 10% on $500 orders. Minimum order, $30. **C**

S.A.V.E
65 E. South Water St.
Chicago, IL 60601
(312) 977-3700
CK, MC, V, AE

S.A.V.E. is the N.A.M.E. of the G.A.M.E. Join the Shopper's Association for Value and Economy—you'll save on family household products. This is a club; when you send in a dollar, you'll receive a $20 designer tote bag along with a surprise gift valued at $20. Sound interesting? After that, you must pay $7.98 every seven weeks, plus a shipping and handling charge. You'll receive a package of groceries valued at $23. There are other ways of saving money. For instance, you can earn an extra gift for answering their "brand opinion poll," etc. No losers in this game, unless you want to return something. There are no refunds or exchanges. **PQ**

SCHAPIRA COFFEE COMPANY
117 W. 10th St.
New York, NY 10011
(212) 675-3733

Coffee, tea, and you can always find me—a sucker for a cup of lapsang souchong (tea) or Kenyan AA water-processed decaffeinated coffee. Any way I can make my life easier is high on my shopping list. Favorite blends were available by the pound (or ½ pound or ¼ pound packs) within their mail-order price lists. BROWN ROAST ($5.65), COSTA RICAN ($5.95), JAMAICA BLUE MOUNTAIN ($14.50)—shipped the day it's roasted to your specifications. Beans are ground to order for the percolator, drip, vacuum, or Melitta. Naturally flavored teas like black currant or raspberry were packed 50 teabags for $3.25 and loose teas by the pound like EARL GREY or DARJEELING were $7.50 to $9.00. **B**

SIMPSON & VAIL, INC.
P.O. Box 309
38 Clinton St.
Pleasantville, NY 10570
(914) 747-1336
CK, MC, V (minimum $15 on credit cards)

Tea and symphony since 1929 for 10% to 15% less plus coffee, accessories, and the accompaniments to both (like chocolates and preserves)

are available through this fine retailer. Now to sweeten the pot further, take another 10% off your first order if you proudly roast you're an *Underground Shopper.* Over 80 varieties of teas to taste, more than 30 high-grown, hard bean coffees from Kenya AA to Mocha-java to water-processed decaffeinateds. Lovely gift-giving canisters filled with teas, teaballs galore, teapots, sugar and creamer sets, maple syrups, pancake and muffin mixes, Scottish soups, pure seafood soups, Louisiana spices . . . all too mouthwatering to enumerate further. This company, more than 50 years old, is owned by Joan and Jim Harron and sells to such famous restaurants as The Russian Tea Room in New York City.

SUGARBUSH FARM
RFD 1, Box 578 U
Woodstock, VT 05091
(802) 457-1757
CK, MC, V, AE, DC, CB

If you want to tap into something delicious, order this family's (made on the farm) maple syrup. What sap could resist any of their seven kinds of Vermont cheeses meticulously packaged in foil and wax. Imagine, two-year-old sharp cheddar (until you try it, you'll never know what two years of aging can do to fresh whole milk cheese); hard-to-find sage cheese (rarely made today and delicious); or naturally smoked cheese (smoked golden for five days over a slow burning maple/hickory log fire). Since 1945, the Ayres family has been delivering naturally good cheese, not processed or colored, at reasonable prices. Gift packs, too. Satisfaction guaranteed. **B**

SULTAN'S DELIGHT INC.
P.O. Box 253
Staten Island, NY 10314
(718) 720-1557
CK, MC, V

Delicacies from the Middle East will melt in your mouth and not in your pocketbook. Their 16-page catalog sumptuously lists their specialties—from tahini (sesame butter), semolina, couscous, bulghur, chick peas, spices, cashews, pistachios, packaged gift items, candied and dried fruits, filo dough, baklava, Turkish coffee to cookbooks. Savings of 10% to 70% including an additional 10% off to readers of *The Underground Shopper* on your first order. Minimum order $15 excluding shipping. Response time—72 hours insures freshness and almost immediate gratification if you're hungry. **C**

TEXAS ROSE COFFEE & TEA
Dept. US
P.O. Box 536
Heidenheimer, TX 76533
(817) 983-3111
CK

If you've got a nose for Rose, your taste buds will be blooming before you know it. This quaint country store carries a selection of freshly roasted coffees, Texas Rose tea (an orange pekoe black tea which they blend and pack), and several varieties of honey, spices, extracts, and other items, although only teas and coffees are sold by mail. Their coffee originates as the finest quality Central American green coffee available, which is then roasted using an old European method of dry roasting. By roasting the coffee beans slowly, the beans retain a richer flavor and stay fresh longer. Besides selling to individuals, they sell their coffee and tea wholesale to gourmet and specialty food stores. A sample pack containing one pound of their special blend coffee and four ounces of tea was $6.25 (they pay shipping). You can also buy larger weight orders of whole bean, filter ground, or percolator ground coffee and loose teas. **F**

WILBUR CHOCOLATE CANDY OUTLET
48 N. Broad St.
Lititz, PA 17543
(717) 626-1131
CK

While my conscience, and Richard Simmons, and Jacki Sorensen "talk a lot," I find I am swayed by a small piece of "chocolate." This company can save "consumers" 20% on their own brand of chocolate and confectionery items. (Any dedicated chocoholic immediately will realize this doesn't necessarily mean 20% savings—it means you can binge on 20% more chocolate for the same price! Like any addict, existence is hand-to-mouth). They carry 500 different confections at outlet prices. Wilbur also has dietetic candies, plus a selection of chocolate and confectioner's coatings in white, pink, green, yellow, and orange sunlight. Delivery takes three weeks, maximum. There is no shipping between June and September—who wants chocolate that "melts in the mail, and not in your mouth" anyway? **PQ**

ZABAR'S
2245 Broadway
New York, NY 10024
(800) 221-3347
(212) 787-2000: NY residents
CK, MC, V, AE, DC

Concerning Zabar's, the famous New York gourmet food store, there's good news and bad news. First, the good news—they have a fascinating little catalog that's crammed with gourmet goodies like Russian coffee cake, milk-fed white veal, and more. Just reading the names of all the scrumptious foods will make your mouth water. Now the bad news—we can't possibly list all the discounted housewares they carry. (As a company's spokesman told us, "That'll take all year!") Nonetheless, they do carry brands like OSTERIZER, WARING, GE, SUNBEAM, KITCHENAID, HAMILTON BEACH, KRUPS, and SANYO at savings of 20% to 40%. Choose from a large inventory of French copperware. You'll save a buck or two on gourmet and hard-to-find coffees such as Jamaican Blue Mountain Style, Kenya, Hawaiian Kona, Mocha Style, Costa Rican, and Colombian. Brew, too, through their selection of decaffeinated blends including espresso and water-processed. All coffees are roasted on Zabar's premises twice a week. If your palate exceeds your pocketbook, call for this catalog immediately. **C**

Freebies

Did you know you could learn winning chess strategies absolutely free? How about arranging for your aged grandparents or friends to get a birthday or anniversary card from the president? You can do that, too, and it's free. Cooking from old New England recipes or giving a Braille cookbook to a blind friend are just two other options that won't cost you a cent. Here are some tips on asking for these "freebies." Ask for just one item at a time—don't be greedy. Specify what you enclose with your request: for example, "I am enclosing a stamped self-addressed envelope." SASE means a 9½-inch long, stamped business envelope addressed to yourself. If you need to send coins, mail as few as possible and tape them inside. Write your name, address, and zip code on both your letter and the envelope. And finally, be patient. Expect to wait a month or two before your request is answered.

AARP (AMERICAN ASSOCIATION OF RETIRED PERSONS)
Health Advocacy Services
AARP
1909 K St., N.W.
Washington, D.C. 20049

For a free booklet about the skyrocketing costs of health care and what you can do about them, write AARP. They offer practical tips on how to save money on medical bills, how to stay healthy, and how to get involved in the fight to hold down health care costs. There's also a brief discussion outlining the scope of the problem.

AMERICAN BABY MAGAZINE
American Baby, Inc.
575 Lexington Ave.
New York, NY 10022
(212) 752-0775

Who says a baby is no bargain? Get a free issue of *American Baby Magazine* for expectant new parents. What kind of articles will you get? The issue that was delivered to us (no, the stork didn't bring it!) contained features such as "Dear Doctor" (answered by Ralph Gause, M.D.), a parent's personal story, "Medical Update," nutrition advice, job-sharing information, and a photo essay of a baby's birth. A yearly subscription's $9.97, with the first six months free. Now, if only the baby would sleep and we weren't so tired, we could read . . . .

AMERICAN FOUNDATION FOR THE BLIND
15 W. 16th St.
New York, NY 10011
(212) 620-2000

This helpful packet will increase understanding of the problems of visually impaired students and friends. A card with raised Braille alphabet and numerals, the life of Louis Braille, and suggestions for teachers who deal with visually handicapped children in the classroom are included. Publications, aids, and appliances for the visually impaired are AFB's specialty, and their catalog of publications for and about the blind can be quite useful. They also offer a free "application kit" for creating a photo-ID card for blind persons. **C**

AMERICAN HEART ASSOCIATION
National Center
7350 Greenville Ave.
Dallas, TX 75231
(214) 373-6300

Do you know that almost one million Americans die of heart disease every year? Do you know how to control high blood pressure? Do you know what major factors contribute to early heart attacks and strokes? You'd know these facts and many others if you read the Heart Association's fact sheet on heart attack, stroke, and risk factors. Diseases of the heart and blood vessels cause more premature death and disability than any other health problem; maybe that's why the American Heart Association provides so many different booklets. A few examples: "Strokes: A Guide for the Family"; "Living With Your Pacemaker"; "Exercise and Your Heart"; "Cholesterol and Your Heart." Please note that we've given you the National Center's address, but the free or nominally charged literature is distributed by the Heart Association's state affiliates and local chapters. To avoid delay, contact the nearest local office; its office should be listed in the phone book.

AMERICAN PAINT HORSE ASSN.
General Store
P.O. Box 18519
Fort Worth, TX 76118

This is the mane source for information on the American Paint Horse. Free information includes a full-color brochure detailing history, breed characteristics, and Association activities. Information is also available on Association services. Videos for loan include the 1984 A.P.H.A. National Championship Show and the 1984 World Championship Show. This comes from a city "where the West begins" and there's a high interest in horses. (Did you know a paint is not the same as a pinto, even though the colors may be the same?)

ANNOUNCEMENTS BY WILLARD SCOTT
"Today" Show Office, Room 304
30 Rockefeller Plaza
New York, NY 10012

Be a star for a day. Willard Scott, the flamboyant weatherman of NBC's "Today" show, will announce birthdays, anniversaries, and charitable events on the air. Couples celebrating their 75th (or beyond) anniversary or individuals who have reached the 100th (or beyond) mark can have their special day announced on national television by Willard Scott. Willard will also announce charitable events on the air. Just send in the name, address, date, and the type of celebration or event at least three to four weeks in advance. For charitable events, send in complete details and press releases with visual aids (if available). For those whose names are not announced, Willard will still send a birthday or anniversary greeting card.

AUTO SAFETY HOTLINE
Consumer Information Center
Department of Transportation
Washington, D.C. 20590
(800) 424-9393

If you're hot to get the facts on auto safety then call the Hotline Monday through Friday, 8 A.M. to 4 P.M. This user-friendly government service provides some 20 booklets on such topics as "Child Restraint Systems"; "How to Fight Drunk Driving"; "Reports on Crash Tests"; "Fuel Economy"; "Motorcycle Safety"; and "Travel Campers' Trailer Safety."

BELL'S GUIDE
RLH Marketing Communication
c/o Bell's Guide
355 Lexington Ave.
New York, NY 10017

Dining out in New York City? Send a postcard to this address and ask for a (free!) guide to 100 of New York's finest restaurants. The guide was compiled by noted New York food critic Bob Lape and contains restaurants in nine categories. You can sample both moderately expensive to very expensive meals from restaurants serving American, Chinese, continental, French, Italian, Japanese, Mexican, Spanish, and seafood. *Bon appétit!*

CONSUMER INFORMATION CATALOG
Consumer Information Center
Pueblo, CO 81009
(303) 948-3334

What's been on your mind lately? Savings, suntans, sensible child raising? Get the scoop by requesting free information booklets from about 30 federal agencies. We saw such best-selling titles as: "The Confusing World of Health Foods"; "Herbs—Magic or Toxic"; "Thrifty Meals for Two"; "Your Key to Energy Efficiency"; "Cholesterol, Fat, and Your Health"; "Antidepressant Drugs"; "Generic Drugs"; "Antihistamines and Aspirin." Confirmed booklet junkies in our office have also broken down and ordered: "Nutrition and Your Health," "Consumers' Resource Handbook," and "Mortgage Money Guide." **C**

DEAK INTERNATIONAL, INC.
Marketing Dept.
29 Broadway
New York, NY 10006
CK, (MC & V*)

The firm that brings you commission-free foreign and U.S. traveler's checks will also send you a currency-by-mail form, rate guide, and brochure on foreign currency needs and investment in precious metals. They sell a currency calculator and send out a quarterly currency guide that is updated for 120 countries. *MC & V for calculator only.

DOVER PUBLICATIONS, INC.
Free Chess Booklet Offer
31 E. 2nd St.
Mineola, NY 11501
(516) 294-7000
CK

"How Do You Play Chess?" guides players through the fundamentals. Dover also has a free catalog of inexpensive chess paperbacks (100 +) to advance a player. Prices start at $2.50. They offer free catalogs in many other areas: fiction, fine arts, music, photography and pictorial archives for professional artists, juvenile, cookbooks, science. They'll take a check, mate. **C**

HOLLYWOOD BREAD
1747 Van Buren St.
Hollywood, FL 33020
(305) 920-7666

Want a handy purse-size calorie and carbohydrate guide to take along to cafes and restaurants? Here's where to get one. It will even slide into wallets. The introductory pages give good advice: "Forget the fad diets, keep this book handy and get to know the foods you eat." About 630 foods are listed. Best of all, the guide won't cost you any dough at all.

JOHNSON & JOHNSON
O.B. Purse Pack
Request Fulfillment Center
P.O. Box 76P
Baltimore, MD 21230
(800) 631-5294 (11:00 A.M.-4:00 P.M. E.S.T.)
(800) 352-4719: MD residents

Write to this place and you'll be sent a sample tampon in a purse-size plastic box about two inches square. It is slightly textured outside with no lettering. The inside is stamped with the O.B. trademark, but not too ob-viously.

L'OREAL GUIDELINE
(800) 631-7358

Why be hair-ried by the hassles of a permanently depressing perm? If you're frazzled by the frizzies or tainted by the tone of your tints, call the experts for free advice. They have a complete team of friendly professional technical consultants who are trained to help consumers. Line open from 10 A.M. to 7 P.M. E.S.T. Monday through Friday.

MARCH OF DIMES BIRTH DEFECTS FOUNDATION
Public Information Office
1275 Mamaroneck Ave.
White Plains, NY 10605
(914) 428-7100

The March of Dimes Birth Defects Foundation provides the public with important information regarding birth defects and genetic disorders. "The Family Health Tree" is a colorful foldout genealogical chart useful for recording family health history. There's also a helpful list of sources for additional research on the back cover. Best of all, the booklet costs . . . $0.00!

MODERN PRODUCTS INC.
Gayelord Hauser Offer
P.O. Box 09398
Milwaukee, WI 53209
(414) 352-3333

Enclose a SASE and receive one sample each of SPIKE, VEGE-SAL, and low-salt VEGIT. Enough comes in each packet to flavor several soup pots. Ingredients are natural salt-of-the-earth seasonings.

MORTON SALT CO.
Salt Dough Brochure
Department of Consumer Affairs
110 N. Wacker Drive
Chicago, IL 60606
(312) 621-5200

"Dough-It-Yourself Christmas Decorations" is a small foldout with directions for salt sculptures. You'll find everything you knead to know to sculpt with dough: basic recipes, tool selection, hardening methods, finishing, and ideas for Christmas ornaments. "The Sodium Content of Popular Prepared Food Items" charts everything from deviled crab to barbeque sauce. Their "Measure Helper" provides data on calories in popular foods. An enticing folder, "Tickle Your Taste Buds," gives eight recipes using Morton's seasoning blend (in soups, pies, and casseroles). Fine info and free!

NEW BEDFORD SEAFOOD COUNCIL
Promotion Department CDAU
17 Hamilton St.
New Bedford, MA 02740
(617) 994-3457

For those who fancy fish, these folks offer free items that'll make your fins flap. Included are an iron-on transfer for you or your mate's T-shirt, a four-inch round blue and gold sticker (both show the council's logo, a sailor boy with a background of rope and nets), plastic litter bag, and a recipe folder of scrumptious seafood dishes that'll hook you in a New Bedford minute. (Limit your request to three items and include SASE.)

OFFICE OF METRIC PROGRAMS
Washington, DC 20230
(202) 377-0944

Give us an inch and we'll take a kilometer. Like it or not, it's coming: the metric system. This office will send you an information sheet and conversion cards ASAP. While we could probably cope with the change, imagine the turmoil faced by the lowly inchworm. Talk about an identity crisis!

PENNZOIL COMPANY
Gumout Division
3675 South Noland Road
Independence, MO 64055
(816) 461-7078

These automotive experts offer three free informative folders: "How to Find Your Way Under the Hood and Around the Car" is appropriately described as "a quick and easy guide to preventive maintenance for the self-service customer (and anyone else who drives)." You'll discover good tips on keeping the old tank in service. "Why Use Fuel Mix Gas Treatment" and "Why Use Gumout" provide facts and figures concerning the solutions and problems of carburetion systems in modern automobiles.

PRESIDENTIAL GREETINGS OFFICE
The White House
Washington, DC 20500
(202) 456-7639

Want someone to get the recognition they deserve? Couples celebrating their golden anniversary (or beyond) and individuals who are 80 years old (and older) can get a congratulatory letter from the president of the United States. To arrange for the greeting to be sent, you need to write six weeks in advance, giving the occasion and the name(s) and address of the recipient-to-be.

RADIO SHACK (any retail store)
Battery-A-Month Card
Your Town, USA

Is this what's meant by a charge card? Not really, but it's a good idea. Once a month, you can get one free battery of your choice (AA, C, D, or 9-volt) from Radio Shack brand bins. No purchase is required to get a card. You may bring your card in for validation anytime during the month and pick out your battery.

RICE COUNCIL OF AMERICA
P.O. Box 740123
Houston, TX 77274
(713) 270-6699

Offerings from this group will tell you everything you need to know about cooking rice. About 30 leaflets are available, but limit your selection to three, and send them an SASE. Subjects include: recipes for people with diabetes and allergies; microwave and conventional cooking; desserts, salads, seafood, and international favorites. "Rush-Hour Recipes" comes in large type and Braille versions (no SASE needed). Write for a complete list of their brochures or request leaflets by title.

ROMAN MEAL COMPANY
Dept. U
P.O. Box 11126
Tacoma, WA 98411

Friends, Romans, brown-baggers: lend us your ears! This company furnishes a variety of fine publications for your use. "Sandwiches Under 200 Calories With Roman Light Bread" is a booklet dieters will appreciate. It gives low calorie recipes for delicious and unique sandwiches. Equally delicious are the menus and calorie counts for a 1,200 calorie, balanced, 14-day diet plan in "Diet and Nutrition." "Bread on the Table" offers 22 pages that will guide you to better nutrition and tell you everything you wanted to know about bread . . . from field to table. *Get Fit and Fiddle in the Kitchen* is a new book Roman Meal is offering for $7.50 (plus $1 postage and handling). It's a creatively written and beautifully illustrated book for children that gives information on nutrition, exercises that are fun to do, and simple recipes for the beginning cook. Send for their complete list of brochures and publications. (Regular size **SASE**)

THE O.M. SCOTT & SONS COMPANY
Marysville, OH 43041
(800) 543-TURF
(800) 762-4010: OH residents

Call (800) 543-TURF ((800) 762-4010 in Ohio) for free lawn care advice. Scott's lawn consultants can tell you the best products and agronomic practices to use for your type of lawn and your region of the country. They can also give you the location of the nearest Lawn Pro® retailer. Free for the asking is *Lawn Care* magazine, a compilation of helpful lawn information published in the spring every year.

U.S. DEPARTMENT OF EDUCATION
Federal Student Aid Program
Dept. J-8
Pueblo, CO 81009-0015
(303) 984-4070

To receive a free copy of "Student Guide; Five Federal Financial Aid Programs, '86-'87," you may call a local office or write to them at the above address in Washington. The new version reflects changes made in 1984 for the Guaranteed Student Loan (GSL) program. Other programs described include: National Direct Student Loans; College Work-Study; Supplemental Educational Opportunity Grants; and Basic Educational Opportunity Grants. Restrictions have been tightened and you can't take financial assistance for granted anymore. It pays to keep current.

WALLCOVERING INFORMATION BUREAU INC.
66 Morris Ave.
Springfield, NJ 07081
(201) 379-1100

Are you climbing the walls? When your walls are singing the glues, hang it up and write for a free information booklet, "Wallcovering How-to Handbook," put out by this nonprofit organization providing educational materials for consumers. Illustrations are large and help you understand the basics such as measuring, necessary tools, cutting, hanging, rolling, and working around tricky places like windows, switchplates, and ceilings. With this booklet, you may get a new wrinkle on wallpaper (and avoid the same).

W.J. HAGERTY & SONS
Dept. US
P.O. Box 1496
South Bend, IN 46624
(800) 348-5162
(219) 288-4991: IN residents
CK, MC, V, COD (with an added charge)

We took a shine to this company's product brochure and free half-ounce sample of silversmith's polish. It's a European formula with tarnish preventative that is sold in jewelry stores throughout the world. Hagerty manufactures their own brand of polish (they know that nothing can tarnish your image faster than a reputation for dullness). Whether you're bringing a shine to old heirlooms or the family tea service, their products can take care of silver, brass, copper, pewter, pearls, wood, and crystal. **B**

WOMEN'S SPORTS FOUNDATION
342 Madison Ave., Suite 728
New York, NY 10017
(800) 227-3988
(212) 972-9170

This nonprofit organization encourages women to be involved in sports. They publish guides, posters, and pamphlets. Their Women in Sports films are available to schools and community groups and the foundation publishes a guide listing scholarships to American colleges and universities. Athletic scholarships range from under $100 to "full ride." The WSF maintains a library for additional resources concerning women and sports. Brochures are available. **B**

Furniture and Accessories

Decorate your home with fine furniture in styles ranging from high-tech to traditional from such manufacturers as BROYHILL, HERITAGE, HENREDON, THOMASVILLE, STANLEY, THAYER COGGIN, and others. If you buy by mail, savings are substantial, often as much as 60%. On large purchases, even after paying shipping, you could still save *hundreds*, even *thousands* of dollars! Look around locally and when you see something you like, send for manufacturer's catalogs or brochures from the companies we list. You'll have to provide the manufacturer's name, a description of the item, the model number, and maybe even a fabric swatch to order. There's a definite trade-off: what you save in dollars you may lose in time. Although shipping times vary widely between companies (a point you should definitely check), don't expect instant delivery. Occasionally the wait can be as long as four to six months. Your local retail store pays freight and you can wait many months paying full price, too.

A BRASS BED SHOPPE
12421 Cedar Road
Cleveland Heights, OH 44106
(216) 371-0400
CK, MC, V, AE, COD

Brass and more comes to you from this store! Brass beds, white iron beds, and daybeds can all be mail-ordered at 50% off retail. The heirloom quality brass and white iron beds offer the best of bedtime beauty with a full refund or exchange guaranteed if not completely satisfied. Special layaway and payment plans make purchasing the perfect bedroom furniture even easier. The prices alone will give you sweet dreams! Orders filled within one week. C $1

ANNEX FURNITURE GALLERIES
616 Greensboro Road
P.O. Box 958
High Point, NC 27260
(800) 334-7391
(919) 884-8088: NC residents
CK, MC, V

Annex-cellent choice for all styles of furniture including contemporary, 18th century, Oriental, French Provincial . . . and some excellent manufacturers: BAKER, DREXEL, HERITAGE, THOMASVILLE, CENTURY, HICKORY, to name but a few. Savings abound from their 45,000-square-foot showroom and usually are 45% from this 42-year-old firm. To find out if what you want is available, supply the manufacturer's name and style number. They will quote prices and arrange delivery (which includes set-up in your home). All orders are shipped COD. B

ARISE FUTON MATTRESS CO.
Dept. US
37 Wooster St.
New York, NY 10013
(212) 925-0310
CK, MC, V, AE

When you're too tired to stand up and be counted, you can always lie down and be discounted. Arise sells its own make of contemporary mattresses that fold up into couches. Their most popular model is their Living Health Futon (Japanese bed roll) that is alternately a sofa or a bed. Aside from five different styles of futons in sizes ranging from crib- to king-size and occupying different price categories—twin-size futons ranged in price from $89 to $225 at approximately $30 increments. Arise carries sofa and bed frames, futon covers, down and cotton quilts and quilt covers, as well as bolster pillows, throw pillows, and a variety of cushions. Our favorite sofa and bed frame bore the name of king-sized KINKO and was $625. By federal law, mattresses are not returnable; other products may be returned for store credit. **B $2**

ARTS BY ALEXANDER'S
Dept. US
701 Greensboro Road
High Point, NC 27260
(919) 884-8062
CK, MC, V

It's the same old story—one thing leads to another. Begun in 1925 as a printing company, Arts by Alexander's soon branched off into picture framing, then into accessories, and finally to furniture. That's quite an evolution. Arts by Alexander's has no ragtime brands—they carry mid-to-upper-echelon lines in accessories, bedroom furniture, chairs, mattresses and sleep products, office furniture, patio and outdoor furniture, rattan, sleepers and sofas, tables, upholstered furniture, and wall systems. Their approximately 200 brands include such names as AMERICAN OF MARTINSVILLE, BERNHARDT, CASA BIQUE, CHAPMAN, HICKORY MANUFACTURING, LINK TAYLOR, and THOMASVILLE. Custom framing is a specialty and they have an extensive gallery of pictures to decorate the home or office. Discounts are 40% to 50% on most lines. **B, PQ**

BACHMAIER & KLEMMER
Postfach 2220
D-8240 Berchestesgaden-2
BRD, West Germany
Germany 8652-5079
CK

Birds of a feather clock together! This German clock factory sells a variety of plain or painted cuckoo clocks. Prices are 45% to 50% lower than comparable American clocks. There's a guarantee on material and workmanship for one year and they'll exchange during this period. If the clock has been damaged in transport, they'll replace it (but an official transport claim by a local post office must be filed). There's no minimum order and no restocking charge. So beak now or forever hold your timepiece! Cuckoo, cuckoo, cuckoo! **C $1**

BARNES & BARNES
190 Commerce Ave.
P.O. Box 1177
Southern Pines, NC 28387
(800) 334-8174
(919) 692-3381: NC residents
CK, MC, V

Cliff Barnes is the marketing director, but you won't find him feuding with J.R. at Southfork. He's more interested in forklifts and shipping merchandise direct from the manufacturer's warehouse to an in-home delivery. Choose from over 200 of America's leading furniture manufacturers. Next time you're feuding with J.R. (Jerky Retail), call Cliff for a peek at his savings. **B, PQ**

BLACKWELDER'S
U.S. Highway 21 North
Statesville, NC 28677
(800) 438-0201
(704) 872-8921: NC residents
CK, MC, V, COD (with 50% deposit)

According to the *Wall Street Journal* (which once gave this company a front-page write-up), Blackwelder's is a savings hot spot for wood-be weekend decorators. Blackwelder's carries walnut, mahogany, cherrywood, rosewood, ash, maple, wicker, and rattan furniture. They're known by the companies they keep: AMERICAN OF MARTINSVILLE, BARCALOUNGER, CHROMCRAFT, FREDERICK COOPER, FITZ & FLOYD, HICKORY, PULASKI, and SELIG plus many, many others. Prices are knot bad—usually 30% to 45% below retail! Blackwelder's even branches off into famous-name brass beds, Persian rugs, KIMBALL pianos, mirrors, and lamps; prices on these items are good, too. Shipping is handled by Blackwelder's own trucking line or by special contract rate with North American Van Lines (that can be lower than a common carrier rate). Blackwelder's does a booming business, so if you can't get through on one of their four in-coming phone lines, keep trying. Their free information request worksheet is an absolute "must" before you buy furniture—it tells you delivery details, available lines, how to get brochures, and how to order Blackwelder's massive $5 catalog. **B, C $5** (refundable)

BOYLES FURNITURE SALES
Dept. US
P.O. Box 2084
High Point, NC 27261
(800) 334-3185
(800) 334-5135: DC, SC, VA, WV, MD, GA residents
(919) 889-4147: NC residents
CK, COD (with one-third deposit)

Boyles carries over 150 lines of furniture, including HENREDON, HERITAGE, DREXEL, CENTURY, HENKEL, and 18th-century reproductions. Prices are 40% off the manufacturer's list price if you live in North Carolina or the surrounding states: it's 30% off list if you live elsewhere. From April through October, High Point has their annual furniture convention for manufacturers. That's a good time for customers to save with old prices. Shipping charges are set by weight and distance—they'll gladly quote the price over the phone, so call and check. They ship by their own carriers and by common carriers. Expect at least an eight- to 12-week wait, and possibly as long as five to six months at the outside. Like many of the North Carolina furniture firms, Boyles doesn't have a single comprehensive catalog, but they'll send you manufacturers' brochures about the particular line you're interested in. **B**

CHERRY HILL FURNITURE, CARPET & INTERIORS
Furnitureland Station
P.O. Box 7405
High Point, NC 27264
(800) 328-0933
(919) 882-0933
CK

Want to know how the no-show showroom saves you up to 50% on home and office furnishings? Look no further than this second generation family business. Established in 1933, you can join the catalog revolution by shopping . . . just with catalogs. Yes, from the hundreds of famous manufacturers, and by shopping direct, you don't have to wait for special sales, closeouts, or dated merchandise. Names like HENREDON, DREXEL, HERITAGE, CENTURY, BAKER, KITTINGER, KARASTAN rugs and carpets, you're only a phone call away. No sales tax outside NC. **C $5, B**

FACTORY DIRECT TABLE PAD CO., INC.
959 N. Holmes Ave.
Indianapolis, IN 46222
(800) 428-4567
(800) 433-3618: IN residents
(317) 631-2577
CK, MC, V, AE, COD

Table pads can be had for a fraction of the retail cost. Eliminate the middleman, the measurer, and save up to 50%. By measuring your own table, you can save a tableful. Factory Direct will send you step-by-step directions, and if that's not enough, their phone service is there to help. If you're not completely satisfied, they'll replace your table pad at no additional cost. All pads are hand-tailored, washable leatherette top, cotton or velour backing, spill-resistant, and fold easily for convenient storage. They also offer table leaf storage pads to protect the finish of your dining room extender against scratches. Material and color selection will be mailed to you to assist you in choosing the right style of pad for your table. Minimum shipping cost, $5.50. **F** (with material and color selection card)

FRAN'S BASKET HOUSE
Dept. US
295 Route 10
Succasunna, NJ 07876
(201) 584-2230
CK, MC, V, AE

Rattan is dandy and wicker is quicker to rearrange from parlor to patio. Find all your lightweight furniture here including dressers, headboards, chaise lounges, rockers, dinettes, bath accessories, porch furniture, even unusual baskets imported direct from Hong Kong, Poland, Spain, and the Phillipines. Two to three weeks is the normal delivery time. The minimum order is $25. There's just no doubt about it: Fran's hefty selection and considerable savings does her peers one up. **C 50 cents**

FURNITURE BARN OF FOREST CITY, INC.
P.O. Box 609, Bypass 74W
Forest City, NC 28043
(704) 287-7106
CK, MC, V, CHOICE

We're barn-again shoppers who religiously check out prices at Furniture Barn. Hay, when they discount 40% to 50% on names like THOMASVILLE, LINK TAYLOR, HICKORY, and CARSONS, we can't resist temptation. They also have accessories, including STIFFEL lamps. Though they're 60 miles from Charlotte or Asheville, they're in the same building as Sybil, the friendly mail-order lady. Just call her or one of the staff with the manufacturer's number and get a price quote or write for a FREE brochure. It's a family business and, praise the lord, they own their own trucks and ship anywhere and will deliver within 1,000 miles. Choose carefully, no refunds. Minimum order $300. **B** (specify style or maker)

FURNITURELAND SOUTH, INC.
Dept. US
2200 S. Main St.
P.O. Box 790
High Point, NC 27261
(800) 334-7393
(919) 885-0116
CK

When furniture comes from Furnitureland, does it follow that it's "soiled" and dirt cheap? We hope not, because we liked what we saw here. Aside from furniture, they carry lamps, accessories, and room-sized rugs at savings averaging 35% to 50% off retail. They have a 40,000-square-foot interior decorated showroom with special prices on already discounted samples and closeouts. Brands include THOMASVILLE, CENTURY, SEALY, HENKEL-HARRIS, LANE, SHERRILL, LA-Z-BOY, WHITE FURNITURE OF MEBANE, and over 400 others. Orders require a 25% deposit (lower than many other firms) with the balance due upon delivery. Delivery time for upholstered goods is 90 days; for wood products 30 to 60 days. There's a 20% restocking charge (plus freight). If they don't travel to your area with their trucks and crews, they'll connect with truck lines who do in-home set-ups. **B**

HENDRICKS FURNITURE, INC.
Route 6, Box 11
1500 N. Main St.
Mocksville, NC 27028
(704) 634-5978
CK

This may sound SEALY but we found bargains on the BARCALOUNGERS and BROWN JORDANS to be at least 40% below retail. You'll find those same savory savings on over 200 lines including DREXEL-HERITAGE, AMERICAN OF MARTINSVILLE, CENTURY, PENNSYLVANIA HOUSE, THOMASVILLE, and others in their 20,000-square-foot showroom. Brochures are available from all the major manufacturers they represent. Freight charges depend on weight and distance: $35 to $45 per 100 pounds is the average. Don't forget, you'll be saving sales tax if you don't live in NC. If the dining room suite is $5,000 retail plus sales tax of 5% ($250) and Hendricks' price is $3,000 and the weight is 800 pounds, you will only be paying $315 for freight. The proof of the savings is in your pocketbook. Most retailers order from NC, too, so when you buy from a store, you're also paying freight charges whether you know it or not. **PQ**

JAMES ROY INC.
Dept. US
15 E. 32nd St.
New York, NY 10016
(212) 679-2565
CK, MC, V

James has no version of a catalog to serve as your Bible on prices, but he will send you (SASE) a free list of over 60 name-brand furniture and carpet lines discounted 30% to 40% off (one-third discount off the manufacturer's suggested retail price is guaranteed). Members of King James' Roy-al entourage include HERITAGE, HENREDON, THOMASVILLE, BAKER, STANLEY, and SEALY. He requires model, style, and color codes before he'll issue a proclamation on prices. Shipping time varies with manufacturer. **B, PQ (SASE)**

KING'S CHANDELIER CO.
Dept. US
Highway 14
P.O. Box 667
Eden, NC 27288
(919) 623-6188
CK (certified), MC, V

Let's shed some light on the subject of chandeliers. King's no jester—every crystal piece in the place is their own design. Lighting fixtures are crystal, brass, and pewter combinations. Chandeliers and sconces hold court in either brass or silver finish. Their 96-page catalog is filled with every style chandelier you can swing from, as well as royal testimonials from customers such as Beverly Sills. Their prices are good compared to those of similar quality merchandise in a retail showroom and their designs are often better. They pay shipping charges east of the Mississippi River. Chandeliers and other items may be returned for full refund within five working days after receipt (customer pays shipping). Orders are usually received in two to four weeks. Debby Boone lights up your life—King's lights up your k-night. **C $2**

L'AMBIANCE FURNITURE
403 N. Elm St.
Greensboro, NC 27401
(800) 833-0061
(919) 373-8115
C, MC, V, AE

In the market for fine furniture for less? This company is just the cure for your ailing decorating demands. Whether it's the bedroom, the dining room, or any other area that needs a new touch, this company will fill the bill—at 40% to 60% off retail prices. Names you know and trust, such as HARDEN, COUNCILL CRAFTSMEN, THOMASVILLE, SOUTHWOOD, and WHITE OF MEBANE make shopping here a genuine joy. A host of household decorating needs can be filled with discount wall units, lamps, occasional tables, and accessories, all with a 100% guarantee. Special orders, however, can't be canceled. A free brochure lists manufacturers and shipping information. Orders are filled immediately. **B**

LAMP WAREHOUSE/NY CEILING FAN CENTER
Dept. US
1073 39th St.
Brooklyn, NY 11219
(212) 436-2207
CK, MC, V

Watt's a nice girl like you doing in a place like Brooklyn? Saving 30% off STIFFEL lamps, and 35% to 40% off every other major name-brand lighting fixture and shade available! If ceiling fans are what you're after, they have over 85 styles on display featuring such major brands such as CASABLANCA, EMERSON, HUNTER, and more. (All discounted.) Although they don't give cash refunds, they do give store credit. **PQ**

LOFTIN-BLACK FURNITURE CO.
111 Sedgehill Drive
Thomasville, NC 27360
(800) 334-7398
(919) 472-6117: NC residents
CK, MC, V, COD

Loftin space? Less-than-lofty prices is one reason for lofting a letter to Loftin-Black. This 40-year-old firm can furnish you with furniture, lamps, and Oriental rugs from over 300 major manufacturers. (HENREDON, THOMASVILLE, CENTURY, PEARSON, BERNHARDT, HICKORY, etc.) Prices generally run about 40% below retail. They require a 50% deposit before they'll ship. Upholstered goods typically take 10 to 12 weeks for delivery; case goods, six to eight weeks. In the event of a return, the restocking charge is 25%. They have their own trucks and will set up your purchase in your home in 35 states. They use common carriers or van lines in the remaining states. **B**

MALLORY'S
P.O. Box 1150-78485
Jacksonville, NC 28540
(800) 334-2340
(919) 353-1828: NC residents
CK

Mallory's should watch their calories: Some of their furniture looks positively stuffed. This firm carries DREXEL, HERITAGE, HENREDON, and over 35 other lines of high-end merchandise (some from Europe and the Middle East). They have 60,000-square-foot showrooms in Jacksonville and Havelock, NC. Prices are discounted to 50%. Their slick 24-page catalog is beautifully photographed; get one, plop down at the kitchen table, and sample their furniture buffet. **C $2, PQ**

MURROW FURNITURE GALLERIES
Dept. US
3514 S. College Road
P.O. Box 4337
Wilmington, NC 28406
(800) 334-1614
(919) 799-4010: NC residents
CK, COD (with 50% deposit)

To Murrow, to Murrow, I'll be there, to Murrow, it's only a stamp away! Located in the heart of this country's home furnishings industry, Murrow's sprawling 23,000-square-foot showroom contains an 8,000-square-foot gallery addition devoted solely to DREXEL and HERITAGE—but that's not all! All told, they represent over 500 famous-name manufacturers including BAKER, DAVIS CABINET, THOMASVILLE, and HICKORY CHAIR. Prices averaged 40% savings off retail and everything's discounted. Resident decorators are available to advise you on choices of furniture, carpeting, and accessories. A 50% deposit with each order is required; balance due on delivery. Custom-made upholstery requires eight to 12 weeks for production and delivery; most furniture manufacturers process orders in two to three weeks. There's a 20% restocking charge on returns. Their brochure gives a partial list of brands and company policies: write for it! **B**

NITE FURNITURE CO.
Dept. US
611 S. Green St.
P.O. Box 249
Morganton, NC 28655
(704) 437-1491
CK

First in discounts since 1945! These folks discount first-quality furniture by 40% and more, and they carry lines from over 200 manufacturers. Brands include THOMASVILLE, DIXIE, WRIGHT

TABLE CO., SOUTHWOOD, DREXEL, HERITAGE, HENREDON, and FREDERICK-EDWARD. (Nite's the only hometown outlet for HENREDON and DREXEL and HERITAGE furniture.) Nite ships anywhere in the country, with prices that are competitive with anyone! Nite has four elegant showrooms of lovely furniture on display. In-stock merchandise can be shipped within a week, but shipping times vary on items that are special-ordered. Twenty-five dollars will get you 10 pounds of catalogs (this amount is refundable with a purchase, or the catalogs may be returned within 30 days for a refund). They have their own brochure; write to get a complete list of the lines they represent, and be sure to tell these folks that you heard about them in *The Underground Shopper.* They are a fully authorized dealer for the lines they represent. **B, C $25, PQ**

NORTH CAROLINA FURNITURE SHOWROOMS
1805 N.W. 38th Ave.
Fort Lauderdale, FL 33311
(800) 227-6060
(305) 739-6945: FL residents
CK

After three generations in the business, these Tarheels are well-heeled! They have a rich inventory featuring furniture lines from 459 leading manufacturers. Discounts range from 20% to 50%, so when you order from their wealth of inventory, you won't land in the poorhouse. Brands include the biggies: HENREDON, THOMASVILLE, BAKER, and CENTURY, among others. They require a 50% deposit to place an order; all sales are final. Most orders are delivered within six to eight weeks. Call for a price quote and be sure to ask about sale prices on samples and closeouts for further discounts. **B, PQ**

PLEXI-CRAFT QUALITY PRODUCTS
Dept. US
514 W. 24th St.
New York, NY 10011
(212) 924-3244
CK, MC, V

Plexi-Craft sells a variety of Lucite® and Plexiglas® acrylic products including furniture, cubes, tables, kitchen and bathroom accessories, and more. Prices were well below what you would pay in department and hardware stores—about 50% less. Plexi-Craft specializes in custom orders, so send a sketch of what you want molded into plastic and they'll send you a price quote. Most orders are received in seven to 14 days. People who identify themselves as *Underground Shopper* readers qualify for an additional 10% discount on their order. **C $2**

PRIBA FURNITURE
Dept. US
5 Wendy Court
P.O. Box 13295
Greensboro, NC 27415
(800) 334-2498
(919) 855-9034
CK, MC, V

Don't be a LA-Z-BOY and pay retail for your home furnishings. Priba offers discounts up to 50% across the table. They carry about 350 major brands of furniture, lamps and accessories, carpets, fabrics and leather, shades and blinds, wallcoverings, and bedding. Brands include HENREDON, BAKER, CENTURY, HICKORY CHAIR, HICKORY MANUFACTURING, and COUNCILL CRAFTSMEN. A 50% deposit is due when placing an order; balance is due prior to shipping. Shipping times vary; most goods are delivered in six to 14 weeks, although case goods typically take six to 12 weeks, and custom upholstery takes 14 weeks. Write or call for a price list or price quote. They'll provide catalogs on request, but you must specify the manufacturer. **B, PQ**

QUALITY FURNITURE MARKET OF LENOIR, INC.
Dept. US
2034 Hickory Blvd., S.W.
Lenoir, NC 28645
(704) 728-2946
CK

Just because you're Quality doesn't mean you can't have quantity, too. This place carries about 150 notable names in furniture, porch and patio lines, and area rugs to outfit the private quarters of your home. After some preliminary scouting around, we saw such major brands as BARCALOUNGER, CHROMCRAFT, DREXEL, HERITAGE, HENREDON, LA-Z-BOY, LEVOLOR BLINDS, SEALY, SERTA, and THOMASVILLE, to trumpet only a few names. Prices on these decorated heroes are wholesale cost plus a 15% to 20% markup; a lot better than the normal 110% to 125% markup. All orders must be paid in full before shipment: most take about 12 weeks for delivery, but this depends on the particular manufacturer. Returns are accepted only in the case of company error. Their motto is "satisfied customers are our only advertising." **PQ**

THE RAM FURNITURE GALLERY, INC.
161 Jordan Road
Ramseur, NC 27316
(919) 824-4295
V

Fine furniture for every room of your home is what this company specializes in. For the traditional look of excellence at a non-traditional price, this company provides only the best. Top brand names including AMERICAN DREW, LINK TAYLOR, HICKORY, and CRAFTIQUE can all be ordered through this company. Prices are a pleasant 40% to 50% off retail prices. For a drastic discount, shop the LINK TAYLOR "Heirloom Gallery" and furnish your home in Chippendale style for a fraction of what you'd expect to pay. China cabinets, buffets, dining room sets, occasional tables, sofa tables, and chests can all be found for next-to-nothing. Brass beds, lamps, fans, and rattan furniture are also included in this storehouse of style and savings. Whether you're looking for traditional, contemporary, or wicker furniture, check these prices before you look anywhere else. Orders require nine to ten weeks for delivery, with repairs or replacement offered on damaged furniture. **B**

ROSE FURNITURE CO.
Dept. US
P.O. Box 1829
214 S. Elm St.
High Point, NC 27261
(800) 334-1045
(919) 882-6871: NC residents
CK, COD (with 30% deposit)

You can Bette your fiddler Rose ain't owned by Midler. Owners Bill and Buck Kester are the grandsons of the founder and they're discounting 300 manufacturers' lines to the tune of 40%. If you're on a Rose bud-get, spend $800 to $1,000 on purchases and save $200 to $300 after freight charges. They require a 20% to 30% deposit for orders to be placed. Rose has 13 trucks with two-man teams to set up furniture in your home. They deliver more furniture themselves than most other stores. Orders are delivered in about eight to 12 weeks, carry the manufacturer's guarantee, and are subject to a 25% restocking charge if returned. With an average of 1,000 pieces to deliver per week, it's no wonder their sales Rose last year. **B, PQ**

SANDMAN
P.O. Box 20437
5139 Schuylkill St.
Columbus, OH 43220
(614) 457-4603
CK, MC, V, COD, MO, CASHIERS CK

Since waterbeds are like sleeping on a floating cloud without the need for any Dramamine, why not save 25% to 70% on your next ensemble? Do-it-yourselfers can choose from INTEX, ROYAL, SMALL WAVES, CALCO HAWAIIAN, and put the waves in motion tonight. These waterbed systems include top of the line free-flow mattresses, stand-up liners, heaters with thermostat, fill kits, pedestals in plywood, not particleboard, decks and frame. Also available are night stands, chests, dressers, mirrors, and other bedroom accessories. Shipping and handling begins at $2.50. **C**

SHAW FURNITURE GALLERIES
131 W. Academy St., 576 US
Randleman, NC 27317
(800) 334-6799
(919) 498-2628: NC residents
MC, V

By George, Bernard! I think Shaw's got it! Not only does "the largest furniture discount house in the Carolinas" sell furniture discounted up to 48%, but they'll even make motel reservations for me and My Fair Lady if we plan to visit their galleries. Shaw represents over 300 top-name furniture manufacturing companies, including: HENREDON, HICKORY CHAIR, THOMASVILLE, COUNCILL CRAFTSMEN, CENTURY, and WOODMARK. They carry brass beds, clocks, lamps, mirrors, bedding, and lighting. They set the stage for savings with the proper discounts. A 30% deposit is required when ordering; balance before shipment. It takes about eight to 12 weeks for orders to be delivered. Returns are subject to a 25% restocking charge. **B, PQ**

SLIPCOVERS OF AMERICA
Dept. F86-510
P.O. Box 590
East Broad and Wood Streets
Bethlehem, PA 18016
(215) 868-7788
CK, MC, V, MO

Slipcovers of America won't give you the slip on good prices. Give your living room a new look with "Custom Look" slipcovers and matching draperies, decorative pillows, and table covers. Carefully designed, premeasured, and cut for the most precise fit possible, they come in dozens of different styles and sizes for most sofas, love-seats, and chairs. Your bedroom is covered, too, with bedspreads, shams, and decorative toss pillows. Create a new atmosphere for your home, from Victorian to High Tech Modern. Don't let these prices slip by, with priscilla curtains priced as low as $37, chair covers at $59, and sofa covers starting at $89. Satisfaction is guaranteed on all products. Within four to six weeks, expect your solution to those living room blues. Shipping and handling based on total price of the merchandise. **C** $1 (refundable)

SOBOL HOUSE
140 Richardson Blvd.
Black Mountain, NC 28711
(704) 669-8031
CK

Sobol sells furniture from over 200 companies at 45% to 50% off retail, so bolster your savings here! You can select from CENTURY, THOMASVILLE, SEALY, CLAYTON MARCUS, AMERICAN DREW, and others. Their most popular line is probably THOMASVILLE—small wonder—it is discounted 50%! There is a 30% restocking charge on returns: orders generally are delivered in eight to 10 weeks. Sobol House will send a helpful "request for quote" form to those who write, along with instructions on how to shop by mail. **C** ($$ varies depending on the manufacturer—refundable with the first order.)

STAR ROUTE HAMMOCKS
Star Route
Box 67-CU
Bridgeville, CA 95526
CK, MO

Hang out with the stars. In a Star Route hammock, you can hang with the best of them. Their inviting hammocks are hand-woven by the Mayan Indians of southern Mexico. Yucatan hammocks are made of the finest quality 100% cotton and are hand-washable. Four sizes were available: The Backpacker, for the lone rocker, was $39.95; The Friendship, a hammock built for two, was $58; The Swinger, for the time when three isn't a crowd; and The Banquet, for a family affair. A variety of solid colors and multicolors are offered. All *Underground Shoppers* receive an additional 10% discount. You won't get stuck holding the sack because the stars will take it back. They offer a 30-day unconditional guarantee. A $5 shipping fee hangs on each order. **B 25 cents**

STUCKEY BROS. FURNITURE CO., INC.
Route 1, Box 527
Stuckey, SC 29554
(800) 334-7794
(803) 558-2591: SC residents
CK, MO

Almost 40 years old and not slowing down one bit, here you can save 35% to 40% on some of the stellars in the furniture world: AMERICAN DREW, CRAFTIQUE, DAVIS CABINET, HENKEL HARRIS, HICKORY CHAIR, WHITE, CLASSIC LEATHER, and more. This showroom boasts a selection that includes 18th century, Oriental, traditional, and contemporary classics. All orders must be placed in writing indicating style numbers, finish, fabric, and quantity. A 25% deposit is required. An additional 1% cash discount is offered if payment is made in full at time of order. Normal delivery eight to 16 weeks. Merchandise cannot be returned without a previously written agreement. Ouch—a 20% handling charge is assessed otherwise on returns. **PQ/SASE**

TURNER-TOLSON, INC.
P.O. Drawer 1507
New Bern, NC 28560
(800) 334-6616
(919) 638-2121
CK, MC, V, COD

Home, sweet home for half the cost! This company offers everything you need to furnish a cozy cottage or a palatial estate. Furniture, rugs, and carpets were available at 40% to 50% off retail price and familiar names included HERITAGE, DREXEL, PENNSYLVANIA HOUSE, THOMASVILLE, and many others. More than 200 of the finest names in home furnishings let you select the style you want to enhance your hearth and home. North Carolina residents pay a 4½% sales tax and everyone pays a 25% restocking fee on returned or canceled orders which can not be canceled with the manufacturers. Same-day response is given to phone orders, one week on mail orders. **PQ**

UTILITY CRAFT, INC.
2630 Eastchester Drive
High Point, NC 27260
(800) 334-3897
(919) 454-6153: NC residents

This utility company sure is a gas—but the pain of high prices is eased considerably with the savings here. Though they specialize in solid wood, 18th century, and colonial reproductions, they do carry all styles and looks in furniture and accessories. KNOB CREEK, CRESCENT, STATTON, HICKORY CHAIR, DAVIS CABINET, GILLIAM, HABERSHAM PLANTATION, THOMASVILLE, and WHITE OF MEBANE in dining room and bedroom; in upholstered pieces, you can sit on BARCALOUNGER, FLAIR, FLEXSTEEL, SELIG, or PEARSON, occasional tables, accessories, casual furniture, brass beds, and bedding by SERTA and KINGS DOWN complete the scene. Utility provides in-home delivery and setup and requires one-third down to place an order. **B**

VARNER WAREHOUSE SALES INC.
2605 Uwharrie Road
High Point, NC 27263
(800) 334-3894
(919) 431-8113: NC residents
CK, MC, V

If you want to garner the wealth of Silas Marner, then you're gonna
wanna' pay a visit to Varner. When furniture prices drove miserly
Silas buggy, he steered his way to VW. (He had a rabbit interest in
saving money.) Discounts were 40% to 50% on first-quality furniture
and dining and bedroom accessories such as upholstery, lamps, etc.
An extra 15% discount was offered on selected floor samples, usually
the cream of the crop, used to impress buyers at trade shows. Varner
ships nationwide and offers a list of manufacturers. Upholstered
items usually take six to eight weeks for delivery; bedroom and dining room case goods take three to four weeks. There are no returns.
B, PQ

WAYSIDE INTERIORS
Dept. US
P.O. Box 207
High Point, NC 27261-0207
(919) 882-8823
(800) 334-8153: orders
CK, COD

It's not hard to imagine that George Washington slept in one of the
rooms pictured in the "DREXEL 18th-Century Classics" brochure we
received promptly from this company. By the Wayside policy, almost
any line on the market can be obtained (over 300 lines are carried),
and each is discounted up to 45%. You name it, they've got it:
CENTURY, HICKORY MANUFACTURING, HICKORY CHAIR, DAVIS CABI-
NET, LANE, THOMASVILLE, WHITE FURNITURE, etc. There are no
returns, although they will exchange damaged items. "Martha!
Bring my slippers while I prop up on this BOLING chair. Items from
that FORGE Company are revolutionary. By George, there's the
ROYAL line, too! Why, it usually costs a king's ransom!"
B (manufacturer's only)

WOOD-ARMFIELD FURNITURE
460 S. Main St.
P.O. Box C
High Point, NC 27261
(800) 334-2744
(919) 889-6522: NC residents
CK, MC, V

They have one of High Point's largest showrooms handling most major manufacturers in upper quality goods. The KNOB CREEK line of furniture is discounted along with many other famous manufacturers. As with other shops in the Furniture District of North Carolina, ordering is basically a hit-or-miss experience. Go to your local furniture store or shop from their catalog to find out if they can get the brand and model you want. Prices are 30% to 50% below retail, and shipping is by their truck or common carrier. Brands we found included THOMASVILLE, CENTURY, HICKORY CHAIR, KNOB CREEK, STATTON, VANGUARD, CLASSIC LEATHER, and DAVIS CABINET. They also offer interior design assistance for their customers. They've been in business since 1939. B

YOUNG'S FURNITURE AND RUG CO.
Dept. US
P.O. Box 5005
High Point, NC 27262
(800) 334-0912: inquiries and orders
(919) 883-4111: NC residents
CK, COD (with one-third deposit)

Call

If you're Young at the heart of the furniture industry, the future belongs to you. This is an ageless source for indoor, outdoor, rattan, and office furniture, as well as bedding, lamps, clocks, and carpet at discounts up to 45% off (special orders receive similar discounts). In the heart of furnitureland, though not as Young as they look, these folks have been in business 42 years and carry over 150 better-quality lines, among them such old-time favorites as BAKER, HENREDON, KITTINGER, DREXEL-HERITAGE, HENKEL-HARRIS, CENTURY, COUNCILL, and HICKORY. Young-at-heart folks can even call toll-free for advice from their staff of trained interior designers. Young's requires a one-third down payment on all orders and has an excellent delivery system with shipping time generally varying from two to five weeks. There are no returns on custom merchandise. If you're vacationing in the area, a look at their 25,000-square-foot furniture showroom could be the High Point of your trip. **B**

ZAMART FOR KIDS
11 W. 37th St.
New York, NY 10018
(212) 869-7606
CK, MC, V, AE

Zamart for Kids offers a zoo of items just for your favorite child. Toys, puzzles, trains, stuffed animals, and a large selection of educational games are among the many items they carry to keep your child zealously busy. They also offer great discounts on strollers, high chairs, and other children's furniture. They get a little zany when it comes to their low prices on brand-name children's clothes. No catalog here; their items change like the zodiac. They will give price quotes though. So zig-zag to Zamart first for all your children's needs. **PQ**

ZARBIN AND ASSOCIATES, INC.
Fourth Floor
401 N. Franklin St.
Chicago, IL 60610
(312) 527-1570
CK

Zarbin is located across the street from the world-famous Merchandise Mart. You can find the largest selection of home furnishings on display in the United States. They can save you 40% and more on famous maker national brands such as CENTURY, DAVIS CABINET, BARCOLOUNGER, HIGHLAND HOUSE, HICKORY CHAIR, LANE, DIRECTIONAL, STIFFEL, CLASSIC GALLERY, FLEXSTEEL, SEALY, and many more. By appointment only, their interior designers will guide you in the selection of your furniture and carpeting exquisitely displayed in the manufacturer's showrooms. They offer home delivery nationwide. If you can't visit them in Chicago, write the manufacturer's name and style numbers for price quotation. **PQ**

Handbags and Luggage

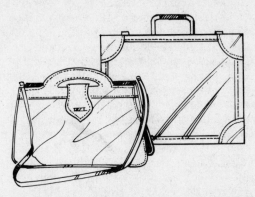

Looking for a set of traveling companions? Get a handle on these suggestions. If you want to bag a lasting bargain, buy the sturdiest, most durable luggage you can find. When it comes to the airlines, no bag has a pass to first-class treatment. Airlines give baggage a beating and you'll need bags tough enough to take it. Another suggestion: if you're a woman in business, consider buying a handbag that doubles as a briefcase. When it comes to buying a bag, know that some listings insist on a description and model number, so be specific. If you are, you'll be more likely to get the olive snakeskin bag by Dior you want, rather than the straw satchel a store clerk is trying to get rid of.

A to Z LUGGAGE
Dept. US
4627 New Utrecht Ave.
Brooklyn, NY 11219
(800) DIAL-011
(718) 435-6330: NY residents
CK, MC, V, AE, DC, CB

How do you spell relief? S-a-v-i-n-g-s! We found everything from attachés to zippered manicure sets at one of their six stores in New York. Christmas comes just once a year, and when it comes, it brings A to Z's only catalog. (But don't miss their periodic sales flyers.) The brimming book contained all kinds of luggage and travel accessories from famous makers such as HARTMANN, ZERO, HALIBURTON, ROLF, TUMI, LACOSTE, and SAMSONITE. Discounts were 20% to 40%. Their imported attaché items represent a particularly good buy. If you're looking for something special, send a detailed description (including style and/or manufacturer's number) of the item you want, along with a SASE, and they will give you a price quote. Their catalog represents only a portion of the A to Z inventory. By calling the company before placing the order, we found out which catalog items were on sale for further reductions. Most orders arrive in about 10 days. An additional 5% will be deducted from the bill if you mention *The Underground Shopper*. **C, PQ**

ACE LEATHER PRODUCTS
2211 Avenue U
Brooklyn, NY 11229
(800) DIAL ACE
(212) 891-9713
CK, MC, V, AE

With 25 years in the business, Ira and Andy are no jokers when it comes to selling handbags, luggage, and briefcases. In fact, they hold a wild card in the bargain game. Selling all types of top-grade luggage, briefcases, attachés, small leather goods, handbags, and gift items makes them an ace: Ace carries brands such as AMERICAN TOURISTER, LE SPORTSAC, LARK, HARTMANN, and LIZ CLAIBORNE. Discounts run 20% to 40% off. Ira and Andy believe that discounts should be calculated by comparison to "real retail" prices. Request the 30- to 40-page color catalog of current merchandise—it's free! Orders are shipped the same day they're received. Exchanges made within 10 days of purchase. **C**

AL'S LUGGAGE
2134 Larimer St.
Denver, CO 80205
(303) 295-9009
CK, MC, V, AE, COD

We shouldn't have to quote scriptures to you about the strength of
SAMSONITE—if you've watched the TV commercials you've probably
seen a testament to its durability. Al's offers some commanding discounts of 40% to 50% off retail on the entire SAMSONITE line. (The
Silhouette 200 line wasn't discounted quite as much: it was 35% off.)
This place is a source for irregular, but perfectly respectable luggage, soft side and hard side casual bags, and attachés. All luggage
carries a two-year guarantee. Orders are shipped in one to two days;
the restocking charge on returns is 15%. If you're planning a trip to
visit the Phil O'Steen's of the Middle East, you can profit with honor
from the savings in this country first. **C $1**

BER SEL HANDBAGS
Dept. US
79 Orchard St.
New York, NY 10002
(212) 966-5517
CK, MC, V, AE

Ber Sel Handbags offers (you guessed it) handbags. Big deal, you
say? Well, in fact, it is a big deal: you can get up to 35% off on a wide
variety of leather, exotic skin and fabric handbags, wallets, belts, and
gloves. Over 20 top manufacturers (ANNE KLEIN, DIOR, PIERRE CAR-
DIN, LISETTE, STONE MOUNTAIN, ISOTONER, and TOTES) are represented. Inquiries must include the manufacturer's style number.
Exchanges are made within 30 days; most orders are received in two
weeks. There's a $2 shipping charge. **PQ**

BETTINGERS LUGGAGE
80 Rivington St.
New York, NY 10002
(212) 475-1690
(212) 674-9411
CK, MC, V, AE

Pack up all your cares and woes and go to Bettingers Luggage for all
your leather needs. Whether it be attachés or briefcases, garment

bags, luggage, small leather goods or trunks, they pack a walloping 30% to 40% off. Names to travel by include HARTMANN, SAMSONITE, SKYWAY, AMERICAN TOURISTER, and LARK. A $5 shipping and handling fee will be added to your minimum purchase of $25. Expect orders in about 15 days from this company that's been fulfilling them for over 65 years. **PQ, SASE**

CAROLE BLOCK LTD.
1413 Avenue M
Brooklyn, NY 11230
(718) 339-1869
CK, MC, V, AE

Carole has a mental Block about charging full price, so she psyches up her customers with 15% to 20% off list in the final analysis. What's more, during her twice-a-year sales, we saved 30% to 50%. The reputation of her merchandise is secure, even if her prices are a bit depressed. Ladies' handbags and small leather goods were available from Italy, the U.S., and South America in such brands as HALSTON, SUSAN GAIL, ALDANA, and VISONA. About 35 brands are carried. There's a $25 minimum order on credit card purchases. Exchanges are accepted for store credit only. Carole's bag has been shrinking prices for over 30 years, but she's still feeling pretty Jung. Write or call for price quote. **PQ**

CARRY ON LUGGAGE
97 Orchard St.
New York, NY 10002
(212) 226-4980
CK, MC, V

A LARK in the hand is worth two at the baggage claim when you can save 35% to 60% on first-quality luggage, garment bags, portfolios, and wallets. Most items are discounted 30% to 35%, but sale items range up to 65% off. Besides LARK, we found VENTURA, WING, LANE, SAMSONITE (up to 50% off), and CHRISTIAN DIOR carrying on with attachés by RONA, YALE, ATLAS, SCULLY, and many Italian lines. Mr. Rubin told us he can special order anything with manufacturer and style number and have it in about two weeks. Shipping is by UPS, usually $5 to $8 for a 14-pound order. **B, C, PQ**

CREATIVE HOUSE
100 Business Parkway
Richardson, TX 75081
(800) 527-5940
(214) 231-3461: TX residents
CK, MC, V, AE

Before you pack it in and become unhinged looking for luggage and
attachés, check out these discounts from 30% to 60% on the moderately crafted WORLD TRAVELER and MASTERCRAFT lines. Their free,
48-page catalog features briefcases and leather attaché cases in
many styles and colors at about half off retail; there's also a line of
leather luggage and garment bags. They had a $200 leather attaché
case for $80. Handbags, wallets, and other leather products are also
available. Several dozen different brands of merchandise are
stocked: familiar names we saw were SAMSONITE, AMERICAN TOUR-
ISTER, AMELIA EARHART, and VERDI. Add $3.75 to your bill for ship-
ping. **C, PQ**

FINE & KLEIN
119 Orchard St.
New York, NY 10002
(212) 674-6720
CK

Julius Fine and Murray Klein opened their tumultuous New York
shop some 40 years ago and business has been good to them. So good,
in fact, that their Fine Klein-tele includes many international celebri-
ties. Today their multi-level stores feature a "tremendous selection"
of exclusive, first-quality ladies' designer handbags, attachés, shoes,
and accessories. Over 1,000 popular brands are carried, among them
KLEIN, GUCCI, HALSTON, and CHRISTIAN DIOR. (The talk of the town is
their better ladies' shoe department above their store aptly called
Sole Above 119 and the jewelry boutique of Bonnie and Toni.) All
items are 30% off their usual retail price. Mr. Klein welcomes everyone to write him for price quotes on particular styles and brands of
merchandise—if you see something in *Vogue*, it's in the bag that Fine
& Klein can get it for you at a substantially lower price. Orders are
shipped the same day they're received. Send a SASE for a prompt
response. **PQ**

HICKS USA
7070 W. 117th St.
Broomfield, CO 80020
(303) 469-3615
CK

For trips to the moon, don't leave earth without the "Faceshuttle"—
a unique cosmetic organizer that doubles as a portable vanity. When
you land, you'll be out only $12. It's heavily padded, comes in all the
fashion colors, is nylon and washable, too. Another out-of-this world
item is their washable duffel bag popular among professional ball
players. It's square, with pockets in both ends and a pocket in the
middle of the bag. Double zippers are lockable, in three sizes with the
smallest a mini version which serves as a handbag as well—$12;
medium, the size of a carry-on case, $18; and the jumbo, $22. All
prices are direct-consumer wholesale prices. Shipping charges, $2
per item. Allow three weeks for delivery. **C (with SASE)**

TRAVEL AUTO BAG CO.
264 W. 40th St.
New York, NY 10018-1574
(212) 840-0025
CK, MC, V, AE

Traveling salesmen purchase their softside luggage from this company and you can, too! (Willie, low man on the totem pole, thought
that lugging around those samples would be the death of him.) Prices
are low! You'll pay 50% to 70% more for comparable quality items in
a department store. Greater discounts are given when you buy in
quantity. The functional Herculon tweed bags we spotted in their 48-
page catalog are stitched extra-heavy and are available with large
casters for greater mobility. A 26-by-20-by-7½-inch piece was just
$32 (approximately 25 pounds shipping weight). They don't carry
famous brands—they sell their own TRAVEL AUTO BAG line
exclusively. Their most popular line is their soft constructed nylon
luggage. They also carry a full line of collapsible garment racks, luggage carriers, steamers, and garment hangers. Prepaid orders
receive first priority, but most orders go out in 24 hours. Returns are
accepted for 30 days with receipt. **C, PQ**

Hard-to-Find and Unique Items

Okay, we'll 'fess up: the following companies (sob, sob) don't sell discounted merchandise. Diehard bargain hunters like us hate to admit it (sniff, sniff), but it's true: you can't get *everything* wholesale. We've put these companies in our book because we felt the nondiscounted (boo-hoo) goods they carried were unusual enough to merit a listing. We've been preaching all along that variety is the name of the game, so thanks to these listings, if you absolutely can't get it wholesale, well, at least you can *get* it. There are times when you just can't find what you want, no matter how hard you try. That's why this section is here. If you shop by mail, you'll have more luck finding what you want. (And that's nothing to cry about!)

ALLEN'S SHELL-A-RAMA
Dept. US
P.O. Box 291327
Fort Lauderdale, FL 33329
(305) 434-2818
CK, COD

Allen's sells seashells by the seashore—at wholesale prices. Wanna good buy on a bivalve? They've got 'em—but that's not all! Craft shells are their biggest sellers, but they've also got decorator, collector, and specimen shells, gas scales, cut and dried shells, exotic tropical air plants; coral, shark's teeth, sea horses, sand dollars, books about shells and shell-craft, original kits unavailable anywhere else, and gifts and novelties. There are over 1,000 all-natural items ranging in price from 10 cents to $200. Five- to seven-inch exotic coral sold here for $7.95 ($20 to $25 retail); a nine- to 10-inch Florida pink conch shell was $7.95; a mother-of-pearl butterfly pin was $1.95. Giant 10- to 12-inch starfish were $6.95. A 16-inch shell Christmas wreath kit was just $14.95. **C $1** ($2 gift certificate)

BANANA REPUBLIC
Box 77133
San Francisco, CA 94107
(800) 527-5200
(415) 777-5200: AK or HA
CK, MC, V, AE, DC

You'll absolutely go bananas looking through the Banana Republic catalog! This company apes no one: the unusual is commonplace here. If you've ever fantasized about joining Teddy Roosevelt on a turn-of-the-century safari, this is the catalog for you. Civilized styles of all-cotton safari clothing would look equally dashing on the wild savanna of Africa or on the beastly streets of Savannah. Prices are comparable to what you might find in a department store, although the clothing, of course, is not. Jackets, multi-pocketed shirts and pants, socks, sweaters, dresses, belts, hats, traveling bags, etc., are all available if you, like Indiana Jones, want to add a bit of adventure to your life. **C**

BEITMAN CO., INC.
P.O. Box 1541
170 Elm St.
Bridgeport, CT 06601
(203) 333-7738
CK

Tired of button your head against the wall? Let Beitman and the Boy Wonder blast out of the Beit-cave in the Beit-mobile and race to your aid. This company custom-covers belts and buttons from fabric, leather, suede, or even plastic that you supply. It's a way of getting the buttons and accessories to match the materials in your own homesewn garments. Everything is made-to-order, except leather tabs and some buckles. Prices are often lower than those found in custom sewing shops, usually about 10% less. There is a $5 minimum order and all merchandise is guaranteed machine washable. Shipping is paid by the company; your order will probably arrive in about a week. Pick up the Beit-phone or write to put these not-so-comic superheroes in stitches. **C**

COMFORTABLY YOURS™
52 W. Hunter Ave.
Maywood, NJ 07607
(201) 368-0400
CK, MC, V, AE, DC, CB, COD

Now, a catalog that says you never have to grin and bear it again. Whatever it is that makes you uncomfortable—whether it's soggy crackers, cigarette smoke, cold feet, or hot steering wheels, here is a company that devotes itself to things that make life easier. For example, if you like to read in bed, there is a compact bed lamp with dimmer to clamp on your headboard. Can't see far enough into your mouth to see where the pain's coming from? A magnifying mirror/ flashlight will take care of that. Exposed sink pipes embarrass you when company comes over? Skirt the issue with a stain-resistant skirt. Handicapped people will find a wide assortment of comforting products from contoured canes to walkers with built-in bags, canteens, Pooper Scoopers, even a split-level bird feeder are featured along with pet taxis, two-way pet doors, leashes, beds, and grooming aids. **C $1**

CONSUMER EDUCATION RESEARCH CENTER
439 Clark St.
South Orange, NJ 07079
(201) 762-7120
(201) 762-6714
Contact: Robert L. Berko

If you're a veteran, dependent, or survivor of a veteran and finding it harder to survive the government bureaucracy than the war, you'll find the 112-page book entitled *The Complete Guide to Government Benefits For Veterans, Their Families and Survivors* to be a lifesaver. For a small investment of $8, you will benefit from perusing this invaluable survival kit, designed to help you claim benefits you never knew you had. Each year billions of dollars in veteran's benefits are unclaimed due to ignorance on the part of the public. This book is published by C.E.R.C. because changing laws make it very difficult to stay current with the latest rules. Complexities also make information difficult to obtain by direct inquiry through local veteran's associations. The book contains a complete guide to every benefit and service available, as well as new rules on eligibility which now includes many people who were formerly ineligible. It also includes a section on where to obtain necessary documents to support claims and complete information on required fees for these documents. Hey, when the government owes you money, you owe it to yourself to collect!

CONSUMERS GUIDE TO HOME REPAIR GRANTS & LOANS
C.E.R.C. Grants
134 Evergreen Place
East Orange, NJ 07018
(800) USA-0121

Write for your copy of this book today if you're one of the many homeowners who are unaware that regardless of your income, there are federal, state, and local programs that will help you with the repairs and remodeling of your home. There are even programs that give you money for repairs that does not have to be repaid or that will loan you money at below market levels or at no interest at all. In many areas, utility companies will either do energy conservation work free or at low cost and in other places will lend homeowners money at no interest to pay the contractor of their choice for the necessary work. Over 4,000 sources of grants and subsidized loans to choose from. Form letters are included to help get your information to the proper agency. **C $9** (including postage, 184 pages)

GLASS HOUSE WORKS CATALOG
10 Church St.
Stewart, OH 45778-0097
(614) 662-2142
CK, MC, V

The "esoterica botanica" in this catalog might tax even the most earnest taxonomist. However, for those of you who know a ficus from a fuchsia, this is an excellent reference work and source for rare and unusual varieties of home and greenhouse plants. If they don't have the plant you want listed in their copious catalog, send them the common name or scientific name, description, where you saw it growing, and a copy of any articles which mention it. The catalog describes color, shape, lighting requirements, prices, and other commentary useful to home growers. Allow six to eight weeks for shipping; add $4.50 for postage on all orders. Add an additional 50 cents per plant for air UPS or air parcel post. Minimum order is $10 plus postage. C $1.50

THE JUGGLING ARTS
Dept. US
612 Calpella Drive
San Jose, CA 95136
(408) 267-8237
(415) 342-6490
CK, COD

This company really goes for the juggler vein with their range of juggling equipment like spinning plates, clubs, fire torches, balls, and such. Perfectly balanced aluminum spinning plates and bowls are their best-selling items. Most of their merchandise is slightly less expensive than other mail-order firms, but their real claim to fame is that "there are no props of equal quality in retail stores." (The business was started when the owner, a member of a family of professional jugglers, could not find quality props for her act.) A set of three cloth balls filled with rice was $10.95, while a set of three rings 11 inches in diameter was $14.95. Fire torches (designated, appropriately enough, "Not for the Beginner") were $10 each. A new line of books including *Just Juggle, Want to Be a Juggler?*, *The Juggler's Manual of Cigar Box Manipulation and Balance* were also available. Delivery usually takes about a week. They'll give a 100% refund if requested. C $1

LEFT HAND CENTER
4400 Excelsior Blvd.
St. Louis Park, MN 55416
(612) 926-6033
(612) 375-0319
CK

Lois Ruby would like to give you a few left-handed compliments, like men's left-handed undershorts for $7.98, or a left-handed can opener for $9.95. The catalog featured an extensive selection of left-opening greeting cards for all occasions. They also have a backwards clock and a left-hander's portfolio. Turns out Miss Ruby has her left *and* right hands in a number of different projects. The Left Hand Center's prices are very good. When ordering the catalog, be sure to request a free Lefty sticker and a $1 refund coupon. **C $1**

THE NON-ELECTRIC HERITAGE CATALOG
Dept. US
Lehman Hardware and Appliances
Box 41
Kidron, OH 44636
(216) 857-5441
MC, V

If your electricity has just been turned off or if you've been turned off by modern times, get back to basics and reacquaint yourself with some quaint and useful appliances. Among the many offerings we found: dough mixers, noodle makers, corn dryers, lard presses, gas and kerosene refrigerators, butter churns, hand-operated clothes washers, hog-scrapers, apple parers, and cream separators. A six-quart WHITE MOUNTAIN ice cream freezer was a bargain at $88.95, and wood stoves were also a good buy, to electric bills, that is. There's a $5 minimum order, and it usually takes between five and 10 days to receive your order. The Lehman family operates two stores in Holmes and Wayne counties right in the heart of Ohio's Amish country. Why are you waiting? Send for their unique 88-page catalog today. **C $2**

OPPORTUNITIES FOR LEARNING, INC.
20417 Nordhoff St.
Chatsworth, CA 91311
(818) 341-2535
CK, MC, V, COD

We did our homework and found educational materials for early education and special education, as well as computer software at opportune prices. Opportunities For Learning provides 10 catalogs "chalked" full of scholastic products. They'll broaden your horizons, but they won't take your lunch money. Some of the titles of their catalogs to sharpen your wits on: *Much Ado About Math, Reading and Language, Expanding Horizons,* and *Materials For Early Education.* That's four + six = ten. All of the catalogs offer microcomputer software, filmstrips and cassettes, books and games, manipulatives, and reproducibles. We discovered wonderful eye-opening books like *Games That Teach,* costing only $9.95 and *My Daycare Book* which costs $3.95. There are just too many items to mention—enough to fill a schoolhouse. So send for their free catalogs and go to the head of the class. You won't be wearing the dunce cap if you are not fully satisfied either; they offer a 30-day guarantee on all products. **C**

PAPRIKAS WEISS IMPORTER
1546 Second Ave.
New York, NY 10028
(212) 288-6117
CK, MC, V, AE

From the wooden shelves of this 100-year-old gourmet food shop come some of the world's finest delectables. Owner Ed Weiss "has to be the greatest and fastest and most complete and thorough source of food information in the world," wrote Maida Heatter, the famous creator of the *New York Times* recipe series. The imported foods and cookware (hard to find on many local fronts) included many Hungarian specialties like double-smoked Hungarian bacon, paprika paste, fresh-baked Dobosh torte (seven-layer cake), even a dumpling machine. Plus cheeses, pâtés, coffees, teas, and candies. Corporate gifts available. **C $1**

THE SOURCE FOR EVERYTHING JEWISH
Hamakor Judaica, Inc.
P.O. Box 59453
6112 N. Lincoln Ave.
Chicago, IL 60659
(800) 431-9003
(312) 463-6187
CK, MC, V, AE, DC, CB

When Christmas comes along and you want to select the perfect Hanukkah gift for your Jewish friends, then this catalog is better than chicken soup. Illuminate your gift-giving to include an electric menorah (imported from Israel) for $50 or a magnificent candelabra showpiece of historic design for $295. Gourmet gifts included an acrylic "nosh box" to a bagel cutter to a make-a-feast for your kosher colleagues. The Bear Mitzvah stuffed animals for $45 are fun for that 13-year-old birthday boy, while the silver-covered bible elaborately embossed with stones and enameled Ten Commandments would be a lasting remembrance of the occasion ($65). Be a real "mensch" if you're really daring and enjoy a game of Chutzpah if you're wanting a hilarious board game ($12.95). **C $2**

THE SOUTHPAW SHOPPE
P.O. Box 2870
San Diego, CA 92112
(619) 239-1731
CK, MC, V, AE

Give this shoppe your paw and they'll send you a flea catalog. The camaraderie among lefties is evident by the number of T-shirts, bumper stickers, buttons, and other paraphernalia having to do with being left-handed. Functional items such as scissors, cooking utensils musical instruments, how-to-books for calligraphy, embroidery, guitar, golf, writing, and even ego-boosting *(The National Superiority of Left Handers)* won't leave you feeling "left out." **C**

U.S. OPTICS
Dept. US
P.O. Box 724808
Atlanta, GA 30339
(404) 252-0703
CK, MC, V

Longing for a pair of chic aviator glasses, but don't want to pay prices that are sky high? Before you give up, give U.S. Optics a try. They carry an exclusive line of aviator glasses priced from $6.95 per pair. Styles include a variety of frames and lenses for a variety of uses. You'll not only look chic, you'll feel comfortable when your eyes are protected from the sun by these polished glass lenses. A free case is provided with each pair. 30-day guarantee. **B**

Hardware and Tools

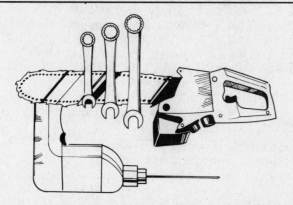

Whether you're renovating your home or just building a classy sandbox, tools and hardware can be expensive. They are often hard to find locally at discount prices and that means you can really get nailed. If you have to spend a fortune on tools, that do-it-yourself home repair project can end up as a do-it-to-yourself budgetary disaster. Hook up with these listings for brass and porcelain faucets, chain saw winches, hydraulic presses, hardware, tools, underwater sweepers, or a pair of woodchopper's chaps. It's no fun getting hammered by high prices and if you use these listings, you won't be.

ARCTIC GLASS & MILLWORK COMPANY
Route 1, Box 157
Spring Valley, WI 54767
(715) 639-3762
(715) 639-2516
CK, MC, V

What a pain in the neck to price-check for windows, doors, patio doors, insulated glass for solar homes, sun rooms, etc. Look through this looking glass first before you buy elsewhere for savings from 50% to 70% off list. A 10-year replacement guarantee is offered on glass seals and a 20-year guarantee on window seals. They can custom-build any size in any shape in double pane or triple, tempered or untempered glass, and are an authorized dealer for WEATHER-SHIELD windows, doors, and patio doors (43% off factory list): they also stock surplus WEATHER-SHIELD windows and doors which are 50% to 70% off. Delivery time—six days to almost every state in the USA (49, actually, to date). **C $2**

BAILEY'S, INC.
P.O. Box 550
Highway 101
Laytonville, CA 95454
(707) 984-6133
CK, MC, V

Paul could have saved himself some Bunyans by using this 76-page cata-log for supplies. We saw items ranging from extra-large dogs (claws) preferred by experienced timberfallers on down to a toy chain saw for the little cut-up. Woodsmen can lumber along in CHIPPEWA brand boots at savings ranging from 30% to 50% off list price. Significant discounts on chain saws didn't go against our grain, either. WORK SAFE, McCULLOCH, PIONEER, HOMELITE, in fact, hundreds of brands were carried and were waiting for the right jerk to make them roar to life. A chain saw winch was a cinch at $379 and a pair of protective forester chaps was $34 to $38, depending on size. Their magnetic first aid kit was a good bargain. Returns that aren't their fault are charged a 10% restocking fee. Be the first chip off your block to axe for a catalog. Folks living in the East or South can write Bailey's at P.O. Box 9088, 1520 S. Highland Drive, Jackson, TN 38314, or phone them at (901) 422-1300. **C**

THE BEVERS
P.O. Box 12
Wills Point, TX 75169
(214) 272-8370 (after 4:00 P.M.)
CK, MC, V

Busy as a beaver building, fixing, and repairing? Then sharpen your teeth on prices 20% to 50% below retail with The Bevers. They supply nuts and bolts by the buckets as well as a den full of general merchandise. No specific brands, just dam bustin' quality at low, low prices. Orders are shipped immediately within three days of their receipt. Money back on returned merchandise. Don't get flooded with the high cost of building, just "Leave It to The Bevers."
C $1 (refundable)

BOWDEN WHOLESALE CO.
111 First St. N.E.
Culman, AL 35055
(800) 633-3272
(205) 739-5056: AL residents
CK, MC, V

To look at the thick Bowden catalog you would think this was a big company and it is. But when we called, Mr. John Bowden answered the phone and told us all about his business. He is a distributor for the BLACK & DECKER line of tools, and he discounts them 30% off list. He discounts MAKITA and RYOBI, two Japanese manufacturers, 30% off list also. We found this catalog to be one of the best for mechanical and woodworking tools with discounts on some brands running as high as 70%. There was an extensive selection of automotive tools in the last catalog. There's a minimum order of $50, but Mr. Bowden says that's just so customers don't get surprised when they order a $3 wrench and it comes with an $8 shipping charge. Isn't that thoughtful? **C $3** (refundable)

CAMELOT ENTERPRISES
Dept. US
P.O. Box 65
Bristol, WI 53104
(414) 857-2695
CK, MC, V, COD

In a kingdom of high prices, it's nice to find a palace priced right. Camelot Enterprises offers a realm of champion tools—fasteners, electric tools, and shop equipment—knightly enough for Sir Lancelot. The empire carried brand names like RAM, ROCKFORD, TRUECRAFT, and VACO. They have enough to fill a moat, at a very noble savings of up to 50%. Orders take one day to two weeks. Tools carry anywhere from a 90-day to a lifetime warranty depending on the manufacturer. No minimum order and there is a 10-day return policy for those of you who might commit treason. So, if you are tired of blue-blooded tool prices, get off your throne and get on the phone. **C $1** (refundable)

CONTINENTAL LAWN MOWER MFG. CO.
Dept. US
3205 E. Abrams
Arlington, TX 76010
(817) 640-1198
CK

Great grass-cutting prices on riding lawn mowers aren't a continent away; they are but a phone call away. With probably the least expensive riding mowers in the country, this manufacturer cuts corners by offering their mowers by mail as well as to customers who save freight by driving to their 43,000-plus square foot factory. Construction on the eight horsepower basic is all steel, parts are under warranty for one year from the factory. The engine is a four-cycle BRIGGS & STRATTON with authorized dealer warranty. It has a three-position with reverse transmission, chain drive, safety clutch, adjustable cutting height, can carry 500 pounds, and comes assembled. Basic price was $529.95 in September 1986. From here, it's like buying a car. You add to the options and price. Pneumatic wheel, four-wheel rear drive, blade, padded and/or spring seat, grass catcher, and high-speed sprocket are some choices. Orders paid in cash or with a money order are received in about one week. There is a 15% restocking charge on unused mowers that are returned. *Underground Shopper* readers qualify for an added 5% discount off the regular low, factory-direct price. **B, PQ**

C.U. RESTORATION SUPPLIES
1414 Cranford Drive
Garland, TX 75041
(214) 271-0319
CK, COD (add $2 to order)

If your Chippendale's chipped, C.U. Restoration Supplies will come to the rescue. In addition to offering a huge selection of tools and products for refinishing, restoring, and repairing antiques, they also carry an extensive line of caning and rush products. Hardware for antique office furniture as well as kitchen cabinets was found in the illustrated catalog, along with doorknobs, keyhole escutcheons, and drawer pulls. Prices are very reasonable, which earns a garland for this Texas merchant. We can C.U. will get some expert help from this company. **C $2**

GILLIOM MANUFACTURING INC.
Dept. US
1700 Scherer Parkway
St. Charles, MO 63303
(314) 724-1812
CK, MC, V

Keep this number handy, man. If you're into power tools, Gilliom has the plans and tools for build-it yourself band saws, lathe drill presses, wood shapers, circular saw tables—all designed to save you $50 to $250. They also carry kits of metal parts so you can build your own power tools. We saw plenty of parts and accessories such as V-pulleys, line shafts, work lights, motors, and sanding drums. Don't expect to find name-brand items: everything's their own GILBILT brand. All parts are heavy duty and guaranteed for five years against mechanical failure due to defects. There is no minimum order; 10% restocking charge on returns. This is definitely a place for things that go bump and grind in the night. **C $1, PQ**

LEICHTUNG "HANDYS"
4944 Commerce Parkway
Cleveland, OH 44128
(800) 321-6840
(216) 831-2555; OH residents
CK, MC, V, Layaway

Leichtung got my attention with their 86-page irresistible catalog of deals. Scattered through the four-color slick shopping book of tools, hardware, gardening equipment, automotive, housewares, and craft kits are "one-cent offers"—where you can buy one and get a second for only a penny. Car kits up to $10 less than ever offered before, a full set of taper drills at $20 off the regular price, the RYOBI ten-inch planer and jigsaw at $146 less than was sold three months earlier, and the world-famous LERVAD workbench at the lowest price since 1975— $275. The ELECTROLUX vacuum for $129.95 made a clean sweep and the 100% merino lambswool mattress and pillow covers guaranteed a good night's sleep—cheap. Returns within 90 days for refund. Satisfaction—rest assured. Minimum order $15. C

MAIL ORDER PLASTICS, INC.
56 Lispenard St.
New York, NY 10013
(212) 226-7308
CK

What do photographers, mad scientists, and high school girls have in common? (No, not a porno flick called "Dr. Tickle and Mistress Hide.") They all find plastic doo-dads for less from this company. Beakers and measuring cups are perfect for the home photo buff. Funnels, trays, vials, and pitchers make the home lab more efficient. A wide assortment of compartmentalized boxes store earrings, buttons, and even love notes for the teenager. If it's plastic, chances are you can get it here at a good price. Case discounts are offered; minimum order of $50. C

MASTER MECHANIC MFG. CO
P.O. Box A
280 S. Pine St.
Burlington, WI 53105
(800) 558-9444
(414) 763-2428
CK, MC, V, AE

Mastermind a plot to save about 20% to 25% on a wide range of mechanical items and tools from this 40-year-old company. We saw hydraulic presses, winches, drill presses, air compressors, electric motors, pumps, electric tools, etc. The Master Mechanic alternators can guard against disaster in case of power outages. The 1,500-watt direct-drive generators (four horsepower with two-year warranty) were $419 and big sellers. There are good prices on gas engines and an 8,000-pound fisherman's winch was just $349 (compare at $500). Brands include BLACK & DECKER, MILWAUKEE TOOL, GRESEN HYDRAULIC, PRINCE HYDRAULIC, BRIGGS & STRATTON, KOHLER, and ONAN GENERATORS. Orders are shipped immediately: most are received in five days. No restocking charge for orders returned within 10 days. Their 68-page catalog is electrifying. C

McKILLIGAN INDUSTRIAL AND SUPPLY CORP.
435 Main St.
Johnson City, NY 13790-1998
(607) 729-6511
CK, MC, V, COD

Selling to industries and high school shop teachers is the main business of McKilligan. Individuals can purchase hardware, tools, electronics, graphic supplies, and craft materials at up to 35% off list prices. The encyclopedic catalog costs $5 (refundable) and lists over 70,000 items. We usually look for companies *without* vises, but at these prices we'll make an exception. Other good buys: a STANLEY Powerlock tape measure with a half-inch blade and a two-meter metric gradation was $4.49 (regularly over $6). A 15-piece homeowner's basic tool kit was $34.97—the tools would cost over $60 if bought individually. Watercolor supplies by GRUMBACHER were discounted 20% to 30%. Kits for stained glass, model cars, model rockets, and miniature houses were available. Ceramics equipment and molds were also featured. The McKilligan catalog is worth buying as a reference work for quick price comparisons. When it comes to variety, we think this is one of the best. C $5 (refundable)

R.B. MASON COMPANY
Lockbox 6074-U
Falmouth, ME 04105
(207) 781-2509
CK, MC, V, COD

If you're into over 10,000 brand names for motors, pumps, fans, engines, tools, blowers, heaters, lights, air compressors and accessories, hydraulics, controls, grinders, bases, office products, water filters, switches, values, and, whew, thermostats, set your sails for this company. Up to 30% savings with another 10% reader discount on DAYTON motors and air tools, TEEL pumps, and SPEEDAIRE air compressors. Other notables included: EMERSON, GE, ROCKWELL, SKIL,

BLACK & DECKER, and MILWAUKEE. A 30-day money back guarantee with usual one-year manufacturer warranties included. **C $7.95** (1,299 pages) **C** Free mini-catalog

RENOVATOR'S SUPPLY—5503
Millers Falls, MA 01349
(413) 659-2211
CK, MC, V

They've got the handle on everything: brass doorknobs, drawer pulls, brass and porcelain faucets, chandelier prisms, door hinges, fancy letter boxes, weathervanes, brass bolts and hooks, copper lanterns, and the "world's largest selection of brass switch plates." They carry over 1,500 hard-to-find hardware items. Everything a renovated home needs to feel pretty is featured in their 48-page catalog at savings up to 70%! (Knock on wood.) Most of the unique items are specially produced for owners Claude and Donna Jeanloz: the others are imported from around the world. They'll exchange items, give credit, or refund the purchase price if not satisfied. Their new magazine *Victorian Homes* is for young couples renovating old homes. **C $2** (refundable)

SAFE EQUIPMENT CO, INC.
Route 1
P.O. Box 61
Wallace, NC 28466
(800) 682-5001: NC residents only
(919) 285-5679
CK (personal and certified)

Better SAFE than sorry. Don't go down the tubes financially paying full price for pumps, suctions, and BRIGGS & STRATTON engines when you can save 35%. There is no minimum order. Orders paid by money order or certified check are shipped immediately. There is no restocking charge because there are very few returns. Happy motoring, folks. **C**

TOOL IMPORTERS WAREHOUSE SALE
650 Huyler St.
P.O. Box 2228
South Hackensack, NJ 07606
(800) 342-8665
CK, MC, V, AE, COD

We thought Boring Heads was a new punk rock band that played in boring bars until we read this 400-page catalog with the bright orange cover. Extensive product specifications, illustrations, and photographs make this a valuable tool for selling everything from small items like drill bits and screws to large-ticket items like band saws and surface grinders. Prices are about 40% to 60% lower than list prices. Some entries had additional deductions, bringing the savings to 80% in some cases. If you're a mechanic, small manufacturer, or weekend handyman, it is well worth your time to look through this catalog. An additional 20% discount is given when checks accompany the order. The minimum order is $25; add $5 to all orders for shipping and handling. **C**

U.S. GENERAL TOOL AND HARDWARE
Dept. US
100 Commercial St.
Plainview, NY 11803
(800) 645-7077: orders
(516) 349-7275: inquiries
CK, MC, V

After over 30 years in business, U.S. General is still battling high prices. We found an army of over 5,000 name-brand hand and power tools and hardware marching to the tune of 40% off in their 200-page coded catalog. Late model items from BLACK & DECKER, ROCKWELL, STANLEY, PROTO, and others got our attention. Those items coded with a "D" are shipped directly from the manufacturer to avoid double shipping costs. Also check into additional discounts with the Volume Discount Plan for orders exceeding $300 and receive a 2% discount; 3% off $500 or more; and 4% for $1,000 orders. $10 minimum on credit card orders; orders are shipped immediately; no restocking charge on returns. Credit cards on phone orders only! Yes sir, that's American! **C $1** (refundable)

WORLD ABRASIVE CO.
1866 "U" Eastern Parkway
Brooklyn, NY 11233
(718) 495-4301
CK

The people here (thankfully) aren't noted for their abrasive person-
alities, even when they're worn out. (They certainly didn't rub us the
wrong way!) World Abrasive has sanding belts, discs, sheets, rolls,
and other sanding accessories at nitty-gritty savings. True grit
prices on standing discs: $6.23 for 25 fine six-inch discs ($10 elsewhere). Their world also includes wire wheels, goggles, oil stones,
and grinding wheels for those who like the grind of everyday life. Top
name-brands like NORTON are available and prices are about 30% to
50% off retail. Most orders are received in one to two weeks. No
restocking charge or minimum order; refund or exchange on
returns. *Underground Shopper* readers can deduct 20% off their
first order. **C, F**

ZIPP-PENN INC.
P.O. Box 15129
Sacramento, CA 95851
(800) 824-8521
(800) 952-5535: CA residents
MC, V

When Charlene the Chain Saw needs a new wardrobe, Zip-Penn zips
in with accessories to outfit her in style. We saw discounts up to 40%
on replacement parts for lawn mowers, chain saws, small tools, and
accessories. (Bargains like that made our chain saw break into a
snaggle-toothed smile.) Chain saws are probably the best buys;
safety equipment for chain saw users is also reasonably priced. They
have a 32-page catalog with eight smaller versions which come out
every six months. Orders are shipped from their warehouse within
24 hours. All merchandise carries an unconditional 30-day warranty.
Write for their famous "Zip-O-Gram" listing many bargains. There
are other locations at 1372 Blounstown Highway, P.O. Box 4248, Tal-
lahassee, FL 32315 or 2008 E. 33rd St., P.O. Box 10308, Erie, PA
16515. **C, PQ**

Hobbies and Crafts

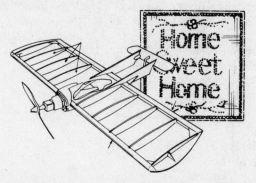

Don't just let the time pass—be creative—let your imagination run wild! Nothing is as satisfying as making something with your own two hands. Whatever your interest is, there is sure to be something here for you. Get yarn, woodworking tools, optical accessories, beekeeping supplies, jewelry-making instruments, dollhouse furniture, leathercrafting materials; almost anything to indulge your creative spirit. Be crafty, order by mail or phone and make bargain-hunting part of your diversion. When it comes to saving money, "where you get it" is as important as "what you get."

AMERICA'S HOBBY CENTER, INC.
Dept. US
146 W. 22nd St.
New York, NY 10011
(212) 675-8922
CK, COD ($15 minimum)

This is *the* source for hobby horses who want to assemble 10% to 40% discounts. If you're a model enthusiast and like to build scaled down airplanes, railroads, ships, or cars—America's Hobby should be the Center of your attention. They advertise "red hot sales" on everything from "little engines that could" to "medium motors that can." If it floats, flies, swims, sinks, roars, or runs, you can bet this place has it. (They've got over 100,000 little things to tinker with.) Call or write for information on their catalog and bulletin prices. There's an exchange policy, but they'll refund if they can't deliver.
C $2.50

BABOURIS HANDICRAFTS
56 Adrianou Str.
105 55 Athens, Greece
01-32-47-561
CK, IMO

See entry page 21.

BELL YARN/WONOCO YARN
10 Box St.
Brooklyn, NY 11222
(718) 389-1904
CK, MO

Bell, book, and craft a yarn or two at this craft consortium. Since 1917, this establishment has been needling their customers with savings of up to 50%: yarn, knitting and crocheting supplies, needlepoint, crewel, latch hook, embroidery supplies and kits, cross stitch and counted cross stitch supplies and kits. Stellar names like MINERVA, COLUMBIA, and BERNAT were reflected in the vast inventory. Refunds made within 90 days, but must be accompanied by receipt. Allow two to three weeks for delivery. Color listings and price lists include color cards when available. There is a $2.00 shipping and handling charge. **PQ (SASE), F**

BERMAN LEATHERCRAFT
25 Melcher St.
Boston, MA 02210-1599
(617) 426-0870
CK, MC, V, AE, DC

Berman has a complete line of leathers and suedes including Gallapava, a fancy name for turkey skin. They also have lizard, snake, and antelope skins as well as the more traditional cowhides (sorry, no buffalo, Bill). Hardware, accessories, dyes, and books on leathercraft are also available. Prices are competitive and better than you'll find many other places, with the best buys coming on quantity orders. They're one of the few companies that sells fashionable metallic leather by the skin, although it's not listed in their 32-page catalog. The minimum order is $15. Send for leather swatches for a garment, belt, wallet, or bag—50 cents each. **C $2**

BOYCAN'S CRAFT AND ART SUPPLIES
Dept. U84
P.O. Box 897
Sharon, PA 16146
(412) 346-5534
CK, MC, V

Boy, can they get some discounts at Boycan's! Their catalog includes over 10,000 supplies and 500 complete kits for needlework, flower making, doll making, dollhouse and accessories, macramé, miniatures, dried flowers, party favors, crafts, holiday decorating, and much more. Items are discounted about 30% off retail, but discounts of an additional 20% on orders over $25. Over 500 books on various craft projects were also listed in this book, boy-oh-boy! **C $2** ($1 is refundable)

CHERRY TREE TOYS, INC.
P.O. Box 369
Belmont, OH 43718
(614) 484-4363
CK, MC, V, COD

Whirligigs—clever variations of weather vanes and wind toys—the ones you used to see atop old barns or fence posts most often in the Northeast or Midwest are available here in do-it-yourself kits. Cherry

Tree Toys liked them so much, they designed 26 new whirligig plans so that you, too, could "forecast" the weather. Know the wind's direction by watching an entire array of whirligigs ranging from mallard ducks, parrots, and roadrunners to a woodchopper, Uncle Sam, or a washerwoman—and many more—spin in the wind. Cherry Tree Toys' full-color catalog not only has whirligigs and toys, but plans, parts, and three varieties of kits for all skill levels. The easiest kits to make are precut and predrilled and require only sandpaper and glue for assembly—while the more challenging kits contain only the plans and the special turned wood or metal parts. Most kit prices range from $4.50 to $22.00. Also available are toy, craft, game, and furniture parts in maple, oak, walnut, and cherry in addition to nontoxic finishes and general toymaking and woodworking supplies. **C $1**

CLOTILDE
237 S.W. 28th St.
Ft. Lauderdale, FL 33315
(305) 761-8655
CK, MC, V, MO

If waiting for your department store credit card bill every month keeps you on pins and needles, maybe you should take up sewing. Clotilde got the notion to compile a catalog of hard-to-find notions such as glass-head steel pins, Teflon iron covers, magnetic pincushions, and many more. The complete line of pressing aids by June Tailor was represented in one issue. We found patterns and books for smocking, quilting, and even French hand sewing. The discounts run about 20% on all items listed in the attractive catalog. **C** ($1 shipping and handling)

COLUMBUS CLAY COMPANY
1049 W. Fifth Ave.
Columbus, OH 43212
(614) 294-1114
(614) 294-7040
CK

At the Columbus Clay Company, they take discounting for granite. In business since 1939, this company is well-known as one of the best sources for ceramic supplies. Owned and run by George Rigrish, a graduate of ceramic engineering at Ohio State, the business manufactures a wide variety of clays and glazes which are sold direct to the public or to schools and studios. They also carry kilns and other instruments for the potter. **C**

COUNTRY HANDCRAFTS MAGAZINE
P.O. Box 643
Milwaukee, WI 53201
(800) 558-1013
(800) 242-6065: WI residents
(414) 423-0100
CK, MC, V, AE

If you were country when country wasn't cool, you may want to pick up this publication. It caters to crafters who want country projects by giving patterns and project instructions in every bimonthly issue. Every pattern is full-size and shown in full-color. They are excellent buys: $12.98 for the magazine.

CRAFTSMAN WOOD SERVICE CO.
1735 W. Cortland Court
Addison, IL 60101
(312) 629-3100
CK, MC, V

Wood you like to pay 15% less for woodcrafting tools like chisels, shaves, drill presses, coping saws plus brass finishes for cabinets and doors? We thought so. Here are some more options: Craftsmen drawings for a gun cabinet cost $8.75; build your own veneer backgammon board from scratch for $29.95. One exceptional bargain was 12 pounds of small pieces of imported wood for $14.98. They've got over 50 brands including BOSCH, DREMEL, AMERICAN MACHINE TOOL, FOREDOM, BENCHMARK, ROCKWALL, and STANLEY, too, so you're not sacrificing quality. Discounts vary, but they give a 10% quantity discount. Minimum order is $10 for cash; $15 for charge cards; and $25 for an open account. There is a 30-day return-for-refund (with approval) period. Merchandise orders should arrive in three to five days. Check out their 144-page catalog for the full story. **C $1** (for postage and handling)

CRAFTWAYS CORPORATION
Dept. U986
4118 Lakeside Drive
Richmond, CA 94806
(415) 223-3144
CK, MC, V, MO

Charted designs and iron-on transfers from Sesame Street, Walt Disney, Norman Rockwell, and the National Football League were

among the many patterns in this catalog. Cheer up any child's room
with favorite characters from Mickey Mouse to the Dallas Cowboys.
The Needlepunch Toolset available from Craftsways is an innovative
way of making "rug" paintings on canvas. If you invest just $5.99 in
the kit, you can create one of three floral designs suitable for framing. **C $2**

CROSS CREEK
4114 Lakeside Drive
Richmond, CA 94806
(800) 538-4942
(800) 421-9948: CA residents
CK, MC, V (for orders over $15)

Cross your fingers to remind you to order this 32-page catalog
stuffed full of crafts from award-winning designers and craftper-
sons. At the top of the list are such items as cross-stitch charts and
books, folk art dolls, wooden dolls and soft sculpture patterns, band
boxes, scherenschnitte (a traditional paper cutting art), and iron-on
transfers. Interspersed between those items are accessories for
stitchers: platinum needles, towels, and potholders with AIDA
inserts, tote bags and many "country" decorating items that include
frames and precut mats, peg racks, wooden cupboards, and towel
racks. All have been selected for highest quality at the most reasonable price. They guarantee everything and you can get that in
stitches. Look for their bimonthly magazine called *Cross Stitch and
Country Crafts* at your local newsstand, subscription price $14.97 a
year. **C $1** (published twice a year)

DEEPAK'S ROKJEMPERL PRODUCTS
61 10th Khetwadi
Bombay 400 004
India
phone: 388031 (dial "01" for operator assistance with the call)
CK, BANK AND POSTAL ORDER, BANK CHECK

Besides owning Deepak's, personable Vijaychand Shah also owns
Shah's Rock Shop, Vijay World Traders, and Gemcraft India International. (He's into everything, and everything seems to be in his brochure.) So many hundreds of items are packed into his brochure, it's
hard for readers to find anything. (It's the mail-order equivalent of
the "can't see the trees for the forest" phenomenon.) If you're per-

sistent, you can draw a bead on beads that you can string up for yourself or give as handmade beaded jewelry to your friends. The cost is next to nothing: about 50% to 80% less than retail. Lapis lazuli, 50 cents per carat; tiger eye, 10 cents per carat; emeralds, $5 per carat; and medium blue Burma sapphires, $10 per carat. Digging through their catalog, we also excavated bone-ivory jewelry, sandalwood and rosewood articles, buffalo horn carvings, mother-of-pearl, brass, and jeweler's tools at inexpensive prices. Quantity purchases equal maximum savings. Orders shipped by sea mail take eight to 12 weeks to arrive, while air mail post parcels take one to two weeks. The minimum order is $25 to get free delivery by air mail or sea mail. Parcels are duly insured by the company. **C, PQ $1** (refundable on the first order)

GINGER SCHLOTE
Box 19523 T
Denver, CO 80219
(303) 936-7763
CK, MO

Jewelry buffs with a penchant for doing it their way will love this mounting parts catalog. Forty-eight pages for the hobbyist with a creative drive and a desire to save 40% to 60%. Jewelry boxes, rings, pendant mountings, chains, and accessories all delivered in one week to 10 days. Policy of fast, friendly service with a quibble-free guarantee is a nice clincher to the deals. **C $1** (refundable with coupon)

GLORYBEE BEE BOX, INC.
1015 Arrowsmith St.
Eugene, OR 97402
(503) 485-1761
CK, MC, V, COD

These folks mean bees-ness! This leading manufacturer of woodenware discounts their products about 30% bee-low retail. That's a honey of a deal! Apiarists (a fancy word for beekeepers) will be buzzing with delight as they look over the complete line of accessories, equipment, and supplies for beekeeping including, of course, live bees and hives displayed in the Glorybee catalog. Bee-ginners will find the catalog interesting and veteran beekeepers will appreciate the fact that Glorybee's discounted prices have taken the sting out of their job or hobby. Additional discounts are offered on a per item basis. Glorybee Natural Sweeteners Inc. features bulk and gift packs of honey and bee pollen at wholesale prices, plus other assorted items. Next time you're in Eugene, dance on by. Bop, bop, bee bop! **C**

THE GOODFELLOW CATALOG OF WONDERFUL THINGS
Dept. US
P.O. Box 4520
Berkeley, CA 94704
(415) 845-2062
CK, MC, V

Here's a source book for handmade items you can mail-order direct from the artisan. This 720-page compendium (priced at $13.95 plus $2.50 for shipping) features 680 selected artisans of jewelry, sculpture, canoes, kayaks, kimonos, teepees, stained glass, roller skates, walking sticks, quilts, rocking horses, photographs, and a myriad of other good and wonderful things. By using this book and ordering direct from the particular craftsperson, you can save at least 20% off the prices charged by fancy boutiques for craft items. Other books from these same goodfellows (each at $14.95 plus $2.25 shipping): *The Goodfellow Catalog of Wonderful Things for Kids of All Ages; The Goodfellow Catalog of Gifts under $50; The Goodfellow Catalog of Wonderful Things to Wear and Wear and Wear; The Goodfellow Christmas Catalog;* and *The Goodfellow Catalog of Things for the Home and Office.* Each book has approximately 150 to 170 artisans and comes complete with ordering information and pictures.
C $13.95 plus $2.50 shipping

GRIEGER'S, INC.
Dept. US
900 South Arroyo Parkway
P.O. Box 93070
Pasadena, CA 91109
(800) 423-4181
(800) 362-7708: CA residents
(818) 795-9775
CK, MC, V

These folks have been in the mail-order business for more than 50 years, so they're definitely doing something right. A glance through their color catalog will tell you what. It's a fact that once you've found this place, you won't need a Grieger-counter to locate precious price-saving craft projects. They've got jewelry mounts for earrings, pendants, rings, chains, bead-stringing kits, wax supplies, tumble-polished gemstones, belt buckles, lariat tie slides, clock parts, stained-glass kits, music boxes, wood burning supplies, soldering supplies, adhesives, kilns, tools, and more. Jewelry mounts and supplies are their most popular items. We didn't find a rhinestone cowboy, but we did see a nice gold-colored unicorn on a chain selling for just $2.95, three for $7.79. A pewter raccoon was just $1.95, $1.60 for a family of six or more. Top brands included FORDOM and DREMAL. They also sell cubic zirconia. There is a $5 minimum order; customers usually receive their order in about a week. C

HOBBY SHACK
18480 Bandilier Circle
Fountain Valley, CA 92728-8610
(800) 854-8471
(800) 472-8456: CA residents
(714) 963-9881
CK, MC, V, COD ($6 charge)

Hobby Shack's color catalog displays hundreds of souped-up, radio-controlled models of boats, planes, and cars bound to stretch the imagination of kids and adults alike. They carry SUTABA radios and THUNDERING TIGER engines; elaborate designs, bright colors, and assorted scale sizes are available. Plenty of accessories, tools, and supplies are available at up to 50% off. Regular customers gain special status and receive the *Sport Flyer,* which touts special sales during the year. There is no minimum order, no restocking charges, and if you place an order, the catalog is free. F

HOBBY SURPLUS SALES
P.O. Box 2170-A
New Britain, CT 06050
(203) 229-9069
CK, MC, V

You're bound to go loco when you see the great prices and selection of LIONEL and AMERICAN FLYER trains and train repair parts. While they have one of the best selections of trains we've seen (from giant size LGB to tiny N gauge), their huge illustrated catalog features over 6,000 items and specializes in offering a full selection of hobby kits and supplies for everyone in your family. You will find a wide variety of new, as well as hard-to-find, out-of-production model cars, trucks, ships, planes, radio tools, and more. Most are on sale for discounts of 25% to 50%. Closeouts and discontinued merchandise went for ridiculously low prices. Want to explore space? Why not build a model rocket that really flies thousands of feet and then parachutes safely back to earth. Feeling steamed up? Their selection of real operating steam engines from Europe will fascinate and educate. For a comprehensive guide to family-centered activities that will open the door to hours of creative fun, get the Hobby Surplus catalog! Shipping is free on orders over $40 and is only $3 for orders less than that magic number. Hobby Surplus guarantees your satisfaction or your money back. Mention *The Underground Shopper* and get their 128-page catalog for $1 (instead of $2, the usual cost). **C $2**

HOLCRAFT CO.
211 El Cajon Ave.
P.O. Box 792
Davis, CA 95616
916-756-3023
CK

The Dutch treats found in this catalog are not meant to be shared except with someone special. Instead of making whoopee, make chocolate from one of the many authentic molds. Inspired by Victorian molds, those sold by Holcraft Co. are nickel-plated and will last forever. They make lovely chocolates in the shape of a teddy bear, Victorian cat, Santa Claus, the Easter bunny, pig, elephant, and others which are decorative and also make excellent wall hangings. Dutch cookie boards (the traditional Dutch spice cookies are called "speculaas") are also sold. Mention *The Underground Shopper* for a 20% discount. **B SASE**

THE H.O.M.E. CRAFT CATALOG
Route 1
Box 10
Orland, ME 04472
(207) 469-7961
CK, MC, V, AE, COD

Homeowners Organized for More Employment not only is a delightful community group, it's a handicrafters haven. If you fancy appliquéd pot holders, pottery, Christmas wreaths, or patchwork quilts like Granny used to make, you'll like what you find in this 8-page brochure. Other items include handwoven towels, mats, and coverlets; hand-knit sweaters, socks, and hats; and stuffed toys and dolls. Pot holders, quilts, and toys are their most popular products because of their craftsmanship and discount prices. These are the genuine articles: everything is handmade. For those of you cynics who wonder just who gets your money, 70% of the item's selling price goes to the Maine craftspeople. Most orders are received in about three weeks, but allow four to six weeks delivery on larger items. Full refunds or exchanges are made, but aren't often needed—everything is inspected by Sister Lucy Polin, president and designated fault-finder. **C $1**

LAMRITE'S
Dept. US
565 Broadway
Bedford, OH 44146
(216) 232-9300
CK, MC, V

Daisy, Daisy, give me your answer do, I'm half crazy over the love of you. It won't be a stylish marriage, but we'll have flowers all over the carriage. Lamrite's carries a full line of wedding supplies discounted approximately 20% off retail. There's a large selection of straw hats that you can decorate and a *huge* selection of ribbons. Their Pretty Petals kits for making silk flowers are a particular favorite with 15 different flowers in 25 colors. There is a $10 minimum order; orders typically are shipped out the same day they're received. (If more people knew about discounted wedding supplies, do you think there would be fewer tears at weddings?) **C $2 (refundable)**

LHL ENTERPRISES
Box 241
Solebury, PA 18963
(215) 345-4749 (orders only)
CK, MC, V, AE, MO

Raising your craft consciousness without raising the prices is a mighty lofty feat. Save, on the average, 25% to 40% off manufacturer's suggested retail prices—the full spectrum of a craftperson's wildest dreams. From needlework, art supplies, books, naturals, stenciling, silk flowers, Pretty Petals™, styrofoam, wood cutouts,

potpourri, Lucite accessories, candlewicking supplies, crochet hooks, lace doilies, straw hats, felt, wire frames . . . got the picture? Expect two to three weeks for a catalog, five days to two weeks for personal checks to clear for merchandise. Minimum order, $10.
C $3, PQ (with SASE)

MEISEL HARDWARE SPECIALTIES
P.O. Box 258
2313 Commerce Blvd.
Mound, MN 55364
(612) 472-5544
CK, MC, V, MO

Near the shores of Lake Minnetonka, Meisel Hardware Specialties await your requests for the latest in woodworker specialty hardware. Wood wheels with rubber tires, metal spoke wheels, doll stroller wheels, brass jewelry box hardware, 24K gold plated cabinet hardware, plans, and parts for classic wood toys and many country and Folk Art projects are available through their 48-page beautifully crafted and discounted catalog. They will sell wholesale to anyone who can meet their $25 minimum order—but are generally 40% below craft store prices and are probably the largest single source of woodworking hardware in the country. **C $1**

NEW ENGLAND FRAMEWORKS
Dept. US 4
Route 1
Wilton, NH 03086
(800) 258-5480: credit card orders only
CK, MC, V, AE

Seeking frame and fortune? Seek no more but sneak a peek at this manufacturer's 24-page catalog; it's free when you send a long SASE with two stamps. The frames and domes here are made to display collector's plates; collector plates are also featured. Display hardware and shelves are also available. All frames are made of wood and are available in many styles. Everything is priced about 50% lower than similar items found in retail stores. "All telephone orders are filled the same day/mail orders are filled immediately," said Bob Edwards, owner of this 11-year-old company. The catalog has a handy frame finder chart which matches frame to your plate size. There is a $15 minimum order. **C (SASE)**

THE POTTER'S SHOP
1844 Commonwealth Ave.
Newton, MA 02166
(617) 965-3959
CK

Has your reading been going to pot lately? Let it go to pottery. Specializing in books on ceramics and pottery, Steve Branfman's mail-order business will keep you fired up about the subject with 15% to 50% discounts and more on a wide range of titles. All books are discounted 15% off list. Discontinued and out-of-print books get discounted further. They have over 250 different titles in stock and on display. Their periodic fliers keep you abreast of special promotions. When you're in the area, visit The Potter's Shop studio and retail store and find the work of local and resident potters for sale. Special orders are welcome and they will investigate the availability of any title you request. **C**

SONSHINE CRAFTS
Dept. 3
437 Clinton Ave.
RD 1
Salt Point, NY 12578
(914) 266-5955
CK, COD (plus $1.90)

If you're pressed for a special something, calligrapher Pat Smith can custom letter and decorate just what would bring that personal touch to gift giving. Allow three to four weeks for delivery of matted and framed verses, and quotes written in calligraphy and accented with pressed flowers. Many quotes (yours or hers) are available in a choice of six frames. Price list and quotes available along with a color catalog. The shopper in me loved "Life is not a dress rehearsal," but the old favorite "Footprints in the Sand" was still appealing. **C 50 cents**

SPLENDOR IN THE GLASS
Dept. 3
9 Mackin Ave.
Beacon, NY 12508
(914) 831-5347
CK

Bask in a reflection of colored glass accessories from this craftsman. Chose either 1) opalescent (a nontransparent glass usually streaked with two colors) or 2) cathedral (transparent textured stained glass in a multitude of colors), and add a touch of glass to your decorative scheme. Picture frames to complement any photograph or picture, window boxes with color-coordinated arrangements of silk and dried flowers, desk accessories with a supply of stationery, potpourri boxes, mirrors, and wall terrariums complete the picture. *Underground Shopper* readers will receive a 5% discount. **B 50 cents**

SQUADRON MAIL ORDER
1115 Crowley Drive
Carrollton, TX 75011-5010
(214) 242-8663
CK, MC, V, AE

Tanks to this defender of discounts, model airplanes, motorcycles, bombers, battleships, tanks, and other "militaria" are available at savings of 30% to 70% off retail. This is one of the country's foremost dealers of airplane kits with a selection that ranges from a simulated World War I biplane to an exact replica of a Navy fighter detailed down to the cockpits and decals. A fascinating selection of books for the model builder is available, many concerning a particular branch of the armed services. Squadron owns their own publishing company and markets publications through this mail-order business. **C $3.50**

SUSAN OF NEWPORT
P.O. Box 3107
Newport Beach, CA 92663
(714) 673-5445
CK

If you can take a ribbon, this may be a critical company for you. Susan's from Newport, but she loves poking around the warehouses and showrooms in the Los Angeles Garment District. That's why you can purchase ribbon and lace at bargain prices. It's fun to shop this catalog. Not only are the prices ridiculously low, but there are bonus coupons, grab bags, and super specials for added savings. To become a Preferred Customer, place one order of $10 plus shipping. After that, you will receive all newsletters, and sale and special buy announcements, indefinitely, at no cost. Quantity discounts are given. **C $2 (includes samples)**

VETERAN LEATHER CO.
Dept. SG
204 25th St.
Brooklyn, NY 11232
(800) 221-7565
(718) 768-0300: NY residents
CK, MC, V, COD

Veteran Leather Co. has a variety of leathers including suede and chamois, and they carry a large assortment of leather working accessories and tools. They stock brands like CRAFTOOL, MIDAS, BASIC, FIEBING, OSBORNE, ORIGINAL MINK OIL, and LEXOL. Most prices are lower than retail with discounts up to 30% on quantity purchases. There is a $25 minimum order (for mail-order) and a 10% restocking charge on returns unless the material is defective. You can examine this 40-year-old family business' catalog (56 pages) or call for a price quote. Mention *The Underground Shopper* for a bonus 5% discount! **C $1.50** (refundable)

Housewares

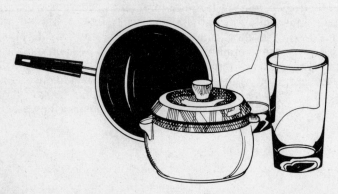

Why go to Belgium for waffles when you can iron out a not-so-syrupy bargain right here? Need some SABATIER knives for slicing that elegant pâté en croute? You'll find some sharp bargains here. Celebrate St. Patrick's Day with a set of genuine Irish ale tankards. Raise your cooking to haute cuisine with CALPHALON cookware. Americans are entertaining more and more in-house and with the right housewares and cookwares, you'll set the culinary standards for good taste at your next progressive dinner party.

ALEXANDER BUTCHER BLOCK AND SUPPLY CORP.
176 Bowery
New York, NY 10012
(212) 226-4021
CK, MC, V, Certified Check

This family-owned store is a chop off the old (retail) block! They fashion their own first-quality furniture, tools, and kitchenware using 100% maple, oak, and some FORMICA. Prices are about 25% off those of a department store. Their selection is extensive; they make 100 different styles of chairs alone. Parquet tables are the hot item. An added benefit: Alexander says they can custom-make a piece of furniture to your specifications in a day's time and will "beat anyone's price." Write or call with your specifications. There's a 20% restocking charge on returns. Orders are usually delivered in about seven days. PQ

A COOK'S WARES
3270 37th St. Ext.
Beaver Falls, PA 15010
CK, MC, V, AE

Gourmet goodies galore! Confirmed cooks and budding bakers alike will enjoy every page of this 28-page catalog. Pots and pans, bakeware, gadgets, food processors, and more are available, all at 20% to 40% off the retail price. Experienced owners personally handle each order and test all equipment before placing it in the catalog. From spice racks to sweet sauces and chocolate to crystal, this business meets all your epicurean needs. Detailed descriptions of the merchandise make your selection simpler. Superior products include HENCKELS cutlery and utensils, CUISINART food processors, LE CREUSET copper pans, KRUPS appliances, TAYLOR WOODCRAFT butcher block tables, PILLVUYT porcelains, and much, much more. With more than 1,300 items packed into these pages, you're sure to find plenty that tastes good to you. Merchandise carries a 30-day unconditional guarantee, and after that, merchandise may be exchanged or returned by mutual consent. All items carry a manufacturer's guarantee. C $1

THE CHEF'S CATALOG
3215 Commercial Ave.
Northbrook, IL 60062
(800) 972-1000: credit card orders
(312) 480-9400
CK, MC, V, AE, DC, CB

Ooh-la-la! Cuisine is an art and this company's 40- to 60-page full-color catalog displays 1,001 gourmet cookware items, fine foods, and imaginative gifts from around the world to help you create those gourmet masterpieces. From the FRUGAL GOURMET's lemon reamer to fresh roasted coffee beans from Trieste, Italy, to a black steel oven apple pancake pan, The Chef's Catalog serves up top brands like CUISINART, CALPHALON, KRUPS coffee makers, HENCKELS knives, SIMAC electric ice cream makers, MOULI salad makers, and more at money-saving, mouth-watering reductions. Discounts range to 40%. A Belgium waffle iron by NORDIC WARE was $31.95, plus $4.50 postage (regularly $40 plus tax in retail stores). An introductory special featured the CUISINART DLC7 Pro Food Processor for $219.99 plus $12.50 shipping for a savings of $75. You'll also see items like the self-stirring SAFFRON saucepan from France and Paul Newman's popcorn. There's a $20 minimum order with credit cards, no restocking charges, and exchanges and refunds are made if you're dissatisfied. Most orders are received within eight working days. Mention *The Underground Shopper* when you call—you'll get an additional 10% discount. **C $2**

CLOTHCRAFTERS
Dept. US
Elkhart Lake, WI 53020
(414) 876-2112
CK, MC, V, MO

Smile and say "cheesecloth"—it's just $2.50 for two yards. Cheesecloth can be used for straining, keeping salad and parsley fresh for weeks, or for a variety of other purposes. For pots that are too hot to handle, order denim pot holders, $2.50, or casserole cushions, $2.50. A complete set of such cushions was a bargain at just $8 and included a seven-inch pad, $2; a nine-inch pad, $3; and a platter pad, $4. There are excellent buys on 100% cotton flannel sheets. Save by buying sheet sets—a set of full-size, flannel sheets was $33; queen size, $38. A white cotton shower curtain needing no liner was $23. There's no minimum order, no restocking charge, and refunds are given on request. **C**

COLLINSWORTH
219 N. Columbus St.
Lancaster, OH 43130
(614) 653-0972
CK, MC, V, AE

Buying glassware at retail prices can be a real pain in the pocket-book—unless you buy here. For 20 years Collinsworth has helped shoppers get their moneysworth. They've helped shatter the high cost with classic hand-cut glassware at see-through savings of up to 50%, plus special discounts for those buying in quantity. Ashtrays, ale tankards, drink glasses, decanters, candleholders, and bud vases are a few examples. They had some crystal-clear bargains: a half-liter wine carafe with four wine glasses at $12.95; a monogrammed sangria pitcher with six glasses at $35.95; a set of four 15-ounce clear tankards monogrammed with one initial at $11.95; and a set of eight 12½-ounce monogrammed tumblers at $14.95. Each set comes with a card signed by the artisan who cut the glass. What class! All merchandise is guaranteed against defects. You'll get your order in two to five weeks; shipping is $3.50. **C, F**

FIVENSON FOOD EQUIPMENT, INC.
324 S. Union St.
Traverse City, MI 49684
(800) 632-7342: MI residents
(616) 946-7760
CK, MC, V, AE, D, Certified CK

You can pay cash or you can lease with Fivenson's own exclusive leasing plan or you can charge it—anyway you cook it, if you're in the kitchen for professional food service equipment and furniture, this is it. Save 40% across the counters for under-counter dishwashers, fryers from 15 to 60 pounds, a three-minute mixer for dough, mixers to handle from five to 140 quarts, a draft beer dispenser ($1693), a heated display food warmer ($595), an old fashioned (eight quarts in 15 minutes) gourmet ice cream machine ($995)—even pizza signs for your car if you want to compete with Domino's. Starting their 50th year, the advantages of buying from their huge inventory is immediate service and great prices. **C** Send **SASE** with two stamps

GRAND FINALE
P.O. Box 620049
Farmers Branch, TX 75262-0049
(214) 243-6200
CK, MC, V, AE, DC

Designer clothing, fine furnishings, and elegant accessories bow out on the pages of Grand Finale, the first catalog company formed to offer luxury merchandise at significant savings. Designers' names are not always given, but imagine ordering a blouse and finding out it's an ALBERT NIPON! A recent catalog featured Beacon Hill sheets by WAMSUTTA ($14.99 for twin, $32.99 for king, an additional $5 charge for monogramming). FIELDCREST linens in a duck paisley pattern were $7.99 for twin and $18.99 for king size. TOWLE's silver plated flatware in a Boston shell design (46-piece set) was $299.99 and would retail at $320. Finally, a PAULINE TRIGERE red and black reversible raincoat that would retail for $270 was just $199. Sound pretty good? Many brands turn up in the catalog and discounts are often 40% to 50%. Expect to receive your order in about 10 to 14 days. Write for Grand Finale's catalog. You'll soon be asking for an encore!
C $2

HANDART EMBROIDERIES
Hing Wai Building, Room 106
36 Queen's Road Central
Hong Kong
Telephone: 011-852-5-235744 (dial direct)
CK, MC, V, AE

We're not above taking a Handart with items like these. This company stocks embroidered tablecloths, kimonos, shirts, blouses, and other Oriental items at about 20% below retail. As we flipped through Handart's Xeroxed price sheets, we saw a 72-inch round hand-crocheted lace table cover for only $25. Children's Kung Fu-style pajamas were $8 and came in sizes 2 through 14. We also saw hand-crocheted doilies and place mats, as well as ladies' pure silk flower-print scarves for $12. Satin sheets for a queen-size bed were $36. Jade ornaments and ivory hand-carved ornaments were reasonably priced, too. Handart goes out on a limb to offer a full refund if the customer is dissatisfied for any reason. C

IMOCO INC.
3225 Premier Drive
P.O. Box 152052
Irving, TX 75015
(214) 580-1122
CK, MC, V, AE, DC, CB, LAYAWAY

Imoco, you're ok. Imoco sells housewares, primarily, and they've got some of the best buys on CORNING WARE items you'll find anywhere. Forty-five-piece sets of CORELLE in popular patterns like Holly Days, Honey Dew, Ginger, and Blueberry are only $69.95—compared to a retail price of $126. Twenty-piece sets in patterns like Spice of Life, French White, Cornflower are also available. Despite a retail price of $171, they're only $69.95 at Imoco. Extra-heavy stainless steel cookware (a set of 19 pieces) that retails for $319.95 is a fantastic bargain at just $129.95. SYLVANIA and MAGNAVOX electronics were discounted 30% to 50%, AMERICAN TOURISTER luggage was reduced by 60%, and we found brands like SINGER, REGINA, HOTPOINT, and ECKO, all at a terrific savings! There's a full refund if merchandise is returned (with authorization) within 30 days, and they'll replace defective items. Shipping is immediate; the cost is $9.95 for anywhere in the U.S.; and it will take two to six weeks before you get your order. **C $2**

KITCHEN BAZAAR
Dept. US
4455 Connecticut Ave. N.W.
Washington, DC 20008
(202) 363-4625
CK, MC, V, AE

The name of this company not only describes our kitchen, but some of our cooking, too! Bizarre! This full-color kitchenware catalog includes gourmet cookware and serving dishes. Some items during their periodic sales are simmering at up to 75% off. (The mere thought sets our blood to boiling!) January is traditionally their clearance month: that's when they gather their slow sellers and slash prices to the bone. Brands included CALPHALON, LE CREUSET, CUISINART, BRAUN WUSTHOF, and COPCO. There are no minimum orders; orders usually arrive in 14 to 21 days. If you're in Washington or its environs, drop in one of their stores. They've been in business for 22 years and the staff is exceptionally knowledgeable. **C**

LILLIAN VERNON
510 S. Fulton Ave.
Mount Vernon, NY 10550
(914) 633-6300
CK, MC, V, AE, DC, CB

Mail-order magic was packed into the pages of this catalog! There's something for every person on any list when you flip through these pages. Puzzles, games, clothing, accessories, and baby items were all offered at low prices. Novel gifts for kids of all ages are sure to bring smiles, such as a set of six animal noses (bear, cat, parrot, pig, mouse, and duck) for year-round fun, or a 26-piece wooden Noah's Ark playset. Elegant gifts for the home included brass toilet paper holders, lamps, sconces, and magazine racks. Gifts in Lucite, crystal, rattan, and linen let you find something for even those hard-to-shop-for friends or relatives. Gifts for the home, office, and automobile gave a unique new approach to gift-giving. From the functional to the fashionable to the far-out, this catalog was just what you'd want to cure the buyer's blues, or to pick up a few personal items for just pennies. Seasonal catalogs offer Christmas ornaments and seasonal gifts. Orders are shipped by UPS and come with a 100% customer satisfaction guarantee. **C**

MAK INC.
P.O. Box 65445 E
West Des Moines, IA 50265
(515) 279-9075
CK, MC, V, COD

How would you like to have dinner with the president? Well, we can't arrange that, but we can tell you which cookware is used in the White House. However, it's a national secret; so sh-h-h. MAK Inc. provides the Reagans with CALPHALON, heavy-duty professional cookware at an unstately price. You'll elect MAK to office with savings of up to 40%. We found capitol deals like the CUISINART Food Processor priced at $224. It retails for $320. A CALPHALON starter set which included an eight-quart stock pot with cover, eight-inch omelette fry pan, one-half-quart sauce pan, and *The Calphalon International Cookbook* with top secret recipes was only $160. That represented a savings of over 25%. Bake up some oval cookies for the office on REMA Bakeware, a cushion-aire insulated baking sheet that goes for $15.95, including shipping. Get a grip on life with COOL HANDLES, the specially designed, heat-resistant handles which permanently replace awkward hot pads. You won't get burned buying them at a cost of only $6.50 each plus 50 cents shipping. You may be waiting until the next election, though, for your order; four to six weeks is the normal delivery time. You may not be able to eat with Ronnie, but you can eat like him with MAK. **C $2** (refundable)

MONSANTO ENGINEERED PRODUCTS
800 N. Lindbergh Blvd.
St. Louis, MO 63167
(314) 694-1000
CK

OK, maybe you never made it as a football hero. Just because you didn't bask in glory in the past doesn't mean you can't bask on the grass in the present. For $1.75 per square foot, you can put stadium ASTROTURF remnants around your pool area, in the kitchen, or on the patio. Rolls are 10 feet to 350 feet long and in 15-foot widths. These folks prefer not to cut existing pieces to exact dimensions, but to select the piece(s) that best meet your requirements. Delivery takes about 10 days and the carpet is not returnable—so if you don't like your rug—turf luck! (Still . . . while you may never be able to cut like O.J. Simpson, you won't have to cut like your Lawn Boy, either). "So let's go, men and remember: When the going gets turf, the turf gets going. Get out there and kick As-troturf!" **PQ**

PARIS BREAD PANS
500 Independence Ave. S.E.
Washington, DC 20003
(202) 544-6858
CK

Founder Clyde Brooks writes that after living in Paris many years, he didn't want to give up French cuisine—especially the light, crusty bread that the French are famous for. He devised his own bread recipe, but unable to find pans like those used in France, he designed his own pans. A set of double pans making four loaves costs $12.50, including postage, and a four-pan set was $17.75, or about 40% less than in retail gourmet shops. New items offered include a San Francisco sourdough pan and recipe, $9.50, and oversize cookie sheets to utilize the whole oven, $8.00 to 8.50. Shipping charges are included in the price. Our Mr. Brooks says you can save plenty of dough by baking your own. **B**

PFALTZGRAFF PFACTORY OUTLET
P.O. Box 2048
York, PA 17405-2048
(717) 757-2200
CK, MC, V, AE, DC

They say it's "pfabulous, pforever, pfantastic!" It's PFALTZGRAFF stoneware, glassware, and copperware. Every piece is made from natural materials, hand-finished, and hand-decorated. They offer a world of ware for your kitchen counter or dinner table—platters, soup tureens, casserole dishes, wine goblets, gravy boats, mugs, copper chambersticks, and cookie cutters. Stoneware is safe in microwave ovens, freezers, and dishwashers and is chip-resistant.
C $1 (refundable)

PLASTIC BAGMART
904 Old Country Road
Westbury, NY 11590
(516) 997-3355
CK, MO

It's in the bag! This factory outlet for plastic bags has a bag full of bargains for you. We found over 300 sizes and strengths of bags. They also have the bag on gloves, film, and compactor bags. Their prices are something to brag about, too. One hundred extra-heavy industrial type bags with a 56-gallon capacity cost $35.95. Santa could put everyone's toys in those bags. Or maybe you're not trying to bag an elephant, in which case, the light kitchen and office bags costing only $20.95 per 1,000 are more your bag. Whether you are baggin' big or storin' small, the Plastic BagMart has them all . . . fat, skinny, short, or tall. You won't get caught holding the bag, though, because shipping is included in the price and there is a money-back guarantee. So get on your Mart, get set, go! F

WESTON BOWL MILL
Weston, VT 05161
(802) 824-6219
CK, MC, V

We were never much for the GE College Bowl, but the Super Bowl's another story. When it comes to fielding a team of quality products, the Weston Bowl just about bowls us over. (Their housewares aren't your everyday run of the mill.) Maple, birch, elm, and beech trees sacrifice their roots to become salad bowls, cheese boards, knife holders, pine sugar buckets, stools, coffee tables, shelves and racks, canisters, and jewelry boxes. Everything is beautiful (as Ray Stevens used to sing), and comes in your choice of natural, dark lacquer, or no finish. About 70% of their inventory is their own; they distribute the remaining 30% for other folks. Prices are reasonable since they are factory direct. Restocking charges vary depending on the item; orders are shipped out in about two or three days. There's a $5 minimum order. Request their retail catalog: there's also a wholesale catalog for businesses buying in bulk (over $50). **C**

YANKEE INGENUITY
Brandy Hill Road
Thompson, CT 06277
(203) 923-2061
CK, MC, V, COD

It takes one Yankee to appreciate another Yankee's ingenuity. Primarily set up to wholesale clock parts to craft shops, ceramic studios, and manufacturers of handcrafted clocks for resale, by ordering through the mail, you, too, can save up to 70% off the retail price. The clock will only register 48 hours for a response to your order with all parts guaranteed for life against factory defects. So, if you're ready to defect, write for their eight-page illustrated brochure today. **C $1**

Investments

Radical changes are taking place in the financial investment market. This has opened up many opportunities to smaller investors. People capable of making their own investment decisions can use discount brokers for their stock trades and save on commissions or they can invest in mutual funds and avoid a sales commission entirely. Discount brokers are less expensive because their commissions are based only on performing the mechanics of the transaction, not on providing financial advice as brokers in major brokerage houses must do. We have also listed several Swiss banks suitable for smaller investors. They welcome mail accounts and have officers fluent in English.

DISCOUNT BROKERS

Discount brokers do not give investment advice, but they will execute your buy and sell orders at fees well below those of "full-service" brokerage houses. Among discount brokers, there is a range of transaction costs depending on the manner of payment and the extent of services. Most brokers set up credit accounts for their clients, with the credit charges reflected in the rates. Check around and find a broker that offers only what you need for the lowest cost. Discount brokers have become very popular, but it's important to remember that clients must obtain their own investment information. If you need investment advice, a good source (to call collect) is: Sam Kesner, 32-year veteran with E.F. Hutton, 2001 Bryan Tower, Suite 3308, Dallas, TX 75201, (214) 744-2511.

BROWN & CO.
20 Winthrop Square
Boston, MA 02110
(800) 225-6707

This company charges a base fee of $25 for the first share traded, and four to eight cents for each remaining share. Customers must have a minimum of five years' trading experience. There's a $5,000 minimum deposit to open an account. Margin accounts are available.

CHARLES SCHWAB & CO., INC.
101 Montgomery
San Francisco, CA 94105
(800) 227-4444
(800) 792-0988: CA residents

Charles Schwab has offices throughout the country and is one of the largest discount brokers. They have added many services such as a money market fund to ease trading, long business hours, cheap term insurance, and 24-hour price quotations. Their minimum commission is $34.

DISCOUNT BROKERAGE CORP.
67 Wall St.
New York, NY 10005
(800) 221-5088
(212) 806-2888: NY residents

Discount Brokerage is one of the least expensive of all discount brokers. Their commissions are 20% to 40% less than those charged by other discount brokers, and they have offices in New York, Philadelphia, Washington, D.C., St. Petersburg, Fort Lauderdale, Houston, Minneapolis, San Francisco, and Los Angeles. They offer a choice of three money market funds (tax free, government, and regular) with "automatic sweep," which means client funds are automatically placed on a daily basis in the fund specified so that they can earn maximum interest. Most discount brokers only do this on a weekly basis. There is no minimum order.

FIDELITY BROKERAGE SERVICE, INC.
82 Devonshire St.
Boston, MA 02109
(800) 544-6666
(800) 523-1919: MA residents

This company has offices throughout the country. One of their most popular financial offerings is Fidelity, U.S.A., an asset management account which includes discount brokerage, a money market fund yield, unlimited check writing, and a credit card. Margins on mutual funds are available and Fidelity will even sell gold. The minimum commission is $30; there is no minimum order.

KENNEDY, CABOT & CO.
9465 Wilshire Blvd.
Beverly Hills, CA 90212
(800) 252-0090

Based upon total customer accounts, Kennedy, Cabot & Co. is the largest independent discount stockbroker. Service to the "little guy" is their forte. Orders are cleared and executed through Securities Settlement Corp., which is a wholly owned subsidiary of Traveler's Insurance. Accordingly, each account is protected up to $10 million, $100,000 of which is cash with the balance in securities. Besides their normal trading activities, they deal in municipal bonds and GNMA's. There is a $20 minimum commission, although this may be reduced due to increasing volume. Clients get two free trades of up to 2,000 shares if they transfer their accounts from competitors, or one free trade of up to 2,000 shares if they open a margin account.

MURIEL SIEBERT & CO., INC.
444 Madison Ave.
New York, NY 10022
(800) USA-0711
(718) SIE-BERT: NY residents
(212) 644-2433

Muriel Siebert, a full-service company, was the first firm in discount brokerage. They offer the full range of products, in equities, options, and fixed income (Ginnie Maes, Municipals, etc.). They offer special rates for active traders—as low as two cents per share and also handle institutional orders for banks, money managers, and investment firms.

OLDE DISCOUNT STOCKBROKERS
735 Griswold
Detroit, MI 48226
(800) 521-1111
(800) 482-4000: MI residents

Founded in 1971 as a traditional brokerage firm, they were one of the first companies to go discount and charge competitive rates. They now have 50 offices. Clients can request a "round trip" which allows them to receive a 50% discount on the commission they're charged when they buy and sell within a 31-day period. Commissions are calculated depending on either the number of shares traded or the size of the transaction in dollars. They also handle institutional accounts for banks, savings and loans, and credit unions nationwide.

OVEST SECURITIES, INC.
90 Broad St.
New York, NY 10004
(800) 255-0700
(212) 668-0600: NY residents

When it comes to trading stocks, you can "share" the wealth or play your cards close to the Ovest. This discount commission stock brokerage firm charges up to 90% less than other brokerage firms. Active traders can find what are perhaps the lowest commissions in the industry. Under this company's "Premier Status" program, traders can pay an annual fee of $1,000 and trade on the New York Stock Exchange (NYSE) and American Stock Exchange (ASE) for

$25 plus three or four cents per share, per trade. Lower charges are available for over-the-counter (OTC) trades; margin accounts are welcome. They're members of the NYSE, National Association of Securities Dealers (NASD), and Securities Investors Protection Corporation (SIPC).

QUICK & REILLY, INC.
120 Wall St.
New York, NY 10005
(800) 221-5220
(800) 522-8712: NY residents

Quick & Reilly was the first NYSE member to discount commissions. This firm has 53 offices nationwide and ranks as the third largest discount broker. There is no minimum order; minimum commission, $35.

ROSE & CO. INVESTMENT BROKERS, INC.
One Financial Place
440 S. LaSalle St.
Chicago, IL 60605
(800) THE-ROSE

Established on St. Patrick's Day in 1972, they were one of the first discount brokers and are owned by the Chase Manhattan Corporation. They are a full-service firm, with the exception of research and recommendations, which they don't offer. Minimum commission is $35; for equity transactions (stocks and warrants) only; no minimum order.

ROYAL, GRIMM AND DAVIS, INC.
20 Exchange Place
New York, NY 10005
(800) 221-9900
(800) 426-6970: Upstate NY residents
(212) 635-0880: NYC residents

This discount stock brokerage firm will give free stock reports and a comprehensive 10-year history on earnings, dividends, payout ratio, book value, etc., to their clients. Transactions can be 50% to 80% less expensive than those handled by regular brokers. The minimum commission per trade is $30. They will trade listed and over-the-counter stocks, put and call options, corporate, government, and municipal bonds. Cash balances of $2,000 or more automatically receive interest. Royal, Grimm and Davis is a member of the NYSE and has access to all principal exchanges and OTC markets, so all the services available in a full-service brokerage house are offered, except financial advice.

TEXAS SECURITIES
4200 S. Hulen, Suite 536
Fort Worth, TX 76109
(817) 732-0130

Fort Worth may bill itself as "Cowtown," but you won't find these stockbrokers at the stockyards. This 10-year-old company is Fort Worth's oldest and largest discount brokerage firm, and they've expanded into such new frontiers as Las Colinas, El Paso, and Graham. Commissions average 50% to 80% lower than those charged by the NASD and SIPC. The firm is a registered securities dealer and they'll work on margin. The minimum order is $25. They will sell blue chip stocks, but for cow chips, you'll have to find a more "bullish" company.

NO-LOAD MUTUAL FUNDS

A mutual fund is an organization through which investors pool their money and have it professionally managed. This can be beneficial to people who either don't have much money to invest or who don't know much about investing. Most mutual funds invest in the stock market, but they can invest in tax exempt bonds, Treasury bills, gold, or new companies. All your deposits and withdrawals are handled through the mail. We recommend you find a "no-load" mutual fund, meaning there is no sales commission attached to your transactions. Some no-load funds advertise in the financial sections of major newspapers. You can also get a list of no-load funds by writing to: The No-Load Mutual Fund Association, 475 Park Ave. S., New York, NY 10016. Or, you can call any of the following companies for information on their mutual funds.

These are toll-free numbers you can use to request shareholder information:

Alliance Capital Reserves:
(800) 221-5672, 9 A.M. to 6 P.M. EST
(800) 221-5672: NY residents

Dreyfus Liquid Assets & Dreyfus Group:
(800) 645-6561, 8 A.M. to 8 P.M. EST
(718) 895-1206: NY residents

Fidelity Daily Income:
(800) 544-6666, 8:30 A.M. to 8 P.M. EST
(617) 523-1919: MA residents

Financial Programs:
(800) 525-9831, 7 A.M. to 4 P.M. MST
(800) 332-9145: CO residents
(303) 779-1233: CO residents

Penn Square:
(800) 523-8440, 9 A.M. to 5 P.M. EST
(215) 376-6771: PA residents

Permanent Portfolio Funds:
(800) 531-5142 9 A.M. to 5 P.M. CST
(512) 453-7558: TX residents and outside the continental U.S.

Scudder Fund Distributing, Inc.
(800) 225-2470, 8 A.M. to 6 P.M. EST
(617) 426-8300: MA residents

T. Rowe Price:
(800) 638-5660, 8 A.M. to 6 P.M. EST
(301) 547-2308: MD residents

Vanguard Group:
(800) 523-7910, 8:30 A.M. to 5:30 P.M. EST
(215) 648-6000: PA residents

Many investment firms accept collect calls from shareholders or those requesting information.

TREASURY NOTES, BONDS, AND BILLS

Buying direct from the Federal Reserve Banks' Securities Department can save you the $25 to $40 commission you pay at the bank. You can enter a noncompetitive bid by mail for the next auction, which means you'll pay the average price of the competitive tenders. Ask for the next mailing and carefully note the deadline. There are

Federal Reserve branches in Atlanta, Boston, Chicago, Dallas, Cleveland, Kansas City (Missouri), Minneapolis, New York City, Philadelphia, Richmond, San Francisco, and St. Louis.

SWISS BANK ACCOUNTS

Swiss banks hold a unique position in worldwide banking. The stable economic characteristics of Switzerland combined with the Swiss traditions of privacy in banking matters offer advantages not found in federally regulated American banks. The following three Swiss banks will open up mail accounts for American investors with small amounts of funds to invest. Each bank has officers fluent in English. Our original source for this data was *Inflation Proofing Your Investments* by Harry Browne and Terry Coxon (New York: William Morrow & Co., 1981).

BANQUE ANKERFINA SA
50 Ave. de la Gare
CH-1003 Lausanne, Switzerland
(021) 20-4741

Minimum to open account is approximately $600. Contact Mrs. Francine Misrahi or Beda Fuerer.

FOREIGN COMMERCE BANK
Bellariastrasse 82
CH-8038 Zurich, Schweiz/Switzerland
(01) 482-66-88

Minimum to open account is $10,000. Contact Roger Badet, Bruno Brodbeck, or Peter Weber.

UEBERSEEBANK AG ZURICH
Limmatquai 2
CH-8024 Zurich, Switzerland
(01) 252-0304

There is no minimum to open an account. Contact Bruno Mattie, Siegfried Herzog, or Kurt Kamber.

Jewelry

Who can resist the pristine glitter and glamour of exquisite jewelry, the sparkle and fire and inner radiance of a fine gem? Many a stone has unlocked the romance and passion of a woman's heart. The mystery and quiet beckoning of beauty, the silent sexiness of lovely jewelry is captivating to all. And whatever your heart desires, you'll find in the following pages. Whether sifted, mined, or plucked from the ocean's floor, it's all here—everything from low-cost gems and cultured pearls from the Orient, to high-grade diamonds from New York's famed jewelers on Forty-Seventh Street. The more specific you can be about what you want, the more satisfied you'll be with your selection. Remember, the bigger the carat, the heavier the stone; and the higher the karat, the purer the gold.

ADCO COMPANY
P.O. Box 10949
Chicago, IL 60610
(312) 337-7804
CK, MC, V

We're talking costume jewelry here, the kind in drugstores, not the stuff that Tiffany charge accounts are made from. But any teenager would find these pages exciting. Earrings represent the largest selection of "fun" jewelry we've seen in one place—ranging in styles from "cultura" pearls to a pair of tropical fishes to dangling strawberries and pencils. For all the fashion trends and fads, the gal on a budget will be well prepared with earrings and necklaces priced from about $3 to $6. With orders over $25, you will receive a special gift.
C 50 cents

BATIKAT
P.O. Box 140266
Dallas, TX 75214
(214) 386-4869
CK, MC, V

Batikat, batikat, Seth Hersh is the Batikat man. He trades exclusively in Indonesian gold work. Each piece of jewelry, whether a ring, bangle, necklace, bracelet, earring, etc., is completely handmade and is guaranteed to be 22K (91.6% pure) gold. Heavy gold necklaces weighing in at about one and a half ounces are Batikat's biggest selling item. The richly burnished luster of this jewelry dramatically conveys the mysterious allure of gold for people throughout the world and throughout history. Batikat has traveled extensively in Indonesia and has developed its own manufacturing facility there (each piece is hallmarked "BKT" and "22K".) By combining the decreased costs of producing its own jewelry and the benefits of mail-order sales, Batikat is able to offer 22K gold jewelry at very affordable prices. Orders are usually delivered in two to three weeks when the merchandise is in stock. (Most is.) Shipping is $7.50: orders are delivered by insured, registered mail. Undamaged merchandise which is returned within two weeks is good for full credit: there are no full cash refunds because of the fluctuations in the price of gold. For more information, check out Batikat's eight-page brochure. **B $1**

BMI
1617 Promenade Bank Building
Richardson, TX 75080
(214) 234-4394
MC, V, AE

If you're thinking about getting into gem-nastics, this company will make you sit up and take notice. They carry brand name watches, and will order and drop ship (at a minimum of 20% to 35% off) such watchable watches as ROLEX, SEIKO, CARTIER, CONCORD, CORUM, and PIAGET. Their inventory consists of 14K and 18K jewelry from diamonds to semiprecious stones. Gold chains in serpentine, cobra, herringbone, and beveled herringbone varieties are about 50% off. This former veteran Zales employee and jewelry rep also offers add-a-beads, fashion earrings, ear jackets, pearls, studs, and a promise that if you can describe it, he can get it for you. Prices fluctuate with the gold market. All jewelry is guaranteed to be represented accurately. Most orders are received in two weeks. Shipping charges are $7.50. The 200+ page, full-size, and full-color catalog has everything from a $50 ring to a $50,000 necklace, all at 50% off suggested retail price. **C** $5 (refundable)

BOULLE, INC.
EUROPEAN DIAMOND IMPORTERS &
CUTTERS, INC.
Suite 95
200 Crescent Court
Dallas, TX 75201
(214) 698-0000

The Boulle brothers are the gems of the diamond business. Their African diamonds are mined in Sierra Leone and offered direct to you. Loose diamonds are available in any shape, color, or size with up to 50% savings below discount store prices. These diamonds can be mounted in any setting or design of your choice. They specialize in 18K European design jewelry. In making your diamond purchase, the Boulles will deal direct with you through your own bank. They will also accept, as a trade, any diamond purchased as credit towards a larger purchase. Because of their expertise and integrity, they guarantee all purchases. **C**

BUTTERFLIES & RAINBOWS, INC.
P.O. Box 1231
Dunedin, FL 34296
(813) 733-6499
CK, MO, COD

Spreading her wings, this entrepreneurial craftswoman manufactures infants' and children's personalized gifts and adorable doll jewelry that winds up in stores for a whole lot more. Golden Beginning® infant keepsakes are exquisite handcrafted booties inscribed in 24K gold and laced in either pink or blue satin ribbon ($29.95 plus $2 shipping—sold elsewhere for $40). A 14K gold infant bracelet was 4 inches surrounded by 3mm 14K gold beads. The baby's first name is spelled out in genuine porcelain alphabet beads and framed with pink or blue glass hearts. Only $19.95 plus $2 shipping through *The Underground Shopper*—sold elsewhere for $32.95. Send baby's first name. Nostalgic genuine hospital baby bracelets ($4.00 plus $1 shipping) and personalized birthstone bracelets ($6 plus $1 shipping) complete the rainbow of items available. **PQ**

CROWN CULTURED PEARL CORP.
580 Eighth Ave.
New York, NY 10018
(212) 719-1540
CK

How do you tell if a pearl is cultured? Easy. Cultured pearls rest in Queen Anne oyster beds. We found carved jade pelicans, hippopotamuses, rhinoceroses, and exotic birds inhabiting the pages of this typed mailer. Pearls from Japan and China, along with ivory, coral, carnelian, onyx, malachite, and other gemstones were formed into rings, necklaces, pendants, earrings, and bracelets. We shook our Buddhas until they were thoroughly jaded, hoping they would give us some fresh pearls of wisdom. The prices we saw in their stapled price sheets ranged from $10 to $1,250, with everything discounted about 20% to 60%. Their minimum order is $15; most orders are received within seven days. Shipping's $2. **B**

EMPIRE DIAMOND CORP.
Dept. US
Empire State Building, 66th Floor
350 Fifth Ave.
New York, NY 10001
(212) 564-4777

This company's building an empire. In business for over 55 years, this well-known diamond cutter and wholesaler sells jewelry at a 25% to 40% discount. Fine quality diamonds, cultured pearls, colored gems, and 14K to 18K gold jewelry ranging from $10 charms to $100,000 diamonds make up their inventory. Their gold seal guarantees your complete satisfaction. Refunds are given within 60 days: there is no minimum order. Their 92-page, full-color catalog is a visual feast.

THE FANTASY COLLECTION
OF 14K GOLD MOUNTED DIAMAGEM©
5952 Royal Lane, Suite 103
Dallas, TX 75230
(800) 527-6983
(800) 492-9209: TX residents
(214) 361-1411
CK, MC, V

Just half the printed price is your price from this 44-page color catalog of faux gems extraordinaire. All stones are the trademarked Diamagems© grade AAA cubic zirconia, machine cut, and hand polished in Europe. Rings are set in 14K yellow or white gold in sizes 6 for ladies, 9 for men. There is a sizing charge for larger or smaller ring sizes. This beautiful collection includes the Emergems© (emerald-like gems that would make your friends green with envy). All fancy shapes: pears, marquises, ovals, emeralds, heart shapes, triangles, and radiants that radiate from the pages. Cultured pearl classics, gold chains (herringbone, rope and cobra), gorgeous as well as genuine ruby, sapphire, and emerald creations are all available. All 50% off the retail prices and a free catalog, to boot, from this Dallas-based manufacturer. **C**

GOLD 'N' STONES
Box 387
Westhope, ND 58793
(701) 245-6356
CK, MO

Finding this gem in North Dakota was no easy matter. Nonetheless, we found it . . . and since 1972, they've generated a loyal following. Specializing in Jade and Hemitite as well as the latest addition—New Zealand Sea Opal (deep blue) jewelry. Gold 'n' Stones also carries a large variety of Alaskan, North Dakotan, and other hat and lapel pins. High-quality, reasonable prices (savings 10% to 40%), and service. All items are real gems and stones, nothing is glass or fake. Most settings in 23K Hamilton gold plate. Two week delivery, a five-year warranty. Orders less than $10, add $1 postage and handling. **C**

HOUSE OF ONYX
Dept. US
#1 North Main
The Rowe Building
Greenville, KY 42345
(800) 626-8352
(800) 992-3260: KY residents
(502) 338-2363: AL, HI residents
CK, MC, V, DC

This house is built on the premise that onyx-ty is the best policy, so if rocks are your quarry, you'll find agates, loose diamonds, opals, sapphires, emeralds, tigereye, malachite, and blue topaz here at 50% less than retail. (With these prices, we could afford twin purchases of these Gem-in-eyes and we could still bask in the lapis of luxury.) Onyx is the specialty of the house; they're the largest dealer in carved onyx in the U.S. All merchandise carries a 100% satisfaction guarantee; the minimum order is $25; and their 56-page catalog is free. Last year, over 2 million orders were processed and not one complaint was registered through the Post Office, action lines, or other consumer protection agencies. Onyx-ly. **C**

INTERNATIONAL IMPORT COMPANY
P.O. Box 747
Stone Mountain, GA 30086
(404) 938-0173
CK, COD, MO

We discovered an International secret: an import company that can save you a national deficit on natural, genuine cut gems. International Import Company offers top secret savings of 33% or more as their top priority. This 56-page document contains the specifications on 3,000 stones out of their 100,000 gem inventory. Choose from a secret file of amethysts, sapphires, garnets, diamonds, emeralds, jade, opals, rubies, and others. You buy nothing prior to your examination and approval. Refunds are made promptly after receipt of your returns, but you must return your unwanted merchandise promptly, too; five days is the limit. There is a $10 minimum order, but no handling fee. **C**

MARCUS & CO.
9460 Wilshire Blvd.
Beverly Hills, CA 90212
(800) 824-5677
(213) 271-6244
CK, MC, V

No Marcus Welby, M.D., here, but there is a successful operation. If the thought of paying retail for a PIAGET, ROLEX, CONCORD, CARTIER, PATEK-PHILLIPE, or other expensive watch makes your pacemaker race, here's a remedy for your malady. Take two aspirins and call them in the morning. Your temperature will go down 40% and you may even get to dicker over a trade-in on your present ticker. **PQ**

RAMA JEWELRY LTD.
OPP Rama Tower Hotel
987 Silom Road
Bangkok, Thailand
phone: 001-66-2-234-7521

Oh Mama, Rama is the Thai that binds the wholesale gems, jewelry, Thai silks, silverware, bronzeware, leather goods, and other local products will help you "Thai one on." Princess rings, diamond rings, and ruby and sapphire rings are their mainstays. Make your choice from hundreds of new and exquisite designs in jewelry. They can create your own exclusive design from a picture, sketch, or description. There is a $100 minimum order in U.S. dollars and mail orders are welcome. Deliveries usually take one to two weeks if sent air mail, and about two months for sea mail. **C, PQ**

R/E KANE ENTERPRISES
15 W. 47th St. #401
New York, NY 10036
(212) 869-5525
CK

More than a good citizen, Kane is a good entrepreneur as well. While you likely won't find her muttering "rosebud" on her deathbed, you may, if you listen closely, hear the words "Cubic Zirconia" pass from her lips. This company delivers Cubic Zirconia for $10 per diamond carat, compared to $85 elsewhere. A round CZ was $10 per diamond carat and $30 for a marquise cut. **PQ (SASE)**

RENNIE ELLEN
15 W. 47th St. #401
New York, NY 10036
(212) 869-5525
CK

If, as Frank Sinatra sings, New York's a city that doesn't sleep, does it follow that this jeweler rocks around the clock? (To quote Bill Haley.) You'll have to find out for yourself—we forgot to ask. But enough of our glittering comedic gems! We left no stone unturned in a fruitful search for bargain diamonds in the Big Apple. Happily, we found Rennie Ellen in the perfect setting. As a consumer advocate and one of the few women in the industry, Rennie's wholesale diamond cutting business will polish up to 75% off the price of all jewelry items. Her 12-page catalog offers pendants, necklaces, bracelets, and chains sparkling with sapphires, rubies, and amethyst stones. There is a money-back guarantee, most orders are delivered in 10 to 15 days. **C $2**

SAMARTH GEM STONES
P.O. Box 6057
Colaba, Bombay 400 005
India
213512
CK, IMO, BANK DRAFT

Since 1965, Samarth has been exporting and manufacturing gemstones at savings of 30% to 75%. To simplify the multitude of inquiries, Samarth has grouped the gemstones in the following ways, but all require the same minimum purchase ($50): Group 1: 12 perfect round ready-to-wear 16-inch genuine carnelian, bloodstone, jasper, agate, White Agate, Black Agate, Crystal Quartz, Rose Quartz, green, pink, blue Aventurine, moss Agate for necklaces—$50, air mail prepaid. Group 2: Six perfect round ready-to-wear 16-inch genuine amethyst, garnet, tigereye, Smokey Quartz, Moonstone, Golden Citrine stones for necklaces—$50, air mail prepaid. Group 3: Chuck (Tumbled) shape, ready-to-wear 16-inch genuine amethyst, garnet, tigereye, lapis lazuli, turquoise, peridot, emerald, multicolor turmuline, aquamarine, multicolor onyx, goldstone, citrine for necklaces—$50, air mail prepaid. Group 4: Cut gemstones of round, oval, emerald, octagon, pear shapes from sizes 1 to 5 carats. Full set of 12 amethyst, aquamarine, peridot, garnet, iolite, golden citrine, lapis lazuli, smokey quartz, Indian Star ruby, moonstone, diopside, enstatite gemstones—$50 air mail prepaid. Group 5: Precious genuine stones—ruby, emerald, and sapphire—three stones of different shapes, ring size 1 to 2 carats—$50, air mail prepaid. **C $1** (refundable)

THE SWISS KONNECTION
5330 Alpha Road, Suite 300
Dallas, TX 75240
(214) 233-0627
CK, MC, V, AE, COD

See entry page 57.

VANITY FAIR (also S.A. PECK & CO.)
55 E. Washington St.
Chicago, IL 60602
(800) 235-3000
(312) 977-0300: IL residents call collect
CK, MC, V, AE, DC

Since 1921, S.A. Peck has been specializing in jewelry design and diamonds. Because they import and manufacture fine jewelry and eliminate the middleman's profit, they offer savings from 35% to 50%. Their merchandise is top-quality and priced perfectly. For example, a modern octagon-shaped GRUEN 18K goldtone Swiss quartz, ultra-thin calendar watch sold for $115, compared to $318 elsewhere. Most items are in this price range. Their 30-day money back guarantee is underwritten by Lloyds of London. They also offer the free service of inspecting and ultrasonically cleaning your jewelry for you. An appraisal is included with all diamond purchases. C

VAN MOPPES DIAMONDS
Albert Cuypstraat 2-6
1072 CT
Amsterdam, Holland
(20) 761242
MC, V, AE, DC

In today's world of inflated diamond prices, you don't have to stick your finger in a dike to get lower prices. Just let your fingers do the walking and give Van Moppes a call. They will be happy to send you their catalog containing selections of 400 designs from their collection of over 2,000 models of jewelry. They have been in business since 1828—longer than Holland has had dikes. This is Amsterdam's most famous diamond factory. Mr. Arnold J. Van Moppes represents the eighth generation in this family business. All of their items are made with 18 carat gold. Their stones are cut with the world-famous Amsterdam cut—a cut above the rest. This family has eliminated the costly middleman to give you the lowest possible prices. These precious diamonds took thousands of years to be created and cannot possibly be described with words. They must be seen to be appreciated. Before you buy a gem for your hand, check prices with this man from tulip land. C $5 (refundable if purchase is made)

VAN PLER & TISSANY
465 S. Beverly Drive
Beverly Hills, CA 90212
(800) 2KARATS
(213) 551-1055
CK, MC, V, AE, DC, CB

There's bargains in them thar' (Beverly) hills! The savings in this catalog were a real gem—such as a 1K Van Pler simulated diamond for only $25. Finely crafted stones were a sensational look-alike for less. Diamonds, emeralds, rubies, and sapphires could be purchased mounted or unmounted in 14K gold or sterling silver. Dazzling displays of jewelry for both men and women at a counterfeit cost let even the most budget-conscious buyers bathe in jewels for a bargain. Unusual settings made shopping here better than buying the real thing! Exotic ivory, noble-looking gold nuggets, and perfect pearls are sure to please the most distinctive jewelry tastes. A 15-day refund policy was offered on jewelry; 30 days on unmounted gems. A lifetime guarantee on the luscious look-alikes and one year on material and workmanship made the transaction more tempting. Unmounted gems were shipped within four working days, jewelry in one to four weeks. A $2 to $3 shipping and handling fee is added to orders. The 24-page catalog was a virtual goldmine! **C**

Kits and Kaboodle

Remember that first do-it-yourself project? You were five, and you used half a paper plate and some crayons to make a gift for your mother, and she thought that it was the most beautiful paper plate-half in the world. You're probably more skillful when it comes to working with paper, crayons, and paint—not to mention wood, cloth, and metal—by now. At least we hope so! (Come to think of it, maybe it's time you made another gift for Mom.) Do-it-yourself projects have come a long way from primitive designs made on paper plates with broken crayons. You can build a grandfather clock or a baby's cradle; assemble a greenhouse; ferment some wine; repair an antique trunk; construct a computer; wire a stereo; or even build a three bedroom house, or a live-aboard boat. All it takes is time, determination, and knowing where to buy your supplies.

THE BARTLEY COLLECTION
Dept. US
3 Airpark Drive
Easton, MD 21601
(301) 820-7722
(800) BARTLEY
CK, MC, V

You take the lowboy and I'll take the highboy from this elegantly photographed catalog of 18th-century antique furniture reproduction kits. These gleaming wood furniture pieces will hold candles, brandy, or the White House china (in reproduction of course), or even your collection of murder mysteries. All kits are complete and include solid brass hardware, all finishing materials, stains and varnish, and complete instructions. There's even a form included for replacement of possibly missing pieces. All kits can be ordered finished or unfinished. Bartley's 16-page catalogs come out eight times per year and each catalog contains a selection of new kits. Refund and exchange privileges extend for 30 days for items returned in their original condition; missing, defective, and freight-damaged parts will be replaced at no charge during the same period. You should receive your order in about 10 days. **C**

BREWMASTER
162 Steam Mill Road
Odessa, NY 14869
(607) 594-3743
CK

Ale, ale, the gang's all here! Is this for you? Of Coors it is! Serious and recreational beer guzzlers nip beer prices in the Bud with their very own Brewmaster beer-making kit. We've known men who became Hamm's after just one taste. (There's many a sip 'twixt cup and lip!) Besides beer-making supplies, we heard through the grapevine that they carry all of the better winemaking supplies, too. A random sampling of items for sale included: Canadian Ale Kit (12 gallons) $13.95; light beer kit (5 gallons) $11.95; Old English Stout Kit (6.5 gallons) $13.95 along with malts, hops, and yeast. The savings are from 40% to 50% below standard prices on these unique delicious homemade brews. These Premium brews from imported hops create an alcohol content of over 5%. Tool kits are available. They also carry New Super Wine Kits that take three weeks to make delicious wine, either red, pink, or white, only $19.95. If you appreciate champagne, you can fizzle the white wine into 25 bottles of old bubbly easily. Orders are shipped via UPS every two days and are subject to a basic $2 handling charge. Customers who order and mention *The Underground Shopper* will receive a 10% discount. Send for a private copy of the "Yankee Bubbler" listing. **B**

BURRO
Dept. US
6885 Boudin St., N.E.
Prior Lake, MN 55372
(800) 328-3592
(612) 447-1090: MN residents call collect
CK, MC, V

If you load up a Burro with all your vacation supplies, you won't have to make a jackass out of yourself. This lightweight, durable trailer costs less to tow than its heavier relative and it can be led by hand. A day or two of assembling will put this beast of burden in working order, and if you're not in the mood to burro-w through the parts yourself, company people will offer a bray of hope by assembling it for you at a reasonable price. The basic kit started at $2,596, and that's a direct-from-factory, wholesale price. Orders are usually delivered in about three weeks, although this can vary depending on the time of year. **B $3**

CANE & BASKET SUPPLY CO.
Dept. US
1283 S. Cochran Ave.
Los Angeles, CA 90019
(213) 939-9644
CK, MC, V, AE, DC, CB

In a Testament to the Genesis of evil, Cane was Able to weave himself a tale of woe. Fortunately, you won't become a basket case if you make the right sacrifices and stay out of trouble. Boasting "the largest selection of caning and basket supplies in the world," these folks can give advice in hand-weaving chair seats, choosing the appropriate tools and materials, or selecting oils and varnishes for the right finishing touches. (And that's the unvarnished truth!) Prices are 20% to 40% lower than you'll find in craft stores carrying similar products. C&B also sells complete kits of woods and weavings for footstools and chairs, for those who want to keep their idle hands busy in their own and not the Devil's workshop. Returns are accepted with no questions asked. Shipping's the same day. Check out their 20-page catalog. **C $1**

CHERRY TREE TOYS, INC.
P.O. Box 369
Belmont, OH 43718
(614) 484-4363
CK, MC, V, COD

See entry page 257.

CLOTHKITS
24 High St., LEWES
E. Sussex BN7 2LB
England
(0273) 477111
MC, V, Sterling Cheques, Sterling Postal/Money Orders, Euro-Cheques made out in Sterling, Access, Eurocard

See entry page 22.

COLONIAL WOODCRAFT
Dept. US
11229 Reading Road
Cincinnati, OH 45241
(513) 563-6666
CK, MC, V, COD (with $2.50 service charge)

We cannot tell a lie. Colonial is following in the footsteps of ol' George Washington. They've taken their hatchets and have cut down and chopped up a forest of black, wild cherry trees for you to assemble and polish into rockers, tilt-top tables, washstands, desks, quilt racks, cheval mirrors, butler tea carts, and beautifully detailed cribs. About 60 different items are carried. A Shenandoah rocker was $169.95 ($8.25 shipping) in kit form, but would retail for $500 if bought assembled at a store. In-stock items are shipped out within 24 hours, most often by UPS. **C, PQ**

CONSTANTINE'S
2050 Eastchester Road
Bronx, NY 10461
(800) 223-8087
(800) 822-1202: NY residents
CK, MC, V, AE, COD

Constantine's claim is "everything for better woodworking" and who would disagree? This 170-plus-year-old company offers kits, materials, tools, and books for everything from backgammon table tops to dollhouse miniatures. With Constantine's supplies you can build a ship model or guitar, or make a cabinet or clock. Inlays, overlays, cane and rush supplies, whatever your pleasure, their 107-page catalog's probably got something to assemble. Prices aren't discounted, but they are competitive: Constantine's merchandise qualifies as hard-to-find items. Their library is as extensive as their selection of specialty tools. There's a $15 minimum order with charge card; a $10 minimum with cash. They stand behind everything they sell, and will give full refunds or exchange if you're not satisfied. Orders are usually delivered in seven to 10 days. **C $1**

E. C. KRAUS
Dept. US
Wine & Beer Making Supplies
9001 E. 24 Highway (Winner Road)
P.O. Box 7850
Independence, MO 64053
(816) 254-7448
MC, V, COD

Destill, my art! A loaf of bread, a jug of watermelon wine, and thou art on the way to enjoying the fermented fruits, flowers, and vegetables of thy labors. Kraus's 16-page illustrated catalog features a library of information, plus a large supply of yeasts, extracts, equipment, and accessories for beer and wine private production. Fruit juices and additives for making wine are their biggest selling items. There is no charge for shipping, satisfaction is guaranteed, and delivery is usually in about a week. No restocking charge on returns, either. If you identify yourself as an *Underground Shopper* reader and request one of their free catalogs, they'll include a coupon for a free wine-making recipe book good with your first purchase of $5 or more. Such a deal! All you need to supply is the women (or men) and song. **C**

EMPEROR CLOCK CO.
Emperor Industrial Park
Fairhope, AL 36532
(205) 928-2316
CK, MC, V, DC

Look at the Emperor's new clocks from the world's largest manufacturer of grandfather clocks. It's no wonder—they sell grandfather clock kits at factory direct prices from $264 to $589 (retail $800 to $1,500). Clock movements are included. (What's a grandfather clock without its pacemaker?) They also have wall clocks in cherry, walnut, and other fine woods. If you're not a handyperson, you can buy the clocks assembled. You'll still save a bundle over retail prices, and you'll save time. Emperor also carries butler tables, chests, and gun cabinet kits. Complete instructions, screws, and hardware are included. Expect your order to arrive in two to four weeks. Movements are warranted for three years; there are 30-day return privileges. **C $1, PQ**

FOUR SEASONS GREENHOUSES
5005 Veterans Memorial Highway
Holbrook, NY 11741
(516) 563-4000
MC, V

This company's greenhouses have been used for many special projects and solar demonstrations, including the Department of Energy's demonstration house at Brookhaven National Laboratory. Their 40-page free catalog provides extensive information, accompanied by excellent photography of the many types of maintenance-free features and accessories that are available. Color charts, diagrams, and other catalog features give facts and figures that can help you make a decision, whether it be for your home or business. Greenhouses range in price from $2,500 to $50,000 (that's a lot of the green stuff!), and delivery usually takes about three to four weeks. **C**

FROSTLINE KITS
2501 Frostline Ave.
Grand Junction, CO 81505
(303) 241-0155
CK, MC, V, AE

Baby bunting and clothes for hunting: saddlebags for mopeds; backpacks for dogs; robes and booties for humans; comforters and tents;

even a do-it-yourself (imitation) bear rug are among Frostline's wide variety of sew-it-yourself outdoor clothing and equipment. Mountain parkas and bike gears are Frostline's biggest selling items. Delivery usually takes about three to four weeks. There's a six-month refund period and they'll exchange in the case of faulty materials. That should take the chill off. **C**

GERRY SHARP, TRUNK DOCTOR
Dept. US
P.O. Box 380511
San Antonio, TX 78280
(512) 695-9437
CK

Mrs. Sharp not only repairs and restores trunks, but she's into trunks like no one else. She's been working on antique trunks since 1968 and has done more than 205 custom jobs. She writes and publishes *Trunk Trix* and *Trunk Tray Trix*, both filled with encyclopedic data on the history and repair of just about any type of trunk. If your Pandora's box is getting a little creaky in the joints, she has leather dyes, straps, hinges, brass nails, slotted handles, drawbolts, corners, ball bearing casters, and various closures for antique trunk restorers. Her bimonthly newsletter is free. "Trix" how-to manuals are $5 each and well worth it. This 5-foot 2-inch lady is a real jewel. You'll save about 10% on the price of trunk hardware and leather on orders over $35. Shipping usually takes about two weeks through the Post Office. Mention *The Underground Shopper* and you'll get $1 credit on hardware or leather. **B (SASE)**

GETTINGER FEATHER CORP.
16 W. 36th St.
New York, NY 10018
(212) 695-9470
CK

Boa, oh boa, we feathered our nest for chicken feed! Not only that, we got ostrich, marabou, turkey, and peacock feathers which tickled our fancy and can be used in all crafts. Pheasant tails were $13 per 100. Your hats will welcome the many styles of feathers available from this company. Our sample packet included a bright green "fashion" feather as well as some beautiful black speckled plumage. Send $1.75 for your own samples without feather delay. **B $1.75**

GO CART
Dept. US
P.O. Box 405
Elkhorn, NE 68022
(402) 289-3994
CK, MC, V, AE

Wheels of fortune? Well, probably not, but you *can* save 20% on a go-cart kit complete with a welded frame, three-horsepower engine, clutch, and chain. Or order a la cart without the engine, $179.95 (retail $239.95). They also make fiberglass mini-cars. Orders are shipped direct from the factory and usually take two weeks to arrive. Their catalog costs $3. **C $3**

GOLF DAY PRODUCTS, INC.
Dept. US
3015 Commercial Ave.
Northbrook, IL 60062
(312) 498-1400
CK, MC, V, AE

Join the club of savvy swingers who repair their own golf clubs. You can save up to $40 on each set of 14 new golf grips, according to the company's 48-page, full-color, repair manual/catalog. That's about 60% savings when compared to a pro shop. $36 savings are possible on refinishing three woods. Unused returned items are accepted for exchange within 45 days. If you're like most folks, you'll get your order in about 10 days. *Underground Shoppers* who come clean and reveal their true identity will get their $2 catalog free. **C $2**

THE GREEN PEPPER
941 Olive St.
Eugene, OR 97401
(503) 345-6665
CK, MC, V, COD

I'm a pepper, you're a pepper, but these folks are Green Peppers (and when you're hot, you're hot!). Buy the patterns alone or the complete kits to make colorful, fashionable clothes for camping, galloping, pedaling, crossing the country, or schussing down the slopes. This company specializes in active sportswear patterns, fabrics and notions in brands like GREEN PEPPER, GORE-TEX, KLIMATE, THINSU-

LATE, and DACRON II HOLOFILL. Hard-to-find fabric for rainproof/ waterproof clothing is their best-selling item. Prices reflect 50% or more savings over comparable ready-mades. We saw patterns for vests, jackets, parkas, ski suits, running suits, as well as book bags, saddle bags, and cargo bags all designated by asterisks to denote the degree of sewing difficulty. Fabrics and notions needed for each pattern are also included in their catalog. They also provide "precut kits" as an educational service to junior and senior high school home economics teachers. Novice to experienced sewers can find something in this 20-page slick, black-and-white photographed catalog. There is no minimum order or restocking charge, and refunds or exchanges are made on merchandise returned in its original condition. Wouldn't you like to be a Pepper, too? **C $1**

GREEN RIVER TRADING CO.
Boston Corners Road
R.D. 2, Box 130
Millerton, NY 12546
(518) 789-3311
CK, COD

See entry page 72.

H. DECOVNICK & SON
1975 Diamond Blvd.
Concord, CA 94520
(415) 837-1244
CK, MC, V, AE, COD

H. DeCovnick & Son stops time in its flight. Your savings won't be fleeting, either. Grandfather clocks are the big sellers here—they can drop ship clocks from such manufacturers as RIDGEWAY, SLIGH BALDWIN, FANCHER, TREND, HOWARD MILLER, and PEARL CLOCKS. Grandfather clocks aren't the only thing for sale: they've also got spare parts for major German manufactured movements. Oils, wood fillers, and polish are also available. Discounts are about 15% off retail. Numerals and pendulums swing out the savings when you mark your own time, too. Most orders are delivered in about three weeks; no restocking charges on returns. If you buy a grandfather clock here, don't forget to tell them you're an *Underground Shopper* reader. They'll engrave your monogram on the pendulum bob of your new purchase absolutely free. **PQ**

HEATHKIT ELECTRONIC CENTER
6825A Green Oaks Road
Fort Worth, TX 76116
(817) 737-8822
CK, MC, V

There's not a room anywhere in your castle that wouldn't benefit from a project from this grand old name in home kit electronics. Solar water heaters, weather indicators, desk computers, metal locators, doorbells, air cleaners, chess challengers, clocks, cradles, radios, and television sets are just a few of the possibilities we found in their 104-page catalog. They have everything from an incredibly accurate atomic clock to an (intelligent!) atomic thermostat. Easy-to-build equipment kits are also available for computers, televisions (ZENITH SYSTEM IIIs with remote control), automotive items, marine test instruments, furniture, stereo, ham radio, and weather equipment. They even offer home study courses. Prices generally range from 30% to 40% lower than retail and they have a complete inventory of replacement parts and repair facilities. There's a liberal return policy; a restocking charge is levied only when a kit has been opened and extensive repacking is required. Parts are guaranteed for 90 days. **C, PQ**

HERITAGE CLOCK CO.
Heritage Industrial Park
Drawer 1577
Lexington, NC 27293
(704) 956-2113
MC, V, AE, DC

When the grandfather clock goes "bong, bong, bong" you know it's high time to check out Heritage. This company carries some very handsome oak, cherry, and walnut grandfather clock kits. Do-it-yourself kits (those without movements) were timeless bargains at $339.50 to $699.50. Solid brass West German movements sold for $234.50 to $1,474.50. If you don't have the time to build a clock yourself, you can buy one fully assembled beginning at $682. They also handle wall clock kits: one kit was $184.50; its already finished counterpart was $319.50. Or you can wind up with their carriage clocks, cuckoo clocks, ship's clocks, anniversary clocks, barometer clocks, Italian import clocks, tambour clocks, and everyday alarm clocks. Finally, when it's time to go to bed, try one of their Heritage brass beds. There's a $5 minimum order, an approximate three-week shipping time; a 30-day refund period; 15% restocking charge. All clock cases and movements are guaranteed for a two-year period. **B**

HERRSCHNERS INC.
Hoover Road
Stevens Point, WI 54481
(715) 341-0604
CK, MC, V, AE

Herrsch-a-buy, herrsch-a-buy, little baby. And rest assured that the selection of handcraft kits for little ones is tremendous. Baby afghans, bibs, mobiles, towels, buntings, sweater sets, and quilts can be made from easy-to-use kits. That's not all—lacy Victorian blouses, pillows, sachets, even garters and hankies can be fashioned. Afghans are the biggest seller at Herrschners if one considers the number of pages devoted to them. Embroidered tablecloths are well-represented. Quilts are too. Christmas ornaments, dolls, latch rugs, and needlepoint kits make this catalog worth ordering. **C**

HOLLYWOOD FANCY FEATHER CO.
Room 807
220 W. 5th St.
Los Angeles, CA 90013
(213) 625-8453 or 625-2883
COD

This is no fly-by-night operation. Birds of a feather, as well as Disneyland execs and movie moguls searching for costume and set design materials, flock here for their wardrobes. (They didn't name names for us—perhaps their customers were shopping under a nom de plume!) Hollywood sells fancy feathers: pheasant, ostrich, guinea hen, turkey, and others. Discounts are about 30% off what others charge. Get your head out of the sand and take flight with ostrich feathers at $6 to $12 per dozen; there are over a dozen colors to choose from including turquoise, gold, and burgundy. That's fit for a peacock! You won't feel fowl parading in your plumage and strutting in your exotic pheasant skins ($12 to $20 per skin) while draped in marabou boas. There's a $50 minimum order, and about a week passes before your order will arrive, so don't get your hackles up. **PQ**

HUDSON GLASS CO. INC.
219 N. Division St.
Peekskill, NY 10566
(800) 431-2964
(914) 737-2124
CK, MC, V, D

If you can't have breakfast at Tiffany's, have breakfast under one. "The Source" catalog from Hudson Glass Co. featured three pages of patterns for Tiffany-style lamps you make yourself. If you don't think that's impressive, the rest of the thick catalog had patterns for stained glass windows, mirrors, boxtops, hangings, and lamp bases. Besides books and patterns, we found 15 types of glass plus tools, hardware, and forms for projects of any level of proficiency. No longer is buying your stained glass-making supplies going to be a pane in the pocketbook. **C $3 (refundable)**

IDENT-IFY LABEL CORP.
P.O. Box 204
Brooklyn, NY 11214-0204
No phone
CK

Crafters will find personalized labels to sew into their gifts available from this mail-order company. Printed in red and black on durable white cotton, the labels are 2½-inch by 1⅛-inch with pinked edges. Forty labels cost $5.75, 100 cost $9.75. Twelve styles are available. Allow two to three weeks for delivery. Campers will find a less expensive tape which can be sewn onto everything. **B**

KUEMPEL CHIME CLOCK WORKS
Dept. US
21195 Minnetonka Blvd.
Excelsior, MN 55331
(612) 474-6177
CK

These grandfather clock kits are made by real grandfathers! Their 22-page, full-color catalog: a) introduces you to the little old clockmakers who create the clocks; b) tells you how the business began; and c) offers accolades and testimonials from satisfied customers. You can buy just the clock plans, just the moulding packages, or an entire kit containing all case pieces. A selection of melodic clockworks is sold separately. If time flies when you're having fun, a project from Kuempel should speed you on your fun-filled way. Catalog is FREE to *Underground Shopper* readers! **C $2**

LUGER BOATS
P.O. Box 1398
St. Joseph, MO 64502
(816) 233-5116
CK

All hands on deck? No way, Jose: the decks and hulls are finished, and all you have to do is install the interiors in these molded fiberglass wake-makers. (We always preferred indoor sports, anyway.) Luger features live-aboard boats, seaworthy surfriders, sailboats, and sport fishing models in their 48-page catalog. An 11-foot model sported a base price of $2,000. Shipping takes about two to six weeks. **C**

MILAN LABORATORY
57 Spring St.
New York, NY 10012
(212) 226-4780
CK, COD

Discover the secrets of Forbidden Fruit, Roman Punch, and other magical nectars of the gods by concocting them in the confines of your own kitchen. Milan is a complete headquarters for beer-bellied brewers and bibulous imbibers of wines and spirits. They have chemicals, extracts, preservatives, barrels, corks, and a host of other supplies to make your alcoholic elixir-making easier. Their $3 catalog (refundable if your order exceeds $50) devotes a whole page to extracts to mix with alcohol, sugar, and water to make instant (and discounted) liqueurs and cordials. Discounts fermented at 50%: the brands were Milan's own. There's even a wine doctor in the house who can diagnose errant brews, mismixed batches, and lifeless spirits. **C $3**

MILES HOMES
P.O. Box 9495
4700 Nathan Lane
Minneapolis, MN 55440
(800) 328-3380
(800) 642-3200: MN residents

Miles to go before you sleep in one of these ranch-style, split-level, one and one-half, and two-story houses. The Miles people specialize in making your impossible dream of home ownership a four-walled reality. Their designs are modern and simple, but solid and homey-looking. Homes are available with decks and vaulted ceilings—some have separate dining rooms. Of course, the homes are precut and build-it-yourself. One of their biggest selling points is that there's no money down and the homes are financed at below market rates. You need good credit and a lot. Miles has 16 national sales offices and five distribution points, plus design centers and model homes. **C**

PYRAMID PRODUCTS
Dept. US
3736 S. Seventh Ave.
Phoenix, AZ 85041
(602) 276-5365

With a Pyramid foundry set, mechanics, hobbyists, artists, inventors, jewelers, and sculptors can make metal castings for models or model parts, figurines, plaques, and jewelry. Precious metal miners can use the Pyramid Furnace for smelting ore. Their furnaces provide the Pyramid power of temperatures up to 2,400°F for melting iron, bronze, aluminum, copper, gold, white metal, and silver. Casting supplies are also available, as you'll see if you check out their 12-page catalog. **C**

ROLLERWALL, INC.
Dept. US
P.O. Box 757
Silver Spring, MD 20901
(301) 589-5516
CK, MC, V

What do you get when you cross a wallpaper pattern with a paint roller? ROLLERWALL, of course! This company claims you don't need any talent (hey, that's us!) and they guarantee "delightful results." Lots of different designs enable users to apply paint on plain walls in intricate designs. Their introductory offer was a "four rollers for the price of three" deal. Four to six weeks is the usual delivery time, there's a 30-day refund or exchange policy, and shipping charges are $3. Some of their letters from satisfied customers are from set designers and hotel owners. **C**

ST. CROIX KITS
423-U S. Main St.
Stillwater, MN 55082
(800) 328-6795, ext. 386
(612) 439-9120
CK, MC, V, AE, COD

Has the high cost of beautiful musical instruments been a cross to bear? Then St. Croix's should bring heavenly music to your ears. They offer a cathedral of 25 different acoustical instruments for you to construct from kits. You can bring the hills alive with the sound of music by constructing a guitar for only $89.95. After it's finished, it would be worth $250. A Mountain Banjo kit was only $129.95, and a mandolin was only $239.95. At these prices, you should be picking and grinning. With a little patience and time, you could build a beautiful gothic harp which, for the price of $399.95, would be worth $995 when finished. That's something to harp about. The company carries a variety of useful kits that could save you a kit and kaboodle—porch swings, hanging chairs, wooden trains, airplanes, kitchen knives, and more. If you decide you can't quite get it together, just return your unfinished kit for a full refund. Make yourself a deal with St. Croix. **C $1 (refundable)**

TEXAS GREENHOUSE CO.
2731 St. Louis Ave.
Fort Worth, TX 76110
(817) 926-5447
CK, MC, V, COD

Red-faced over greenhouse prices? There is no reason to be hotheaded over hothouses with Texas Greenhouse kits. (When you build your own greenhouse, only your plants will get steamed.) Since 1948, this company has manufactured their own greenhouses and accessories so their prices are factory direct. About 15 to 20 brands are carried, including MODINE heaters and CHAMPION coolers. Prices are competitive. Most orders come in six to eight weeks; there is a one-year guarantee; a 15% restocking charge on returns. You'll have to put down a 50% deposit with your order, balance due on delivery. *Underground Shopper* readers get an extra 5% discount so don't be shy about who you are! C

THE TOYMAKER SUPPLY CO.
105 Weiler Road
Arlington Heights, IL 60005
(800) 624-3938
(800) 358-4208: IL residents
CK, MC, V

In this case, the toymaker is you, Mom or Dad. This company sells patterns for a variety of toys including wooden animals, jigsaw puzzles, trains, cars, and rocking horses. If you know your way around a hammer and handsaw, you can build these inexpensive toys in a few hours. Your kids may get such a kick out of what you're doing that they'll want to help (for which there is another catalog).
C $1 each

TRI-STEEL STRUCTURES, INC.
1400 Crescent
Denton, TX 76201
(817) 566-7081: customer service
(817) 566-1386: sales
(817) 566-3000: building sales
CK

Anyone afraid of having their house blown down by a hurricane should try steel. According to Tri-Steel Structures, the nation's largest designer and manufacturer of steel frame homes, steel frames allow quicker erection at a lower cost than conventional wood frame homes. High-strength hurricanes are unable to knock steel structures down. They claim that energy savings of up to 60% can be realized and that you don't have to maintain the exterior because of the lifetime guarantee on Alcoa aluminum siding. Tri-Steel homes are shipped to the erection site on trucks where the owner or builder either can do the work himself or contract to have it done. You can purchase the home in shell form from Tri-Steel for about $10 per square foot and finish the home for a total of only $25 to $35 per square foot depending on custom touches and local costs. **B**

TURN-O-CARVE TOOL CO.
P.O. Box 8315
Tampa, FL 33674-8315
(813) 933-2730
CK

The only original lathe top wood-turning duplicators sold worldwide for over 35 years. Make pro-like duplicate turnings easy and fast on almost any lathe. Make money at home full- or part-time like thousands of others. Make spindles, knobs, trays, lamp bases, ball bats, fishing rod handles, and much more. Design original turnings on flat templates and make duplicates of same in any amount desired. Sell your products to stores, hobby shows, flea markets, church groups, etc. The market is limitless. **B $1** (refundable with first order)

VIKING CLOCK DIVISION
The Viking Building, Box 490
Foley, AL 36536
(800) 321-1089
(205) 943-5081
CK, V, AE, DC

It's easy to tell what makes Viking tick—a collection of several hundred clock kits ranging from grandfather-size to wall-mounted and mantelpiece models. Their Model 900 Grandfather Clock is their most popular offering. Prices, while not discount, are competitive, and they're certainly lower than they'd be for a fully assembled, non-kit clock. They'll refund on returns for 30 days; no restocking charges. Please call their toll-free number for more information. **C**

WILDERNESS LOG HOMES
Rural Route 2, U.S. 85
Plymouth, WI 53073
(800) 237-8564 (Spell: 800-BEST LOG)
(800) 852-5647: WI residents
CK, MC, V, COD (on house with 50% down)

Want your kids to grow up to be president? Raise them right—in a log cabin! Wilderness Log Homes provide just what their name says, but their dwellings are not the rough-hewn, thatch-as-thatch-can variety. The logs are hand-crafted and (would you believe it?) custom-designed. Homes have a woodsy charm and blend in well with their environment provided you don't erect one in midtown Manhattan! They're available with up to five bedrooms, cathedral ceilings, studies, dining rooms, and almost as much elbow room as the great outdoors. Their most popular model is the "Cumberland," a 1,700-square-foot cabin with two porches and cathedral ceilings. Those favoring modern comforts and energy efficiency will be interested in their "Insulog Kits" in which the logs have been split and filled with insulation and the interior finished with sheetrock. These units have ceilings with an R-value of 40 and side walls are R-30. Prices are good when compared with others in the same business, not surprising as they own their own mill. Kits are shipped on flatbed trucks, and usually go out about four weeks after you place your order. *Underground Shoppers* can get $1 off on their catalog. **C $6**

Medical Products and Supplies

The next time your doctor writes you a long-term prescription, don't rush to the corner drugstore to have it filled. Send it to a prescription service! You can save as much as an additional 60% over their discounted prices, for example, by substituting generic compounds for brand-name drugs. Whether you're buying a prosthesis, juice extractor, contact lens or hearing aid, compare prices before you buy and be specific about your requirements and shop by mail!

AMERICAN HEALTH SERVICE, INC.
1413-G Golf Road
Waukegan, IL 60087
(312) 662-4707
CK, MC, V

Eh, what's that? WE SAID WE'LL WAX ELOQUENT over the earful of savings available here, so listen up and we won't have to drum it in. AHS has got names in hearing aids and health care products we've all heard before, and at savings of 30% to 60% off. You'll get good vibrations from hearing aids by AUDIOTONE, BOSCH, DAHLBERG, DANAVOX, ELECTONE, FIDELITY, FINETONE, MAICO, OTICON, PHILLIPS, PHONIC EAR, QUALITONE, RADIOEAR, RION, SIEMENS, TELEX, UNITRON, and other top brands at unheard of savings. Replacement hearing aids are a specialty, so obtain your first one from a local dealer, and then maintain your financial equilibrium by getting a replacement through the mail. All hearing aids come with the manufacturer's warranty and satisfaction is guaranteed. There's a 30-day unconditional return policy. Orders under $10 are billed $1.25 for postage and handling. Tune in to a good pick-up—our experience shows AHS ships promptly and conscientiously. *Underground Shopper* readers qualify for an additional 10% off the prices listed in their 32-page catalog. Remember, you heard it hear first. **C**

AMERICA'S PHARMACY SERVICE, INC.
P.O. Box 10490
Des Moines, IA 50306
(800) 247-1003
(515) 287-6872
CK, MC, V

One of the largest mail-order pharmacies in the country (they stock over 10,000 prescription and non-prescription items), America's Pharmacy expresses the sentiment that "you can save more money by buying generic vitamins and prescriptions instead of higher priced national brands." America's prices on generic alternatives represent savings of 25% to 60% off the cost of advertised brands. Generic equivalents are chemically identical to brand-name products and are approved by the FDA. They also carry vitamins and minerals, A through zinc; aspirin, cold capsules, sleep aids, creams and ointments; even hearing aid batteries and blood pressure kits. All orders are guaranteed to be correct in quantity and strength. Refunds or exchanges are made within 30 days. There is no charge

for shipping via UPS or parcel post, although there *is* a 75-cent handling fee. Check out their 32-page catalog for more information.
C, PQ

BRUCE MEDICAL SUPPLY
411 Waverley Oaks Road
Waltham, MA 02254
(800) 225-8446
(617) 894-6262: MA residents
CK, MC, V, COD

A professional no-pin-stop sphygmomanometer (doesn't exactly roll off the tongue, does it?) may not be your idea of an im-pulse purchase, but at least you can get a blood pressure reading without getting the squeeze put on your wallet, too. This company's 36-page catalog offers a complete line of medical supplies (in such brand names as SQUIBB, HOLLISTER, UNITED, 3M, DANSAL, NV HOPE, AHENDS, COLO-PLAST, BAUSCH & LOMB, MENTOR, DEPENDS, and BARD) at savings of 20% to 60%. Coupons are offered on select items. Heating pads, walking aids, bathroom aids, and a wide range of ostomy products bring medical and monetary relief to those with colostomies, ileostomies, and urostomies. (Ostomy products are what they're best known for.) Bruce gives full refunds within 30 days, 80% refunds between 30 and 60 days, and there's no restocking charge. Credit card orders are shipped out the same day as they're received; orders paid by check are held until the check clears. **C**

CONNEY SAFETY PRODUCTS
3202 Latham Drive
P.O. Box 4190
Madison, WI 53711
(800) 356-9100
(800) 362-9150: WI residents
CK, MC, V, AE

Solving safety problems built this company into a major source for saving money in the workplace or on the home front. Accidents can occur anywhere, and after 40 years in the business, Conney's catalog offers discounts on safety equipment as well as fast service. You can buy first aid supplies at a quantity discount based on your annual first aid dollar purchases, as well as take advantage of the Big Buck Savings throughout this four-color 64-page catalog. You can save up to 50% on Conney brands. Products include safety glasses, dust masks, disposable earplugs (great to block out your teenager's rock music), fire extinguishers, rubber gloves, Band-Aids, Ace bandages, antiseptics, burn remedies, feminine hygiene, and more. **C**

**CONTINENTAL ASSN. OF FUNERAL &
MEMORIAL SOCIETIES**
Dept. US
2001 S St. N.W.
Suite 530
Washington, DC 20009
(202) 745-0634

You don't have to be a dead-icated *Underground Shopper* to avoid a grave mistake on a funeral. There are 160 nonprofit Memorial Societies in the U.S., another 25 in Canada. Most are staffed by volunteers. These folks are committed to "simplicity, dignity, and economy in funeral arrangements." While most members emphasize services with closed caskets and immediate burial (or a memorial service following cremation), you can nail down a traditional American funeral at lower cost with pre-need counseling. Call or write: they'll send a packet that includes a donor's card, list of societies in your area, plus *all* members listed with them. It could help you avoid coffin up your estate in your move from here to the hereafter. **PQ**

CREATIVE HEALTH PRODUCTS
5148 Saddle Ridge Road
Plymouth, MI 48170
(800) 742-4478
(313) 453-5309: MI residents
CK, MO

See entry page 169.

DUK KWONG OPTICAL CENTER
Fourth Floor
27 Cameron Road
Tsimshatsui, Kowloon
Hong Kong
(3) 668019

Their eyes of fashion can be upon you—and you won't have to squint at the prices at this worldwide mail-order source. Eyeglass frames and sunglasses (prescription and non-prescription) come in a range of styles priced from $7 to $67 (CHRISTIAN DIOR). Most averaged around the $20 to $30 range. Also available, safety frames and hard ($45) and soft ($100) contacts ground to your prescription or duplicated from your current lenses. To determine size of glasses, just draw a simple outline of your current frames. Delivery time: 24 to 48 hours after receipt of your order. Additional 10% off for orders of two pairs, 15% off for three pairs or more. $3 per pair, air mail postage charge. **B**

LINGERIE FOR LESS
11075 Erhard
Dallas, TX 75228
(214) 341-9575
CK

This company sells their own SOFT TOUCH BREAST FORM for $42.00 (plus $2.50 postage and handling). We couldn't find one comparable for under $75 anywhere—many are as high as $185. A truly unique product, the breast forms were developed by a physician who specializes in creating prostheses from synthetic gels. The molded gel feels soft and conforms to the body like a natural breast. The breast forms come in seven sizes and fit any type bra. Just state your bra size when ordering. Each breast form comes with a one-year unconditional guarantee. Their lingerie items (in many major brands including VANITY FAIR, VASSARETTE, MAIDENFORM, and PLAYTEX) are 20% to 60% off retail, but are sold in-store only, so local yokels take note. Orders are usually delivered in about two weeks. Exchanges and refunds are given. **PQ**

MAJESTIC DRUG CO., INC.
711 E. 134th St.
Bronx, NY 10454
(212) 292-1310
CK

When you're out on a camping trip and your filling plunks into your cup of coffee, DENTEMP can fill in for a dentist. This filling mix, developed by a dentist, temporarily replaces lost fillings, loose caps, crowns, or inlays so you can keep on talking while the stuff is caulking. A single application costs $3.25. They also carry health and skin care products (which they manufacture) at prices roughly comparable to retail, but you get 10% off on a $25 order. There's a 10% restocking charge on returns and no minimum order. Orders are shipped out within 24 hours; most are received in five to 10 days. **B**

MENDEL WEISS
91 Orchard St.
New York, NY 10002
(212) 925-6815
CK, MC, V, COD (when over $50)

See entry page 52.

THE NATIONAL CONTACT LENS CENTER
Santa Rosa Optometry Center
1188 Montgomery Drive
Santa Rosa, CA 95405
(707) 542-3407
CK, MC, V

Save 40% to 70% on all nationally available brands of soft contact lenses. Paying to see clearly at cost plus $15 (paid only once on as many lenses ordered) is just what the doctor ordered. Great for replacement lenses and not original prescription. You will receive their eight-page brochure describing and listing company policies, price list, order blank, and guarantee in just a few days. Order time— approximately one to two weeks. **C**

PARAGON MEDICAL PRODUCTS
P.O. Box 834068
Richardson, TX 75083
(214) 783-8064
CK

Savings of up to 55% are paramount at Paragon Medical Products. For the senior shopper or handicapped consumer needing exercise, home health care products and appropriate and useful gifts, this place is a godsend. Little items including utensils with extra-large handles, wall-mounted jar openers, and two-handled cups are just a few of the over 1,000 possibilities. A treadmill listing for $3,600 was discounted to $2,995; scales $280/$219/; scooter $2,495/$1,895. Brands like TROTTER, LANCER, PACER, HEALTHOMETER, E & J,

INVACARE all usually have one year warranties. And remember, some of these items may still be tax deductible. **C** (no fee for small C, $1 for large C, up to 500 pages)

RIC CLARK
Dept. US
9530 Langdon Ave.
Sepulveda, CA 91343
(818) 892-6636
CK

You'll grin ear-to-ear to hear of 50% and more savings on nationally advertised brand-name hearing aids. Ric can't mention the manufacturers' names, so he used substitute names in his free catalog. They'll create prescription aids from your audiogram, but they don't make custom ear molds, so you must buy yours locally. An in-the-ear aid that they sell for $239 would cost about $480 retail; their top-of-the-line aid was $289 and would retail for about $900. Although we found no savings on batteries, repair costs averaged $35 compared with $60 elsewhere. A $10 deposit is required—they'll refund it if you're dissatisfied and apply it to the price of your order if you're happy. There's a one-year guarantee and 30-day trial period. Orders are air mailed first-class the same day they're received. Sounds good—particularly when you consider this business was begun 15 years ago as an adjunct to retirement. **C**

RITE-WAY HEARING AID CO.
P.O. Box 59451
Chicago, IL 60659
(312) 539-6620
CK (terms, too)

Hear ye! Hear ye! Are you oppressed by excessive hearing aid prices? Have manufacturers got you by the eustachian tubes? Rise up, one and all, for the days of lib-ear-ation are at hand. Make a price pilgrimage to a land of economic freedom, to a new land of discounts! Rite-Way sells hearing aids the right way—at 50% off! Batteries are 25% off and repairs are about 25% lower than you'll find in the retail Homeland. Brand names include ROYALTONE, DANAVOX, and others occasionally, and all aids are available for a 30-day trial and carry a one-year unconditional guarantee (and a six-month warranty on repairs). They'll send you an impression kit for custom ear molds.

Select from behind-the-ear, all-in-the-ear, eyeglass, and body aids. You've got nothing to lose but your pains (pricewise). **B, PQ**

Musical Instruments

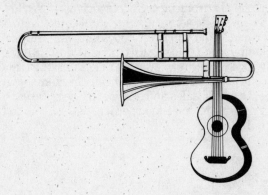

You may have a musical gift, but like a St. Bernard puppy, that's an expensive gift to have. The cost of music lessons, a good quality instrument, and sheet music can really sound a sour note. By careful shopping you can usually get your instrument for less than retail without sacrificing quality. Consult a professional to get advice on what to buy for your skill level, then shop by mail. Most major manufacturers are carried by the companies listed in this section. Some offer group discounts, trade-in policies, and free trial periods. That leaves us with a song in our heart.

A.L.A.S. ACCORDION-O-RAMA
16 W. 19th St.
New York, NY 10011
(212) 675-9089
CK, MC, V

No wonder their competition keeps saying "Alas!" A.L.A.S. squeezes out almost unbeatable savings of 15% to 45% on accordions, concertinas, electronic accordions, and amps. They're known in the industry as "the electronic accordion specialist." While that might not sound impressive to some, it's gotten them on "Late Night With David Letterman," and you can't knock success. They carry all top brands, including EXCELSIOR, PAOLO SOPRANI, HOHNER, CORDOVOX, ELKA, POLYTONE, FARFISA, SCANDALLI, ARPEGGIO, and AVANTI; that's not so surprising since they've been direct importers of musical instruments and in sales and service for over 30 years. There's a 10% restocking charge on returns; orders can take up to two weeks to be delivered. C

CARVIN
1155 Industrial Ave.
Escondida, CA 92025
(800) 854-2235
(800) 542-6070: CA residents
(619) 747-1710
MC, V, COD*

Trivia pursuit: what on earth do Frank Zappa and Roy Clark have in common? (No, not generic quiche or the sound of one wave slapping.) Here's a clue: Jefferson Starship, Rush, and Heart are also strung-in on this deal. Give up? The answer is Carvin, a manufacturer who has drummed up quite a reputation among professional musicians. No one's got the blues over their "X" amps (a hot number in their line of amplifiers), and their electric guitars are good pickin'. Not only are these goodies available at a 40% savings when rated against comparable name-brands, but they offer a 10-day free trial period, and if not satisfied you can return the product with "no strings attached." Delivery is in two weeks. Their 1987 color catalog is 84 pages is far-out and free. *COD only for under 10 pounds or $200. C

FRED'S STRING WAREHOUSE
P.O. Box 225
Shillington, PA 19607
(215) 777-FRED (3733)
CK, MC, V, MO

Don't fret over the high prices of strings today. If you're a guitar, bass, banjo, violin, or any other stringed instrument player, you'll save up to 40% at this warehouse. All items are either shipped directly in the factory carton or inspected thoroughly at the warehouse before packing. Experienced musicians man the phones and can answer most musical questions. MARTIN, MARQUIS, VEGA, GIBSON, D'ADDARIO, LABELLA, ROTO SOUND are just a few names you're likely to hear. C

FREEPORT MUSIC
41-R Shore Drive
Huntington Bay, NY 11743
(516) 549-4108
CK, MC, V, COD (with 25% deposit)

Thar she blows! Moby Dick could have made a euphonious wail playing the instruments listed in this catalog. We don't mind spouting off about the savings here: discounts ranging from 30% to 60% off didn't harpoon our budget. Organs, amplifiers, synthesizers, and every other kind of musical instrument and accessory you need to transform your home into a concert hall or disco is available. We saw a complete piano tuning kit for $39.95, a musical saw with an instruction book for $29.95, and a wireless microphone guitar attachment for $39.95. Harboring brands like LUDWIG, TAMA, GIBSON, IBANEZ, BOSS, FENDER, OVATION, SELMER, KING, BENGE, ARMSTRONG, SIGNET, and RICKENBACKER, this 54-year-old company also offers a complete repair service. Call or write for an estimate. There's a $10 minimum order with cash; $25 with charge. Defective items will be exchanged or repaired at no cost except shipping, but there's a 15% restocking charge on returns. To get on their mailing list and receive semi-monthly fliers for only $1.00, refundable on your first order— their discounted instruments won't set you to blubbering. F

JAZZ AIDS
P.O. Box 1244
New Albany, IN 47150
(812) 945-3142
CK

Established as a leader in the jazz education field for over 20 years,
this company carries about 400 instructional jazz and jazz improvisa-
tion items. They are well-known for selling the PLAY-A-LONG book
and record sets, but their wide range of music and books should keep
you jamming long into the night. For the beginning student or established pro, a romp through this catalog will stir up feelings of desire,
so have your checkbook handy. **C**

MANDOLIN BROS.
629 Forest Ave.
Staten Island, NY 10310
(718) 981-3226
CK, MC, V, AE, COD

If strings are your thing, put the finger on these guys and strum up
some savings. Their 64-page catalog displays electric and acoustic
guitars, banjos, autoharps, and, of course, mandolins at prices that
won't make you fret. They specialize in the "vintage" instrument
(1833 to 1969) but they also carry the finest brands of new instruments. A few of their more notable customers have been Bob Dylan,
Joni Mitchell, Mike Seeger, Stephen Stills, Judy Collins, and Elliot
Easton of The Cars. Discounts are 30% to 40% on brands like GUILD,
C.F. MARTIN, OVATION, SIGMA, GIBSON, YAMAHA, DOBRO guitars;
GIBSON, STELLING, GOLD STAR, WILDWOOD, and WASHBURN banjos;
and GIBSON, FLATIRON, KENTUCKY, and MARTIN & MONTELEONE in
mandolins. Mandolin Bros. is the largest dealer in the world for C.F.
MARTIN guitars and they sell many vintage MARTIN guitars and
GIBSON mandolins. Shipping charges are $20 for customers who live
east of the Rockies; $35 for those who are "far-out" on the West
coast. There's a full guarantee on all items shipped, with a 72-hour
trial privilege. (Customers should phone them during the trial period
if they're dissatisfied and return the instrument by UPS or mail for a
full refund of their purchase price, less shipping charges). A deal like
that shouldn't cause any unpleasant reverberations. **C**

MOGISH STRING COMPANY
34950 Miles Road
Chagrin Falls, OH 44022
(216) 248-9502
CK, MC, V, COD

Nine years and 14,000 customers later, they haven't had one complaint yet. If you prefer not to be strung along any further, then I have to admit I'm bullish on Mogish. Don't fret—almost 50% off the full line of strings for guitars, violins, mandolins, banjos, and basses. Then there's their guitars, violins, and mandolins (electric, classical, and folk). All accessories including picks, straps, signal processing devices, cords, metronomes, tuners, and amplifiers. Incomparable brands: MARTIN, D'ADDARIO, GIBSON, GUILD, GHS, FENDER, CASIO, CREMONA, ARION, and SHURE, for sure. Same day shipment. Write for their free 24-page catalog which gives detailed product description and prices—and you will sing or play their praises forever. C

NATIONAL MUSIC SUPPLY
Dept. US
P.O. Box 14421
St. Petersburg, FL 33733
(813) 823-6666
CK, MC, V

When it comes to musical accessories this company has them coming out the old kazoo! National Music Supply is a national supply house for schools of music as well as a main supply source for professional and student musicians. They offer special boutique items as well as VCR equipment, clocks, and repair tools. The 196-page catalog features over 1,300 items discounted 30% to 60% from retail. While the majority of products are accessories such as microphones and music stands, NMS does carry some instruments. A SELMA BUNDY 1400 clarinet was $167 (retail $349.50); and a BACH STRAD trumpet was $640 (retail $1040). Every conceivable accessory from mouthpieces and ligatures to drumsticks and cymbals is represented at substantial savings. Looking for a xylophone? They have those, too! They offer 15% savings on all music orders from major publishers. They also have a 72-page orchestra catalog for stringed instruments. Both catalogs are free. C

NEMC
Dept. UGS
P.O. Box 1130
Mountainside, NJ 07092
(800) 526-4593
(201) 232-6700: NJ residents
MC, V, AE

At NEMC (National Educational Music Company), you can picc-o-lo priced instrument from a clarinet to a violin. They carry over 900 instruments and prices are up to 50% off the list price. Inflation-fighter offers deserve an additional round of applause. All major manufacturers are represented (ARMSTRONG, SIGNET, and others) and what they don't have in stock, they'll special order. An ARMSTRONG flute that would regularly retail for $369.50 was just $183—small wonder it's their best seller! Your order should come in 10 days to two weeks; there are no restocking charges levied for returned merchandise. If your child is taking music lessons, this is a good place to pick up a horn without blowing a lot of cash. **B**

PLAYER'S MUSIC, U.S.A.
166 W. 48th St.
New York, NY 10036
(212) 869-3870
MC, V, AE

Accord-ion to this dynamic duet, for over 50 years they've been sup-plying up-and-strumming musicians with the instruments of their trade. (And they're no lyres!) They sell new, used, and vintage musi-cal instruments and accessories at 30% to 50% discounts. (There is a variance in price depending on age, use, and instrument quality, but most new instruments are about 40% off.) About 15 different brands are available, including GIBSON, FENDER, and ARIA. Guitars and PA systems are their biggest sellers. Customers usually receive their orders in about two weeks when the merchandise they ordered is in stock. There are no refunds, but Player's Music will replace damaged merchandise. All new merchandise is covered under a one-year war-ranty. There are no strings attached when you write and ask for information, so that won't leave you on a sour note. Player's Music must be doing something right—they've sold to B.B. King, Stewart Copeland of The Police, Pat Metheny, and Steely Dan. **PQ**

P.M.I.
Dept. US
P.O. Box 827
Union City, NJ 07087
(201) 863-2200
Money Order

"When you're looking for that big break, P.M.I. can be instrumental" was their line, not ours. We'll toot their horn, too, for lines of first-quality, professional musical instruments and accessories in over 100 major brands, including GIBSON, ROLAND, FOSTEX, and PRO AUDIO PRODUCTS. Discounts ranged from 30% to 40%. We learned from their 58-page catalog that they are the only mail-order company that deals in custom made and modified guitars. They've done a number of instruments for rock groups. Besides guitars, they have keyboards, brass and woodwind instruments, and multi-recorders. Orders are drop-shipped directly from the manufacturer when P.M.I. gets your order and full payment. Additional freight charges run about 3%. There's a $20 minimum order, 30-day exchange or refund policy, and 15% restocking charge on returns. Free catalog available upon request. **C, B, PQ**

RHYTHM BAND, INC.
Dept. US
P.O. Box 126
1212 E. Lancaster
Fort Worth, TX 76101
(817) 335-2561
CK, MC, V, DC, COD (for preferred customers)

What's a band without Rhythm? This company principally sells to elementary schools, although they do sell to individuals at the same reduced rates. (There's no minimum order.) Prices are about 20% lower than you'll find in retail music stores. Their 48-page, full-color catalog displays rhythm instruments like bells, bongos, castanets, cymbals, drums, glockenspiels, kazoos, maracas, rhythm sticks, ukuleles, and xylophones, but their Chromaharp® (something like a zither) is their most popular item. Everything shown is their own RBI brand. Their catalog also includes music software for APPLE, COMMODORE, and IBM computers. Every purchase must meet with complete customer satisfaction and approval or it can be returned (at Rhythm Band's expense) for a refund or exchange within 90 days.

Orders arrive in about a week. This company set our hearts to pounding (rhythmically). **C**

SAM ASH MUSIC CORP.
Dept. US
124 Fulton Ave.
Hempstead, NY 11550
(800) 4-SAM-ASH
(718) 347-7757: NY residents
CK, MC, V, AE

There's so-nata bagpipe, marimba, or accordion Sam can't lay his hands on! Sam Ash, with its seven stores and over six-million dollar inventory, is trying their darnedest to be the lowest priced, best quality music store in the country. They've got "one of the world's largest inventories of musical instruments, amplification, sound reinforcement, professional audio equipment, sheet music, and accessories." They're not kidding around—they've even got stage lighting and industrial video equipment. Founded in 1924 by prominent New York violinist and bandleader, Sam Ash, the business offers every major name brand in instruments, synthesizers, and sheet music. Synthesizers are their hottest selling item. Prices are excellent, usually 30% to 70% off retail. Triple guarantees are offered on all instruments including original factory guarantee, Sam Ash's guarantee and a guaranteed trade-in policy. There's a $25 minimum order; orders usually are received in about two weeks. They don't have a catalog or brochure because, in their words, they have "too much stuff." **PQ**

SHAR PRODUCTS COMPANY
2465 S. Industrial Highway
P.O. Box 1411
Ann Arbor, MI 48106
(313) 665-7711
CK, MC, V, COD

The family that plays together, stays together. (At least that's the impression the family photo in their catalog gives.) For over 25 years, the Avsharians have stood for selection, service, and low prices (25% lower on instruments and accessories) for folks strung out on stringed instruments. They've got strings, accessories, cases, instruments, and repair supplies at respectable discounts, while

Suzuki materials, books, and reams of sheet music are available at full price. (They don't restrict themselves when it comes to brands, their policy is to "straddle various" manufacturers.) Strings, cases, and accessories are their biggest selling items. We saw plush Continental and London Suspensionair and Non-Suspension cases by AMERICAN CASE COMPANY discounted $100 to $200, with less spectacular savings on lower-priced cases by JAEGER, FREISTAT AND LIFTON, and M.A. GORDGE. Orders arrive in about a week; satisfaction is guaranteed; there's a $2 restocking charge on returned sheet music. Shar's regular discount catalog and their catalog of 600 most requested sheet music pieces for strings are free, but the complete sheet music catalog is $2.50. **C**

THE WOODWIND/THE BRASSWIND
Dept. US
50741 U.S. 31 N.
South Bend, IN 46637
(800) 348-5003
(219) 272-8266: IN residents
MC, V, AE, COD

We don't remember the question, but the answers my friend, are blowing in The Woodwind and The Brasswind catalogs. Despite sounding like twin condo developments, The Brasswind and The Woodwind are stores specializing in instruments for serious musicians. If you specify your catalog preference, you can rustle through their price sheets and select from a very extensive list of quality instruments discounted about 40%. A BUFFET Clarinet listing for $1,500 was only $645, and a LEBLANC L-200 Clarinet was $495, $1,450 list. A KING Cornet sold for $209, $359 list. Other instruments include piccolos, flutes, bassoons, oboes, saxes (and accessories) in the Woodwind catalog; fluegelhorns, trombones, trumpets, French horns, euphoniums in Brasswind. They make repairs, too. There's a two-week return privilege, and even an installment plan on some instruments where no interest is charged. All instruments are completely tested before shipment. Shipping is $7. Check out their Woodwind 40-page catalog, Brasswind 30-page catalog, or 60-page drum catalog. Anyone mentioning *The Underground Shopper* will get free shipping with their order. **C**

Novelties

Novelty" means "new thing" and these companies will make a new person (or gorilla or sea creature) out of you. You can twist balloons into dachshunds, star-spangle the night sky with a breath-taking fireworks display, or dig into a tin of delicious popcorn or fortune cookies. Hundreds of fun-loving and novel treasures are available from the companies found on the following pages. If you think there's nothing new under the sun (or underwater), check here—but watch out for motorized shark fins!

ACE FIREWORKS
Dept. US
P.O. Box 221
Conneaut, OH 44030
(216) 593-4751
MC, V, Cashier Check

You light up my night! Connoisseurs of the finer things of light can shatter the stillness and split the night skies with any one of 1,000 different types of fireworks available here. They've got bottle rockets (their biggest seller), Roman candles, ladyfingers, and countless firecrackers, and everything is priced 20% to 30% below average retail. You can get "Class C common fireworks" including "happy lamps" and "baby magic blooms" in two to three days by mail. There's a $25 minimum order, but there's no charge for shipping. You must be 18 or older to order. Satisfaction guaranteed and apparently a lot of folks are satisfied: Ace has been in business for 28 years. **C $1**

ARCHIE McPHEE & COMPANY
Box 30852
Seattle, WA 98103
(206) 547-2467
CK, MC, V

Everything from the avant-garde to the extremely bizarre is yours for the buying from Archie McPhee & Company. Those hard-to-find items you'd forgotten you wanted as a child are available at nearly the same prices they were back then. If you're in the market for rubber insects, rodents, or fish, this is the place to shop. And the pink lawn flamingos are an absolute steal at only $9.50 a pair. More selective shoppers, however, may go for the deluxe set, covered in flattering pink feathers! Potato guns, voodoo dolls, wind-up wiper glasses, and punk dolls from outer space make gift-buying from this catalog outright outrageous. The 48-page catalog, free upon request, also stocks trolls, rubber chickens, inflatables, disguises, and glow-in-the-dark goods. Prices are all 10% to 30% below retail and there's a 15-day 100% satisfaction guarantee. Requests and orders are shipped within 15 days of receipt, and a flat $3 charge is added to all orders for shipping and handling. Mention *The Underground Shopper* and get $1 in McPhee Money, good for your next order. **C**

BITS & PIECES:
THE GREAT INTERNATIONAL PUZZLE COLLECTION
1 Puzzle Place
Ridgely, MD 21685

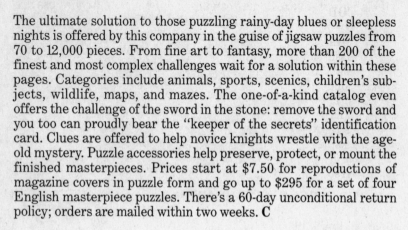

125 Walnut St.
Watertown, MA 02172
(800) JIGSAWS
(301) 634-1000
CK, MC, V, AE

The ultimate solution to those puzzling rainy-day blues or sleepless nights is offered by this company in the guise of jigsaw puzzles from 70 to 12,000 pieces. From fine art to fantasy, more than 200 of the finest and most complex challenges wait for a solution within these pages. Categories include animals, sports, scenics, children's subjects, wildlife, maps, and mazes. The one-of-a-kind catalog even offers the challenge of the sword in the stone: remove the sword and you too can proudly bear the "keeper of the secrets" identification card. Clues are offered to help novice knights wrestle with the age-old mystery. Puzzle accessories help preserve, protect, or mount the finished masterpieces. Prices start at $7.50 for reproductions of magazine covers in puzzle form and go up to $295 for a set of four English masterpiece puzzles. There's a 60-day unconditional return policy; orders are mailed within two weeks. **C**

B.J. ALAN
Dept. US
P.O. Box 3
12900 Columbiana-Canfield Road
Columbiana, OH 44408
(800) 321-9071
(800) 362-1034: OH residents
CK, MC, V

Dyno-mite! Well, not really, but you can at least have a blast if you're the type who likes to pop off. This fireworks company offers 500 items at discounted prices. Top brands (THUNDER-BOMB, BLACK CAT, RED LANTERN) come in candles, fountains, ground spinners, missiles, rockets, parachutes, sparklers, bottle rockets, smoke items, and snakes, as well as many other bang-up bargains. There's a $25 minimum order, an offer of gift certificates or refunds for "valid reasons," and a charge of 20% for restocking. Stock up for New Year's,

July 4th, or even add a little drama to the night you "pop the question." (She can't refuse!) You must be 18 to buy. **C** $1 (refundable)

CARRIAGE TRADE CREATIONS
Dept. US
P.O. Box 116
Lincoln, RI 02865
(401) 724-4655
CK, V, COD

Mr. and Mrs. Reuter have been running this company a long time and want to assure their customers of their concern for quality. (People in Rhode Island have that quality.) Monogrammed acrylic keyholders, $4, and solid brass GI dog tags on an 18-inch chain, $8, were definite bargains. Their write-it-yourself desk markers are tempting for anyone who has ever wanted to put a sign on their desk that reads "Where's the beef?" Minimum order: $25. Delivery takes three to four weeks, add an extra week if you've paid by check. They offer readers of *The Underground Shopper* a 33% discount off already low-priced personalized gifts. **C** $1 (refundable)

CURRENT
Dept. T3T1
The Current Building
Colorado Springs, CO 80941
(303) 594-4100
CK, MC, V

In the high country of Colorado, Current carries stationery and gift items, and if you go with the flow, it's hard to go wrong. The current Current catalog is over 88 pages and displays calendars, all-occasion cards, gifts, date books, stationery, wrapping paper, recipe cards, and birthday party kits in many attractive designs. They carry 500 to 600 different items. Gift wrap and greeting cards are their big sellers. Discounts depend on the number of items ordered: price breaks come with the eighth and 16th item ordered, and savings can reach 45%. (It's another way to save some Current-cy.) Their guarantee's a good one: you must be totally satisfied or they'll replace your order or refund the money. It's comforting to know you won't have to fight against the Current. **C**

DAZIAN, INC.
2014 Commerce St.
Dallas, TX 75201
(214) 748-3450
CK, COD

Once upon a time, there was a fairy princess, one king, two butterflies, and a white rabbit . . . sound like a story you know? You can
bring it to life with Dazian. Their 32-page catalog offers theatrical
fabrics, trimmings, leotards, and much, much more. Whether you
are going to a costume ball or putting on your own play, you'll dazzle
your audience on opening night with sequins and spangles, or you
could be the king with a jewel-encrusted crown and a regal scepter.
Being in business 144 years is nothing to drop a hat at, and hats they
have, in several different styles. A top hat goes for only $4.75, while a
paper Uncle Sam hat was patriotically priced at $1. Overall, their
prices deserved a standing ovation. For a good ending to the story
. . . live happily ever after with "the world's largest and oldest theatrical fabric organization." There's no minimum order, but returns
and exchanges must be made within 30 days, or it's curtains. The
End. **C**

FAIR & SQUARE
Dept. US
22 Huron St.
Port Jefferson Station, NY 11776
(516) 928-8707
CK

OK, they're fair, but are they square? Not likely, since they circle the
globe looking for out-of-this-world bargains in rock 'n' roll collectibles, toys, gifts, novelties, and more unusual finds. Popular items
include stuffed talking bears and talking dogs. If you're looking for
just the right gift for that not-so-right person, this is the place to
look. Bumper stickers and key chains are also popular. For an extra
15% savings, tell 'em you read about 'em in *The Underground Shopper*. **C $5** (refundable)

FRONT ROW PHOTOS
Box 484-U
Nesconset, NY 11767
(516) 585-8297
CK, MO

Experience the stars vicariously through these knockout photos of rock stars in concert. The highest quality with the lowest prices—major rock, new wave, and heavy metal bands from the '60s, '70s, and '80s. Minimum order $5. Postal Money Orders are preferred. Their 60-page catalog offers thousands of opportunities to reach to the stars—The Who, Police, Jimi Hendrix, Olivia, Bowie, Adam Ant, Van Halen—the best, all for $1.50 (less when more are purchased). Response time—a mere seven days. **C $2** (including a sample photo of customer's choice)

GOOD 'N' LUCKY PROMOTIONS
P.O. Box 370
Henderson, NV 89015
(800) 645-8259: orders only
(702) 564-3895
CK, MC, V, COD

Always looking for the lucky charms? This is your lucky day! We found them; frosted heart pendants, key chains, earrings, rings, and butterfly buckles were just a few of the lucky buck-savers we discovered. You won't need a leprechaun to find savings of about 75%. These Good 'N' Lucky charmers handle more than just charming charms. For instance, they carry bankrupt stock, closeouts, and overruns. Approximately 1,000 items are stocked year round. Lotsa' luck finding a bigger selection anywhere. You'll need the luck of the Irish to find lower prices than these. Ladies' rings were just $5.80 per dozen, and pocket watches were only $7.80 each. Fad items such as the popular DEMON BALLS, which retail as much as $5 a piece were bouncing at $16.80 per dozen. Samples are offered on many items. You don't have to be Irish, just an *Underground Shopper* fan to receive an additional 10% discount. Remember, items are sold "as is." **C $1**

INTO THE WIND
2047-US Broadway
Boulder, CO 80302
(303) 449-5356
CK, MC, V

Don't let your plans for starting a new hobby be up in the air. Send for this catalog but beware, there *are* strings attached. Into The Wind offers one of the largest selections of kites and wind socks available by mail. Kites range from traditional silk Chinese birds and butterflies to space-age nylon airfoils. Each kite's description in the colorful catalog offers information on flying characteristics and features as well the level of proficiency required to operate it. There are kites just for children, kites for fighting other kites, and kites for decorating your pad. Prices range from a modest $4.50 airfoil to the $160 "Wave Stratoscoop." Boomerangs and wind chimes were also found in this catalog. **C**

JOHNSON SMITH CO.
4514 19th St., Court East
Bradenton, FL 34203
(813) 747-6645
CK, MC, V

After getting a whiff of the Johnson Smith catalog, I was ready to place my order for a Herculean wristband, rotating spaghetti forks, a leather bullwhip, a ventriloquist's dummy, live "sea monkeys," character masks (for those with minor personality disorders?), phony blood, alien ears, monster teeth, motorized shark fins, an electric talking toilet, liquor lollipops, and The Last Supper purse wallets. Over 1,600 unusual offerings from around the world are available. This 72-year-old company has two good-sized catalogs: *World of Fun* and *The Lighter Side*. They contain almost everything you could ever want in the way of jokes, novelties, costume jewelry, hobby items, electronics and radio stuff, magic and Halloween items. Prices are generally below retail. Delivery time is about three to four weeks, but they'll give refunds or make exchanges immediately if there's a problem. **C**

LA PINATA
Dept. US
Number 2 Patio Market
Old Town
Albuquerque, NM 87104
(505) 242-2400
CK, MC, V, COD

These amigos are piñata perfectionists! Vent your frustrations on traditional motifs (bull, donkey, pedro, star) or seasonal characters (reindeer, Santa, pumpkins and witches, Easter rabbits). They come in three sizes ranging from $3.50 to $12.98. This family-run business has a life-size bull that's been no small provocation to the shop cat for many years. If you want a custom job done (they've created a sexy lady, a four-foot Idaho Potato, and a Dallas Cowboy . . . no relation), just provide a picture and the size and they'll give you a price quote. Send SASE for current price list. Most orders can be delivered within a week (via UPS); a special two-day service is available. They will refund or replace your order if not satisfied. Be sure to mention *The Underground Shopper* for a special 10% discount. **B, PQ**

LAURENCE CORNER
62/64 Hampstead Road
London N.W. 1 2NU
England
Phone: 011-44-1-01-388-6811
CK, MC, AE, DC, CB, ACCESS, BARCLAYCARD, POSTAL ORDER

Forget the lampshade at your next party and make your grand entrance in checkered trousers, prison pj's, oxygen mask, and fez hat. Laurence Corner sells new and used theatrical costumes, lightweight party costumes, inexpensive props, government surplus, medical lab instruments, and much more at "ridiculous" prices. If you want to get ahead with a hat that's different, check out their huge selection of unusual headgear from Civil War caps to Quaker hats. **B**

LETTER BOX
Dept. US
Box 371
Woodbury, NY 11797
(516) 933-1919
CK, MC, V

Is your creative self expressed best in traditional, elegant, or contemporarily bold writing papers? Does your pen whirl through Victorian swirls or dance across art deco-rations? The Letter Box will sign, seal, and deliver personalized designer stationery to you—and everything's enveloped in savings of 15% to 50%. The more you order, the more you'll save. The rage in personalized pages these days is the mini-pad (legal looks, graph paper with your name etched in contemporary or traditional designs). They're all 25% below retail. Write for their brochure—it comes with samples of imprints on various paper stocks. No orders are taken by phone; everything must be printed clearly. Shipping charges are determined by the amount of your order. Expect your order in four to six weeks. They'll reprint if the imprint is incorrect, but there are no returns for obvious reasons. **B, samples $1**

LINCOLN HOUSE
Dept. US
300 Greenbrier Road
Summersville, WV 26651
(800) 821-5293
(304) 872-3000: WV residents
CK, MC, V

Gift-giving ideas just seem to multiply in this house undivided against itself. Honest, Abe, Lincoln logs in fine candles, inexpensive gifts, and stationery in an attractive catalog. There are over 300 different items to choose from. We found cookie tins and other kitchen gadgets, calendars with different themes as well as two-year pocket calendars, children's toys—choose from a large assortment of gift products—something for everyone on your gift list. Prices were 20% to 40% off retail, and satisfaction is guaranteed, so they ain't just whistling Dixie. There are three discounts in effect depending on the number of items you buy. Expect to receive your order in two to three weeks. There are no shipping charges—100% satisfaction guaranteed or you'll get a complete refund or replacement if you're unhappy. Do you suppose everything bears the Union label? **C**

PARADISE PRODUCTS
P.O. Box 568
El Cerrito, CA 94530
(415) 524-8300
CK, MC, V

We thought Paradise Products consisted of apples, fig leaves, and serpents until we looked through their catalog and discovered nothing was lost. They've got party goods for 23 international and nine seasonal themes with tempting discounts of 25% on an assortment of favors, posters, crepe paper, hats, banners, flags, and masks (in their Party Host line). Say "Aloha!" to Hawaiian orchids and packets of beach sand or "How!" to an Indian peace pipe. You can even save a fortune, cookie, on fortune cookies for your next Chinese party. Finding the proper decorations to set the mood for a fifties or sixties party is no problem when you flip through this company's 72-page catalog. There's a $30 minimum order—if you order less than this amount enclose $4 as a service charge. All items are guaranteed to be as represented in the catalog with shipments guaranteed to arrive on time (not fashionably late) for the party and in perfect condition, or they'll cheerfully refund your money. **C $2**

SPENCER GIFTS, INC.
1050 Black Horse Pike
Pleasantville, NJ 08232
(609) 645-5587
CK, MC, V, AE

Seventy-seven Sunset tricks! Here's an innovative catalog that won't let the sun set without the assistance of a gadget or gizmo to make your life easier. Some of the more bizarre items we found included a "wrist pen," which doubles as a rubbery piece of jewelry for $1.99, a nifty "pop-top lifter" for $1.49, a banana harmonica also $1.49, and a beer mug shaped in the form of the female anatomy. Don't leave foam without it, $2.99. Save up to 65% over prices found on similar items at airport gift shops. Full refund if not completely satisfied. Minimum order $10 by phone. **C**

Office Supplies

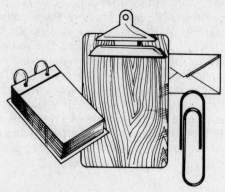

You've got to spend money to make money." How often have you heard that? It's a business cliché and it's true—most of the time. It's not true, though, when it comes to shelling out for office supplies. They're not investments, they're expenses, and if you don't watch your costs, before you know it your company will be expended rather than expanded. Kaput. So what can you do? Cut corners! Buying office supplies and equipment from a discounter is a good way to begin. Forms, ribbons, pencils, pens, calendars, etc., are all available at a discount through the mail. Larger purchases such as typewriters, computers, word processors, Dictaphones, and floppy discs are also discounted. Shop around and try different products, but when it comes to reordering, place your order by mail. It may take a little longer to get your order, but like that other cliché says, "Haste makes waste."

ALLIED BUSINESS MACHINE SYSTEMS
9281 Earl St.
La Mesa, CA 92041
(619) 461-6361
CK, MC, V

The ABM system we encountered here was far from hit-or-missile. Their 40- to 60-page catalogs list items from reconditioned IBM typewriters to computer paper, with shredders, binders, tape recorders, answering machines, calculators, and desk files filed in between. Popular brands include IBM, SANYO, and OLIVETTI computers and typewriters. Their selection of ribbons for printers really threw us for a loop. Prices were up to 70% less than conventional office suppliers. Their prices to repair IBM typewriter elements insure that they do a booming business—this is their real claim to fame. Generally there are no returns, although this varies. (Does this mean it's "Bombs away?") Orders are processed in a few days. We hadn't expected such an explosion of office options, and we have to admit we were caught with our defenses down. **C $1.50**

THE AMERICAN STATIONERY CO., INC.
300 Park Ave.
Peru, IN 46970
(800) 428-0379
(317) 473-4438
CK, MC, V

Since 1919, this company has been providing the Write Stuff and saving you up to 50% in the process. Personalized Stationery, wedding stationery, and accessories (reception needs) is the American Way. Wedding invitations, thank-you notes, embossed stationery, hand-drawn calligraphy stationery, Crane papers with exclusive designs on some, well, what are you waiting for, start writing for their free catalog now. No minimum orders with an incredible response time of two days. **C**

AMITY HALLMARK LTD.
149-44 41st Ave.
Flushing, NY 11355
(212) 939-2323
CK, COD

They don't need red trucks, hoses, and loud sirens to put out the fliers down at the station. Amity Hallmark offers full graphic services along with a wide variety of computerized typesetting and off-set printing services for letterheads, envelopes, booklets, and business cards. "Extra services" such as padding, punching, and stapling are available at nominal prices. They are a big operation and because they use the latest technology in printing equipment, they can pass their savings from increased efficiency on to consumers in the form of lower prices. Certain jobs take longer—such as cards, carbonless forms, booklets, envelopes, and colored ink. Shipping is free to the New England states, Pennsylvania, Ohio, West Virginia, Virginia, Maryland, New Jersey, New York, and Washington, D.C. **B**

B & I FURNITURE CO.
Dept. US
611 N. Broadway
Milwaukee, WI 53202
(800) 558-8662
(800) 242-7200: WI residents
(414) 272-6080
CK, MC, V, AE

If you want industrial, commercial, and business furniture, you've come to the right place. B&I's got all kinds of brands, including LA-Z-BOY, COLE, HON, KRUEGER, and NATIONAL OFFICE. Everything is first-quality. The biggest part of their business is small business/office computer furniture. Everything in their 80-page catalog carries at least a six-year guarantee on materials and workmanship; some items are guaranteed up to 30 years. Products are shipped directly from the plant to the customer in four to six weeks (normal ship) or 10 to 15 days (quick ship). **C**

BUSINESS ENVELOPE MANUFACTURERS
Dept. US
900 Grand Blvd.
Deer Park, NY 11729
(800) 645-5235
(800) 222-2418: NY residents
(516) 667-8500
CK, MC, V

Don't feel sorry for these envelopes—they're made to take a lickin'! BEM will "envelope" you in business statements, invoices, stationery, ledgers, labels, ribbons, jumbo markers, and more at factory direct prices. Imprinted business envelopes were priced a good 35% below retail (a discount that definitely didn't leave a bad taste in our mouth). With savings like that, it's not surprising that envelopes are their most popular item. It you don't believe us, just take a look at their 40-page catalog! There is a 500 envelope minimum order, everything's fully guaranteed, and you can expect to receive your order in about 10 days. Open credit accounts are available. **C**

BUY DIRECT, INC.
216 W. 18th St.
New York, NY 10011
(212) 255-4424
CK, COD

Bye, bye, blackboard; welcome to the space age! Hello, word processors that need their own set of supplies. Progress doesn't come easy or cheap, but at least with guys like Buy Direct, it's easier and cheaper than most places. This company carries all kinds of business forms (including snap-out and computer forms), labels, and assorted printing items. They've got the latest stock of computer, mini-computer, and word processing supplies—like special binders, disc cartridges, storage systems, and print wheels. Computer forms and BUSH computer furniture are their most popular items. Prices at this wholesale distributor are consistently 15% to 30% below retail. There's no minimum order (except on computer forms, 1,000), returns are credited, and there's a 10% restocking charge on returns. Their 144-page catalog is in glowing color. **C $2**

COLWELL BUSINESS PRODUCTS
201 Kenyon Road
Champaign, IL 61820
(800) 248-7000
(800) 252-6920: IL residents
(800) 252-6960: IL residents
CK, MC, V, AE

Make it your business to send for this catalog. Their motto is "stationery and forms for price-conscious businesses." They have a catalog devoted exclusively to computer and word processing forms and supplies. Over 300 software packages are included with forms for accounts payable, payroll, statements, labels, and invoices. Colwell had the best prices we found on printed business cards. Five hundred white vellum cards with black ink were just $14.95 for raised letter imprint and $12.95 for flat letter imprint. **C**

COMMERCIAL OFFICE PRODUCTS
1000 East Higgins Road
Elk Grove Village, IL 60007
(312) 364-0440
CK, MC, V, COD (payable 100% by certified check)

Time for a Commercial: "There are over eight million stories in the Naked City. This is just one of them. It was a dark, rainy night. I was at Joe's Bar when I responded to an 852—typing without a ribbon. I'd dealt with this type before. The victim was named SMITH-CORONA: the suspect, Mike Masher. I'd caught him once before and he promised not to return. Now he had two strikes against him. I dusted the keys for fingerprints. I guessed this guy Corona to be a big ticket item, but I was 35% off. I don't know why Masher had attacked SMITH-CORONA: it would have been just as easy for him to pound on SHARP, IBM, ROYAL, or OLYMPIA. Masher had a record of cold, calculating assaults with a battery in the TI and HP cases, too. HP calculators were one of his favorite targets, particularly here. Why did he do it? I guessed Masher was trying to save the $4.95 shipping, but now he'd be shipped up the river. He'd be gone within 24 hours with a 30-day exchange period. At 10:15, I got a call on my RECORD-O-CALL ($249, $349 elsewhere) from the Chief: Get some milk on the way home. Case closed." **C**

ESC ENVELOPE SALES CO.
Normandy, TN 37360-0060
No phone
CK

One of our readers advised us to become pen pals with this printer and we found ink-credible savings. If you're a small businessman or a lover of *les belles lettres*, you can get 1,000 #10 business envelopes printed for $21.50 plus a small shipping charge. A local quick printer charged $36.95 for the same job. Allow two weeks for delivery. **PQ**

FIDELITY PRODUCTS CO.
5601 International Parkway
P.O. Box 155
Minneapolis, MN 55440
(800) 328-3034
(612) 536-6500: MN residents
CK, MC, V, AE, DC, CB

Fidelity's own brand of opaque correction fluid was incorrigible at 39 cents per bottle, but the buys on corrugated modular storage systems ranked even higher in our files. We didn't see the writing on the wall with their anti-graffiti urethane, $26.95 a gallon, which protects against aerosol spray paint, felt pen, and most other staples of visual vandalism. They carry over 1,800 products for the office, factory, or warehouse, including temporary files, packaging tapes and containers, and first aid kits (OSHA approved). Prices are about 15% to 20% less than retail, and up to 40% savings on quantity purchases. Thirty-day free trial with a full refund during that time. Delivery of orders is usually within seven to 10 days. There are two catalogs: a 120-page job for business and industry and a 52-page one for data processing. **C**

FRANK EASTERN CO.
625 Broadway
New York, NY 10012
(800) 221-4914
(212) 677-9100: collect in NY
CK, MC, V

Message from the boss: Keep this company on file—under "M" for memo-rable. Savings are up to 50% off retail on business and institutional equipment. They've got chairs, files, bookcases, storage units, panel wall systems, desks, tables and a wide selection of computer workstations. Over 300 prominent office brands are carried, including LA-Z-BOY. Ergonomic chairs are a specialty. There's no minimum order; standard manufacturer's warranties apply. You'll get your order in about three weeks. They've been in business for 40 years. Check out their catalog with its complete selection of office and institutional seating in wood, chrome, plastic, or combinations. **C $1**

JILOR DISCOUNTS
1020 Broadway
Woodmere, NY 11598
(516) 374-5806
CK, MC, V

The daily grind is easy with the right office machines. Jilor brews bargains on calculators reduced 20% and more by makers like SANYO, CANON, SHARP, and VICTOR. Or get keyed up on typewriters by SMITH-CORONA, OLYMPIA, SILVER-REED, and OLIVETTI. Get the message? They've got answering machines by SANYO, CODE-A-PHONE, RECORD-A-CALL, GE, and PANASONIC recording record savings. Are you a wheeler-dealer? Then dial and while away the hours on a cordless, and one or two line decorator-style telephone by ITT, PANASONIC, TELEQUEST, and PAC TEL. Also available is ORANGE MAGIC, the wonder all-purpose cleaner that whisks away stains and dirt, grease, ink, and gum from cars, motors, boats, driveways, pet stains—just about anything. It's the stuff New York is using to remove the graffiti from its subways—so here's proof that at least our recommendation need not be erased. Call if you require service on calculators, answering machines, or dictation equipment. There's a $25 minimum order and $5 shipping charge. There are no refunds, but they will exchange. **PQ**

LANDMARK SPECIALTIES, INC.
1588 Gwen Drive
Pocatello, ID 83204
(208) 232-4809
CK, MC, V

Looking for a computer that won't spindle, fold, and mutilate the company budget? Check the lineup of computers on-line here. This company serves as a broker, so your job is to shop around and find what you want, then contact LANDMARK for current prices. Just give the brand name, model number, and other identifying information. Besides computers, Landmark has CRTs, terminals, monitors, boards and accessories, software, modems and supplies. Everything from A (ALTOS) to Z (ZENITH) is available, including hard-to-find computers and related items. Prices are from 15% to 40% below manufacturer's list on new equipment—more on used or refurbished. No catalog is available because of the rapidly changing market. Write or call for a price quote. **PQ**

L & D PRESS
Box 641
78 Randall St.
Rockville Center, NY 11570
(516) 593-5058
CK

Congratulations! You're starting your own business. You'll probably be needing the following items from L & D Press: business cards, envelopes, letterhead, announcements, stock forms, reply messages, invoices . . . the list is endless, but there is a light at the end of the tunnel. You can save up to 50% on printing and office supplies with L & D Press. We found incredible deals on business cards. They were available in 18 popular type styles. A very convenient order form is provided for guaranteed accuracy. Prices ranged from $14.95 to $29.95 (per 1,000), depending on the selection made. Maybe you're tying the knot instead, and want to announce it to the world. You can shout it from the rooftops or order announcements from L & D and save. Correspond in style with luxurious stationery at notably low prices. Select from two styles: 100 Princess or 80 Monarch with matching envelopes only $10.95. Twenty years in business is very impress-ive, too. If you don't want to save money, it's none of our business! **B, F**

NATIONAL BUSINESS FURNITURE, INC.
Dept. US
222 E. Michigan St.
Milwaukee, WI 53202
(800) 558-1010
(800) 558-9803: customer service
(800) 242-0030: WI residents
CK, MC, V

Far-out! This company outfitted the new wing of the American Embassy in Senegal. Apparently word reached those diplomats in Africa about the diplomatic prices charged here. Nothing is as revolutionary as evenhanded pricing! What's that to you? Well, you don't have to be a continent or two away to take advantage of the incontinent bargains here. In fact, you can shop for over 40 top-drawer brands without ever leaving your desk, just by flipping through one of NBF's 48-page catalogs. Names like COLE, GLOBE/COSCO, LA-Z-BOY, HIGH POINT, INDIANA DESK, O'SULLIVAN, DOLLY MADISON, and SAMSONITE are all available direct from the manufacturer, not to mention computer furniture starting at just $79. Discounts run about 30%, volume orders get bigger savings. They arrange for your order to be drop-shipped from the manufacturer in about three to five weeks, with reasonable freight charges tacked on. Merchandise is returnable, but it's subject to a restocking charge of 25%. **C, PQ**

NEBS
500 Main St.
Groton, MA 01471
(800) 225-6380
CK

Make your office feel all-write by taking care of business with discounts on carbonless business forms, sales slips, envelopes, invoices, labels, files, and check-writing systems. Prices won't put you out of business: 12 large (100 sheets) legal pads for $9.50 ($10.50 elsewhere), raised print business cards, $19.95 for 1,000 ($27 elsewhere). Most of their over 300 items carry the NEBS brand. Small businesses are their biggest customers. No shipping charges on prepaid orders; orders come in about six working days. Check out their 108-page catalog for the full story. **C**

OLYMPIC SALES
Dept. US
839 S. Labrea
Los Angeles, CA 90036
(800) 421-8045: orders only
(213) 937-3221: CA residents
CK, MC, V

When it comes to courtesy, Olympic didn't exactly come forth with an Olympian effort. Their abrupt response to our inquiry was "The prices in the catalog are what we charge and, no, we don't take requests for catalogs over the phone!" (We'll leave the gold medal with the people who make flour; these guys weren't even in the race.) If you're trying to get ahead in the race to the top (and aren't predisposed to judge), Olympic still might be worth a try. They carry a large assortment of computers and printers, calculators, typewriters, cassette recorders, VCRs, stereo equipment, and video games. You'll find IBM and SANYO computers, and TEXAS INSTRUMENTS, SHARP, and HEWLETT-PACKARD calculators. H-P calculators may be their best buy. Orders usually arrive in about 10 days. Check out the prices in their catalog, but remember, *write* for it. **C $2**

PEARL BROTHERS TYPEWRITERS
476 Smith St.
Brooklyn, NY 11231
(718) 875-3024
CK

Net one, Pearl two, and save up to 50% on typewriters with more than a few years shell-f life. The retail oyster was shucked open to reveal lustrous 10% to 40% discounts on name brands like IBM, OLYMPIA, SMITH-CORONA. The ADLER line of typewriters is the best buy here: the ADLER-ROYAL SATELLITE I was just $325 (regularly $575). They also have calculators and word processors. Their service department will repair any make of typewriter. All merchandise carries an unconditional 90-day guarantee. Write for more information and wait for good tide-ings. **PQ**

QUILL® CORPORATION
Dept. US
100 S. Schelter Road
Lincolnshire, IL 60198-4700
(312) 634-4800: orders
(312) 634-4850: inquiries
Open accounts with credit confirmation

Quill may sound like a name inspired by a porcupine, but the prices here are anything but prickly. This company serves only businesses, institutions, and professional offices. With over 600,000 accounts, their business-to-business business needles their competition. As the largest mail-order office products firm in the nation, Quill has outstanding values down the line. The TI 5130II calculator was just $69.99; 3M Post-it® notepads were as low as $2.99 per dozen; and hanging folders for file drawers were just $6.49 per box. Their thick, slick, full-color, 344-page catalog is well worth a look: you'll find everything from 3M diskettes (at 31% to 45% off), typewriters, lamps, attachés, and office furniture, to those important office incidentals like tape, staplers, assorted pads and paper, pens, ROLODEX files, and printer ribbons, to name only a few. All things considered (and they do have all things!), we'll save our barbed comments for a company less fortified with merchandise than Quill. **C**

ROCHESTER 100, INC.
P.O. Box 1261
851 Joseph Ave.
Rochester, NY 14603
(716) 544-3414 (call collect)
CK

Buy directly from this manufacturer of vinyl plastic envelopes and holders. These holders are "clearly" invaluable to organize, transport, store or protect important documents, manuscripts, proposals, floppy discs, mag, tab, or data cards and sheets, word processing records, and related data. Their modern factory produces hundreds of different dies and has the capacity to manufacture holders up to 26x38 sizes. Fast service and low prices are their buyline since they sell by mail and phone only. No follow-up salesman will call you if you request information. Call collect for further information and free samples on request. **PQ**

S-100 INC.
Division of 696 Corp.
Suite C
14455 N. 79th St.
Scottsdale, AZ 85260
(602) 991-7870
CK, MC, V, COD

In this computer age, Barnum & Bailey would say life is a circuit. S-100's full-color, 100-page catalog has debt-defying prices of 15% to 35% off on high-wire supplies like microcomputers and peripheral devices—floppy discs, "Murrow" memory boards, alphanumeric line printers, video boards, music synthesizer boards, and terminals you'd die for. Over 100 brands such as CROMEMCO, GODBOUT, NORTH STAR, SEATTLE, TRANSCEND, TELEVIDEO, QUME, MCPI, LUKE, DATACOM, NW, COLUMBIA COMPUTER SYSTEMS, IBM, STB, AST, and EPSON. Computer systems and WINCHESTER drives are their biggest selling items. Their multi-tiered pricing system helps out in these days of double-digital inflation. Payment by check or money order will entitle you to the biggest discount; there's a small deduction for credit card and COD orders. They'll replace and exchange defective merchandise; orders go out in two to five days. **C**

THE STATIONERY HOUSE INC.
1000 Florida Ave.
Hagerstown, MD 21740
(800) 638-3033
(301) 739-4487: MD residents
CK, MC, V, AE, DC, CB

Foiled again, but this time it's gold foil stamping at the Stationery House. These folks cater toward businesses, although they do have many gold-stamped, thermograved raised print designs suitable for personal stationery as well. Selection is adequate and includes stock logos and designs ideal for a new business in need of a professional look at low cost. Let's face it—you're saving up to 40% by ordering thermograved stationery direct rather than through a printer, and you won't incur any extra typesetting or paste-up charge. The Stationery House claims they can match your current design or artwork, regardless of your choice of paper, ink, colors, or type styles, whether it be thermograved raised print, flat offset lithography, genuine engraving, hot foil stamping, or blind embossing. They claim to do all this for a lower price. C

THRIFTY PRINTS, INC.
103 Hotel St.
Brooklyn, WI 53521
CK, MC, V

Save 25% to 40% on your printing and typesetting needs through Thrifty Prints, Inc. Thrifty Prints offers printing on a wide range of paper stocks and colors. Professional typesetting is prepared by competently trained personnel on the most up-to-date commercial equipment. Send a self-addressed stamped envelope for complete details.

TYPEX BUSINESS MACHINES INC.
23 W. 23rd St.
New York, NY 10010
(800) 221-9332
(212) 243-8086: NY residents
MC, V

Typex doesn't sell Brand X: only ROYAL, SCM, SILVER REED, OLIVETTI, OLYMPIA, IBM, ADLER, and BROTHER typewriters including hard-to-find foreign language varieties. They also have calculators, copiers, and PANASONIC and SONY dictating equipment. Savvy shoppers can key into savings from 30% to 40% off. They have an X-cellent service department to repair any make of typewriter. Their minimum order is $50. Write or call for more information.

WINDFALL MAILING LISTS
P.O. Box 268
Lyman, SC 29365-0268

430 Oak Grove Road
Spartanburg, SC 29301
(803) 574-7732
CK, MC, V, AE, COD, MO

What a blessing in disguise! Windfall eliminates the middleman and blows tremendous savings your way. You'll discover factory direct, computerized mailing list in several categories. Multi-level enthusiasts, mailing list compilers, brokers, book buyers, and mail-order operators, to mention a few, are potential buyers. *Underground Shopper* readers will receive an unexpected gain with an extra 30% discount. You'll stir up a hurricane when you catch wind of these prices. Fifty labels were only $8, or for you bigger stickers, 100,000 run for $1,500. Your names will be printed on pressure-sensitive, peel-and-stick labels. You won't be squalling if you're not satisfied. If one name is not delivered, you will receive 10 free. Minimum order is 50. All orders are processed and shipped within 72 hours. So, you'll get your order in a breeze. Send an SASE for a free sample. "You can't buy better lists, but you can buy more expensive ones." Need we say more? **F (SASE)**

WOLFF OFFICE EQUIPMENT
Dept. US
1841 Broadway
New York, NY 10023
(212) 581-9080
CK, MC, V, COD

Shepherding the company finances? "Cry Wolff" for savings on typewriters, computers, and office equipment. These folks are ready to flock to your rescue. Savings run 30% to 35% on names like OLYMPIA, OLIVETTI, SMITH-CORONA, SHARP, BROTHER, SANYO, VIC-

TOR, TEAL, KAYPRO, CANON, SCM, IBM, and others. SMITH-CORONAand OLIVETTI typewriters are the big sellers. Check out the electric check-writers, dictating machines, and office furniture. Their minimum order is $100, with a 15% restocking charge on returns. Orders are usually received in about a week; there's a 90-day guarantee. Not baaaa-d. **F, PQ**

Pet and Ranch Animals

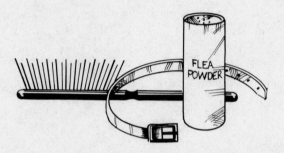

Four-footed family members need love just like everyone else, but they also need their own supplies. You may not know it, but there are mail-order companies specializing in pet supplies. You don't have to rove all over town to find Rover a leash. Collar a bargain on a dog or cat collar, or buy toys, grooming supplies, vitamins and medical supplies, hair clippers or hoof trimmers for your racehorse, ocelot, or Great Dane. Some mail-order firms even keep a veterinarian on staff to give you free advice. That's a deal that should set everyone's tail to wagging!

AVP (ANIMAL VETERINARY PRODUCTS, INC.)
P.O. Box 1267
Galesburg, IL 61401
(800) 634-7001: West Coast states
(800) 447-8192: Midwestern states
(800) 345-3042: East Coast states
(309) 342-9511
CK, MC, V

Our pet peeve has always been paying too much for animal health care products. No more, my pet. AVP is *the* catalog to consult whenever purchasing pet care products. A division of Dick Blick Co., their merchandise includes HAUGEN Pet Products. From simple ("cosmic catnip") to specialized (poodle hair dryer), the items fulfill every need a pet owner or pet shop keeper might have. Feeders, furniture, scoopers, skin care, chokes and chewies, clippers, collars, piddle pads, vitamins, odor eaters, and litter pans . . . are you getting excited! Instead of saying "Out, damn Spot," treat your pet like a member of the family. After all, it's a dog-eat-dog world out there. **C**

ECHO PRODUCTS, INC.
Dept. US
32841 Park Lane
Garden City, MI 48135
(313) 425-5293
CK, MC, V

Echo's a place for resounding bargains in small animal food and hardware, especially for tropical fish. You'll be tankful for the watered-down prices (25% off) on aquariums, fish filters, and live fish. Other discounts range up to 40%. They'll ship *fish*. Tropical fish are drop-shipped, with the only delay occurring in cold weather. Live delivery is guaranteed. Branded items are available, including SUPREME filters; VORTEX filters; GEISLER foods for dogs, cats, and birds; and TETRA fish food. A complete line of 250 books on pets and pet care was their newest offering and was discounted 25%. Check out their 40-page catalog—you won't want to miss the amusing "Tropical Fish Problem Solver Chart" that's included. Give 'em a holler and wait to hear back. **C $1** (refundable)

THE KENNEL VET CORPORATION
P.O. Box 835
1811 Newbridge Road
Bellmore, NY 11710
(516) 783-5400
CK, MC, V, AE, D, COD

This company is the purr-fect place to fill your small pet supply needs! A full range of products for dogs, cats, and other small animals takes care of health, grooming, and playtime needs for the pet in your life. A complete line of vaccines, sprays, ointments, and grooming aids keeps your pet looking and feeling its finest at prices that are sure to make you feel good, too! Tools for professional care include grooming tables, stand dryers, clippers, trimmers, and nail groomers. Latex and hard rubber toys for pets offer plenty to keep you both entertained for hours. Brand-name supplies such as LAMBERT KAY, VET KEM, ST. AUBREY, RING 5, OSTER, MID-WEST, and GENERAL are all available below retail cost. Learn more about caring for your pet with an extensive selection of pet care books from publishers such as Alpine, Howell, TFH, and Denlinger. Orders of $50 or more receive an additional 10% discount and customers outside of New York don't pay sales tax. Orders shipped via UPS. **C**

NORTHERN WHOLESALE VETERINARY SUPPLY
Dept. US
5570 Frontage Road North
Onalaska, WI 54650
(800) 356-5852
(800) 362-8025: WI residents
(608) 783-0300
CK, MC, V, COD

Ro-meow, Ro-meow, wherefore art thou with my chow? The Montagues and Cat-ulets may have been battling tooth and claw in Shakespeare's day, but today when it comes to problems like worms and fleas, the battle's over. Northern Wholesale carries a complete line of 6,000 animal health products (including PFIZER and ELANCO brands) discounted 15%. Check 'em out: the minimum order is $20, and their 112-page catalog is free. A veterinarian is available to answer questions. What more can you ask? **C** (Specify large or small animal catalog)

OMAHA VACCINE COMPANY
P.O. Box 7228
3030 "L" St.
Omaha, NE 68107
(402) 731-9600
(402) 731-1155: Phone orders
CK, MC, V, MO, COD

My doggie door cost $79.95; in the catalog, a comparable one was $10.25. So—even the best of 'em strays from the path of good sense and admits she's been had. Whether it's for your dog, cat, or horse, you're sure to find something and save 20% to 35% while you're at it. Over 22 years of customer and vet satisfaction, you can expect their jam-packed, illustrated 104-page catalog in about 10 days and another week for your order. Tell them you're an *Underground Shopper* and you'll get a free gift. I'll let you know what it is after I order my cat nail clipper ($4.25), my mini-cargo kennel ($6.86), and some ADAMS FLEA OFF MIST (1 gallon—$29.00). C

PETCO ANIMAL SUPPLIES
Dept. US
9151 Rehco Road
P.O. Box 1076
San Diego, CA 92121
(619) 469-2111
CK, MC, V, COD

This cat-alog is the purr-fect Santa Claws wish book for felines, canines, and their human pets. Petco carries a full line of brand-name supplies for cats, dogs, horses, birds, and fish at prices of 10% to 50% off retail. Most are about 30% below retail. Their catalog of grooming supplies, collars, leads, toys, vaccines, remedies, and veterinary supplies also devotes 10 pages to vitamins. Satisfaction is guaranteed; there's a $5 minimum order; there's no restocking charge on returns. We'll bet your pet can convince you to get something—ours certainly gave us paws. C

TOMAHAWK LIVE TRAP CO.
Dept. US
P.O. Box 323
Tomahawk, WI 54487
(715) 453-3550
CK, COD

Honest Injun, palefaced animal lovers can snare savings without having the bite put on their four-footed friends. Tomahawk Live Trap makes humane traps and box-type cages for catching, holding and/or transporting wild and not-so-wild beasts like mice, chipmunks, beavers, raccoons, skunks, rabbits, cats, dogs, squirrels, turtles, pigeons, fish, and rats. A raccoon/cat trap-cage (#108) was just $24, but would retail for over $48; it's a favorite purchase of humane societies. This is the only company that makes traps approved by the U.S. government for humane societies. All traps are built to last. (One long-term customer wrote: "Your traps and Zippo lighters are the only products that have kept their quality throughout the years.") Prices are excellent, since they're factory direct. Orders are shipped out the same day. Get set to spring into action! **B**

UNITED PHARMACAL CO., INC.
Dept. US
P.O. Box 969
St. Joseph, MO 64502
(816) 233-8800
CK, MC, V

We wanted to throw rice when we saw all the bridle and grooming supplies in United Pharmacal Company's 130-page catalog. This place is no mirage made in heaven. We found 20% to 40% discounts on antibiotics, vitamins, insecticides, and horse tack—in fact, on everything we needed to care for a dog, cat, or horse. Shout "I do, I do" by buying do-it-yourself vaccines. You'll save about 80% off vet's fees with no prescription needed for catalog items. Flea collars were just 75 cents each when you order 12 or more. Fall specials included Barbara Woodhouse choke chains for $2.50, $27.50 per dozen and her book *No Bad Dogs* was just $6.50 ($13.95 retail). Who could forget the pin-striped sweaters for preppie puppies for $2.15 each? Shipping is $1.75 to $2.25; there's a $5 minimum order. Special premiums given for cash orders, and additional discounts of up to 10% for quantity purchases make this more than a puppy love affair. **C**

THE WHOLESALE VETERINARY SUPPLY, INC.
Dept. US
P.O. Box 2256
Rockford, IL 61131
(800) 435-6940
(800) 892-6996: IL residents
(815) 877-0209: Rockford residents
CK, MC, V

Get it wholesale at Wholesale! From hair clippers to hoof trimmers, they've got everything you need in vitamins, supplements, prescriptions, medical supplies, shampoos, and insecticides for your Flicka, Benji, or Morris. Everything is discounted up to 50%, including popular brands like LAMBERT KAY, FARNAM, and PET-TABS (pet vitamins). You'll also find items like wonder wormers, anti-mating spray (works only on four-legged animals—shucks!), spray cologne and deodorant, flea bombs, JIM DANDY horse treats, and carrying cages. For something even more exotic, buy a cow chip penholder for $11.95. There's a full-time, in-house veterinarian who answers your questions at no charge. Their 112-page catalog is $1, first-class mail; the price is refundable with your first order. About 80% of their items are shipped free—the others are marked FOB in the catalog. There's no restocking charge on orders returned within 30 days, but you must call first. **C $1** (refundable)

Plants, Flowers, Gardens, and Farming

Grow your own fruits and vegetables, raise chickens, repair your tractor, landscape your yard—you'll reap the benefits of a healthier lifestyle and a heartier bank account. Start with high-quality seeds, add good soil and weather, fertilize with tender loving care, and—voilà!—you'll have everything from apples to zucchini all ripe for the picking. When ordering live plants or seeds, be sure to consider your native soil conditions and local weather. If you're not sure a white flowering dogwood will make it through your winter, consult a local nursery or the mail-order supplier before you order.

BIO-CONTROL
Dept. US
P.O. Box 337
Berrycreek, CA 95916
(916) 589-5227
CK, MO

Question: What winged wonder fearlessly fights for your garden's glory, risking life and limb in a never-ending struggle against those horticultural hell-raisers, insects that feast on your foliage? It's Ladybug! (No, this is not some flipped-out refugee from a religious cult, or a six-legged feminist crusader of the insect world—the Green Hornet doesn't have a wife.) Ladybugs are insects that brunch on the bugs that munch on your flowers, shrubs, and trees. They make gourmet meals of mealy bugs (mealy bug Bourguignonne), leafhoppers (hoppers au gratin, with bay leaf), and aphids (aphids à la mode). If beetles in your beans and crawlies in your clover are driving you buggy, write Bio-Control for a price list of their beneficial bugs. Lacewings, Chinese praying mantises, and trichogramma are also available. Biological warfare can be cheaper and safer than insecticides, and all these antennaed mercenaries ask for is a free lunch. Live delivery is guaranteed; shipping charges are included in the price. **C, PQ**

BLUESTONE PERENNIALS INC.
Dept. A
7211 Middle Ridge Road
Madison, OH 44057
(216) 428-7535
CK, MC, V, AE

The Bluestone catalog kind of grows on you. The 350 or so varieties of perennial plants remind us of birthdays; they crop up every year with practically no coaxing. If you admire the beauty of flowers found bordering lawns or being grown in gardens for display, here's a chance to try your green thumb at saving some green cash. Not only does Bluestone offer an outstanding array of flowers, but their prices are very reasonable. Care is taken to package the plants and a full money back guarantee is given. The four-color catalog features a description of all plants, shade and lighting requirements, price, and, in some cases, photographs. Colorful reading. **C**

BROOKFIELD NURSERY & TREE PLANTATION
P.O. Box 2490
1970 Palmer St.
Christiansburg, VA 24068
(800) 443-8733
(703) 382-9099
CK, MC, V

Bah! Humbug! It's Christmas time again. Time for the annual, hectic hunt for a tree in a forest of high prices. Here is a version of *The Christmas Carol* that will lift even Scrooge's spirits: The Spirit of Christmas Past—Humbug! Bruised, crushed, dried-out trees that were shipped thousands of miles and show every mile. Your living room floor is blanketed with needles, and your wallet is a lot thinner. The tree is dead, and the special day hasn't even arrived yet. Besides that, you had to fight the crowds for a not so jolly tree. The Spirit of Christmas Present—Ho! Ho! Ho! Capture the elegance and tradition of a Christmas spent in the Blue Ridge Mountains of Virginia. Brookfield Plantation offers a very unique service that will make your Christmas merry. They deliver beautiful, carefully nurtured, handselected, fresh trees directly to your door. Each tree is guaranteed to bring joy to your heart, or you will get a full refund. Mike and David have one of the largest evergreen farms on the East coast. It contains one-half million of the very best white pines. They are the first growers to ship a tree direct to your door. Every tree arrives fresh and crisp in its own package since it's shipped the same day it's cut. The prices will make you Dancer and Prancer on the rooftops. One white pine, approximately five feet in height, cost only $24.95 plus $10 shipping and handling. Santa couldn't deliver a better deal. The Spirit of Christmas Future—Noel! Noel! No more tree hassles, ever! You can relax, Ebenezer; throw out that plastic tree and bring the wonderful fragrance of fresh pine home. Get beautiful, handcrafted, fresh, pine wreaths for a dear price of $9.95 plus $3 shipping and handling. What a terrific present to welcome the new season! For the holiday enthusiasts, two pounds of evergreen boughs for decorating is offered at a trim $6.95 plus $3 shipping and handling. Another of Santa's helpers is the lifetime tree stand uniquely designed to eliminate the need to trim those beautiful lower branches for only $19.95. Fraser firs and blue spruces are offered for the pickier, their price a little stickier. Now, that's a Christmas carol even Dickens would appreciate. Here's a little stocking stuffer we almost forgot: all orders must be placed each year by December 17. **B**

BUTTERBROOKE FARM
78 Barry Road
Oxford, CT 06483

It's back to nature for mail-order shoppers. Whether gardening for pleasure, profit, recreation or appetite, Butterbrooke Farm has the seeds to start it all. For 35 cents a packet (compared to 50 cents to one dollar elsewhere), this company will provide a wide variety of seeds to choose from. Butterbrooke Farm caters to the vegetable gardener by offering 70 varieties of seeds in their catalog. These seeds are pure, open-pollinated strains, which means any seeds you save from your own produce will grow to be just as beautiful as their parents. Because these seeds require a short growing season, they are ideal in areas like New England. Furthermore, these seeds are chemical-free which should please the organic purists among us. Butterbrooke owners Tom and Judy Butterworth have formed a seed co-op. Membership is $6 per year. **C**

CAPRILANDS HERB FARM
Dept. US
Silver Street
Route 44
Coventry, CT 06238
(203) 742-7244
CK

Travelers will be glad to know owner Adelma Simmons conducts tours through the farm from April 1 to December 27 for a small fee. The next best thing to being there is receiving a copy of their very concise brochure, which includes a healthy selection of medicinal and decorative herbs ranging from rosebuds and lavender to musk, clove, and orange blossoms. Most herbs are sold in small packages, but you can get quarter-pound packages of lemon verbena and half-pound packages of rosebuds and lavender blossoms. Books, postcards, incense, potpourri, coat hangers, note paper, necklaces, and spinning wheels are also available. There are three shops: a gift shop, a greenhouse, and a book store. Prices are reasonable, although they are not discounted. There is a $5 minimum order; delivery's in one to two weeks. Many herbal wreaths are too fragile to ship. **B**

CENTRAL MICHIGAN TRACTOR AND PARTS
2903 North U.S. 27
St. Johns, MI 48879
(800) 248-9263
(800) 292-9233: MI residents
(517) 224-6802
MC, V, COD

Till we till again, here's a source for 50% savings on "good used tractor and combine parts" for the farm. When they answer the phone, expect them to say "Tractor Salvage." They have parts for all makes and models, rebuilt starters, reground crankshafts, reconditioned cylinder heads, plus cylinder blocks. Discounted diesel and gas engines for tractors and combines are also available. There's a 30-day guarantee on all parts, with refunds given. Orders are shipped within 24 to 48 hours. **PQ**

COUNTRY HILLS GREENHOUSE
Route 2
Corning, OH 43730
No phone
CK, MC, V

Country Hills Greenhouse specializes in growing and selling a wide range of gesneriads. If that statement doesn't send you rushing for a postage stamp, try this. They sell African violets, lots of 'em. Hey, get your oddball flowering plants here. Unusual African violets are just part of their repertoire. You can find lipstick plants, geraniums, and many other flowering and foliage plants listed in their catalog. It's the Bloomingdale's of horticulture. There is a $10 minimum order, but you won't have trouble filling that with prices of about $2 to $5 per plant. **C $1.50**

COUNTRYSIDE HERB FARM
Dept. SG
Conneautville, PA 16406
(814) 587-2736
CK, COD

Countryside is the largest herb farm in the northeastern U.S.; they supply much of the retail herb industry. Some 300 varieties of herbs are grown for craft use: herbs with fragrant names such as Simmering Potpourri (their best seller), Holiday Spice, Fragrant Oil, Aroma

Glow, and Summer Garden are available. Countryside also imports spices. All products are sold at discounts of up to 50% below retail. Shipping is free; delivery usually takes about 10 days. **C**

DAIRY ASSOCIATION COMPANY, INC.
Dept. US
Lyndonville, VT 05851
(802) 626-3610
CK, COD

Hay, a horse is a horse, of course, of course, and it behooves him to have, what else, soft hooves. (If you don't believe us, just ask Mr. Ed!). Along with the GREEN MOUNTAIN HOOF SOFTENER, get a supply of BAG BALM dilators to keep Elsie from uddering sounds of distress during milking. (BAG BALM's their best-selling item.) KOW KARE and TACKMASTER products are also available at considerable savings. Credit is issued on receipt of returned merchandise, but call first; they accept on a prepaid postage basis upon their authorization. **B**

DUTCH GARDENS
P.O. Box 200
Adelphia, NJ 07710
(201) 391-4366
CK, MC, V

Go Dutch. This company deals exclusively in narcissus, iris, daffodils, amaryllis, lilies, dahlias, tulip bulbs, and other flowers shipped direct from Holland. Prices average about 30% below retail; some prices were comparable to retail. Tulip bulbs are their biggest selling item. Each flower they carry is pictured in full bloom in their exceptionally attractive 174-page catalog, with the growing time, bloom size, and other pertinent information. Free delivery is offered if your order totals $40 or more; an additional cash discount of 10% is offered if your order is $70 or more; 15% if your order totals $500 or more. They will replace bulbs that don't grow the first year. Though they appreciate payment with orders, they will extend credit 30 days after receipt of bulbs. **C**

FLICKINGER'S NURSERY
Sagamore, PA 16250
(412) 783-6528
CK, COD

Is the Little Woman pining for some firs? You don't have to think mink to spruce up your love life! For 36 years Flickinger's has been needling their customers and providing a hedge against inflation. Small trees are their specialty and prices are from 50% to 75% lower than you'll find in most nurseries. We saw seedlings and transplants of bristlecone pine, Colorado blue spruce, Douglas fir, Canadian hemlock, European white birch, and white flowering dogwood. There's a $30 minimum order, so you may need to branch out and chop up your order with friends. How does 100 five- to nine-inch Japanese black pine seedlings for $24 sound? Stumped? One thousand are just $120. Don't beat around the bush (or go barking up the wrong tree)—write for a free catalog. Note: This company's stock is grown for the Northeast, Midwest and some coastal Southern states, so westerners will have to look elsewhere. **C**

FRANS ROOZEN
Vogelenzangseweg 49
2114 BB Vogelenzang
Holland

For over 50 years, this family has been tiptoeing through the tulips and singing a song of savings on over 1,000 different varieties of bulbs. Prices are comparable to other discount bulb importers from Holland, with savings planted in the 10% range. There is a $20 minimum order with a money back guarantee if your complaint is reasonable. Flowers are guaranteed. **C**

FRED'S PLANT FARM
Route 1
P.O. Box 707
Dresden, TN 38225-0707
(901) 364-5419
(901) 364-3754
CK, COD

One potato, two potato, three potato, four; and a lot, lot more. Fred's Plant Farm grows ten varieties of sweet, sweet spuds. Centennials,

Nancy Halls, Jewells, Vardeman, Red Nuggets, White Yams, Yellow Yams, Jaspers, and Algolds were the sugar-coated varieties offered this spring. "We grow our own seeds and plants." Fred guarantees to ship strong, well-rooted plants or your money back. No dud spuds in his garden or yours. You won't be caught holding the hot potato. Fred pays all shipping charges and sends you a free "growing guide" with each shipment, to guide all you green growers. You won't be yammering over these wholesale prices either. Twelve plants cost only $3.98, or for the bigger grower, 2,000 plants cost only $67.95. There's no minimum order, so, don't be a potato head, order from Fred. **B**

GURNEY'S SEED & NURSERY CO.
Yankton, SD 57079
(605) 665-4451
CK

If the grass is always greener on your neighbor's side of the fence, try Gurney's. They carry more hybrid plants, bulbs, trees, seeds, and gardening supplies than you've probably ever seen before. Over 4,000 items from African violets to zucchini are bursting out in their colorful 66-page catalog. Prices are better than you'll find in most retail plant and gardening stores. We've grown fond of their one-cent sale, too. Their crop of novelty items like grow-your-own bird seed, yard-long cucumbers, loofah sponges, tobacco, horseradish, and even praying mantises represents good buys. A nice perk, Gurney's "Complete Growing Guide," is sent with all orders. **C**

HICKORY HILL NURSERY
Dept. US
Route 1, Box 390A
Fisherville, VA 22939
(703) 942-3871

These Hickory Hillbillies aren't afraid to turn over a new leaf, or an entire layer of topsoil, with their TROY-BILT ROTO-TILLER POWER COMPOSTERS manufactured by the Garden Way Manufacturing Company. Their price list showed 12 models of roto-tillers ranging in price from $535 to $1,231, with most discounted 10% to 20%. Prices on various attachments are also discounted. (Discounts vary with the season.) Our experience with roto-tillers has been akin to plowing behind a bucking Brahma bull while gripping a jackhammer, but at least here, the prices won't shake you up. **C**

HOFFMAN HATCHERY, INC.
Gratz, PA 17030
(717) 365-3694
CK

They've been hatching since 1948, and the Hoffmans think that's a feather in their cap. If you think a bird in the hand is worth two in the mail, just look at their prices (cheep, cheep!). Commercial and fancy breeds of chickens, ducks, geese, quail, turkeys, hens, swans, even peafowl are available. Some of these fine-feathered friends carry hefty price tags—a pair of White Royal mute swans cost $595 and must be picked up at the airport. Fifteen Rhode Island Red chicks, on the other hand, will be shipped to your local post office for $11.00 plus $4.95 postage and handling. In addition to animals, Hoffman's carries equipment for small flock raisers. Brooders, feeders, coops, picker fingers . . . everything you always wanted to know about chicks but were too busy to ask is contained in this brochure. In case you haven't been able to put one aside, they even sell plastic nest eggs for $3.75 a dozen. A copy of "Basic Fundamentals on Raising Goslings, Ducklings, Guineas, Chicks, and Turkeys" ($2.25) is indispensable reading, as is the bulletin concerning the raising and feeding of ducks on a budget, $2.50. **B**

J. E. MILLER NURSERIES, INC.
5060 W. Lake Road
Canandaigua, NY 14424
(800) 828-9630
(800) 462-9601: NY residents
MC, V, AE

No need to be a John E. Appleseed with John E. Miller. His 56-page catalog includes 11 pages of apple strains including "old-fashioned" favorites along with many other quality fruit trees, too. Prices are competitive, with walnuts being their most popular line. Everything comes with a one-year guarantee against failure. Replacements are offered at no charge ($1 handling fee only) until August 1; after that, they'll replace at one-half the purchase price. There's a $10 minimum on charge orders. Their catalog is packed with facts and tips on all aspects of growing. **C**

LONG DISTANCE ROSES
P.O. Box 7790
Colorado Springs, CO 80933
(800) LD-ROSES
(303) 537-6737
MC, V, AE, DC, CB

Flowers to go! Fresh roses and orchids can be sent almost anywhere in the United States via Federal Express at a price lower than your neighborhood florist. Overnight floral delight is offered for most areas, with a few locations requiring up to two days. Roses come in your choice of colors—red, pink, or yellow, with other colors available on special occasions. Roses are guaranteed and available for only $39.95 per dozen. Mention *The Underground Shopper* and get orders for only $34.95! Dendroduim orchids from Hawaii can also be ordered for $34.95 per dozen with delivery promised within two days. Flowers are guaranteed fresh, or a complete refund or replacement is provided. **B**

NOWETA GARDENS
Dept. US
900 Whitewater Ave.
St. Charles, MN 55972
(507) 932-4859

Carl Fischer, founder of "Beautiful Gardens" (translation of the Indian word "noweta"), has been growing gladiolus for 57 years and he's glad, which is to be expected from a man surrounded by happy friendship flowers. Varieties for sale are Buttercup Dancer, Gladheart Hallmark, High Seas, and Lavender Dream. Minimum bulb order is $15, but you receive a 20% discount with orders of $250 or more. Usual shipping season runs from March to June; orders are sent by UPS and filled in accordance with planting seasons in customers' regional areas. They send out 10,000 catalogs a year, so get in line for a free one. **C**

PONY CREEK NURSERY
Tilleda, WI 54978
(715) 787-3889
CK, MC, V, COD (with 25% down)

Are visions of sugarplums and cherries break-dancing in your head? That's the pits, man. Maybe you've been aiming for an organic diet or maybe you are just a flower fancier. Whatever your plant preference, you can stock your greenhouse with seeds, fertilizers, insect repellents, and more from Pony Creek. Sugar snap peas and other hybrids were just 69 cents (but 69 cents to $1.25 at retail stores); Hummingbird Feeders, $3.98; Plant-Rite Row Seeders, $19.95. A full assortment of ORTHO garden products, plus tree seedlings of all varieties including their best-seller, Colorado blue spruce, was available. Price breaks mean the more seedlings you buy, the better your savings. Get on your way to healthier eating, beautiful landscaping, and sizable savings. Canning, drying, and freezing supplies will help you achieve self-sufficiency or stockpile foodstuffs for the approach of Armageddon. Orders are shipped in April and May only. Pony Creek will replace (ONCE!) any shrub, tree or evergreen that dies in its first growing season and is returned with the guarantee slip by November 1 of the year it was purchased. **C**

PRENTISS COURT GROUND COVERS
Box 8662
Greenville, SC 29607
(803) 277-4037
MC, V

They've got you covered! Give your lawn a new look with cushioning ground covers. A variety of textures add that special touch to banks, slopes, and rock gardens. More than 50 varieties of ground covers, including day lilies, fig vine, algerian ivy, honeysuckle, and phlox let you choose the creative—and inexpensive—landscape option. And, at 40% to 60% below retail cost, these ground covers are a beautiful buy for any budget. Ajuga, pachysandra, and cotoneaster are also available. These practical problem-solvers are the scenic solution to humdrum lawns. Top-grade stock lets you enjoy maximum ground coverage for a minimal price. A large selection of varieties and colors creates covers with a refreshing new look. Prices include shipping and handling, and orders are shipped within one week. **C 25 cents**

RAINBOW GARDENS
NURSERY & BOOKSHOP
Dept. US
P.O. Box 721
La Habra, CA 90633-0721
(213) 697-1488
CK, MC, V

Somewhere over the rainbow, bluebirds fly and plants bloom in such abundance that it's hard not to believe you're in plant heaven. This plethora of plants includes epiphyllums and other rain forest cacti from aporophyllum moonlight, King Midas, Cadet, and Pegasus to whet your appetite on the cover of their 24 page, four-color catalog. The selection of cacti is staggering. The Christmas and Easter cactus were mouth-watering as was their excellent collection of books to cultivate and nurture you every step of the way. The minimum order is $14 with a 10% off discount to *Underground Shoppers* for orders over $50. **C $1**

REICH POULTRY FARMS, INC.
Dept. US
Box 14, R.F.D. 1
Marietta, PA 17547
(717) 426-3411
COD

If your poultry has been looking paltry, you've come to the Reich place. Mr. Reich's been in the poultry biz for 42 years and ships baby chicks from February through November. All orders are shipped Air Parcel Post, Priority Mail—and usually arrive anywhere in the U.S. or Canada overnight. Savings come with volume. If you buy only 15 or so chicks, the price may be better in a local feed store. (Hens-forth, we'll order in large quantities to get the better price.) Besides chickens, Reich ships exotic geese, turkeys, quail, and seven kinds of ducks, plus equipment and veterinary supplies. Their minimum order is eight baby turkeys, 15 baby chicks, or 10 baby ducks. Reich sends out over 100,000 of their six-page brochures each year, so join the flock.

ROYAL GARDENS
Dept. AIC
P.O. Box 588
Farmingdale, NJ 07727
(201) 780-2713
CK, MC, V, AE

Bargains are always blooming when you browse through this book of bulbs. Hundreds of varieties and colors bring a breath of fresh air to indoor and outdoor gardeners year round. King-size hyacinths in a dazzling display of color will bloom indoors or outdoors, and grow to eight inches in height. Unusual accents to any garden can be added with clusters of anemones, alliums, grape hyacinths, and more, all of which come in mixtures of seven to ten bulbs. Giant tulips, rock garden tulips, and hybrid tulips create a scene sure to flatter your garden. Tiger lilies, trumpets, peonies, irises, and bleeding hearts come in king-size varieties to create a scent-sational flower bed. Hundreds of varieties and colors as well as fertilizers and books are packed into the pages of this catalog. Prices are 20% to 50% lower than competitors, with up to 50% off for early orders. All orders carry a 100% guarantee—replace, credit, or refund—it's your choice. If bulbs fail to bloom in the first season, Royal Gardens will refund or replace with no questions asked. **C $1**

SMALLHOLDING SUPPLIES
Little Burcott, Nr Wells
Somerset, BA 5 INQ, U.K.
(0749) 72127
CK, MC, V, ACCESS, EUROCARD

Are you starting your own small farm? A lot of families are nowadays. Maybe you operate a larger corporate farm. If so, you may find Smallholding Supplies can save you moo-cho dollars. They are the cream of the crop when it comes to supplying the farmer with any imaginable farm item. Items long forgotten can be found here at prices of long ago. We found their 26-page catalog filled with hundreds of items. A new Italian milking machine was priced at $745.20. That should make your cow jump over the moon in delight. Listen to these cheesy deals. Cheesecloth, molds, butter churns, yogurt machines, and other milky items were offered at prices way below retail. A five-gallon milk churn was only $44.25. Tether your cow in the heather with a tethering stake, only $7.76. Shear your sheep cheap for only $240 per pair of electric shears. Not a baaa-d deal. Prices will be quoted and discounts negotiated for large consignments. Remember it's coming from England, so it might not make it for tea. **C $5**

SMITH & HAWKEN
25 Corte Madera
Mill Valley, CA 94951
(415) 383-4050
CK, MC, V, AE

Gardeners on the grow will love every page of this catalog! Indoor and outdoor gardening is made simple with the items offered by Smith and Hawken. Year-round gardeners everywhere will appreci-

ate the English cottage greenhouse with coordinating shelving, staging, and benches to make the most of your plants. Garden furniture in a weather-resistant teak finish lets you enjoy your self-made Eden, or if redwood is more to your liking, enjoy the hand-carved redwood seating group. Aluminum garden furniture in a Victorian style was available, also. To help your garden grow, look into the large selection of tools, pruners, and garden accessories. Everything for the gardener was available in this 32-page full-color catalog. All you add is sunshine and enthusiasm! An unconditional guarantee was offered on all items. Orders shipped within one week of receipt.
C

Records and Tapes

Hear ye, hear ye! Are your ears itching for some music? Scratch the itch, but avoid a pain in your pocketbook. Mail-order companies offer sound bargains on records and tapes. Loop-the-loop with cassette tapes of your favorite crooner, or get in the groove with albums at irresistible prices. Whether you lull yourself to sleep with a lullaby, or set your eardrums to throbbing with the pounding and roaring of New Wave as it crashes onto the sandy beach of your brain, you'll find what you want at a price you can afford. And that's a deal worth hearing about.

ANDRE PERRAULT
Dept. US
P.O. Box 5629
Virginia Beach, VA 23455
(804) 460-1999
MC, V

This fellow holds a lot of records, but you won't find him in the record books—his records are all full of holes. (What's more, while it's often said that records are made to be broken, his records are made to be played.) If you haven't guessed by now, Andre's into music. He has an unbelievable selection of classical records from Arthur Rubinstein to Zubin Mehta, Brahms to Strauss. If you give a Wolf(gang) whistle, you can get Amadeus Mozart; for the cost of a stamp you can quit beating the bushes for Beethoven and get their monthly newsletter. They carry all domestic classical records and foreign labels such as EMI, DEK, HYPERION, ARGO, CHANDOF, ABBY, PATHÉ MARCONI, RCA FRANCE, RCA GERMANY, ELECTROLA, SCHWANN MUSICA MUNDI, ACANTA, TELEFUNKEN, PSALLITE (specializes in organ music) to name a few. No one else can match their selection of domestic and foreign label classical records. Prices are reasonable. Save even more; subscribe to their monthly catalog for $13 a year and receive special subscribers' prices on many of their items. Orders are usually received in six to eight weeks. Canadians can order from: C.P. 250, St.-Hyacinthe, Quebec J257B6. Got to go—they're playing our song! C

CRI COMPOSERS RECORDINGS INC.
170 W. 74th St.
New York, NY 10023
(212) 873-1250
CK, MC, V

Compose yourself and compose a letter to CRI. Their catalog will put you in touch with a wealth of musical compositions recorded by a variety of orchestras. For example, we found a recording of the Louisville orchestra for $5.95 and another by the University of Michigan for $5.50. When it comes to locating extraordinary or unusual performances or compositions, these folks know the score. C

THE CULTURAL GUILD
P.O. Box 5468
Richardson, TX 75080
(214) 239-3140
MC, V, AE

If you're watching a bunch of people shouting at each other, waving their arms, and cavorting to beat the band (and none of what you're seeing or hearing makes any sense), then you're either at the opera or at the state capitol. The Cultural Guild has created a series of cassette tapes to help you become more familiar with the world's best-loved operas. You'll learn to recognize the key musical themes and arias from the operas and to understand their characters, plots, dialogues, and meanings. There are no intimidating overtones, just explanations in both conversational and musical language. You can bone up on *La Boheme* on the way to work or give your boss *Madame Butterfly*. (Fluttery will get you everywhere.) Orders are received in about one month. When these folks can figure a way to make politics comprehensible, we'll *really* shout "Bravo!" **B**

DOUBLE-TIME JAZZ RECORDS
1211 Aebersold Drive
New Albany, IN 47150
(812) 945-3142
CK

Double-Time is working overtime to bring you hard-to-find jazz records in half the time at half the price. Whew! Jamie Aebersold has made a name for himself (and apparently a street, too) in the jazz business. Collectors know whom to call for cutouts, out-of-print, and esoteric jazz selections from the '30s to the present. Mainstream, bebop, modern, and swing are well-represented in this huge inventory. **C**

HARMONIA MUNDI—USA
3364 S. Robertson Blvd.
Los Angeles, CA 90034
(213) 559-0802
MC, V, MO, Cashier Check

Send your money to Harmonia Mundi—not for Blondie but for imported recordings on the HARMONIA MUNDI, RCA, HYPERION, UNICORN-KANCHANA, CHANDOS, PERFORMANCE RECORDINGS, HONG

KONG, and ORFEO labels among others. This company, a division of Harmonia Mundi—France, is a wholesaler to record stores, although they will help individuals get unusual items. If you know records, this may be a valuable source for hard-to-find titles. **C**

HOUSE DISTRIBUTORS
2000 E. Prairie Circle
Olathe, KS 66062
(913) 829-6691
CK, MC, V, AE

Contrary to what the name suggests, this company does not distribute duplexes, nor do they retail ranch homes. They sell mainly jazz music, with some blues, bluegrass, folk, and contemporary thrown in for variety. If you're looking for some obscure song on an even more obscure small label, they probably can get it faster here than anywhere else. It's worth a try since prices are generally at least $1 below list price. They carry LPs and cassettes. Titles date back to the 1920s—we got a recording of the Glen Miller radio show. There is no minimum order; if you buy three or more records, shipping is free. **C**

MUSIC IN THE MAIL
P.O. Box 1
Brightwaters, NY 11718
No phone
CK

We've received plenty of notes in the mail, but never one with such sound advice. Music in the Mail operates as a cooperative classical buyers' service for serious record collectors. They offer factory-sealed classical recordings for 50 cents to $1 above dealer's cost. They don't keep an inventory, but order direct from the factory in Europe once your order has been received, so delivery of your order takes from six to eight weeks. They request that all correspondence be accompanied by a SASE. **C $1**

THE RECORD HUNTER
Dept. US
507 Fifth Ave.
New York, NY 10017
(212) 697-8970
MC, V, AE

Got a minuet? If you've got a bad case of Saturday Night Fever and have been itching for some entertainment, step out in style to the classical big symphony sound of Mozart, Haydn, Beethoven, Schubert, Strauss, or Mendelssohn at good discounts. Names like Dvorak, Smetana, Borodin, and Khachaturian compose a Slavonic festival of sound. The Record Hunter has more than just classical music, though—a lot more! They stock records of all types of music and have probably the biggest selection of compact laser discs in the U.S. Top 20 albums, normally $8.98 each, are just $5.98. Another feature sets them apart: They operate a search service and will ferret out any record or title that is still in print. Most orders are received in seven to 10 days. Shipping charges are $2 for the first disc and 25 cents each thereafter. C

ROCOCO RECORDS LTD.
P.O. Box 3275
Station "D" Willowdale
Ontario, Canada M2R 3G6
CK

We went loco for Rococo! High-quality transfers and pressings of hundreds of live or historical vocal and instrumental performances are available. Nearly all of the great and near-great vocalists, instrumentalists, and conductors can be found in the detailed supplements for $4. In addition to the supplements, which date back to 1967, current release sheets are sent to anyone who is interested. Prices are very reasonable. B

ROSE RECORDS
412 S. Wabash Ave.
Chicago, IL 60604
(312) 987-9044
MC, V

Everything's coming up Rose's. Record prices can present a thorny problem, but this place can soft-petal a solution. While we never promised you a Rose bargain, albums at 20% off list smelled like a pretty sweet deal. Budding classical music lovers will find scores of selections, although folk, pop, blues, soul, and jazz albums also sprout in their 20-page catalog and are available for the picking. Cutout LPs (LPs "cutout" of a record company's regular stock) started blooming at $2.99; with a list price of $4.98, their price was $3.98; $5.98 albums cost $4.75. If you're like most folks, you'll receive your order in about a week. A nice arrangement for those who like to face the music without paying the piper. **C**

Shoes

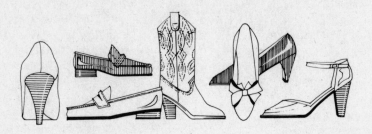

You'll take a shine to the fancy footwork listed in this section. In fact, it's a "shoe-in!" How about buying a pair of old-fashioned cowboy boots, just for kicks? Good savings could spur you on. And if Chief Big Foot's been on the warpath lately, don't criticize until you've walked a mile in his moccasins. Maybe he doesn't know about all the size AAAAA to EEEE shoes available by mail. Want something even more unusual? Get a toehold on comfortable, well-constructed wooden clogs from the Netherlands. For loafers, tassels, topsiders, saddles, espadrilles, or sneakers, look here first for special buys. You'd be a heel not to.

A.W. GOTTEN
Albert Cuypstraat 102-104-106
1072 CZ Amsterdam-z
The Netherlands
Telefoon 729724
CK, V, POSTAL ORDER

Go Dutch! This 85-year-old company is a Dutch treat with their shoe tree full of Dutch and Danish wooden shoes and clogs (klompen) for the whole family. Prices are about half what you would pay if you bought domestically (so maybe you Otten to buy in the States!). Feel the difference of having shoes from a Nether-land. Better yet, a pair of wooden shoes lasts almost forever. Once you've mastered the technical task of converting your shoe size to inches, and then to something called "maat," you'll have one foot in the door. Using the monetary conversion chart supplied by A.W.G. Otten, we estimated a pair of ladies' clogs would cost around $10.55. It costs about $10 just to rent wooden shoes in the U.S. Allow four to five weeks for delivery and add $6.50 (U.S.) for postage. Request their free brochure, "The Story of Dutch Wooden Shoes," to really get into the spirit of things, and to answer your friends' questions. **B**

THE BEST CHOICE
P.O. Box 13
1251 E. Chocolate Ave.
Hershey, PA 17033
(717) 533-8339
CK, MC, V, AE, DC, D, COD

For chocoholics into fitness, this is the best choice to take the bite out of the price of running and tennis shoes and apparel. Save 15% to 25% but splurge on the additional calories while visiting the town. Delicious names: NIKE, NEW BALANCE, ADIDAS, TIGER, AVIA, and REEBOK, men's and women's running shorts by SPORTCO, season sweats and sunglasses. Accessories such as their JOG BRA, tennis and running socks and insoles are just a few of their best choices. Expect to get into the swing of things in two to three weeks. Shipping and handling, $2.25. **B**

BLUM'S
1 Milton St.
Dansville, NY 14437
(716) 335-2266
CK, MC, V

Take steps to save your feet before you're Blum out of luck. Softly constructed of comfortable materials, the canvas and urethane shoes sold by this mail-order house will keep your tootsies from being too pooped to pop. If you stand on the job or walk a lot, invest a few dollars in a pair of comfortable shoes and take a load off your feet— and mind! **C**

BOOT TOWN
Dept. US
5909 Belt Line, Suite 101
Dallas, TX 75240
(214) 385-3052: collect
CK, MC, V, AE, DC, CB

One of Dallas's finest boot merchants mails his boots out of town for the same 25% to 40% discounts. Over 30 top-quality brands are available: LUCCHESE, TONY LAMA, RIOS, JUSTIN, DAN POST, NOCONA, ACME, LARRY MAHAN . . . in the most exotic skins of lizard, snake, ostrich, antelope, cowhide, and more. Sizes 6½ to 13 for men, 4 to 10 for women, and children's sizes. Call for customer assistance with the brand and size and Boot Town will ship within a few days. They also carry the popular "name blank" belts, hats by RESISTOL and other major brands, and a variety of buckles ($8 to $50) including CRUMRINE initials. Western shirts and jeans by LEVI, WRANGLER, LEE, and PANHANDLE SLIM, to boot. Expect your order to arrive in about two weeks. They'll give refunds or exchanges on unworn boots; there's no restocking charge on returns. *Underground Shoppers* putting in an order for over $200 will receive a free bootjack. **B, PQ**

CALIFORNIA CARGO
P.O. Box 4178
Dept. 63
Carlsbad, CA 92008
(800) 223-2526
(800) 445-4343: CA residents
CK, MC, V, MO

See entry page 168.

CARLSEN IMPORT SHOES
Dept. US
524 Broadway
New York, NY 10012
(212) 431-5940
CK

Imagine the Los Angeles Coliseum filled to capacity as over 100,000 sports fans watched an Olympian performance. Now imagine that every one of those people took off their shoes and left them in the stadium—100,000 pairs of shoes. Now imagine one store with an equivalent inventory of shoes and call it Carlsen Import Shoes. That's a lot of track shoes to keep track of! This is where athletes truly foot the bill for less. Carlsen carries all types of running footgear (track shoes are their specialty), in brands like PUMA, PONY, PATRICK, BROOKS, SPALDING, AUTRY, and ADIDAS. Order their free catalog and dash through sports equipment like bags, balls, and track suits. Discounts range from 15% to 30% off retail. Unused items are returnable. All orders must be prepaid; they're shipped out within 48 hours. Carlsen's been in business for some 50 years and was the first company to outfit school teams with ADIDAS shoes. C

CARR'S
P.O. Box 2511
Waco, TX 76702-2511
(512) 824-9228
MC, V, AE, DC, CB, D

Carr's is linked into some of the crème de la crème shoe stores in the country. End of the season merchandise is regrouped and shipped from some of the best retail stores to Carr's and repriced at 33% to 70% off. Brands carried: CHARLES JOURDAN, STUART WEITZMAN, AMALFI, BANDOLINO, PAPPAGALLO, NINA, J. RENEE, and LIZ CLAIBORNE . . . more than 30,000 shoes! They also carry handbags. Just call or write with a description of the shoe you want and your size. Add $2.50 shipping and handling cost per item. Refunds or exchanges are given on returned shoes.

CHERNIN'S SHOES
1001 S. Clinton
Chicago, IL 60607
(312) 922-5900
CK, MC, V

Our hearts churned after discovering Chernin's. We didn't even have
to butter up our husbands to order our shoes. Prices are so reasonable, even a stubborn cow would be moo-ved to buy a pair of men's
calfskin tassel loafers for $36.95 or ladies' snakeskin dress pumps for
$59.95. The names are withheld at the request of Chernin's, but thou-
sands of famous brands are sold at reasonable prices. Extra-narrow,
extra-wide, extra-long, extra-short . . . size 'em up. Their selection of
wingtips, oxfords, demi-boots, boat mocs, hiking boots, penny flats,
pumps, boots, and athletic shoes for men, women, and children is an
amazing "feet." Five locations in the Chicago area. **C**

FINE & KLEIN
119 Orchard St.
New York, NY 10002
(212) 674-6720
CK

See entry page 235.

HILL BROTHERS
99 Ninth St.
Lynchburg, VA 24504
(804) 528-1000
MC, V, AE, DC, CB, COD

Put your best foot forward with your feet outfitted with shoes from
Hill Brothers. HB deals exclusively in women's shoes and they carry
shoes in sizes 3 to 13 and widths AAAAA to EEEE. (The range of
shoe sizes varies depending on the shoe style; there are over 600 different styles.) That means that sufferers of five-digit inflation no
longer need to have a Cinderella complex about the size of their hard-
to-fit feet. Some shoes carry ritzy names like CHLOE, CHER, and
ANDRA, while others bear the decidedly less glamorous appelations
VERNA, AGNES, BERNIE, and RONA. Prices are competitive; satisfaction is guaranteed. Orders are shipped within 24 hours; shipping
charges are $3.25. If you return your shoes within 14 days, they'll

make an exchange or give a full refund. Their free, 64-page, full-color catalog is perking with savings. **C**

JUST JUSTIN TAKE OUT BOOTS
Dept. US
9090 Stemmons
Dallas, TX 75247
(800) 458-7846: nationwide
(800) 258-7846: TX residents
(214) 630-2858: local residents
CK, MC, V, AE, COD

Are high-priced cowboy boots about to put you on Boot Hill? Get some relief! Discounts run 40% to 70% off normal retail here—that should spur you on to action! The selection's great (they have over 15,000 pairs of boots in stock), but just as you'd expect with a name like Just Justin, you won't find any labels besides JUSTIN. To order, send your size in regular shoes (men's or women's) and Justin will send you the size you need. Shipping's preset at $5 for a pair of boots; you'll probably receive your order in about two weeks. They'll exchange or give refunds if there's a problem. **C**

J.W. BRAY
Dept. US
305 E. Hawthorne
P.O. Box 189
Dalton, GA 30720
(414) 226-2729
CK, MC, V

We've got good news and bad news about this 42-year-old company. First the good news: You can slip into women's soft slipper scuffs, and slip off half the retail price. Attractive women's terry and tricot wedges and scuffs were offered for $5 to $6 ($9 to $11 suggested list). The bad news is: There's a $25 minimum order, so unless you're a centipede, you're going to really have to stock up. (There *are* disadvantages to having low prices!) Besides slippers, their own line of men's, women's, and children's leisure and casual footwear is available at 20% to 40% less than retail. They guarantee 100% customer satisfaction or you can return the merchandise. You'll probably get your order in about two weeks. Their motto ought to be, "We try softer." **B, C**

NELSON'S
Dept. US
201 South Park
Fairfax, MN 55332
(507) 426-7216
CK, COD

With our boots on your tootsies, your soles can take flight. (On the other hand, who wants soar feet?) This firm isn't afraid to put a full-Nelson on high prices, especially on U.S. made boots and casual shoes. You can lace up a $13 discount on safety insulated boots, $10 savings on slip-on boots, or $15 on insulated boots. U.S. made boots and casual shoes are probably the best bargain here. The owner handles his mail-order business during workday lulls at his store, so he doesn't have additional help for this end of the business. Prices are about 15% below retail and include shipping and handling costs. Orders usually come in about a week or 10 days. We're no arch-enemies of Nelson's, in fact, we'll stomp up a storm on one heel of a good buy. **B**

ORCHARD STREET BOOTERY
75 Orchard St.
New York, NY 10002
(212) 966-0688
MC, V, AE

We almost couldn't see the tree-mendous discounts through the forest of inventory at Orchard. There's nothing seedy about this establishment—when it comes to footwear, they're the apple of our eye. You can't help but pick something from Orchard's crop of shoes for the well-heeled woman. GOLO, STANLEY PHILIPSON, PALIZZIO, JACQUES COHEN, BANDOLINO, ANDREW GELLER, MARTINEZ VERLO, FERRAGAMO, NINA, VERSANI, PETER KAISER, and others are available in leather and vinyl "slush boots," loafers, sandals, slippers, and evening wear. Prices are unseasonably reasonable at 25% to 30% below retail. Harvest a 20% savings on shoes to cover sizes 5 to 10, in B and C widths. There are no refunds; they exchange or give store credit. Orders go out the same day as received. Write or call for more information; be sure to have the style and model number of the item you want. **PQ**

PL PREMIUM LEATHER BY HANOVER
P.O. Box 340
Hanover, PA 17331
(800) 345-8500 ext. 33
(717) 632-7575
CK, MC, V, AE, DC, CB, COD

You'll save money Hanover foot here with factory direct savings on first-quality men's and women's shoes. The selection is excellent: HANOVER, CLARKS, and NEW BALANCE are just three of the dozen or so brands they carry. Classic styles included wingtips, loafers, tassels, topsiders, saddles, espadrilles, and sneakers. Their line of premium-quality, comfort-constructed dress shoes is probably their best value. Shoe widths run from AA to EEE; shoe sizes from 6 to 15. All shoes carry a free 10-day trial with a refund available at the end of that period if you decide "the goods ain't good enough." Shirts, socks, ties, and belts were also featured in their 40-page color catalog. Delivery usually takes about a week. PL is owned by a very well-respected manufacturer, Clarks of England, and they've been in business since 1899. C

ROAD RUNNER SPORTS
Suite K
11211 Sorrento Valley Road
San Diego, CA 92121
(619) 455-0558
(800) 551-5558
CK, MC, V, AE, MO

This company will run circles around their nearest competitors. Guaranteed the lowest prices on the best names in running shoes, business, dress, and golf shoes all by FOOT-JOY. The original SAUCONY (my personal favorite) was $39.95 (retail $64), and SAUCONY's latest aerobic shoes (men's and ladies'), regular $56 was $38.95. Half-price GORE-TEX running suits by TIGER were $79.95. Names like NIKE, ADIDAS, NEW BALANCE, BROOKS, AVIA, and ETONIC were all jumping out at me with some dollar savings as much as $45. Call toll free and speak to any of the shoe experts where you can not only expect advice but shipment in 24 hours. Over 20,000 running shoes in stock. And that's just the beginning to the wonderful Road Runner story. C

Sporting Goods

Whether you're a middle-aged athlete fighting off flabby thighs and a growing paunch, or a superbly conditioned young adult with the body of a Greek god, outdoor athletes will find everything they need for sports outdoors (or even indoors!). You can find everything from basketballs to bass lures by mail. When ordering hiking boots or running shoes, always send along an outline of your foot since sizes can vary, even within the same brand. If you telephone for information, ask if there's a floor model of what you're looking for that's for sale. Buying a floor model is a great way to save even more on what you want.

ALLYN AIR SEAT CO.
18 Millstream Road
Woodstock, NY 12498
(914) 679-2051
CK, COD

Who cares about "fanny fatigue"? Lots of people, that's who. If you are a peddle pusher, truck driver, taxi driver, cycle rider, or just going down the highway, you care about your derriere. Is your rump in the dumps? Never fear, Allyn Air Seat Co. is here. We found the perfect solution for tired tooshies. Allyn's offers air cushions for just about everyone and you won't be paying out the bazooka for them. An air-filled seat cover for a motorcycle was only $30 including shipping. The model attaches in minutes and stores easily when not in use. The seats bring up the rear only one-fourth inch and never need refilling. No butts about it—these seats are the "kiss of comfort." Some new products being offered include The Frame Bag, offering carrying convenience for the pampered peddler. It is aerodynamically cut to prevent wind resistance and costs only $15. Cover your rear safely with the Big E-Z-VU Bar End Mirror costing only $9. Here's a treat for your seats; the prices. They are 25% below retail and deliveries are mailed immediately upon order. So move your tail and get your order in the mail. **B (SASE)**

AUSTAD'S
Dept. US
4500 E. 10th St.
P.O. Box 1428
Sioux Falls, SD 57101
1-800-843-6828 (except SD, AL, HI)
(605) 336-3135
CK, MC, V, AE, DC, CB

Como está, Austad? If you've been engolfed with the urge to hit a little white ball, bogie on down and putt in an order here. Since 1963 Austad's has stocked a complete line of quality golf gear (RAM, WILSON, MACGREGOR, and other leading manufacturers) at prices up to 40% less than retail. With an outstanding selection at fair prices, Austad's won't put a divot in your green. Their full-color catalog features clubs, bags, carts, shoes, training aids, sportswear, accessories, gifts, and even exotic golf vacations. Many items are made exclusively for Austad's by leading golf manufacturers. Orders are shipped within 48 hours, usually by UPS, so most orders are received within one week, two weeks maximum. If golf is your handicap, this store and mail-order company should treat you in a fairway. **C**

BART'S WATER SKI CENTER, INC.
P.O. Box 294
North Webster, IN 46555
(800) 348-5016
(800) 552-2336: IN residents
(219) 834-7666
MC, V, AE, COD

Are you having trouble keeping your head above water skiing costs? We didn't find that sink-or-swim attitude at Bart's. He carries slaloms, ski vests, swim suits, T-shirts, and many other water skiing accessories. You'll be jumping over the wakes when you see his lake of brand names: CONNELLY, JOBE, and AMERICAN to mention a few. He's your HOTLINE to values. Would we KIDDER you? Just look at these bargains: the top of the line CONNELLY slalom skis retail at $425, his price, $297.98; a three-buckle ski-vest retailing at $44.95 was $37.98; for your skiing pooch, a doggie vest was $17.98. What a hotdog of a deal! Bart's 40-page full-color catalog is especial-ski nice. You won't get splashed in the face if you don't like your order; Bart accepts returns up to 30 days for any reason. **C**

BASS PRO SHOPS
P.O. Box 4046
Dept. BP01
Springfield, MO 65808
(800) 227-7776
(417) 883-4960: AL, HI residents
CK, MC, V

Something's fishy in the state of Missouri, Mark. It's the Bass Pro Shop. They lure mail-order shoppers with a huge catalog baiting them with savings up to 50% off retail. We fell for it hook, line, and sinker and found boats, rods, reels, line, hooks, clothing, and more. We had a sinking feeling the high-quality would cost a lot. But holy mackerel, were we ever convinced. A whale of a deal! **C $2**

BIKE NASHBAR
4111 Simon Road
Youngstown, OH 44512
(800) 345-BIKE
(800) 654-BIKE: OH residents
(216) 782-2244
CK, MC, V, D

Sports enthusiasts will move right along to catch the bargains in this biker's shopping bible. For both the serious and semi-sedentary biker, Bike Nashbar carries the finest equipment at the finest prices we've seen in a long time. Racing and recreational bikes, touring bikes, and street bikes are all available from this company. All major brands, such as CITADEL, SHIMANO, VITUS, COLNAGO, CINELLI, GUERCIOTT, and the Bike Nashbar brand were carried at up to 60% off retail price. Accessories such as bike pumps, water bottles, shoulder holders, helmets, shoes, and mirrors were included in the bargains. Already own a bike you just can't part with? Chances are, you can order its repair and replacement parts through this catalog, such as chains, brake levers, cranksets, and flywheels. Deluxe seats, tires, fenders, and tool kits are also available at discount prices. Indoor enthusiasts will appreciate the stationary trainers to keep in shape year-round. Sporty racing jerseys, caps, and sunglasses round out the racing gear. Orders receive fast shipping and a 100% guarantee of satisfaction. **C $1** (six issues)

BOWHUNTERS DISCOUNT WAREHOUSE
Dept. US
P.O. Box 158
Zeigler Road
Wellsville, PA 17365
(717) 432-8611: orders
(717) 432-8651: customer service
CK (certified), COD

We wanted to talk to an expert, so we asked William to Tell us where to target in on discount hunting bows. (We figured he must know something—he was wearing an Arrow shirt.) Since he aimed to please, we got the point instead of the shaft. It's no surprise he referred us here—this company is the world's largest archery distributor with over 7,500 bows in stock. BROWNING, BEAR, JENNINGS, TSE, DARTON, and MARTIN hunting bows can all be sighted in their 108-page catalog at a discount! Tree stands, targets, broadheads, camouflage clothing, and accessories were also available. Less discriminating single girls a-quiver with the notion of doing a little beau-hunting can even find a selection of turkey calls to help them bag a Tom (or Dick or Harry). Bowhunters Discount Warehouse carries about 150 different brands with discounts running 40% off retail. The best bets for bargain-hunting come during the Christmas season. There's a $10 minimum order; a 20% restocking charge on returns; orders are shipped within 24 hours. *Underground Shoppers* get one free pair of bowstring silencers with their order. **C**

CABELA'S
812 13th Ave.
Sidney, NE 69160
(800) 237-4444: orders
(800) 237-8888: customer service
CK, MC, V

Anyone for singing praises in a Cabela's choir? While we're big believers in being in harmony with nature and in tune with the outdoors, our voices may be a bit too corn-husky for this Nebraska firm. Prices are good—from 10% to 75% off on their own brand of high-quality outdoor gear. They handle all kinds of equipment and clothes for fishing, hunting, and camping (but no guns), with their own brand of down jackets being particularly popular. There is no restocking charge and no minimum order. Five catalogs are issued annually. **C**

CARLSEN IMPORT SHOES
Dept. US
524 Broadway
New York, NY 10012
(212) 431-5940
CK

See entry page 387.

CAMPMOR
810 Route 17 N.
P.O. Box 999—5JD
Paramus, NJ 07653-0999
(800) 526-4784
(201) 445-5000: NJ residents
CK, MC, V

Get on a camping campaign with Campmor! Prices are 15% to 20% off on brand-name camping and outdoor supplies. Eureka tents may be their best value, but they also have CAMP 7 goose-down sleeping bags, CANNONDALE bicycle touring accessories, WILDERNESS EXPERIENCE and KELTY backpacks, COLEMAN stoves and lots more—everything you'll need to survive in the outdoors is displayed in their 88-page catalog. Other brands you'll discover include WOOLRICH, NORTH FACE, and COLUMBIA. We compared the price of VICTORINOX, the original Swiss Army knife, with the prices charged by local retailers and found a 30% savings. Refunds are given within six months of your purchase. Most items have a flat $3 shipping fee and are shipped UPS. (Look for your purchase in seven to 10 days.) Visit their showroom for additional savings when you're in the Garden State. C (five times a year)

CUSTOM GOLF CLUBS, INC.
10206 N. Interregional
Austin, TX 78753
(800) 531-5025
(800) 252-8108: TX residents
(512) 837-4810
CK, MC, V, COD

From a most humble beginning in the basement of his Plainfield, N.J., house in 1969 and a few hundred dollars, Carl and his brother, Frank Paul still operate from spartan surroundings but are selling $9 million worth of golf equipment and accessories. They might be the world's largest supplier of custom clubs, repair components, and accessories even though the majority of those sales outside of their Austin retail locations is by mail order. If you want to tighten your grip on prices, too, plan on saving 10% to 30% or more off suggested retail prices. Minimum order, $10. C (112 pages—Clubmaking components and supplies) C (80 pages—accessory merchandise)

CYCLE GOODS CORP.
2735 Hennepin Ave. South
Minneapolis, MN 55408
(800) 328-5213
CK, MC, V, AE, DC, CB

Are you failing your cycle class? Are you finding the high prices above your level? Maybe you need *The Handbook of CYCL-OLOGY* published by Cycle Goods Corp. It will offer financial aid with savings of 10% to 30% and have you aceing the course. This handbook offers 150 brands of bicycles and related clothing, accessories, and parts.

You'll pass your finals with flying colors with brands like TAILWIND, KIRTLAND, BLAZER, ECLIPSE, CYCLONE, and others. We found schol-arly deals in the Spring Price Schedule; a triwheel carrier was priced at $49.95. Other high-classed deals offered an ATMOS pump only $17.95 and a kickstand only $2.95. We scheduled our classes in style, wearing BATA BIKER shoes and AVOCET skin shorts. Cycle Goods has a liberal refund policy and a 30-day guarantee, so you won't have to cram for a refund. Pass Cycl-ology and graduate from high prices. **C**

DINN BROS.
68 Winter St.
P.O. Box 111
Holyoke, MA 01041
(413) 536-3816
CK, MC, V

There's a soccer (player) born every minute. Why else would the brothers Dinn sell so many trophies and plaques? (Just for kicks?) We saw every conceivable type of trophy, ribbon, medal, wall plaque, desk accessory, etc., in their 48-page catalog, with factory direct wholesale prices up to 70% lower than retail. Swimmers, golfers, runners, bowlers, skiers, skaters, weight lifters, tennis-baseball-bas-ketball-football players, as well as speakers, champion dogs, horses, bulls, and big fish are all represented in walnut and marble-based trophies. A 12½-inch tennis trophy was $8.75 (retail $26.25) and a 5½-inch track trophy was $3.50 (retail $12). Engraving is free. Orders over $200 are shipped free; no minimum order. Most orders are received within 72 hours. **C**

EISNER BROS.
76 Orchard St.
New York, NY 10002
(212) 431-8800
(212) 475-6868
CK, (CERTIFIED ONLY), COD

Eisner Bros. is the world's largest headquarters for all activewear and printables. They carry T-shirts in white and over 20 colors. They also carry sweatshirts, sweatpants, minidress sweatshirts, oversized T-shirts and sweatshirts, night shirts, tank tops, golf shirts, jackets, and baseball caps. They stock sizes from 6 months through adult 4XL in a full variety of colors. Eisner Bros. is a distributor for FRUIT OF

THE LOOM, HANES PRINTABLES, HANES HEADWEAR, PANNILL SWEAT-
SHIRTS BY MONSANTO, RUSSELL CORP., SCREEN STARS as well as their
own brand. The minimum order is a dozen of the same size and color.
Orders are shipped the same day they are placed. **C**

F & M SPORTS OUTLET
Dept. US
679 Belmont St.
Brockton, MA 02401
(617) 583-3782
CK (seven-day clearance), MC, V, COD

This outlet is one of the biggest ETONIC dealers in the country, but
they also give 15% to 20% off BROOKS, CONVERSE, TIGER, BASSETT
AND WALKER, PUMA, FRANK SHORTER, AVIA, HIND, MOVING COMFORT,
FOX RIVER, and STARTER (makers of the official team jackets of the
NFL) brands. Discounts vary depending on the brand. Approximately 60% of their merchandise consists of athletic and golf shoes,
while the remaining 40% consists of clothing. Clothing sizes range
from S to XXL. Most items are first-quality; there are a few seconds
and factory irregulars. Orders are usually shipped "right away" by
UPS and are usually received within five to 15 days. The minimum
order is $20. *Underground Shopper* readers who identify themselves
qualify for an additional 5% discount. On your mark . . . get set . . . .
go for it!! **PQ**

FOLKS ON BUCK HILL
Dept. US
P.O. Box 306
North Industry, OH 44707
(800) 321-0200
(800) 362-6540: OH residents
CK, MC, V

We won't take any potshots at these Folks just because they live on
Buck Hill—though the only thing we've ever poached was an egg.
This company offers outdoor sporting goods (hunting, fishing, camping gear) at about 20% below retail. Their 72-page catalog displays
outdoor items such as archery equipment, fishing lures, bullets, lanterns, guns, sights, sleeping bags, etc., as well as hard-to-find items
in several hundred brand names easily recognizable to outdoorspeo-
ple. DAIWA and REDFIELD in hard goods, and TEN X and WOOLRICH in

clothing are just a few examples. There's a $25 minimum order and a 10% restocking charge on returns. Most orders are received within seven to 10 days. **C**

FUNCTIONAL CLOTHING, LTD.
Wilderspool Causeway
Causeway Avenue
Warrington WA4 6QQ, England
Warrington (STD 0925 or 92) 53111
Telex 627625 FCLWAR G
CK

Their name says it all: functional clothing for work and play is their specialty. Whether you're going on an Arctic fishing expedition, climbing the Himalayas, caravanning across Europe, sailing the Love Boat, or merely birdwatching in your snowy backyard, the patented Airflow construction of their all-weather wear will keep you warm in winter, cool in summer. Coats, jackets, leggings, mitts, headwarmers, thermal clothing, and seagoing overtrousers for men and women are waterproof and windproof, and have removable thermal liners. Granted, you may not make the annual best-dressed list, but then again, who cares what the penguins think? **C**

GOLF AND TENNIS WORLD
1456 South Federal Highway
Deerfield Beach, FL 33441
(800) 327-1760
(305) 428-3780
CK, MC, V, AE, COD

Pay less green for all you need on the green or on the court. They double-guarantee their name-brand equipment and promise to meet any competitor's price on any golf item. Prices you can't putt down: AGI custom woods, $46 to $64 (retail $75 to $100); deluxe nine-inch golf bags, $65 (retail $90); AGI golf carts, $59.95 to $79.95 (retail $70 to $110). A $28 umbrella was just $17.95 and a pair of spikeless shoes retailing for $48 was just $39. They've got all kinds of footwear, fuzzy headcovers, gloves, plus tennis rackets, balls, graphite string, wrist bands, and shoes. They even do golf club customizing to your specifications, with custom irons going for $35 to $55. Expect your order to arrive in about 10 days. **PQ**

GOLF HAUS
Dept. US
700 N. Pennsylvania
Lansing, MI 48906
(517) 484-8842
CK, MC, V

'Fore you swing into action and get teed off, tally up the savings here!
With prices slicing 40% to 60% off retail, you can make your pitch to
Golf Haus and save yourself a long drive, as well as some green. Golf
Haus carries 15 to 20 brands, including all those normally found on
the leader board: SPALDING, DUNLOP, WILSON, TITLEIST, LYNX, PING,
etc. A set of WILSON GE clubs (1, 3, 5 woods plus irons) listing for
$727 was discounted to $350. FOOT-JOY and ETONIC golf shoes averaged almost 50% off retail; MACGREGOR, MAXFLI, and TITLEIST golf
balls also rolled in at rough-ly 50% off. There's a $50 minimum order;
exchanges or full refunds are given on returns. Most folks get their
order in 10 days. *Underground Shoppers* who identify themselves
and buy a set of golf clubs will receive a free set of headcovers (worth
$15) for their clubs. They ship freight free within the continental
United States, and have a free catalog upon request. **C, B, PQ**

GREAT LAKES SPORTSWEAR
11371 E. State Fair
Detroit, MI 48234
(313) 372-4500
CK, MC, V, COD

Ski-p the slopes and head for the après-ski activities in cheap chic.
The Great Lakes factory offers their own brand of nylon jackets,
vests, and arctic gear sold in their outlet store. The more you buy, the
more you'll save. Their full-color, 16-page catalog displayed their own
brand of racing jackets, sport and mopar jackets, astronaut and
bomber jackets, and even water-repellent arctic jackets and vests.
Jackets were unlined, lined with Kasha (a lightweight flannel), or
pile-lined in a rainbow of bright colors. Prices were excellent, about
50% off conventional retail and ranging from $9 for a lightweight
unlined jacket to $23 for the pile-lined bomber-style arctic jacket.
They'll exchange damaged products; there's no restocking charge.
Off-season orders are shipped out the same day, but beware, orders
placed between September and Christmas may take two to six weeks
to arrive. Send for their catalog to get the snow down on bargains. **C**

HILL'S COURT
1 Tennis Way
East Dorset, VT 05253
(802) 362-1200
CK, MC, V, AE

Hill's Court is for all of you who are dreaming about becoming the next Chris Evert Lloyd. Lots of brand-name tennis and active gear here at good prices, with some hard-to-find items like the incredibly sexy white unitard by PONY (was $49.95). Lacoste-style shirts in yummy colors for $22.95 if you order two or more, MICKEY MOUSE tennis whites, and lace panties are among the many items you can find from Hill's Courts. C

HOLABIRD SPORTS DISCOUNTERS
Rossville Industrial Park
9004 Yellow Brick Road
Baltimore, MD 21237
(301) 687-6400
CK, MC, V, C

A little birdie told us where you can save up to 35% on major brand-name sporting goods. Holabird Sports Discounters will have you strutting proud as a peacock in REEBOK, PRINCE, AMF HEAD, SPALDING, YAMAHA, DUNLOP, and an entire flock of others. Whether you are into squash, racquetball, tennis, golf, or running, you can find all the accessories and equipment you need cheep, cheep at Holabird. We were happy as a lark about the bargains we found in their flier. For example, squash balls were $26 per dozen. A PRINCE shoulder tote was only $19.95, and T-shirts were as low as $3.95. Holabird is a song-bird of savings. Here is something to make you sing: they will ship your order within two days. Be a bird in paradise with Holabird. You have to be a fast flyer if you want a refund; you must return your unused merchandise within seven days. B

KIRKHAM'S OUTDOOR PRODUCTS
Dept. US
3125 S. State St.
Salt Lake City, UT 84115
(800) 453-7756
(801) 486-4161: UT residents
CK, MC, V, AE

After a hard day of camping and hiking, at night we like to sleep in-tents-ly. Kirkham's carries the exclusive line of SPRINGBAR® tents, manufactured in their factory. Kirkham's tents are sold only factory direct, without dealers or distributors, resulting in a direct price to the consumer, so it's difficult to compare prices, although prices are certainly competitive. Price comparisons are difficult because Kirkham's tents often have more features and better quality materials used in their construction. Choose from many styles and sizes; from one-person pup tents (for dogged outdoor buffs), to family tents sleeping six (for those into group sacks). Kirkham's refund policy is hardly tent-ative: SPRINGBAR® tents are warranted to be free from defects in materials or workmanship for 10 years. There's no restocking charge; most orders are shipped within 24 hours. C

LAS VEGAS DISCOUNT GOLF AND TENNIS
Dept. US
4813 Paradise Road
Las Vegas, NV 89109
(800) 634-6743
(702) 798-6300
MC, V, AE, DC, CB

You have to know when to hold 'em and know when to sell 'em at a discount. Since 1974, Las Vegas has gambled on selling the very latest in golf and tennis equipment, at prices far below retail, and the gamble's paid off. Over 50 major brands in pro-line golf clubs, shoes, bags, racquets, balls, gloves, as well as a complete line of accessories are slotted in their company, and when we pulled the right lever, brands like WILSON, BEN HOGAN, PING, SPALDING, ST. ANDREWS, PRINCE, ADIDAS, BORG, and ELLESE came up. Bowling equipment and accessories have been added to their vast stock. Discounts range from 20% to 60%. IZOD sweaters were $26.95 (regularly $40). Most orders are delivered in seven to 10 days; shipping charges are $4.95. Federal Express is available for a reduced, special rate. Returns are subject to a 10% restocking fee ($5 minimum). Ninety percent of their merchandise is stocked; 10% must be drop shipped. They put all their cards in their free 72-page catalog and continue to come up a winner. C, B

LOMBARD'S SPORTING GOODS
1840 N.E. 164th St.
North Miami Beach, FL 33162
(305) 944-1166
CK, MC, V

Lombard's prices on name-brand sporting goods, including golf items, won't put a hole in your pocket. For instance, a BEN HOGAN

Tour Wood Vector Shaft was $224 (four woods price), while FOOT-JOY Super Softies cost just $49.95. Besides golf gear, Lombard's sells tennis, squash, and racquetball gear. Every racket you'll hear of is stocked. The STING mid-sized racket is just $91.95, while the HEAD Competition Edge, which retails for $110, is just $60.95. The accessory line is complete, ranging from nets to bags to ball machines. Gut and nylon string prices are the best we've seen so far: gut was $16.25, nylon went from $2 to $8.75. Don't drive, just putt your order in at Lombard's for savings of 30% to 60%. There's no minimum order; orders are processed within 48 hours. There's a 20% restocking charge on unused custom orders. Their catalog is free, but to get on their mailing list to receive periodic fliers, send a buck separate from your order. C, B $1

NEW ENGLAND DIVERS INC.
131 Rantoul St.
Beverly, MA 01915
(617) 922-6951
CK, MC, V, AE

When in a sink-or-swim situation, give special tanks to New England Divers. They've been in business since 1951 and, now, with seven stores, they claim they are the world's largest distributor of scuba gear. Dive in for famous brands like U.S. DIVER'S, DACOR, FARALLON, OCEANIC, UNDERWATER, PARKWAY, KINETICS, POSEIDON, and MAKO and bubble over their 20% to 25% discounts. In-stock orders are shipped within 24 hours; out-of-stock items that must be ordered typically take around three weeks. If you don't see what you want in their catalog, call them and see if they can fish it out of stock for you. C, PQ

PRO SHOP WORLD OF GOLF
Dept. US
8130 N. Lincoln Ave.
Skokie, IL 60077
(800) 323-4047 (for price quote)
(312) 675-5286
CK, MC, V, D

High prices are enough to knock the dimples off any Titleist, so why fall into the (sand) trap of paying retail? Stay away from the rough— you can stop driving and start to putter around at home if you trust a

Pro. This place claims to have "the largest golf inventory in the world." Hazards are few with names like WILSON, LYNX, MAC-GREGOR, BEN HOGAN, PING, RAM, SPALDING, and other brands in clubs, golf carts, golf balls, drivers, wedges, utility irons, shoes, and gloves—especially when prices are 20% to 50% off! PRO LINE golf equipment is their most famous line. They don't give refunds, but do make exchanges. Credit card orders are shipped the next day; orders paid by check are delayed until the check clears the bank. Most orders are received within seven days. The shipping charge is $5: there's a 10% restocking charge on non-defective returns. Since everything is first-quality, you can rest assured that when it comes to ordering a bag, shirt, etc., you won't find a hole-in-one. **C, F, PQ**

RAYCO TENNIS PRODUCTS
(800) 854-6692
(800) 854-6902: California residents
(619) 421-9822
CK, MC, V, COD

The string's the thing! Tighten those purse strings with savings on strings, tennis rackets, and racket-stringing machines at Rayco. Most of their customers are folks who've set up their own racket-stringing business, but that could be you. Stringing your own racket would save you the double markup on strings plus a labor charge. Order delivery times vary: strings are stocked, and you can get them the next day if requested; rackets and stringing machines are drop shipped from the manufacturer. (Some stringing machine manufacturers are in Europe.) There's a $4 service charge on orders under $20; $2 service charge on orders between $20 and $40. **F, PQ**

REED TACKLE
Dept. US
P.O. Box 1348
Fairfield, NJ 07007
(201) 227-0409
CK, MC, V, COD

"The merchandise we carry makes us special," according to store owner Richard Reed. He just may be right: since 1944, they've been offering some very good dyed-fly buys, not to mention lure parts and rod building supplies and components. Popular brands abound including MUSTAD hooks and SWISS SWING lures. Pricing is competitive. Orders are sent out within 48 hours. Shipping charges vary depending on size and weight, but start at $1.90. If you want more information about their fishing supplies, you'll have to worm it out of them yourself. **C, PQ**

REI CO-OP
P.O. Box C-88125
Seattle, WA 98188
(800) 426-4840
(800) 562-4894: WA residents
MC, V

Aside from their eight walk-in stores, REI has one of the best catalogs (96 pages and full-color) displaying outdoor clothing and equipment. Their niche is high-technology hiking, climbing, and camping gear, cross-country skiing, bicycling items and fashion sportswear. Mountain climbing gear is their claim to fame. (Jim Whittaker, one of the first Americans to climb Mt. Everest, was a former president.) Mail-order prices are somewhat below full retail. REI's more than one million members (membership fees are $5) save even more. REI carries many top-quality products by famous-name manufacturers like JANSPORT, SIERRA DESIGNS, WOOLRICH, KELTY, CHOUNARD, and MOUNTAIN HOUSE, to name a few. Their own PEAK VALUE brand offers comparable quality to big-name brands but at reduced prices, a good way to save on the cost of outdoor recreational gear. Also, for a $5 membership fee, you can share in the company's profits at year's end and receive a rebate of what usually amounts to about 10% of the cost of your year's purchases. **C**

ROAD RUNNER SPORTS
Suite K
11211 Sorrento Valley Road
San Diego, CA 92121
(619) 455-0558
(800) 551-5558
CK, MC, V, AE, MO

See entry page 391.

THE SHOTGUN NEWS
P.O. Box 669
Hastings, NE 68901
(402) 463-4589
CK

We got a kick out of the reaction they triggered. This high-caliber publication aims to offer "the finest gun buys and trades in the U.S." Shoot, for only $15 you'll be hit with 36 issues; that's one issue three times per month (or 72 issues for $29.50). You can really get loaded on 108 issues for $44. If you want a sample copy to rifle through before you subscribe lock, stock, and barrel, send $3. After you subscribe expect to wait four to six weeks before you receive your first issue.

SKATE STOP
P.O. Box 950
Great Falls, MT 59403
(406) 453-0101
CK, MC, V

Treading on thin ice with your sporting goods budget? Shop the Skate Stop and you'll have it made in the blade. They discount a wide array of ice skating gear about 20% to 35% off retail. One of their most popular brands is REIDELL, the maker of skate boots, another is WILSON, the blade company. They also carry sports apparel. Write and ask to be put on their mailing list and start saving cold cash. You'll also receive periodic sale fliers throughout the year. **C**

SOCCER INTERNATIONAL, INC.
P.O. Box 7222
Dept. USG6
Arlington, VA 22207
(703) 524-4333: 6:30 A.M. to 10:30 P.M. EST
CK, COD

Is your goal saving money? Well, we have found the place for you. With Soccer International, you can sock away brand-name products without getting socked in the savings. They handle uniforms, equipment, books, games, novelties, bumper stickers, patches, and more—all with soccer motifs. Baby, they'll sock it to you with savings up to 40%. They also offer quantity discounts. They are possibly the only place in the country that stocks soccer items in team quantities. That's the team spirit! Names like UMBRO, WIGWAM, BRINE, STAR, and DODGER will have you scoring points for your team. For starlight soccer players, we kicked up a lighted soccer ball costing $19.95. For crib kickers, we found a soccer ball crib toy with a foot that kicks to music. It's price was $1—plus $1 postage. How about Snoopy playing soccer on a bathmat for only $15? Has soccer gone to your head? Then you'll love their soccer caps that look like a soccer ball. They only cost $5 plus $1 shipping. There is a liberal refund policy that will have you kicking down the field. **C $1** (includes an "I Love Soccer" bumper sticker)

SPORTS HUT
1311 Bell Ridge Drive
Kingsport, TN 37660
(615) 247-3987
CK, MC, V

Come to this Mann's hut and find some savage savings on cutlery. Sports Hut is a national distributor for SCHRADE, CASE, FROST, and COLONIAL brands of cutlery. Sports Hut offers discounts of 40% to 50% on these products because they're a big-volume dealer. If you're the sporting type that needs pocket, hunting, fillet, or butterfly knives, you'll feel right at home at the Hut. If you're the type that likes to be in the kitchen, there's a big selection of knives for you, too. These products are all first-quality and fully guaranteed.
C $2 (refundable)

STEPHENSONS WARMLITE EQUIPMENT
RFD 4 #145
Hook Road
Gilfore, NH 03246

This small family-owned business began as a project to secure better mountaineering gear and slowly, through word-of-mouth advertising, expanded to custom-sewn and crafted gear insuring the quality not often provided in mass produced items. The equipment was developed over many years by an aerodynamicist and mechanical engineer in an effort to improve the warmth, comfort, and convenience of outdoors equipment while keeping the weight to a minimum. The result—warm, ultra-light sleeping bags, the first down bags with integral foam bottoms and double side zippers; the lightest weight, most wind stabled tents; improved ponchos; backpacks and more. Prices appropriate for the quality, but very reasonable. Warning, catalog reflects some nudity in models shown with products in this very descriptive (too wordy, frankly) catalog. **C $3/Basic**

STUYVESANT BICYCLE
349 W. 14th St.
New York, NY 10014
(212) 254-5200: sales
(212) 675-2160: parts
Certified CKs only, MC, V, AE

Don't let your exercise program be gone with the SCHWINN! Get into gear with quality bikes, exercisers, rowers, treadmills, scooters, wagons, and tricycles wheeling such names as ATALIA, RALEIGH, BIANCHI, ROSS, TUNTURI, and CARNELLI. (RALEIGH and ATALIA bikes are what they're most famous for.) They've got accessories at 10% to 30% discounts. There's a $25 minimum order; exchanges only, no refunds. Orders are usually received within two weeks. A spokesman told us Stuyvesant's been in business since 1939. That's a long cycle! **B, C $2.50** (refundable)

TBC
Dept. US
Box 13
1251 E. Chocolate Ave.
Hershey, PA 17033
(717) 533-8339
CK, MC, V, AE, COD (cash only)

At first we thought "TBC" meant "The Best Chocolate," but it's really "The Best Choice." Their free, 45-page catalog won't melt in your hand but you *will* find mouth-watering savings on running, tennis, and hiking shoes, as well as on clothing for men and women. Choices include NIKE, ADIDAS, NEW BALANCE, AVIA, and BILL RODGERS, among others. Bite off a 10% to 20% discount on clothing, a 20% discount on shoes. In-stock items are shipped via UPS within 24 hours. There's a $5 restocking charge on returns. **B, PQ**

TELEPRO GOLF SHOP
17642 Armstrong Ave.
Irvine, CA 92714-5728
(800) 854-3687
(714) 250-9142: CA residents
CK, MC, V

When a professional golfer answers the phone, that's *not* par for the course. This company goes a little further to make mail-order shopping easy. Their catalog features a large selection of famous-name golf clubs in a variety of precise specifications. You'll match these clubs to your shaft flex, shaft length, and swing weight to get the right one. If you don't know all of these things, there is a helpful chart available or ask the pro by phone. A little birdie told us we'd find discounts of up to 60% and he was right. Telepro has three retail outlets in southern California. **C**

TROPHYLAND USA, INC.
Dept. US
7001 W. 20th Ave.
P.O. Box 4606
Hialeah, FL 33014
(800) 327-5820
(800) 432-3528: FL residents
CK, MC, V, AE

By now you must be an accomplished reader of catalogs. This one is full-color and 88 pages, and it comes out once every three years. Why not reward yourself for your expertise and give yourself a medal, plaque, award, or trophy from this family-owned store and mail-order company? After all, you've earned it. Trophyland carries a complete line of trophies, medals, plaques, desk sets, charms, and show ribbons at factory direct savings up to 70% off! All wood is walnut and the marble is imported from Italy. Engraving is free. Most orders are received within four days. They'll replace orders in the case of their error; otherwise there are no refunds or returns. There is no minimum order, although they prefer orders over $25. Shipping is prepaid on orders over $200. **C $2.50, PQ**

WIDE WORLD OF SPORTING GOODS
Dept. US
220 S. University
Plantation, FL 33324
(305) 475-9800
CK, MO

Been looking for some sporting shoes to complement your sporting life? Well, the Wide World of Sporting Goods (formerly The Athlete's Corner) is a great place to tie one on. This place has six styles of NIKE basketball shoes, ranging from canvas shoes at $15.99 to leather ones at $29.95 (retail $29 to $42). Good sports will find sporting goods for tennis, racquetball, running, and basketball—shoes, rackets, and clothing. Leading brands in sporting goods like NIKE, ADIDAS, NEW BALANCE, and EKTELON huddle here before making tracks to go a-courtin'. Clothing brands include OCEAN PACIFIC, DOLPHIN, RAISINS, HOBIE, and HEAD. The POWELL skateboard (followed closely by SIMS, DARIFLEY, and G&S brands) is their biggest seller. Savings were around 30% to 40% on most items; team orders are welcome. Unused merchandise can be exchanged or money refunded; there's a 15% restocking charge on returns. Most orders are shipped within 48 hours and are received within seven days. **C, B, F, PQ**

Stereo and Video

Audiophiles and video-nuts should pick up the relevant issue of *Consumer Reports* at their local library for the lowdown on high fidelity. With so many self-proclaimed audio advisers offering their opinions, you'd be smart to start with the *facts* about turntables, readouts and the rest of what you need. *Consumer Reports's* specialty is unbiased reporting on the advantages, disadvantages, quality, and prices of all major models of stereo and video equipment. You can save yourself a lot of trouble if you do your research before you buy, and then buy through the mail.

ANNEX OUTLET LTD.
43 Warren St.
New York, NY 10007
(212) 964-8661
CK

Annex marks the spot for savings up to 40% on over 30 different brands of video recorders, videotapes, video cameras, TVs, and home and car stereos. They carry such brands as SANYO, SONY, PANASONIC, PIONEER, TOSHIBA, TECHNICS, HITACHI, AIWA, AKAI, RCA, TDK, and JVC. There's a $4 minimum order; no restocking charge; they'll exchange damaged merchandise within seven days. Most orders are received in seven to 14 days. Their slender, black-and-white catalogs come out quarterly—call or write (enclosing a SASE) if you don't see what you want. **C, PQ**

AUDIO ADVISOR, INC.
Dept. US
225 Oakes, S.E.
Grand Rapids, MI 49503
(616) 451-3868
MC, V, AE

Dear Audy: My husband is tweeting me badly. Last month, he hit me and I slipped a disc. He still wants me to cook his tuner casserole before he gets home from work. More than that, if he woofs at me one more time, I'm going to unleash my fury. I can't take his constant needling. It's like a broken record. My head is spinning. What should I do to turn the tables? Signed, Played Out in Yonkers. Dear Miss Out: Take my advice: Get rid of the bozo who's bonkers in Yonkers and check out this company. Prices average 15% to 50% less than retail and they carry over 200 brands in mid-to-high-priced, high-quality stereo and video products. Most orders are delivered in seven to 10 days. There's a restocking charge of 15% on returns. **B**

CALIFORNIA SOUND
5784 Miramar
San Diego, CA 92121
(619) 455-1633
(619) 578-9692: San Diego, AK, HI residents
MC, V, AE

With what frequency have you searched for the perfect car stereo, only to encounter amplified prices and salespeople speaking on another wavelength about tweeters, woofers, wow, and flutter? Treble yourself no further. Listen, "America's car stereo experts" pull the plug on high-priced car stereo equipment with five-year warranties and free shipping. They carry seven brands of stereos and speakers. At the top of the charts were SANYO, JENSEN, METRO SOUND, SHERWOOD, CLARION, SONY, and BLAUPUNKT. (BLAUPUNKT is their most popular line.) All merchandise is priced 20% to 50% less than retail. Their 60-page catalog provides advice on what to consider in component systems and an easy-to-understand glossary of technical terms. There is no restocking charge. Most orders go out in three to four days. **C**

CRUTCHFIELD
1 Crutchfield Park
Charlottesville, VA 22906
(800) 446-1640: orders only
(800) 336-5566: catalog request
(800) 552-3961: VA residents
(804) 973-1811
MC, V, AE, D, DC, CB, CK, COD to business address

Use this crutch to play the field and save 15% to 40% on an extensive line of car stereo and home audio equipment. Highly trained technical advisers run the company and answer questions about Crutchfield's products. Even with this attention to service, prices are still very reasonable. Crutchfield's catalog looks and reads like *Stereo Review* magazine. Helpful buying tips are interspersed throughout. They're authorized dealers for all their products. Brands we found in audio components included: SONY, AKAI, PIONEER, and ADVENT, among others. In-dash car stereos are a big seller; Crutchfield carries an astounding selection from CONCORD, CLARION, JVC, JENSEN, PIONEER, and SONY. The catalog also has an installation guide making it easy to install your own car stereo system and save over buying it from a new car dealership. In addition, Crutchfield carries video products from SONY, CANON, JVC, and AKAI, and telephones and answering machines by SONY, PANASONIC, and PHONE-MATE. If you are buying a stereo for home or car, send for this catalog first. Everyone needs a crutch when it comes to saving money, and they ship in 24 hours. **C** (three times a year, free to readers of *The Underground Shopper*)

CSC MARKETING, INC.
P.O. Box 59433
Dallas, TX 75229
(214) 350-6706
CK, MC, V, AE

Hey, what does CSC mean? "Celebrate sensible costs?" "Consumers save cash?" Maybe it's "Canny shoppers' cakewalk." How about "Calculate saving currency?" or even "Call someone cheap?" Well, whatever the letters CSC stand for, this *company* stands for good buys on televisions and video systems. PANASONIC and RCA are the big brands; discounts run from 25% to 40%. There's no catalog, but they do have price sheets and they'll send photos if you ask. You must supply the manufacturer and model number to order or request information. Their SANYO 19-inch and 13-inch TVs are very popular, but we liked their 5-inch ZYCCOR black-and-white portable TVs which came complete with AM/FM shortwave radio, cassette recorder, and a choice of A/C cord, cigarette lighter cord, or battery power. We've seen this TV priced at up to $199 elsewhere, but it was just $149. Items are drop shipped from New Jersey; shipping charges are included in the price quote so hidden charges won't sneak up on you. Only video equipment is shipped COD; COD isn't accepted on other products. **PQ**

J & R MUSIC WORLD
23 Park Row
New York, NY 10038
(212) 732-8600
MC, V, AE, D

High fidelity is a sound virtue, 'cause nobody likes a speaker that squeaks around. This maestro of music mail-order houses blends 25% to 70% discounts with a huge selection of products. Over 150 brands are available; in fact, every major brand you could want. Their catalog of audio, video, and electronics stuff is about 325 pages (over 10,000 products and over 6,000 titles of videos) and conducts a symphony of famous-name cartridges, headphones, audio and video-tapes, video electronics, computers, communications items, car stereos, calculators, and video games. Their record and tape catalog consists mostly of 80 pages with over 5,000 titles of popular and disco music, although sound tracks, jazz, reggae, C&W oldies, and easy listening are featured, too. Classical records were fugue and far between because only a few titles are published in the catalog

(although their retail outlet carries the largest selection of classical records, tapes and compact discs in New York). The most common record price was $6.99. There's a $25 minimum order; a 10% restocking charge on returns that do not follow described return procedures; an exchange or refund on returns within 30 days of receipt of merchandise (as long as the item is in its original carton).
C ($1 is requested to offset postage costs)

LYLE CARTRIDGES
Box 158 Dept. G
115 S. Corona Ave.
Valley Stream, NY 11582
(516) 599-1112
MC, V

Lyle be seeing you in all the familiar places . . . wherever there's a phonograph. Cartridges, replacement needles, and record care items from 12 different manufacturers including SHURE, PICKERING, STANTON, AUDIO-TECHNICA, EMPIRE, GRADO, ADC, SONUS, ORTOFON, GRACE, B & D, DYNAVECTOR, and MONSTER CABLE PRODUCTS are all discounted 15% to 75%. They also carry old 78 RPM diamond styli to play 78 RPM recordings. The minimum order is $25 by credit card. Most orders are received in seven to 10 days; shipping is by UPS. Send a SASE for a free catalog or price quote. **C, PQ (SASE)**

McALISTERS, INC.
926E Fremont
Sunnyvale, CA 94087
(408) 739-2605
CK, MC, V, AE, COD

We had a Big Mac attack when we saw the prices at McAlisters. They previously offered discount prices and various repair services only to insurance companies which purchased merchandise to replace fire and burglary claims. Now their incredible selection of big screen televisions, VCRs, stereos, microwave ovens, computers, burglar alarms, and musical instruments is available to the public. We compared another discounter in this book with McAlisters and found you simply have to compare each item as discounts fluctuated. The BLAUPUNKT Manhattan in-dash receiver, for example, retails for $300. McAlister sold it for $240 and another discounter sold it for

$269. Yet the SONY XR-15 radio cassette player retailed for $239; was $187 at McAlisters and $159 at the other discounter. Savings of 20% were found on COBRA, CONCORD, FULTRON, SONY, and PANASONIC products. Savings of 30% to 40% were found on JENSEN, KENWOOD, SANYO, ACOUSTIC, and DATRON. The greatest savings (between 40% and 65%) were found on MOTOROLA products although they claim they will not be undersold on VCRs. The computer readout price list is endless. If you know your stereos and electronic equipment, McAlisters offers the best savings on off-brands. **C $5** (refundable with your first order)

SOUND REPRODUCTION, INC.
7 Industrial Road
Fairfield, NJ 07006
(201) 227-6720
MC, V

"OK youse guys, sound off: Brands?" TECHNICS! SONY! SANSUI! PIONEER! AKAI! *"I can't hear you!"* PANASONIC! SHARP! *"Louder!"* KOSS! JENSEN! *"At ease."* For 29 years this company has taken its orders for audio components, etc., from the public and they're not about to quit after so many years of distinguished service. Prices are about 20% to 40% off retail on about 40 brands. Shipping charges are 5% of your purchase price. Enlist the aid of their 40-page catalog before you march somewhere else for your next audio purchase. **C $1** (refundable)

S & S SOUND CITY
Dept. US
58 W. 45th St.
New York, NY 10036
(800) 223-0360
(212) 575-0210
MC, V, COD (certified check)

Morris coded an SOS to S & S and they dashed to our rescue with the information we requested. They carry TVs, video equipment, electronics, appliances, air conditioners, and microwaves at 5% to 10% above cost. Almost every brand imaginable is in stock: SONY, PANASONIC, RCA, ZENITH, AMANA, TOSHIBA, LITTON, HITACHI, FRIEDRICH, and AIR TEMP. S & S has shipped merchandise to customers around the world. There's a $30 minimum; a seven-day return policy as long as the purchased item is in the factory carton with all packing material intact; no restocking charge. Orders are usually received in seven to 10 days. Standard manufacturer's warranties apply. All things considered, we'd say S & S is a City built on a "sound" foundation. **C**

STEREO DISCOUNTERS ELECTRONIC WORLD
Dept. US
6730 Santa Barbara Court
Baltimore, MD 21227
(800) 638-3920
MC, V, AE, DC, COD (with 25% deposit)

If you live back East, you may already be familiar with this company. Stereo Discounters runs the largest consumer electronic show on the East coast every year, with shows in Philadelphia and Baltimore. That's pretty good, but that's not all. They've also been selected "Audio and Video Retailer of the Year" for the past two years. Brands include PIONEER, PANASONIC, and TECHNICS, and discounts range all the way from 15% to 60% off. And if that's not enough, they guarantee the lowest prices. Their 132-page catalog comes out twice a year (fliers come out six times annually); categories range from receivers, amps and tuners, turntables and changers, cartridges, cassette decks, speakers, stereo systems to you-name-it. Compact Discs, VCRs and Camcorders are their hottest selling item. Shipping charges are 5½% of the cost of your order. Most orders are delivered in seven to 14 days. **C, PQ**

Surplus and Volume Sales

Ever wondered where to find uniforms for medical technicians, seafood restaurant waiters, or French maids? (You
haven't?) Do you know where to get Portuguese camouflage
berets, utility paint tanks, and deluxe naked leather and down
vests? (You don't?) Well, maybe you were just thinking about
where to get Korean War-vintage genuine U.S. Army issue
hand-powered generators, and grenade belts from World War
I? (You weren't! Amazing!) If you answered "yes" to any of the
above questions, you've come to the right places. Buying overstocks or buying in multiples usually means savings, as you'll
see from the following dealers. (Incidentally, if you didn't do
very well on our test, don't feel badly. Many people don't.
We're easy—so you can look through this section anyway. And
better luck next time.)

AMERICA'S BEST
P.O. Box 91717
Mobile, AL 36691
(800) 633-6750
(800) 672-1321: AL residents
MC, V

Looking for some of America's best products to use as a fund-raiser for your club or organization? Gift wrap, candles, holiday ornaments, candy, calendars, and more. This company with over 20 years of fund-raising experience has hand-picked proven, top-selling items manufactured by nationally advertised companies. Also available are opportunities to earn bonus cases of products and rebate coupons. Products are priced retail with profits spelled out in the catalog. For example, on the $2 box of HERSHEY's Golden Almonds, you make $45 profit per case of 60 plus $120 for each bonus case. The most unusual offering was the disposal BREATH BRUSH®, available through this catalog exclusively. You could make a clean sweep with this hot-selling item. **C**

ANKA CO.
Dept. US
90 Greenwich Ave.
Warwick, RI 02886
(800) 556-7768
(401) 737-8107: RI residents
MC, V, COD

Pull up the Anka and sell away. Anka Co. sells over 1,000 different items in some 4,000 styles. Their merchandise consists of inexpensive sterling silver, and 10K or 14K gold-filled and goldplate rings geared toward folks who want to buy and then turn around and resell at a profit, thus acting as small dealers. Pearl, opal, star sapphire, and jade jewelry sets were discounted up to 80% from retail, while "kiddie rings" and a line of jewelry for men also were available. From engagement/wedding sets to professional truck driver rings ($72), you'll find it here. The company also provides literature on how to become an Anka dealer. They claim discounts of "200% below retail" which, when you think about it, is pretty astounding. (We suspect someone wasn't too good in math—hopefully it's not their book-keeper!) Their minimum order is $30; shipping charges are preset at $2.50. **C $1** (refundable)

THE BASE EXCHANGE
Store:
10341 Venice Blvd.
Los Angeles, CA 90034

Mail Orders:
P.O. Box 2727
Culver City, CA 90231
(213) 870-4687
(213) 870-4409: credit card orders
MC, V, AE, COD

Salute the selection from this base of paramilitary, survival supplies, clothing, and camping equipment. High fashion millinery fashions for the military look: berets, a Bombay bowler, a safari hunter's hat, an Aussie Bush hat, a Swedish army mountain hat—if you're into hats. Paratrooper boots ($54.50), a genuine goatskin navy flight jacket ($179.50), an officer's bridge coat ($109.50), emblems, badges, wings and insignias, outdoor cookware, camouflage clothing, survival knives, rescue lights, handcuffs . . . a military nirvana. Unique, one-of-a-kind items as well as authentic surplus are shipped within four to seven days. A good sizing guideline is depicted for ease when ordering clothing. With over 40 years in the business, we can commend their four-star unblemished record. **C**

BLAIR
1000 Robins Road
Lynchburg, VA 24506
(804) 845-7073
MC, V, COD

Mary, this is O-Kay. Without being caddy, we were in the pink with all these BLAIR beauty products at wholesale prices. This plan operates as a dealership but you determine your own quota. Buy for yourself or for friends at wholesale prices. Cosmetics, fragrances, health aids, costume jewelry, home products, and small gifts, plus food products such as spices are available. Blair guarantees products and has been in business since 1920. For more information, check out their 32-page catalog. **C**

JERRYCO, INC.
5700 Northwest Highway
Chicago, IL 60646
(312) 763-0313
MC, V

We'll trumpet the praises of Jerryco, 'cause the prices were so low our wallets didn't go tumblin' down the counters in fright. Army and industrial surplus goods were up to 95% off. Their wonderful, pun-filled catalog contained a bewildering collection of scientific curios, and modern-day curiosities that would send even the most inventive of inventors, creative crafts people, and the true tinkerer off the deep end. Anyone for a pacemaker control box, some multi-colored plastic mesh, or 150,000 surgical scrub brushes? What, no takers? A later catalog, *Surplusopolis,* included such beauties as giant church rings, miniature lab flasks, a selection of genuine French military washbasins. They're open to suggestions for future offerings. (From the looks of things, they don't turn down much!) After looking through one of these catalogs and being prompted with all the possibilities, you'll never think of surplus as "junk" again. There's a $10 minimum order. Shipping's the same day as the order's received; full refunds are given within 30 days; no restocking charge on returned items. There is a flat $3 shipping charge for any size order. Their 48-page catalog is free to *Underground Shoppers.* **C 50 cents**

MASS. ARMY AND NAVY STORE
895 Boylston St.
Boston, MA 02115
(800) 343-7749
(617) 783-1250
CK, MC, V, AE, MO

You can a-Mass a marvelous eclectic wardrobe here complete with genuine U.S. and European military garb, like Foreign Legion caps and Vietnam jungle boots. Names like LEE, LEVI, SCHOTT, BATES, EAST-PAK, WIGWAM, DUOFOLD, and HERMAN are campy collections for your camping or survival gear as well as outdoor clothing. Their 52-page, mostly color catalog is jam-packed with a multitude of interesting and unique military surplus, gift items—some even useful and practical. They have two stores in the Boston area; one at 433 Massachusetts Avenue, known as Central War Surplus and one on Boylston Street, which is also their mail-order center. Satisfaction guaranteed or your money back. Find the same item at a lower price

in any mail-order catalog, and they will gladly refund the difference.
C

RSP DISTRIBUTING COMPANY
P.O. Box 2345
Redondo Beach, CA 90278
(213) 542-0431
CK, MO

Talk about closeout heaven. This 200-page catalog sure offers enough items: jewelry, gifts, novelties, housewares, cutlery, survival products, auto accessories, tools, toys, office supplies and accessories, clothing, electronics . . . whew, exhaustive enough to tire even the consummate shopper. Save up to 90% on closeout merchandise; and save up to 60% on suggested retail items in their catalog. You can start playing with your orders usually within 24 hours. You can choose to be the ultimate consumer of these goods, or resell them for a profit. Many products covered by factory warranty; others can be returned postpaid to RSP within 30 days for credit. **C $6** (refundable), **B** and **Sales Kit $2**

RUVEL
Dept. US
3037 N. Clark St.
Chicago, IL 60657
(312) 248-1922
CK, MC, V

Boy, did the military serve us when we enlisted the help of Ruvel's catalog. This store has all types of army-navy surplus goods. Clothing (flier's jackets, pith helmets), camping goods (sleeping bags, snowshoes), dummy grenades, gas masks, knives, British hurrican lamps, poison-resistant full-body aprons, and blood pressure kits are just a few of the items from their extensive inventory. Most items are about 20% less than retail. A 100% down-filled vest (80% Northern goose, 20% other down) was $35.95 and electric socks were $14.95. No license or permit necessary to buy any of their merchandise. There's a 30-day policy on items returned in the same condition as when shipped; items ordered in error or returned for a refund are subject to a 20% restocking charge. **C $2**

THE SURPLUS CENTER
1000-15 W. "O" St.
P.O. Box 82209
Lincoln, NE 68501
(402) 474-4366
MC, V, AE, D, COD

Surplus plus! Their inventory may not quite run from A to Z but it
does range from air-operated tools to wire. In between, you'll find
paint spray-guns and pulleys, batteries and blowers, tanks and telephones, hacksaws and horns at up to 85% off retail prices. Overall,
their slant is more toward electrical and mechanical items for business, industry, farm, and home rather than military gear like
clothing or weaponry. They do have some good brand-name items
available: we spotted such brands as BRIGGS & STRATTON, BOSCH,
WINCO, DERMEL, API ALARMS, PRINCE, SANBORN, AIR COMPRESSOR,
JET POWER EQUIPMENT, and NAPCO. Savings were up to 85% off
retail. Orders are usually received in about 10 days. Items carry a 90-
day warranty; they'll exchange or refund in the case of returns; $3
return charge. Their 64-page, black-and-white catalog is both attractive and straightforward. C

UNCLE DAN'S LTD.
Dept. US
2440 N. Lincoln Ave.
Chicago, IL 60614
(312) 477-1918

also at:
Dept. US
1365 W. Dundee
Buffalo Grove, IL 60090
(312) 259-2001
CK, MC, V, COD

Now you've got an uncle in army surplus besides Uncle Sam! "We
can get you anything you desire," they say with avuncular pride, so if
you're looking for army-navy surplus, camping goods, and recycled
clothing, this just might be a foxhole worth looking into. You'll find
many regular prices, but Unc' has some relative-ly good bargains,
too. 100% wool "like new" army pants were a good buy as were used
army fatigue pants. A COLEMAN lantern was discounted almost 30%
off its retail prices and other COLEMAN camping goods were priced

well, too. EUREKA tents, original issue M-65 fold jackets, LEE jeans, Swiss army knives, TIMBERLAND shoes, PRIMUS propane lanterns and stoves, EAST-PAK duffel bags, and all camping equipment was discounted. Martini-lovers and military martinets will OD on the olive drab! Military memorabilia is bought and sold, too. There's a $15 minimum; full refund or exchange privileges; about a 10-day wait to receive your order. C

UNIVERSAL SUPPLIERS
P.O. Box 4803
GPO.
Hong Kong
phone 001-852-5-224-768

Susie can't go Wong with this Hong Kong supplier! They've got ivory carvings, photographic and stereo equipment, SEIKO and ROLEX watches, eyeglasses and contact lenses—and everything carries a one-year guarantee. A ROLEX stainless steel case with steel oyster bracelet was $589 ($800 in the U.S.); a 14K gold-plated French eyeglass frame by MOREL was $32.70; and replacement contact lenses (by AMERICAN OPTICAL) were $20 per lens or $32.50 per pair. Savings were 50% on eyewear. Hand-carved ivory ball earrings were $7.50, but would cost $33.95 in the U.S. Intricately carved ivory chess pieces, dragons, fans, figurines, and vases were also available.
C $1.50

WEISS AND MAHONEY
Dept. US
142 Fifth Ave.
New York, NY 10011
(212) 675-1915
CK, MC, V, AE

Weiss and Mahoney, "the peaceful little army and navy store," has declared war on high prices. Their bargains are no bombs, either. They sell the usual army surplus store merchandise including clothing, camping equipment, and miscellaneous military surplus. Regulation uniforms for all the armed forces as well as flags from over 50 countries are in stock. Your friends won't think you're all wet in a Marine Corps waterproof coverall for just $19.98. We found uncamouflaged brand names like SCHOTT in outerwear and KIRKHAM in tents and camping equipment in their 50-page catalog, but the big discounts went undetected. There's a $10 minimum order; about a two-week delay before you'll receive your order; exchanges but no refunds. **C $1**

Telephone Services

Southern Belles have changed a lot since the days of Alexander Graham Bell. So have telephones. They now come in all shapes, sizes, and colors. You can get video displays, speakers, cordless models, and computer hook-ups, as well as such features as automatic redial, mute buttons, call waiting, call forwarding, and gadgets that even James Bond couldn't get. If you leave home without one, you haven't read our Electronics section and found out where to drive a bargain on car telephones. Nowadays, even books are typeset through telephone hook-ups. More business is conducted over the wire than ever before, creating the need for WATS time-sharing and other cost-cutting services. Want to know more about putting your phone bill on hold? Check these listings for alternative ways to reach out and touch someone for less.

ADDS TELEMARKETING
155 Pasadena Ave.
South Pasadena, CA 91030
(800) 233-7487 ext. 90
(213) 259-8000

Where else but in California would you find a commune for corpora-
tions? This enterprising eight-year-old company is basically a
corporate order department and sales force extension. Firms unable
or unwilling to staff 24 hours a day and seven days a week or needing
a nationwide sales force can use this service to handle all their calls.
PQ

ATC SATELCO
1 Satelco Plaza
San Antonio, TX 78205
(800) 292-1007
CK, MC, V, AE

If this name doesn't ring a Bell, ma guess is, it soon will. They're
getting the busy signal from price-conscious ding-a-lings all over.
Many customers can dial long distance to anywhere in the U.S. at
savings of 11% to 65%. Satelco's Telesaver Service for evening and
night service offers residential users service without a service or
sign-up charge. Depending on the number of long-distance calls you
make, savings can be substantial. **B, F, PQ**

MCI TELECOMMUNICATIONS CORP.
1133 19th St. NW
Washington, D.C. 20036
(800) 241-5371: MS, AL, FL, NC, SC, TN, KY residents
(800) 624-6240

For across-the-switchboard savings that are far from phony, MCI
offers a long-distance alternative to calling Mom using Ma Bell. If
your monthly long-distance telephone bill is $25 or more and you
have a touch-tone phone, savings per call can range from 15% to 50%,
depending on when you call. For a $5 or $10 monthly charge (no
deposit or installation fees) and then a per call charge similar to Bell's
(only cheaper), you're hooked up. People in many parts of the country
now can call anywhere in the U.S. Installation time averages a two-
week wait. **PQ**

SBS SKYLINE
8283 Greensboro Drive
McLean, VA 22102
(800) 252-1777
(703) 442-5000
CK only

Check out the Skyline—there's nothing hazy here. Rates here are 40% to 60% below Bell and they divide your time on the telephone into six-second increments instead of minutes. That means they measure time on the phone more accurately, which means their bill is fairer. You aren't billed for calls that you don't complete, either. There's no installation fee to use their service and no service charge, but you must use the service to the tune of $15 per month. Folks who pay their bills promptly get a 2% discount.

US SPRINT COMMUNICATIONS
P.O. Box 52501
Irving, TX 75015-2051
(800) 527-0777
(214) 506-1000
CK

These folks should get the no-Bell prize for economy. If you like to talk till you're blue in the face, A.T.&T.'s bill can put you in the red. "Sprint" is a godsend for those who run at the mouth. Savings per call vary depending on time and distance, but run up to 35% less than A.T.&T. One significant advantage is that "Sprint" has an extensive "travel call" network that's available to those who are often on the road. Travelers can use "Sprint" from any city in the U.S. at a very modest surcharge. Service extends throughout the U.S.—including Alaska and Hawaii—the U.S. Virgin Islands, and Puerto Rico. Sprint also serves over 30 foreign countries and by year-end 1987 will serve 90% of the countries that A.T.&T. serves. A wide variety of features is available from Sprint including new operator services and 800 service. As with other systems, a touch-tone phone or adapter is required. **B, PQ**

U.S. TRANSMISSIONS SYSTEMS
ITT Longer Distance
333 Meadowland Parkway
Secaucus, NJ 07094
(800) 526-3000
(800) 526-7270
(800) 652-2871: NJ residents

If you've been getting long bills for long distance, don't let your long-windedness send your savings up in smoke. Dial ITT for some fast relief—it'll be a feather in your (thinking) cap. Their long-distance rates can save you plenty of wampum and that's a whole lot better than getting the clap-per from Ma Bell.

Tobacco

Modern literature has elevated smoking to an art form. Who can imagine Ashenden without an Indian cheroot, Lady Brett without a Gauloise, or Hercule Poirot or Sherlock Holmes without their pensive pipely puffings? It's almost inconceivable that a deep-thinking detective would not, at some point during his ruminations, light up his pipe and surround himself with slowly curling and snaking wisps of smoke. Maybe you haven't been immortalized (yet) on the big screen or in a steamy bestseller—no matter, you can still find the pleasure and relaxation of a pipe or after-dinner cigar one of life's small satisfactions. From the mundane to the exotic, from corncob pipes to handmade cigars—order your supplies by mail. The merchants in our book offer a great selection and the savings are even greater.

FAMOUS SMOKE SHOP
Dept. US
55 W. 39th St.
New York, NY 10018
(800) 672-5544
(212) 221-1408: NY residents
CK, COD (plus $2.00)

Handmade, all-tobacco cigars are shipped anywhere in the world within a few days ($1 for the first box, 50 cents each additional box). You can't use your Visa for a TE-AMO PRESIDENTE, but you may open up an account and charge all you like. Send PARTAGAS to your papa or MACANUDOS to your mama. The huge selection (2,000) of name-brand cigars and tobaccos was discounted as much as 35%. Their catalog is free and informative so why don't you pick one up and . . . read it sometime. Minimum order: one box of cigars. **C**

FRED STOKER & SONS
Box 707
Route 1
Dresden, TN 38225
(901) 364-3754
(901) 364-5421
CK, COD

One dip or two? Aromatic cherry, mild Cavendish, Stoker's pistachio, vanilla nut, peach, pineapple, or apple. Ice cream anyone? No, not ice cream, but sweet cigars and pipe and chewing tobaccos for the choosy chewer or picky puffer. Stoke on this: Fred has been in business since 1948. Now that's something to chew on. Peter Piper picked a peck of BRIAR pipes and then he smoked them. The prices, they didn't choke him—only $12.50 to $25. You're not a chewer? How about popping your top over genuine, yellow hybrid popcorn? A 10 pound can was only $12. Slurrrp on this sweet deal: sorghum-flavored table syrup, a 4¼ pound tin was only $8.95. Get a scoop on this: old-fashioned, home-spun twists cost $40 per 5 pounds. You'll want to put Fred Stoker & Sons tobacco in your pipe and smoke it at these bulk-rate savings. **B**

HAYIM PINHAS
P.O. Box 500
Istanbul, Turkey
011-90-1-522-93-02
011-90-1-528-69-51
CK

Pinhas is your pipe-line for hand-carved meerschaum pipes. Their prices (about 20% lower) blow smoke rings around the competition. Order a pipe shaped to resemble a lion's head, Lincoln, Cleopatra, Shakespeare, Socrates, a mermaid, a skull, a Viking, or even Mickey Mouse. Match that with a carved cigar and cigarette holder ($1.50). The minimum order is two pipes, insurance is extra. Put that in your pipe and smoke it! **C** (issued every three years)

J-R TOBACCO CO.
Dept. US
277 Route 46 West
Fairfield, NJ 07006
(800) JR-CIGAR
(201) 882-0050
CK, MC, V, AE, COD

When in Dallas, J.R. likes ch-Ewing his tobacco, but in New York, he joins the fogies in puffing stogies at 30% to 60% off. This company sells 40% of the premium cigars bought in the U.S.! JR carries hand-made cigars (every quality brand offered) from such exotic lands as the Dominican Republic, Jamaica, the Phillipines, Honduras, Brazil, Costa Rica, Nicaragua, and Mexico. They also have the JR alternative cigars which are discounted reproductions (40% to 60% savings) of such renowned smokes as EL CAUDILLO, FLAMENCO, CREME DE JAMAICA, DON TOMAS, DON DIEGO, MONTECRUZ, HOYO EXCALIBUR, HOYO DE MONTERREY, MACANUDO, PARTAGAS, RAMON ALLONES, REY DEL MUNDO, ROMEO Y JULIETA, ROYAL JAMAICA, JOYA DE NICARAGUA, FLOR DEL CARIBE, and CUESTA REY. JR carries THOMAS CROWN and ROTHMAN cigars, too. To go with their alternative cigars, you'll enjoy their offbeat catalog. If you're huffin' and puffin' to smoke your house up, the mail's your trail to this Southfork of New York cigars. **C**

NURHAN CEVAHIR
Istiklal Caddesi
Bekar sokak No. 12/4
Beyoglu, Istanbul
144-41-23
144-35-10
**IMO, BANK DRAFT (through Osmanli Bankasi,
Karakoy, Istanbul)**

If you're an *Underground Shopper,* you can take 10% off the quoted price and put that in a hand-carved genuine block meerschaum pipe and smoke it. Comparable pipes are at least twice as expensive. Each pipe is guaranteed first quality and comes loose inside the bowl with a label insuring the quality of meerschaum used. Each pipe is wrapped in a plastic envelope and individually packed in a cardboard box with the picture and style of the pipe. **F**

Toys

Toys aren't just for kids! From the smallest to the tallest, from the youngest to the oldest, you can find something special for the perennial young at heart. Let your fingers do the walking through a wonderland of toys from dinosaurs to dolls, bears to balloons. You don't have to wait for Santa's sleigh, these catalogs are available year-round. So plan ahead for that special "child," big or small, sit back, and watch 'em have a ball.

CHERRY TREE TOYS, INC.
P.O. Box 369
Belmont, OH 43718
(614) 484-4363
CK, MC, V, COD

See entry page 257.

CLOTHKITS
24 High St., LEWES
E. Sussex BN7 2LB
England
(0273) 477111
MC, V, Sterling Cheques, Sterling Postal/Money Orders,
Euro-Cheques made out in Sterling, Access, Eurocard

See entry page 22.

DINOSAUR CATALOG
P.O. Box 546
Tallman, NY 10982
(914) 634-7579
CK, MC, V, MO

Don't have enough dinosaurs? Boy, did we dig up some prehistoric bones for you! The Dinosaur Catalog is erupting with cute creatures to adopt. Buy a British Museum of Natural History replica set, for an Ice Age price of $14.95. If you are in search of a new pet for your cave, you will find hundreds offered here. Leapin' lizzards! Look at these prices: Buy dinosaurs by the pound and be sure to get enough at a low price of $8.95. You can dig up T-shirts, models, kits, books, games, jewelry, ties, totes, soap, stationery, and cassettes, all at competitive prices. You may see another Ice Age before you receive your catalog though; the waiting time is two to three months. Orders, however, are filled much quicker—within two weeks. Old, but not forgotten, these ancient reptiles hold the imagination of everyone. Rex assured you will find something in the catalog for even the most vivid imagination. You won't be getting stuck in a tar pit if you're not satisfied with your fossils; they offer a complete refund. Snatch some up while they are still roaming the face of the earth. **C $2**

DOLLSVILLE DOLLS AND BEARSVILLE BEARS
461 N. Palm Canyon Drive
Palm Springs, CA 92262
(800) CAL-BEAR (credit card orders only)
(619) 325-DOLL (3655)
(619) 325-2241
CK, MC, V, AE

The store with an English accent would love to save you 20% and more on their collector teddy bears and dolls, dollhouses and accessories, doll and bear books, clothing and jewelry. They try harder and will beat any price as well as ship free. Specials on DAKIN "ELEGANTE" dolls, WORLD dolls, NEW GORHAM dolls, COROLLE FRENCH dolls, and LENCI dolls pre-1986. "The Royal Wedding" by The House of Nisbet included the bone china doll of Sarah Ferguson. Write for your *free* sample newsletter just for saying you're an *Underground Shopper.* Satisfaction guaranteed—a three-day return privilege. $2, Newsletter yearly subscription/refundable, including $2 beary discount coupons.

FAIR & SQUARE
Dept. US
22 Huron St.
Port Jefferson Station, NY 11776
(516) 928-8707
CK

OK, they're fair, but are they square? Not likely, since they circle the globe looking for out-of-this-world bargains in rock 'n' roll collectibles, toys, gifts, novelties, and more unusual finds. Popular items include stuffed talking bears and talking dogs. If you're looking for an unusual gift for an unusual person, this is the place to look. Bumper stickers and key chains are also popular. For an extra 15% savings, tell 'em you read about 'em in *The Underground Shopper.* C $5 (refundable)

TOY BALLOON CORPORATION
204 E. 38th St.
New York, NY 10016
(212) 682-3803
CK, MO

You could go around the world with their balloons and still not run out of ideas for your next party. There's plenty of hot air around—

helium balloons, latex balloons (all sizes). Mylar balloons with custom imprinting available. Since 1985, this has been a complete center for balloon accessories and party supplies. Three dozen minimum on custom printing. The more you buy, the more you'll save—as much as 70% over your neighborhood party store. Exchanges on unprinted materials less 20% handling charge provided goods are returned unused in good condition. $3.00 minimum charge for shipping and handling. C

THE TOYMAKER SUPPLY CO.
105 Weiler Road
Arlington Heights, IL 60005
(800) 624-3938
(800) 358-4208: IL residents
CK, MC, V

See entry page 314.

ZAMART FOR KIDS
11 W. 37th St.
New York, NY 10018
(212) 869-7606
CK, MC, V, AE

See entry page 230.

Travel

Get out of the house! If the world is your oyster, get up out of your oyster bed and listen to these pearls of wisdom. You don't have to be rich to travel first-class. Try an airline broker or contact one of the travel clubs who offer a country club atmosphere, group travel rates, and the camaraderie and fellowship of fellow sightseers to the world's ports-of-call. Pack your bags at a discount (see Handbags and Luggage), and have your "Travel America at Half Price" coupon book in hand. For reservations, without mental reservations, book a room through the many Bed & Breakfast programs available—all confirm reservations in advance. See the countryside on your bicycle or trade your Pacific condo for a picturesque bungalow in Kennebunk. The sky is the limit—not your pocketbook!

AMERICAN YOUTH HOSTELS, INC.
Suite 800-UF
1332 "I" St., N.W.
Washington, DC 20005
(800) 424-9426: April to September only
(202) 783-6161

Students who want to see the U.S.A. or foreign countries have resorted to this inexpensive housing alternative for years. With over 5,000 hostels located in 62 countries, AYH appeals to travelers of all ages who think spending from $4 to $10 a night for a "delightful surprise" is the best deal in the land. Dorm rooms are the norm. Fees are reasonable: a Junior Pass (17 years and under) is $10; a Senior Pass (18-59 years) is $20; and a Senior Citizen Pass (60 years and over) is $10. Family Passes cost $30; Organizational Passes cost $150; and Life Passes are $200. Members receive a friendly 50-page catalog of hostel facilities that costs non-members $3, including postage. Hostel-la vista! **B, C $3**

BENT TREE TRAVEL
Suite 306
16000 Preston Road
Dallas, TX 75248
(214) 490-1122
(214) 458-8545: 24-hour service
CK, MC, V, AE, DC

Tired of faring poorly in the confusing travel market? Try calling Judy Nurre or any of her highly trained staff at Bent Tree Travel for personalized service. They'll guarantee the lowest fares or refund the difference. You won't get bent out of shape when you learn they don't exclude reservations for airlines such as People's Express, Braniff, and other low-fare airlines. Planning a trip to a tropical beach? A free tote bag is yours for reserving your trip through Bent Tree Travel. Going to Las Vegas? Ask for "Cash for Chips," a cash rebate you can use for those roulette tables when you arrive. Bent Tree handles corporate accounts as well as leisure clients, offering free ticket delivery and round-the-clock service. How's that for a fare deal? **PQ**

BIKE VERMONT, INC.
P.O. Box 207-LF
Woodstock, VT 05091
(802) 457-3553
CK

Roll over rolling hills and tour the verdant countryside, quaint towns, and historic inns of Vermont, one of the most scenic states. Weekend bike tours are approximately $175 for adults and $150 for children which includes two nights in a historic Vermont inn. Midweek tours begin with a Sunday dinner and end Friday evening; they cost $450 for adults and $410 for kids. Midweek tour patrons receive lodging in a different inn each evening. Tours are leisurely and are suitable for beginning to advanced cyclists. Friendly leaders conduct the tours; they're able mechanics, too. A support van carries luggage for the (comfortably small) group. Reservations require a deposit of $100 per person for weekend tours and $200 for midweek tours. (The fee is fully refundable up to two weeks before the tour is scheduled.) BYOB, or rent a bicycle from them. As a nice touch, the tour director will write a personal note of acknowledgment to signees. **B**

CAMPUS TRAVEL SERVICE
1303 E. Balboa Blvd.
Newport Beach, CA 92661
(714) 675-9891
CK

What a way to go! Just write for a copy of *U.S. and Worldwide Travel Accommodations Guide* and get in on college and university guest lodgings for just $6 to $16 a day. Just send a check for $9.95 to the above address and receive the 1986-1987 edition of this invaluable guide to more than 425 colleges in the U.S. and 235 universities listed in 25 countries where dormitory lodgings ($11 a day) are available by the day, week, or month. They vary from single and double rooms to bedroom apartments and suites with kitchens. Most are open to the public during the summer—some year-round. Fifty universities in England alone offer bed and breakfast for only $14 per day. The guide provides daily room rates, available dates, types of accommodations, activities, food services, addresses, phone numbers, and housing officials to contact for reservations. **C $9.95**

CLUB COSTA
Suite 535
9200 Ward Parkway
Kansas City, MO 64114
(816) 361-8404

After joining this club, the sign on your door might read "Here today, gone to Maui." The club can save you money on accommodations, cruises, car rentals, and airline tickets. Ex-airline pilot Dick Bodner found a way to bring to the public the same discounts offered to air-line employees such as pilots and flight attendants. Members pay $49 a year to join and receive four quarterly issues of *Club Costa* maga-zine plus four issues of "Hotline Update," the club's newsletter. In one issue, we found rental properties in Hawaii, Florida, the Bahamas, Mexico, Colorado, the Caribbean, and California. A 50% discount was offered on a one-bedroom condominium at Maui's Kapulua villas resort. **C**

COUNCIL ON INTERNATIONAL EDUCATIONAL
EXCHANGE (CIEE)
Dept. US
205 E. 42nd St.
New York, NY 10017
(212) 661-1414

The free *Student Work/Study/Travel Catalog* lists all kinds of travel bargains and study abroad opportunities available to high school and university students. The International Student ID Card, for ex-ample, can save up to 50% on air fares, rail tickets (international and domestic), bus tickets, ship and ferry tickets, tours, accommoda-tions, and even department stores and boutiques. In addition, the Council offers work programs in Great Britain, Ireland, France, New Zealand, and other countries. Study Abroad language pro-grams for all levels are offered year round for anyone over 17. Tuition and accommodations with meals in a French household were just $495 for three weeks. Write for their catalog (enclose $1 for postage and handling) to discover a whole new world open to everyone. Sev-eral other offices are located in travel agencies throughout the coun-try and in Paris and Tokyo. **C $1**

THE COUPON BROKER
Dept. US
1780 S. Bellaire St., Suite 125
Denver, CO 80222
(303) 757-8144
CK, MC, V, AE

In business since 1979, David Kenny goes for broke. As a buyer and seller of discount airline and hotel coupons, vouchers, and certificates, consumers can fly first class at prices close to coach. Savings from 25% to 60% aren't uncommon. Products that are transferable are bought from frequent-flyers, airline stockholders, and other bartering offers (script). The closer to expiration date, the lower your price. This service is offered primarily for long-distance, coach-class domestic trips, but coach flights to Australia and New Zealand are probably The Coupon Broker's best deal. Customers receive a newsletter describing current deals. The Coupon Broker will give *Underground Shopper* readers (who utilize their service) a bonus coupon for a free weekend rental car or 50% off a two-day hotel stay. (That's a good deal, even though you'll still have to pay taxes and insurance.) **B**

THE EAST WOODS PRESS
429 East Boulevard
Charlotte, NC 28203
(704) 334-0897
MC, V

This company publishes a number of well-written guides to inexpensive travel as well as guides to the outdoors. *The Best Bed & Breakfast In The World* ($10.95 paperback) describes hundreds of accommodations in England, Ireland, Scotland, and Wales with a special section on London. *The Mid-Atlantic Bed and Breakfast Book* ($8.95) lists bed & breakfasts in New York, Pennsylvania, New Jersey, Delaware, Maryland, and West Virginia with accommodating hosts. Other books are available for New England and the South. *What To Do With The Kids This Year* ($8.95) describes 100 family vacation places. Outdoor books include *Wildflower Folklore*, a 256-page hardback ($16.95) by Laura Martin describing the legends and medicinal properties of 105 familiar wildflowers (plus how they got their names). Mention us: shipping is free to *Underground Shopper* readers. (Shipping is free to non-commercial accounts only.) **C**

ELKIN TRAVEL INC./CRUISES ONLY!
25950 Greenfield Road
Oak Park, MI 48237
(800) 445-1666
(800) 445-2024: MI residents
Credit is determined by each tour company

Travel plans up in the air? Elkin can bring the expenses down to earth. Now you can trip the flights fantastic, have a wingding and not create a flap! From North American Elk(in) hunts in the Canadian Rockies to African safaris in the shadow of Kilimanjaro, these folks will arrange the details of your trip so you're left with the fun-in-the-sun fundamentals of having a good time. Travel without travail! ET/CO's owner, Annette Langwald, has great contacts with all the cruise companies, and Cruises Only! has developed the most thorough list of cruise vacations in the country. Shake your marimbas on the Royal Caribbean or Norwegian Caribbean cruises, or find yourself a Czech mate on an international cruise. The best part is that Cruises Only! gives a gift certificate worth up to $100 for booking cruises or tours to Mexico, Europe, Hawaii, or the Caribbean. **B**

ENTERTAINMENT PUBLICATIONS
1400 N. Woodward
Birmingham, MI 48055
(800) 521-9640
(313) 642-8300: MI residents
CK, MC, V

Remember *A Tale of Two Cities*? Well, here's a tale about cities and two-fers. *Entertainment '87*, a thick coupon travel book published for 79 major national and international markets, enabled us to get 50% discounts on hotel rooms, gourmet dinners, football games, jazz concerts—everything from submarine sandwiches to symphony seats. The price of the books varies from city to city: it's $25 in Cincinnati, $38 in Seattle, and $60 in Copenhagen, Denmark. The books are attractive and include menus, reviews, and glossy photos of participating restaurants. Many books have $6,000 to $10,000 or more in cumulative savings if one were to consume the entire book. Another book, *Travel America At Half Price*, includes 1,100 half-price hotel coupons around the U.S. and Canada. There is even now, a *Travel Canada* at half price. More good news: this 26-year-old company is expanding into new markets every year and is now offering savings on air travel and luxury condo rentals. Deals like that beat the Dickens out of paying full price. Call for more information. **F**

THE EVERGREEN BED & BREAKFAST CLUB
P.O. Box 44094
Washington, D.C. 20026
(703) 237-9777
CK, MO

If you're over 50 and dream of traveling throughout the United States, this club has just the ticket for you. Membership here lets you make the most of your travel money by providing accommodations for only $10 per day for a single person or $15 per day for couples. Members of the Evergreen Bed & Breakfast Club are singles and couples above the age of 50 who have a spare room or two in their home that they can share with fellow club members traveling through the area. Accommodations range from the simple to the stately, but prices remain the same—and even include a full breakfast! Homes include an 1886 house in California, a home on the Mississippi River with a public boat launch just down the block, homes near Pikes Peak in Colorado, and many, many more. You make your choice from the extensive list of accommodations provided through a complete directory which lists names and addresses of members, occupations and interests, and special nearby attractions to help you plan the perfect vacation. You make reservations directly with your host. Annual club dues of $25 provide a membership card, annual membership directory, and quarterly newsletters. **B, SASE**

FORD'S FREIGHTER GUIDE
19448 Londelius St.
Northridge, CA 91324

Some people have to get away come hull or high water. Freight travel can cut costs way down and from what some salty dog adventurers say, "It isn't bad!" Oftentimes you'll have access to the passenger lounges, dining rooms, studies, and outdoor decks. The food is excellent, the ride is smooth, and the boat's not as crowded as they claim. To find out more about the 46 cargo/passenger lines, send $7.95. CA residents, please add 6½% tax. **C $7.95**

GUIDE TO THE GUIDES (EUROPE)
Smooth Sailing for the Traveler
P.O. Box 3626
Carson City, NV 89702
(702) 883-9014
CK, MO, CASHIER CK

This quick directory reviews the many guides that are offered the traveler today. It helps the reader wade through the mountains of books on traveling in Europe. Especially notable are the books reviewed for the handicapped, discounts offered to travelers over 55, affordable travel guides, home exchange opportunities, and work opportunities. Also, in the back is a descriptive listing of all the series travel guides such as the *American Express Pocket Guides, Berlitz Phrase Books, Citywalks, Fodor's Budget Guides, Frommer's $-A-Day Guides,* and more. **C $4.95**

JESS MILLER PUBLISHING CO.
P.O. Box 370
Indian River, MI 49749
(616) 238-7116
CK, MO

Go back to college at a fraction of the cost, and don't worry about making the grade this time! This nationwide guide to inexpensive travel offers low-cost lodging on campuses across the nation. The catalog of colleges contains information on staying in a college dorm, what extras you might need to pack for the adventure, and what recreational facilities are available near each campus. Colleges are listed by states and include activities, nearby tourist attractions, and more. Space accommodations, nightly rates (starting at $4.50 a night), and dates of availability are also listed. Satisfaction guaranteed or your money is returned within ten days of mailing date. Catalog orders shipped within 24 hours. **C $8**

RELOCATION RESEARCH
Box 864
Bend, OR 97709
(503) 382-5833
(503) 389-4272: OR residents
CK, MO

Disenchanted city dwellers, take note: relocating away from the rat race can be a reality. This complete guide to greener pastures provides the perfect solution to urbanites feeling the urgency to escape to faraway islands, overseas Edens, or small towns. The 16-page catalog listed publications which will help you find your own paradise, plus tells you a little bit about the folks who penned the books. Catalogs, books, and brochures on every imaginable move were listed. Topics covered "How to Buy Rural Land," "Relocation Planning," "Champagne Living on a Beer Budget," "Planning Your Next Move," and "Employment Business Opportunities." Listings covered long or short-term getaways to every place from agricultural settings to Alaska. Publications offering advice on applying for jobs in a countryside setting, surviving in personal privacy, and living in the tropics were gathered neatly together to make this your easiest move ever. An unconditional money-back guarantee was offered on all items published by Relocation Research. Orders filled within one month. **C $1**

STAND-BUYS LTD.
Suite 4141
311 W. Superior St.
Chicago, IL 60610
(800) 225-0200: only for brochures containing company
information
(313) 352-4876
CK, MC, V, AE

While Tammy Wynette stands by her man, you can stand by for savings with Stand-Buys. By phoning these innocent buy-standers up to three weeks in advance, you can find yourself winging your way to some far off, exotic land. Savings average 35% off the price of charter flights, tours and cruises, and you always get a confirmed reservation. This company is the first (thus the oldest and most experienced) travel clearinghouse in the U.S. They receive 35 to 40 offers daily from travel suppliers—both package tours and cruises. A one-week package tour from Cleveland to Ireland (talk about culture shock!) on 14 days' notice last summer cost $499 (retail $799). Subscribers pay $45 each year and get access to a toll-free member hot line number where they can get information on the status of excursions. Trips originate from all parts of the country. We know a couple who has five sets of luggage packed with clothes for different climates: they're always standing by. **PQ**

TANGLEPOINT TRAVEL, INC.
1551 Avenue K
Plano, TX 75074
(214) 423-6555
Telex 794794
CK, MC, V, AE, DC, CB

In business since 1974, this full retail and wholesale travel agency specializes in international travel (particularly the Middle East and Europe). Call and ask for Bob Bullard for travel savings savvy, par excellence. They'll send tickets by express mail for a fee. **B, PQ**

TRAVEL COMPANION EXCHANGE, INC.
Dept. US
P.O. Box 833
Amityville, NY 11701
(516) 454-0880
CK, MC, V, AE

This is no Amityville horror! The Travel Companion Exchange has served thousands of single, divorced, and widowed people all over North America since 1982. It is the only successful nationwide service of its kind. This company has been featured on "PM Magazine" and in articles in other major newspapers such as the *Los Angeles Times*, the *New York Times*, and *Boston Globe*. Travel Companion Exchange is run by Jens Jurgen, a veteran consumer-oriented travel writer. "It's a great way to make new and interesting friends and save money at the same time," says Jens. Membership rates vary from $4 to $10 a month depending on your age group and duration of initial membership plan chosen. Readers who mention they're *Underground Shopper* readers may deduct another 25% off regular dues. **B**

URBAN VENTURES, INC.
P.O. Box 426
New York, NY 10024
(212) 594-5650
CK, MC, V, AE

We'll venture that urbane urbanites (or others) venturing to the Big Apple aren't after some seedy, slice-of-life slum as an abode to abide in. Most folks aren't. If that describes you, you'll find Urban Ventures to be very accommodating. This service offers single rooms, private suites, and elegant apartments in good neighborhoods right in the core of the Apple. Prices range from $23 to $55 for single rooms; $32 to $70 for a double. Apartment prices range from $55 to $100 a night. (They are the only place in New York where short stays in apartments can be booked.) We're told that their prices are about 30% to 40% less than those charged by other services. Urban Ventures also offers additional services such as securing theater tickets, steering you to moderately priced restaurants, and guiding you to top tourist attractions. If you opt out, there's a $15 cancellation fee that is applied to any future booking: no-shows and same-day cancellations must pay for that night. **B**

VACATIONS TO GO
5901 D-Westheimer
Houston, TX 77057
(800) 624-7338
(800) 833-8047: TX residents
CK, MC, V, AE

Want to take a slow boat to China? Well, you can hop aboard a two-week Orient cruise retailing at $2,455—but with a Vacations to Go membership, you can pay only $1665. Vacations to Go, the fastest growing travel concept today, offers savings up to 50%. Houston-based founders Alan Fox and Robert Carney (he's Texas Air's director and president of Jet Capital Corporation) buy unsold space on airlines, cruise ships, and hotels and resell it to their members at a reduced rate. Members can book cruises as far as six months in advance, while weekend getaways to destinations like Mexico and Las Vegas require a week to ten days notice. Depart in style and save at the same time. Membership is $29.95 yearly and applicable to your entire family or your traveling companion. What a way to go on Vacations to Go! Go!

WORLDWIDE DISCOUNT TRAVEL CLUB
1674 Meridian Ave., Suite 304
Miami Beach, FL 33139
(305) 534-2082
CK, MO

Take off on your dream vacation and take up to 65% off what you'd expect to pay. Cruises, air tours, and international air fares are all included in club packages. Club members must be ready to travel on short notice. Worldwide Discount Travel Club specializes in filling slots on cruise ships, charter trips, and tours that remain empty close to departure dates. Every third Friday, their Travelog newsletter informs members of upcoming excursions. Members pay a $45 annual family membership fee to keep abreast of vacation savings. This club caters to retired people, teachers with long vacations, and busy professionals who can't plan several months in advance for their vacations. Discounters go through tour operators, cruise lines, airlines, and charter wholesalers to find out space availability and discounts. Air transportation packages are available one to six weeks before departure and cruises are offered from one week to several months before departure. Travelers get the same treatment as those who pay full fare. Trips are non-cancellable and non-refundable upon purchase. *Underground Shoppers* are offered a one-year membership for only $30. **B**

THE Y'S WAY
356 W. 34th St.
New York, NY 10001
(212) 760-5856/57/92/40

Y spend? The network of YMCA overnight centers spans North America from coast to coast in 67 cities in the U.S. and Canada. There are 61 overnight centers in 19 countries overseas. Family vacation centers, located in the Blue Ridge, Adirondack, and Rocky Mountains, as well as the foothills of the Berkshires, are also available. Low-cost package tours to New York, Hollywood, and Seattle are perfect for those who don't care for fancy hotels and just want to travel the Y's Way. Information is available at most local YMCA's, but trip arrangements must be made through the New York office. Payment must be made in advance and in full. Free brochure with SASE, No. 10 size with $.39 postage. **B**

Budget Motels with Toll-Free Numbers

"Budget motels" are an alternative to luxury hotels or motel chains with cocktail lounges and conference rooms. All of these no-frills lodging chains offer a clean room with the basic comforts, but without a high price. Different parts of the country have different chains, but here are some with toll-free numbers so you can check 'em out. (Hint: Have paper, pencil, and major credit card available when calling 800 lines for reservations.) For a national directory of budget bunks write: Motel 6, 51 Hitchcock Way, Santa Barbara, CA 93105; phone (805) 682-6666.

NAME	NUMBER	HOME OFFICE
Chalet Suisse	(800) 258-1980	Wilton, NH
	(800) 572-1880: NH residents	
Days Inns	(800) 325-2525	Atlanta, GA
Econo Travel Motor Hotels	(800) 446-6900 (800) 446-6914: VA residents	Charlotte, NC
Family Inns of America	(800) 251-9752	Pigeon Forge, TN
Red Roof Inns	(800) 848-7878	Columbus, OH
Scottish Inns of America	(800) 251-1962	Atlanta, GA

Windows and Walls

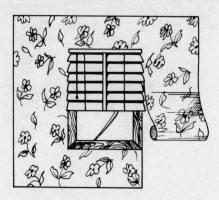

Here's a tip on how to measure your windows when buying blinds. To avoid any confusion when giving the sizes for your blinds inside a window, remember the *width* is the measurement taken from left to right, the *length* is taken from top to bottom, and the *sill* height is the measurement taken from the floor (or counter top) to the window sill. Ask for free installation instructions when ordering your blinds. Installing them yourself isn't difficult and will save you labor charges.

ALEXANDER WALLPAPER
2964 Gallows Road
Falls Church, VA 22042
(703) 560-5524
CK, MC, V

This may sound a little spacey, but if you get high, you can unroll your own grasscloth. Alexander carries ARIRANG™, their own design of grasscloth handmade in Korea, as well as another type of grasscloth, plus cork, two lines of silk string, and hand-sliced woods. SCHUMACHER and a few other brands are carried as closeouts and are priced about 50% off. Most discounts are about 25% to 30% off. The minimum order is a unit package—that's one double roll. Orders are filled and shipped within 24 hours; their refund policy is 30 days from the date of invoice shipment if the package is unopened, subject to a 20% restocking charge. **C $2.25**

AMERICAN DISCOUNT WALLCOVERINGS
1411 5th Ave.
Pittsburgh, PA 15219
(800) 245-1768
(412) 471-6941: PA residents call collect
CK, MC, V

We didn't give this discounter their walking papers with brands like SCHUMACHER, WALLTEX, IMPERIAL, KATZENBACH, and WARREN, and pleated shades and mini-blinds from KIRSCH, LEVOLOR, BALI, and FLEXALUM at 25% or more off. Give them the length and width of window, pattern name, color, and trim specs and you'll get a price quote quicker than you can say LEVOLOR, LEVOLOR, LEVOLOR. There's no minimum order; wallcovering orders are usually received in about seven to 10 days; window treatments in four to five weeks. There's a 20-day exchange or refund period on full bolts of wallcovering (less 20% restocking charge); no returns on custom window treatments. **PQ**

BEST BROS. PAINT & WALLPAPER OUTLET
Dept. US
4900 Fifth St. Highway
Route 222—Temple
Reading, PA 19560
(215) 921-3566
(215) 921-8591
CK, MC, V

What the Best Bros. Paint & Wallpaper Outlet lacks in modesty is more than made up for in savings. They specialize in paint, wallcoverings, carrying such brands as YORK, KINNEY, WALLTEX, WALLMATE, and all the other famous brands; and window blinds like DELMAR, LOUVER DRAPE, BALI, GRABER, and more. These folks sell at 25% to 75% lower than full-price retail stores (and if there's one thing we hate, it's wall-owing in high prices). There is a full refund on in-stock items and a 20% restocking charge on specially ordered merchandise. Paint the town red with the money you save on paints, or walls across the country with the bargains on discontinued wallpapers. **PQ**

THE BLIND SPOT
Dept. US
2067 N. Central Expressway
Suite 102
Richardson, TX 75080
(800) 527-4585
(800) 442-4636: TX residents
(214) 750-9600
CK, MC, V, AE

If you want elegant window treatments at affordable prices, you've got it made in the shade with The Blind Spot. They've got LEVOLOR and BALI mini-blinds, LOUVERDRAPE and GRABER vertical blinds, and woven woods and window shades at up to 60% off of suggested list. Everything is first-quality and custom made. Other brands include ROBERT ALLEN, LAURA ASHLEY (fabrics), SCHUMACHER, and JOANNA SHADES. Supply style, color, size, and model number and the store will send you an informative product brochure that tells you how to measure your windows for blinds and shades. They'll also send you a price list to determine the cost. Great selection of fabrics, bedspreads, baskets, and feather dusters at discounted prices. **B, PQ**

CUSTOM WINDOWS & WALLS
32525 Stephenson Highway
Madison Heights, MI 48071
(800) 772-1947
(313) 585-3026
CK, MC, V

Make the most of your windows and walls without making a dent in your budget. This mail-order company carries micro- and mini-blinds at maximum savings, with discounts of up to 60%. Choose from LEVOLOR, DEL MAR, BALI, and LOUVERDRAPE to add the newest fashion trends to your windows. Roman shades by KIRSCH let you cover your windows with woven wood to save energy and add beauty to your home. Pleated shades and wood slat blinds offer additional style—and savings! Your walls could be covered by names including WALLTEX, BIRGE, and IMPERIAL at 25% to 50% below retail prices. A complete selection of colors and patterns were available in a variety of textures. No refunds available on custom-made products and limited refunds offered on wallpaper. Lifetime warranties from manufacturers offered on most window treatments. Michigan residents pay 4% sales tax and all orders are shipped promptly. **B**

HARMONY SUPPLY INC.
18 High St.
Medford, MA 02155
(617) 395-2600
CK, MC, V

Does your wallpaper hang limp as a wilted wallflower? Well, then write Harmony and give your roomful of blues something to sing about! Smart women would rather use Harmony than his money when 60% to 80% savings are in store. This company carries over 2,500 patterns in wallcoverings as well as FLEXALUM and LEVOLOR blinds. They've got whatever wallpaper you could want, including their own Korean grasscloth and string for just $10.95 (the retail price would be $30 to $35). Discounts on special orders run 30% to 50% off, while in-stock merchandise is an even bigger bargain. In-stock merchandise can be returned for a full refund; 20% restocking charge on special orders. Orders usually take about seven to 10 days to arrive. No brochures or price lists; send them a pattern number and Harmony will send you the pitch. **PQ** (phone)

INTERIORS BY SANZ
P.O. Box 1794
1105 E. Lexington Ave.
High Point, NC 27262
(919) 882-6212
CK, MO

From inside out, Sanz's Interiors make others inferiors. Prices were an incredible 30% to 90% below manufacturers' suggested list price on wallpapers, fabrics, and grasscloths. They have virtually all brands of wallpaper, about 90% of which are from nationally known fabric companies. Hang out with famous names like BRUNSCHWIG & FILS, SCALAMANDRE SILKS, LOUIS BOWEN, SCHUMACHER, WAVERLEY, EISENHART, YORK WALLCOVERINGS, and IMPERIAL PAPERS, as well as almost 60 others (with more added monthly). There are over 150,000 rolls in stock, so they're worth calling if you know the pattern number. There's no minimum order; complete refunds on in-stock orders are given within 30 days. Returns on special orders mean a 25% restocking charge. It makes Sanz to shop at Sanz—particularly since there's free freight for *Underground Shoppers*.
B, PQ

PAINT & PATTERN
Dept. US
2901 Avenue K
Plano, TX 75074
(214) 423-2684
CK

Step right up, friends! You say you want fabric and upholstery? Carpets and floorcoverings? Wallpaper and wallcoverings? Draperies and blinds? Well, folks, they've got all that and more! WAVERLEY, DELMAR, LEVOLOR, ARMSTRONG, CONGOLEUM—you name it, they've got it. Designer SOLARIUM floor covering was just $16.50 per yard (six-feet wide)—way below the prices quoted at full-price retail stores. And all carpet was only 10% over their cost! Yessir—builders' prices to everyone! And if we didn't paint a good picture with our patter, then write them with the item, model, and pattern description and see for yourself! **PQ**

ROBINSON'S WALLCOVERINGS
Dept. L01
225 W. Spring St.
Titusville, PA 16354
(814) 827-1893
CK, MC, V, AE

Robinson's Wallcoverings carries a complete selection of wallcovering and vinyl, prepasted, and unpasted wallcovering from manufacturers such as IMPERIAL, LENNON, SUNWORTHY, and WALDEC at discounts up to 50% off and prices as low as $2.89 per single metric roll. Borders and coordinating fabrics, along with a complete selection of bedspreads, curtains, and matching accessories for a "total decorator look" without the decorator expense are waiting to be ensembled. Most orders shipped within 24 hours via U.P.S. Satisfaction guaranteed; refunds given within 30 days. Custom Order Service is available on almost any wallcovering from nearly any manufacturer. Their 73-page catalog with actual wallcovering samples was available for only $2, refundable on your first order. C $2 (refundable)

RONNIE DRAPERIES
145 Broad Ave.
Fairview, NJ 07022
(212) 964-1480: NY residents
(201) 945-1900
CK, MC, V, AE

Since 1925 Ronnie has sold its own original designs in draperies, bedspreads, and curtains at 20% to 50% savings. There's a wide selection and many styles are comparable to those found in the best retail stores. Bedspreads and draperies come lined or unlined, and Ronnie also offers thermal insulated draperies. LEVOLOR verticals and mini-blinds are also available. There's a $20 minimum order, no restocking charge, and most orders are delivered in two to three weeks. Check the section in their 48-page, full-color catalog on how to measure for draperies before ordering. C

SHIBUI WALLCOVERINGS
Dept. US
P.O. Box 1638
Rohnert Park, CA 94928
(800) 824-3030
(707) 526-6170: CA residents
CK, MC, V, COD

Shibui knows the paper chase can leave you climbing the walls. This company carries handcrafted textiles, grasscloths, and string wall coverings (all imported from the Orient) at approximately 50% to 60% savings. Wallcoverings are natural in texture, color, and material. Their kit of 80 samples of wallcoverings costs $2 that is deductible from your first order. Do-it-yourself instructions and tools are available. There's no minimum order; the restocking charge is 10% on returns; orders are shipped within two days; shipping charges are $7.80 for orders under $100, no charge on bigger orders.
C $2 (refundable)

SILVER WALLCOVERING, INC.
3001-11 Kensington Ave.
Philadelphia, PA 19134
(800) 426-6600
(215) 426-7600
CK, MC, V, AE, D, COD

Wonderful walls can be yours at a price that's pure gold from Silver Wallcovering, Inc. Home decorating at a discount isn't just a dream, it's a way of doing business with this company. Many of the things needed to complete or create the atmosphere to make your house a home can be found here, all at 30% to 50% below what you'd pay in other stores. Wallcoverings, window treatments, and wall decor were all included in the selection of savings. We found most national brands with no minimum purchase required, so check here first, no matter how large or small your decorating needs may be. A 30-day return or refund was offered on damaged materials, and the catalog included extra savings with discount coupons on selected items. Prices included shipping and handling and response time was only three to seven days. C

WALLPAPER NOW
3511 S. Main St.
Archdale, NC 27263
(919) 431-6341
(919) 434-1598
CK, MC, V

Also known as Your-Hang-It-Now™ Discount Wallpaper stores, this five-year-old company wasn't born yesterday when it comes to discounts. They lop off a whopping 30% to 90% off the price of each roll, so don't put off until tomorrow what you can Wallpaper Now! This company offers 25,000 papers and coverings, so if you can't find something you like, it's not their fault. Brands like SUNWORTHY, YORK, MILLBROOK, UNITED, and IMPERIAL are worth looking into and SCHUMACHER's sure to make you order. Grasscloths are particularly popular—not surprising since they're priced at $7.95 to $14.95 and would retail for $25 to $45. Wallpaper Now will match the cuttings you send and will mail out samples. Prices range from 96 cents to $8.95 per single roll, with quality ranging from "paint store" inventory and up. They pay shipping. **PQ**

WELLS INTERIORS, INC.
Dept. US
7171 Amador Valley Plaza
Dublin, CA 94566
(800) 547-8982
CK, MC, V

This company is a leading supplier of window and floor covering products at blinding discounts of 50 to 60% off conventional retail and 80% off department store prices. They carry a diverse inventory of window blinds, carpeting, blind cleaners, mini-blinds, verticals, and pleated shades: all types of window coverings. Nationally known brands make up about 95% of the inventory and include LEVOLOR, LOUVERDRAPE, KIRSCH, and DELMAR. No minimum order; shipping is usually free; most orders come in about four weeks. Orders are accepted by phone, but writing them reduces the possibility of error. Remember to measure your windows correctly; there are no returns on custom-cut orders. All's well that ends well at Wells. **B, PQ**

NATIONAL CHAINS: YOUR HOMETOWN LINK TO SAVINGS

Now that you know how to shop the underground by mail, how about turning up some new turf in your own town or when you're on the road again? There are "off-price retailers" located in most major cities and you can save anywhere from 20% to 90% if you know where to look.

Just what is sold at an outlet? Is it a dumping ground for seconds, irregulars, or out-of-date merchandise? That assumption couldn't be further from the truth. Most outlets carry current, first-quality goods (just like those shipped to retail stores) and are generally staffed by friendly, knowledgeable salespeople. Occasionally, you might find an outlet selling damaged goods, but look for rock-bottom reductions tagging along.

Almost anything can be found at the stores we've included in this section. You'll find sources for suits, shoes, shirts, pants, underwear, bathing suits, china, crystal, pottery, gifts, linens, fabrics, wallpaper, hardware, appliances, sporting goods, toys, and much more located a few miles from where you live. Just check the telephone directory or write to the company for a complete list of store locations. When planning your next trip consult this section and don't leave home without it!

Apparel: Children's

Carter's Children's Wear Factory Outlet: They're no newcomers to town: for 120 years they've been selling a large selection of pajamas, outerwear, and swimwear for kids in sizes from newborn to 14. Garments come in both first-quality and irregular at 20% to 60% off. Some stores carry ladies' and men's sportswear. 62 stores. Headquarters: 963 Highland Ave., Needham Heights, MA 02194.

The Children's Outlet (also The Children's Place): These bargains come from Federated Department Stores with styles ranging from infant to 14. Discounts of at least 20% on such brands as HEALTH-TEX, ON-TRACK, FRENCH COAST, RAINDROPS, ROB ROY, BUSTER BROWN, JORDACHE, BEAR TREE, BLUE DUCK, and FAME. Stores have carpeted play areas and video screens for keeping kids occupied! 78 stores. Headquarters: 25 Riverside Drive, Pinebrook, NJ 07058.

Chocolate Soup: Factory direct prices from this popular manufacturer of children's fashions amount to 30% to 40% off the price you'd pay for comparable looks at a department store. Besides carrying the distinctive CHOCOLATE SOUP styles (appliquéd jumpers and shortalls, for example), they carry IZOD, OSHKOSH, CALABASH, and other famous brands discounted 20% on an average day. 11 stores. Headquarters: 6515 Railroad St., Raytown, MO 64133.

Fabulous Julie's: Since 1956 their slogan has been: "Quality name-brand children's wear at bargain prices." It's true, and for the products of ROB ROY, BILLY THE KID, IZOD, AILEEN, DANSKIN, LITTLE TOPSY, MIGHTY MISS, THOMAS TEXTILE, TRIMFIT, LEE, CHIPS 'N TWIGS, HANES, and DR. DENTON'S. The low prices (25% to 50% off) include PIERRE CARDIN for boys, and JORDACHE, SERGIO VALENTE, YOUNG, and TRENDSETTER for girls. Check out their "Julie Money." 19 stores. Headquarters: 140 Jericho Turnpike, Mineola, NY 11507.

Jolene Children's Factory Outlet: Jolene manufactures girls' dresses for Sears (private label WINNIE THE POOH) as well as for J.C. Penney and other major department stores. Their outlets sell other brands such as HAPPY KIDS and TOM SAWYER with discounts usually ranging from 20% to 70% for first-quality items, closeouts, overruns, and seconds. 14 stores. Headquarters: 1050 W. 350 South, P.O. Box 1446, Provo, UT 84603.

Kids Mart: Kids and their mothers are smart if they shop at Kids Mart, an off-price, value-oriented venture of Holtzman's Little Folk Shop. Labels include SWAT, FAME, LEVI'S, BRITTANIA, OUR GANG,

GOODLAND, HEALTH-TEX, TRIMFIT, OCEAN PACIFIC, CANDLESTICK, SERGIO VALENTE, and OUR GIRL. Prices are an average of 30% below comparable retail, with some sale items reduced up to 80%. Sizes: infants and toddlers; boys 4 to 7 and 8 to 14; girls 4 to 6X and 7 to 14. 167 stores. Headquarters: P.O. Box 3387, City of Industry, CA 91744.

Kids Port, U.S.A.: Get on the good ship to savings at any Kids Port, U.S.A. As the outlet for HEALTH-TEX, one of the leading brands of children's clothes, their merchandise is first-quality and current-season. Playwear, swimwear, and nightwear sold at an average of 25% off. Great buys in infantswear. They carry OUR GIRL and OUR GANG labels, too. 30 stores. Headquarters: 33 Benedict Place, Greenwich, CT 06830.

Kids 'R' Us: A spin-off of the highly successful Toys 'R' Us stores, the concept fits well in kids' clothing. Stylish and discounted brands such as IZOD LA COSTE, JET SET, and ADIDAS are bargains not to kid about. Rapidly expanding, this new chain is likely to be around when the kids are grown up. 43 stores. Headquarters: 395 W. Passaic St., Rochelle Park, NJ 07662.

Polly Flinders Factory Stores: Strictly for little girls (and their older sisters or girlfriends), you'll find the FLINDERS line in all sizes. Merchandise at these outlets is first-quality, even in irregular overruns and cancellations, with savings up to 75%. Their hand-smocked dresses are a must for every girl. Underwear and sportswear, too. 18 stores. Headquarters: 224 E. 8th St., Cincinnati, OH 45202.

Apparel: Family

Beno's: Beno's knows their business because they've been selling off-price since the 1950s. Discounts of 20% to 60% are offered on name-brand, moderately priced apparel for the whole family from business suits to bikinis. Brands: LEVI'S, LEE, WRANGLER, JORDACHE, CALVIN KLEIN, VAN HEUSEN, OCEAN PACIFIC, CAMPUS, BRAXTON, INTERWOVEN, HANES, PLAYTEX, and GARANIMALS. 42 stores. Headquarters: 1515 Santee St., Los Angeles, CA 90015.

Blue Bell Factory Outlet: It's not an ice cream store with 28 flavors; it's a factory outlet with thousands of pairs of WRANGLER jeans and sportswear for the family. One of the many manufacturers located in North Carolina, they've been selling their own brands (and others) at

30% to 60% off like lickety-split. Sizes abound from 1 to 50. Head-quarters: P.O. Box 21488, Greensboro, NC 27420.

Burlington Coat Factory: Get on the right track with the Burlington line: name-brand, in-season, first-quality garments for the family on the move. Discounts are usually 30% to 60% for coats, jackets, suits, sportswear, lingeries, gloves, and more. Save on EVAN-PICONE, MISTY HARBOR, BILL BLASS, IZOD, PIERRE CARDIN, HEALTH-TEX, LIZ CLAIBORNE, CALVIN KLEIN, LONDON FOG, JONATHAN LOGAN, HARVE BENARD, OSCAR DE LA RENTA, PAULINE TRIGERE, WHITE STAG, ASPEN, DONMOOR, LARKLAND, ZERO KING, HANES, BVD, and ISOTONER. This giant company has 82 stores. Headquarters: 263 W. 38th St., New York, NY 10018.

Cluett Factory Stores: Features a large assortment of first-quality current season family apparel overruns at savings of at least 40% below retail. Owned and operated by Cluett, Peabody and Co., Inc.; makers of ARROW shirts and sportswear, GOLD TOE socks, LADY ARROW blouses and sportswear, R.P.M. and JON MARC slacks, SATURDAYS, SUNDAYS, and COLOURS BY ALEXANDER JULIAN sportswear, ARROW boyswear, and DOBIE children's wear. Additional savings on clearly marked slight irregulars and salesman's samples. 29 stores. Headquarters: 1450 Route 22, Mountainside, NJ 07092.

Designer Depot: Stop off at the Depot for a pleasant visit. You might lose some time but you'll get a ticket to Savingsville. This is K mart's entry into high-fashion (and off-price) merchandising, with designer items and brand names at 20% to 70% below regular retail. Brands: YVES ST. LAURENT, IZOD, BILLY THE KID, CALVIN KLEIN, and CHRISTIAN DIOR might not seem like K mart items, but the train is coming, so hop on. 30 stores. Headquarters: 3100 Big Beaver Road, Troy, MI 48084.

Fashion Gal (also Fashionation, Tempo, Show Off, Fashion Mine, The Right Price): One of the nation's largest off-price specialty chains, this group of Gateway Apparel stores offers super bargains on the newest designer and name-brand fashions, in both junior and misses sizes. Discounts range from 15% to 70%, on brands like LEE, FORENZA, LIMITED EXPRESS, GLORIA VANDERBILT, LEVI'S, CALVIN KLEIN, JORDACHE, PALMETTOS, HANG TEN, COUNTERPARTS, BRITTANIA, LADY ARROW, HAPPY LEGS, and LIZ CLAIBORNE. 130 stores. And brand-new under the Gateway Apparel umbrella . . . outlet stores with first-quality name-brand fashions at the right price . . .

$12.99 or *less*! For the store nearest you, write Gateway Apparel, 8500 Valcour, P.O. Box 6990, St. Louis, MO 63123.

Gentlemen's Wearhouse & Ladies Factory Outlet (also Bristol County): The anonymous parent company of this chain is one of the largest producers of private-label garments for department and specialty stores on the East coast. Their off-price outlets offer discounts of 40% to 60% and cater primarily to the 20- to 50-year-old man shopping for contemporary suits, sport coats, and slacks (especially wool). 38 stores. Headquarters: 194 Riverside Ave., New Bedford, MA 02746.

Hathaway Factory Outlet: Hath not a man without a shirt sought shelter in a Hathaway? It is so, says the master of the shirt world. Styles, colors, and sizes for shoppers with tastes ranging from executive to sporting to flamboyant. Men's and women's irregulars are sold for practically nothing. They carry CHAPS and other brands. Prices generally 30% to 50% below usual Hathaway retail. 10 stores. Headquarters: 10 Water St., Waterville, MI 04901.

House of Leather (also Moss Street Menswear, Reading Clothing Outlet, Reading Menswear Outlet, Bag N Bootery, Coat Rack/ Clothes Line, Penn Leather & Coat Co.): This house has a different address for every door, but they all lead to the same 20% to 50% discounts on a wealth of leather coats, boots, and shoes. Brands include BOTANY 500, LONDON FOG, ARROW, CALVIN KLEIN, VANITY FAIR, FRYE, DINGO, BASS, DEXTER, GLORIA VANDERBILT, SASSON, and MISTY HARBOR. 10 stores. Headquarters: Stinson Drive and Old Airport Road, RD 9164, Reading, PA 19605.

Jos. A Bank Clothiers, Inc.: If you like Quaker's oats you'll love their coats because the same people who can feed you can clothe you. Traditional styles for men and women at 30% off retail are available from their manufacturing plant. Investment dressing is the key to their success: Oxford cloth shirts, silk ties, suits, and accessories for conservatives wanting to look like they're rich without becoming poor in the process. 16 stores. Headquarters: 109 Market Place, Baltimore, MD 21202.

Just Labels: "Quality labels, discount prices" is what this off-price division of Beall's Department Stores is all about. Just Labels sells moderate-to-better-quality men's, women's, and junior apparel and accessories at discounts from 20% to 60%. If you've been to Beall's (which, no doubt, you have if you are reading this book), you know their sales are just right for the budget-minded buyer. 12 stores. Headquarters: 3923 Manatee Ave. W., P.O. Box N, Bradenton, FL 33506.

Manhattan Factory Outlet (also Brand Name Fashion): Gotham City is famous for its Seventh Avenue styles (not to mention Eighth Avenue) and now they are spread out across half of America's states. Discounts up to 60% off are distributed properly throughout their MANHATTAN and LADY MANHATTAN brands, as well as on garments from other leading manufacturers. A factory-owned and operated division of Manhattan Industries, first-quality men's and ladies apparel and irregulars make up their inventory. 54 stores. Headquarters: 1501 Broadway, Fairlawn, NJ 07410.

Mill Outlet (also The Clothes Hound, The Clothing Warehouse, The StockRoom, Evan-Picone Factory Store, Haspel Factory Outlet, Palm Beach Mill Outlet): Down by the old mill stream you can outfit yourself and your village queen with some of the best buys in the underground. First-quality brands with emphasis on tailored designs: GANT, AUSTIN HILL, EVAN-PICONE, PALM BEACH, HASPEL, EAGLE, PIERRE CARDIN. Men's suits, sport coats, pants, sweaters, and shirts. Women's Missy and Petite blazers, skirts, slacks, sweaters, and blouses. 20 stores. Headquarters: 626 Bernard Ave., Knoxville, TN 37921.

Newport Sportswear: Newport Sportswear was news in 1981 when The Block Industries opened up this chain. As manufacturers of current-season, first-quality men's shirts, sweaters, activewear, and outerwear, they are still in the main scene. Brands: CLEAR CREEK, NEWSPORT, OCEAN ISLE, NEWPORT, NEWPORT II, and BREAKERS POINT. 28 stores. Headquarters: P.O. Box 420, Wilmington, NC 28402.

The Outlet: One of the best-known (but "nameless") manufacturers of swimwear and sportswear, they made a big splash more than 15 years ago when they jumped into the off-price market. They offer countless styles for men, women, and children in activewear, sportswear, swimwear, and large-size fashions. End-of-the-season sales are especially luring so write and get on their mailing list! 14 stores. Headquarters: 6015 Bandini Blvd., Los Angeles, CA 90040.

Rolane Factory Outlet: Go rolling down the river of "the world's largest seller of hosiery for men, women, and children at great prices." Beach at the islands of name-brand sportswear, suits, and swimwear, all discounted at 40%. 33 stores. Headquarters: P.O. Box 5407, Greensboro, NC 27403.

Syms: Shopping at Syms is a him and her situation: CALVIN KLEIN, STANLEY BLACKER, JOHN WEITZ, PIERRE CARDIN, CERRUTI, GIORGIO ST. ANGELO, YVES ST. LAURENT, GANT, RALPH LAUREN, TED LAPIDUS, CHRISTIAN DIOR, and more at discounts of 30% to 70%. Family clothing includes suits, tuxedoes, overcoats, slacks, shirts, sweaters, shoes, hats, gloves, pajamas, and underwear. 16 stores. Headquarters: 300 Chubb Ave., Lyndhurst, NJ 07071.

Talbott Factory Outlet: The Talbott tag is their best buy, since they're one of the oldest knitting mills in America. Brands vary depending upon availability, but they always have the world-famous French designer line, QUI. Prices are about 30% to 70% off nationally advertised retail prices. Talbott is most famous for traveler's fabric—a wrinkle-free, double-knit yarn bouclé, used in sweaters, blazers, skirts, and blouses. They sell ladies' coordinates and a full line of menswear. 28 stores. Headquarters: North 6th St., Reading, PA 19603.

Van Heusen Factory Store: Their shirts speak for themselves, what can we say? Men's and women's shirts as well as current sportswear, outerwear, sweaters, knits, and personal furnishings. Labels include GEOFFREY BEENE, AIGNER, CACHAREL, HENNESSEY, and LADY VAN HEUSEN. All clothing is first-quality and you don't have to go Dutch to afford them. 111 stores. Headquarters: 281 Centennial Ave., Piscataway, NJ 08854.

Winona Knits: Their business formula is simple: Top-quality, American-made garments at factory direct prices backed by an unconditional guarantee. Their 20 stores feature tops, bottoms, activewear, and outerwear, their specialty being sweaters. 100% wool, wool blends, cottons, and acrylics make up their line of exceptional sweater jackets, V-necks, crew necks, cowl necks, turtlenecks, and vests. Headquarters: 1200 Storr's Pond Road, Winona, MN 55987.

Apparel: Lingerie, Underwear, and Hosiery

Bare Necessities: The current-season, first-quality, name-brand, and designer intimate apparel and lingerie offered by these outlets will barely affect your bank account. Loungewear, panties, bras, robes, and gowns are discounted 20% to 60%. Besides the BARE label you'll find BALI, WARNER, OLGA, VASSARETTE, DIANE VON FURSTEN-BERG, and others in sizes from petite to extra-large. Particularly nice is their personalized service when fitting bras. 25 stores. Headquarters: 350 Warren St., Jersey City, NJ 07302.

Danskin Factory Outlet: Not just for dancing. Join the chorus line, though, and shop for 40% to 60% savings. The premier choreographer in leotards and tights now has a strong line of other activewear, as well as big-name lingerie, panty hose, and cosmetics. Some designer and sportswear also in the show. Four stores, more coming soon. Headquarters: 700 Fairfield Ave., Stamford, CT 06904.

Delta Hosiery Outlet: Deltas have always been sources of plenty and these outlets are in the mainstream of today's off-price merchandising. Save 30% to 70% on panty hose, stockings, panties, girdles, bras, slips, teddies, camisoles, socks, and underwear. HANES, BURLINGTON, NO NONSENSE, and ROUND THE CLOCK are but a few of the labels there. 66 stores. Headquarters: P.O. Box 3158, Reading, PA 19604.

Formfit Outlet: If the apparel fits, wear it while you smile: 40% savings on discontinued styles, closeouts, overruns, and designer lines, as well as fabrics, zippers, and other accessories. Sleepwear, robes, pajamas, teddies, gowns, slips, camisoles, and related clothing form their inventory, a fitting tribute to the female form. 21 stores. Headquarters: The Linnehan Building, The Triangle, Ellsworth, ME 04605.

Gossard Outlet (also Signal Mill Factory Outlet, Athens Mill Factory Outlet, May Hosiery Mills Factory Outlet): At these outlets, usually located in small towns, Gossard sells family apparel at 25% to 50% savings. DEE CEE and CHIC jeans, PINEHURST and CAROLE lingerie, and GOSSARD products are available. Merchandise is a mixed bag of first-quality items in closeouts and irregulars. 20 stores. Headquarters: P.O. Box 1207, 425 E. Chestnut, Nashville, TN 37202.

Munsingwear Factory Outlet: You'll see more penguins (the famous Munsingwear trademark) here than in *National Geographic!* Beyond their sportswear and underwear lines there are women's lingerie and foundations by VASSARETTE. Merchandise ranges from first-quality closeouts to seconds and irregulars at savings of 50% to

70%. 18 stores. Headquarters: 724 N. 1st St., P.O. Box 1369, Minneapolis, MN 55440.

Olga Factory Surplus: We don't know if they have free coffee at their outlets, but there's no doubt that this factory can perk you up with their 20% to 50% discounts. Ogle over the discontinued and irregular nighties, gowns, robes, camisoles, body stockings, panties, and bras. Selection is far from scanty and prices scandalously low. 10 stores. Headquarters: 7900 Haskell Ave., Van Nuys, CA 91409.

The Red Flannel Factory: Red flannel has kept many a person warm and snug, be it by the fire or at the kitchen table. The factory sells their own line so you know it's got to be the best deal in town. We're talking *warm!* But prices are cool and a good 25% lower than retail store prices for flannel clothing. Write for their mail-order catalog. 2 stores. Headquarters: P.O. Box 370, 73 S. Main St., Cedar Springs, MI 49319.

Shapes Activewear Outlet: Get in shape with this outlet's activewear: leotards, hosiery, fleecewear sweats, socks, tights (from stirrups to high gloss), exercisewear, dancewear, warm-ups, and more—most from an "unnamed" 300-store hosiery manufacturer. Save 40% on first-quality and 60% on irregulars. Flashy and aerobic atmosphere of stores make shopping fun. 30 stores. Headquarters: 1540 Turnpike, New Hyde Park, NY 11040.

Socks 'N Such: Sock it to me, baby, you're such a deal on first-quality fashion hosiery at prices 20% to 40% off suggested retail. Accessories for infants, children, men and women are stocked, along with socks, and more socks. All items carry the company's label and are sold from kiosks in high-traffic zones of malls. 25 stores. Headquarters: 3320-C2 Vineland Road, Orlando, FL 32811.

Apparel: Men's

Adam's Warehouse: You won't find any fig leaves in this warehouse, but you can cover up with some polyester "perfect for the bowling alley" leisure suits to haute couture designs by YVES ST. LAURENT, PIERRE CARDIN, and other top brands. Also famous for their black suits, Adam's has discounts of 20% to 50% on most items. 15 stores. Headquarters: 123 Beach St., Boston, MA 02111.

Anders: Wander no more, friend, for Anders is your store. Part of a large buying cooperative (150 member stores), they receive regular shipments of first-quality name-brand and designer men's clothing and furnishings discounted by 20% to 50%. Labels: EAGLE, GIORGIO SAINT ANGELO, ETIENNE CARON. 34 stores. Headquarters: 1231 Roosevelt Ave., York, PA 17404.

Barry Manufacturing Company (also Zeeman Manufacturing): Barry is Zee-man for the budget-minded shopper. Right off the manufacturers' assembly lines, their apparel runs heavily toward wool blend suits, sport coats, and slacks. Inventory contains mostly their own label suits in sizes ranging from 35S to 60L and 58XL. 34 stores. Headquarters: 2303 John Glenn Drive, Chamblee, GA 30341.

Clothing Clearance Centers: Clean out the closet and clear some shelves for the savings you'll get when you shop at these centers. Every item of a man's wardrobe can be found at 30% to 50% below retail: suits, jackets, raincoats, dress shirts, ties, and hosiery. Brands: ADOLFO, HALSTON, BOTANY 500, PIERRE CARDIN, and STANLEY BLACKER. 13 stores. Headquarters: 350 Fifth Ave., New York, NY 10118.

Kuppenheimer Factory Stores: Hartmarx (formerly Hart, Schaffner and Marx) bought this off-price chain in 1983, so don't take your brothers to the races, go to Kuppenheimer's outlets. They manufacture suits, sport coats, and slacks for men and sell them at factory-direct prices; comparable to a 35% or more cut below average retail. NOTE: Kuppenheimer stores in Texas are not owned by Hartmarx and are not bound by the off-price format. 143 stores. Headquarters: P.O. Box 7050, 5555 Oakbrook Parkway, Norcross, GA 30091.

The Men's Wearhouse: These stores house some great buys at 20% to 30% discounts and welcome you to come and see their classy merchandise: BOTANY 500, NINO CERRUTI, OSCAR DE LA RENTA, YSL, DANIEL HECHTER, CHAPS, GIVENCHY, and ADOLFO. Tailors are on premises and alterations are billed only when extraordinary adjustments are required. 31 stores including ones in San Francisco, San Jose, and Sacramento. Headquarters: 5507 Renwick, Houston, TX 77081.

NBO (National Brands Outlet): NBO could be *Nothing But Opportunities* to walk out of NBO's stores wearing some fine threads. Designer menswear everywhere: suits, sport coats, jackets, and activewear. Everything imaginable is on the racks, which are filled with the lines of 200-plus designer and brand-name labels at discounts ranging from 30% to 70%. NBO is close to being the zenith of men's off-price chains in America and is expanding. Nine stores. Headquarters: 60 Enterprise Ave., Secaucus, NJ 07094.

Prince Fashion Outlet: You can dress like a prince without turning into a pauper at these outlets when you buy direct from the manufacturer. PRINCE brand ruffled shirts, silk trousers, jackets, blazers, and even jogging suits (without armor) are marked down 50% with additional savings on specials. Seven stores. Headquarters: 1201 N. Interstate 35, Carrollton, TX 75006.

S & K Famous Brands: S & K went into the off-price menswear business back in 1967 and is into what's up (the latest styles) and what's down (prices, usually 30% to 50% below retail). This "quiet outlet" chain features a complete selection of menswear from the finest department stores (BLOOMINGDALE'S, LORD & TAYLOR'S), traditional retailers, and manufacturers. 48 stores. Headquarters: P.O. Box 31800, Richmond, VA 23294-1800.

Webster Warehouse Outlet: A large inventory for the definitive man whose tastes turn toward big labels: OLEG CASSINI, BRITTANY, MEMBERS ONLY, COVERAGE, and more all at 35% to 70% off. Everything, from suede sport coats, shirts, sweaters, and suits, is ready-to-wear. No irregulars. Four stores. Headquarters: 1800 Woodlawn Drive, Baltimore, MD 21207.

Apparel: Women's

Ann Michele Originals: (also Carolyn's): Ann Michele is the original southern belle when it comes to off-price, moderate-to-better ladies' apparel (sportswear, dresses, and accessories). Discounts run 60% off of its own Ann Michele Originals Moderate Missy Sportswear line. Other labels with 25% off are ALFRED DUNNER, CRICKET LANE, CETRO, DANIELLE B, STONYBROOK, LAURA MAE, HERE'S A HUG, THIRD GENERATION, SULTRA, PENGUIN ISLE KNITS, CRYSTAL, CHRISTOPHER ALAN, and MARISA EVAN. Four stores. Headquarters: 130 S. Walnut Circle, Greensboro, NC 27409.

Apparel America: Eighty-eight units operating four value-oriented chains—Vogue International specializes in junior apparel; Fashion World (misses to mature); Special Sizes, for petite and large size women; and 990 Shops which serve as clearing centers. One of the fastest growing independent chains in the country. Headquarters: 5353 N.W. 35th Ave., Fort Lauderdale, FL 33309, (305) 733-3331.

Artie's: Artie's may not sound like the name of a women's apparel store, but it is, especially for activewear items including sweat suits. They carry clothing for the whole family. Prices on irregulars, overruns, closeouts, and other first-quality items can approach 60% off. 22 stores. Headquarters: 1670 Republic Road, Huntington Valley, PA 19006.

Audrey's Hideaway (also The Competition): This is the fashion place for young, contemporary working women. Daily exposure in both the New York and California markets brings the newest fashions to its customers at the sharpest available price. Among the latest fashions we found here were CALVIN KLEIN, LIZ CLAIBORNE, ESPRIT, SANTA CRUZ, TANGIERS, JORDACHE, CHAUS, I.V. DIFFUSION, OUTLANDERS, and more. Audrey's Hideaway relies on strong creative buying to deliver value to its customers. 20 stores. Headquarters: 2 Cedar St., P.O. Box 507, Woburn, MA 08101.

The Banker's Note: If this banker calls you in—you're in luck—and it can be in red or black, or brown or blue or . . . as long as you sign on the dotted line for designer sportswear, dresses, and suits in styles from traditional to contemporary. This banker's assets include CHAUS, VILLAGER, PANTHER, LIZ CLAIBORNE, EVAN-PICONE, STUART LANG, GLORIA VANDERBILT, and ILLA and ARIELLA (the last two are the Banker's private stock). High turnover and savings of at least 20%. 62 stores. Headquarters: 3358 Canton Road, Marietta, GA 30066.

Brenda Allen: It's All-en a day's work, discounting first-quality misses, ladies', and junior fashions, that is. Large-volume purchases and low overhead translate into 40% to 60% savings on such brandnames as VILLAGER, SASSON, CHIC, LEE, and LIZ CLAIBORNE. 19 stores. Headquarters: 1625 Atwood, Pensacola, FL 32504.

Cap Tree Factory Store (also Vanderbilt Fashions, Vanderbilt Factory Outlet, Langtry Ltd. Shirt Co.): This tree has a bunch of branches and they all can save you some "green." Top-of-the-line blouses, dresses, pants, blazers, and sweaters are sold at well-trimmed prices. In addition to the LANGTRY and VANDERBILT manufactured lines, these outlets offer LANDING GEAR, CHELSEA GIRLS, ESPRIT, TOM BOY, and many more labels at an average of 30% off retail, although specials go up to 65%. 19 stores. Headquarters: P.O. Box 851, Asheville, NC 28802.

ClothesTime: It shouldn't take much time to find one of these successful outlets, a huge chain founded by two men who sold dresses from a van at flea markets. ClothesTime sells designer and brand-name women's wear, for junior and missy sizes (sportswear a specialty). GUESS, CHEROKEE, BRITTANIA, and BONJOUR are but a few of the big labels sold at 30% to 70% off retail. (Much of the merchandise is made especially for CT and has no retail equivalent.) 275 stores. Headquarters: 5325 E. Hunter Ave., Anaheim, CA 92807 (714) 779-5881.

Clothesworks: These clothes work to make you feel good and save you money, especially if you're a seasoned shopper looking for JACK WINTER and other famous maker sportswear. From blouses to jackets, pants to skirts, sweaters to shirts, always save 20% to 60% off retail at these manufacturer's outlets. 85 stores. Headquarters: 810 N. Teutonia Ave., Milwaukee, WI 53209.

Corner House: Dress like the girl next door or better, corner the market on career-conscious clothing from these outlets. Misses and junior sizes in sportswear, suits, coats, shoes, activewear, lingerie, and accessories are sold at 15% to 25% off retail; labels include CALVIN KLEIN, SERGIO VALENTE, LIZ CLAIBORNE, JONATHAN MARTIN, SASSON, ETIENNE AIGNER. 14 stores. Headquarters: Route 663, Quakertown, PA 18951.

Dimensions in Fashion (also Show Off, Clothes to You, Sportique, Something Special, Discovery in Fashions): The spacious stores in this big chain add some new dimensions to shopping for first-quality, name-brand, and designer labels in misses and junior apparel. Discounts run from 30% to 70% on CALVIN KLEIN, JONES NEW YORK, JORDACHE, NORMA KAMALI, BON JOUR, JOHN HENRY, and GLENORA. 60 stores. Headquarters: 1 Northeast Way, Braintree, MA 02184.

Donlevy's Backroom: You don't have to go through the back door to get to great savings when you shop at these stores. Better ladies' apparel and accessories (sportswear, dresses, and coats a specialty) are available for the Mary Cunningham-type fashion-conscious. Prices are 40% to 70% below retail, even for EVAN-PICONE, PIERRE CARDIN, CALVIN KLEIN, GLORIA VANDERBILT, HARVÉ BENARD, YVES ST. LAURENT, and CHANCERY LANE (store label). 53 stores. Headquarters: 1440 Broadway, Suite 1952, New York, NY 10018.

Dress Barn (also L.J.'s Clothes Barn): You don't have to be a small-town girl to go for the big town bargains in these barns. Hey! They've got famous labels, but we've got to keep them cooped up in our files. Overall, there's an excellent selection of first-quality misses' and juniors' sportswear, dresses, coats, swimwear, and accessories discounted 20%; end-of-the-season sales knock 50% off already discontinued lines. Shop and save 'til the cows come home. 208 stores. Headquarters: 88 Hamilton St., P.O. Box 10220, Stamford, CT 06904.

Fashion Barn: One of the most extensive selections of off-price fashions for women of all ages and sizes. Famous labels and brand names throughout the store in junior, missy, queen, and half sizes always 25% to 60% below department store or nationally advertised prices. Over 500 well-known companies are presented in all categories including dresses, coordinates, separates, activewear, sportswear, jeans, skirts, and swimwear. All price tags indicate original retail prices. 115 stores are scattered across the country. Headquarters: 270 Market St., Saddle Brook, NJ 07662.

Fashion Gallery: You'll look pretty as a picture after shopping at these stores, which are owned by Spencer Companies, a multifaceted corporation with 50 years' experience in retailing. Specialists in brand-name juniors' and misses' sportswear (and brand-name shoes), they carry SASSON, JORDACHE, CHOCOLATE CHIPS, MISS LIZ, LANDLUBBER, and WEST SIDE ACTIVE WEAR. 20 stores. Headquarters: 450 Summer St., Boston, MA 02210.

Flemington Fashion Outlet: A friend to the working woman, this Pennsylvania-based outlet chain has a vast inventory of moderate-to-better designer women's fashions in coats, sportswear, and dresses, in sizes from missy to junior. Past-season samples sell for 25% to 75% off retail; brands include VIVANTI, ACT III, TRISSI, LONDON FOG, LIZ CLAIBORNE, and STANLEY BLACKER. 12 stores. Headquarters: 1920 S. 5th St., Allentown, PA 18103.

The Great Factory Store (also Jo Harper, Fashion Works): One of the many off-price chains that have headquarters in Reading, Pennsylvania, the Great Factory Stores carry first-quality junior and missy designer brands: SASSON, ELLEN TRACY, DIANE VON FURSTENBERG, ROSEANNA, CHAUS, VILLAGER, BILL BLASS, TAHARI, and CALVIN KLEIN at 20% to 50% below retail. 22 stores. Headquarters: P.O. Box 265, Morgantown, PA 19543.

Hit or Miss: The odds are that this chain will *hit* more than miss: the Zayre Corporation (big daddy of T.J. Maxx) plans on having 800 of these outlets operating by 1986! That just goes to show that all those nickles add up. Selling in such volume, they can afford to give the consumers a true break; typical discounts on merchandise are 20% to 40%. Top-brand labels abound but Zayre would hit the ceiling if we tell all. More than 400 stores. Headquarters: 100 Campanelli Parkway, Stoughton, MA 02072.

Hurrah!: Three cheers and a hurrah for trendy brand-names and 30% to 50% savings on sportswear/accessories by RICKI, ANDREW ST. JOHN, SEGERMAN, CRABGRASS, JUSTIN ALLEN, LEVI'S, ROCKY MOUNTAIN, QUE PASAI, JONI-BLAIR, JOHN SCOTT & CO., LEE, and ZENA. Especially worth celebrating for a young girl beginning her wardrobe. 38 stores. Headquarters: 7400 Excelsior Blvd., P.O. Box 1435, Minneapolis, MN 55440.

Inlook Outlet: Look before you leap, then jump in and let your fancy lead you to some "in" styles at off-priced savings of 30% to 70%. This manufacturer of junior and missy apparel has JERREL, STRAIT LANE, MELISSA LANE, and other fine labels in a variety of fashions, so don't go out without looking at their business and evening suits, blouses, dresses, loungewear, and cocktail dresses. Labels not cut out let us see some good buys of SMART PARTS, LADY ARROW, ANNE KLEIN, SASSON, NOTCHES, CHIC, and JOHN MARTIN. 11 stores. Headquarters: 1240 Titan, Dallas, TX 75247.

Loehmann's: Founded by famed bargain mogul Frieda Loehmann in Brooklyn in 1921, this famous off-price chain now offers coast-to-coast cost cutting. Huge stores draw crowds of rich and not-so-rich, all searching for dresses, suits, evening gowns, sportswear, outerwear, lingerie, and accessories made by leading designers and manufacturers from 30% to 60% below retail. Their famous Back Room features exclusive couture ensembles and formal wear at prices 20% to 50% less than usual. Almost 100 stores. Headquarters: 2500 Halsey St., Bronx, NY 10461.

Old Mill: The old mill's still churning out the bargains, especially in their own lines: COUNTRY MISS, COUNTRY SUBURBAN, HANDMACHER, and WEATHERVANE COORDINATES. Their moderate-to-better sportswear, sweaters, tops, suits, dresses, activewear, and coordinated separates are all first-quality, current-season, and discounted 25% to 70%. Sizes range from 4 to 18 and 4P to 16P. 63 stores. Headquarters: P.O. Box 769, Easton, PA 18042.

Oxford Sportswear Outlet (also Champion Retail): One of the largest sportswear manufacturers in the U.S.A. provides a plethora of overruns, irregulars, and discontinued lines of ladies' casualwear (and men's fashions) to these outlets, and everything is sold at 50% below retail. You don't have to be an Oxford graduate to recognize quality in their labels: COS COB, MERONA, RALPH LAUREN/POLO, and many others. 19 stores. Headquarters: 222 Piedmont, Atlanta, GA 30308.

Plus Sizes: Big is better when you're talking savings (and bank accounts, and Christmas bonuses, and so forth). This chain specializes in no small market and offers prices reduced by 20% to 50% for the fuller-figured woman. If you are burdened by swelling inflation and want to trim down on your wardrobe budget, jog to their stores to see the youthful and fashion-forward styles; big-name brands in sizes 38 to 52. 36 stores. Headquarters: 85 Union, Memphis, TN 38103.

Post Horn: Honk if you love bargains. This chain is owned by J.G. Hook, the preppie proprietor of colorful Oxford cloth blouses, which are for sale along with khaki shirts, Madras bermudas, navy blazers, and many other traditional styles for women. Most first-quality merchandise is discounted 30%. 16 stores. Headquarters: 1300 Belmont Ave., Philadelphia, PA 19104.

Ship 'n Shore (also Ladies Factory Outlet): Get on the good ship (take a lollipop with you) and head for the savings shore. Be careful or you'll get lost in a sea of designer wear and sportswear, from the SHIP 'N SHORE label to DONALD BROOK and PIERRE CARDIN. First-quality garments at 40% off, seconds at 50%. 22 stores. Headquarters: Bridgewater Road, Aston, PA 19104.

Sizes Unlimited (also Smart Size): Strange, but true: The Limited, Inc., owns Sizes Unlimited outlets. However, there are no limits to the fully stocked inventory that invites the full-figured, budget-minded, moderate-income woman to save 25% to 50% on apparel in sizes 16½ to 38 up to 52. Brands: SASSON, LEVI, TRISSI, LADY DEVON, FIRE ISLANDER, HARVÉ BENARD, and PLAYTEX (and SIGNATURE A, their private label). 86 stores. Headquarters: 469 Fifth Ave., New York, NY 10017.

Sportswear Mart: Smart shoppers make the Sportswear Mart one of their first stops when they're looking for competitive prices. Tailored fashions come from LIZ CLAIBORNE, JH COLLECTIBLES, VIL-

LAGER, GIORGIO SAINT ANGELO, and HARVÉ BENARD, all at 20% to 70% off. 12 stores. Headquarters: 720 W. Main St., Louisville, KY 40202.

Suzanne's: Fashion-conscious shoppers have put Suzanne's at the top of the list for first-rate quality merchandise offered at 20% to 50% off department store prices. The selections are the newest and most current around, including labels such as: LIZ CLAIBORNE, CHAUS, CHEROKEE, JONATHAN MARTIN, and J.H. COLLECTIBLES. Shipments arrive daily, stocking stores full of new enticements. Suzanne's is definitely worth discovering! 50 stores. Headquarters: 3236 Skyline Drive, Dallas, TX 75006.

T. H. Mandy: Every woman needs a Mandy bargain around the house and some say the more the merrier! Owned by U.S. Shoe Corporation, this chain sells misses apparel in moderate-to-designer lines: 25% to 50% off on name-brand merchandise . Experts in the off-price business, they offer fine service and savings. 16 stores. Stores in the Washington, D.C., Philadelphia, Chicago, and Dallas metropolitan areas.

Virginia Alan Ltd.: She's come a long way and she's not afraid of wolves or bogeymen; nor is she likely to run from 20% to 60% discounts on current-season and first-quality merchandise from top-name manufacturers (sorry, unlisted). They carry women's ready-to-wear with emphasis on suits, separates, blouses, and dresses for the professional woman. 18 stores. Headquarters: 40 Mead St., Stratford, CT 06497.

The Way Station: Hold the horses, stop the wagon! Got to get to the Way Station to make a connection: dresses, bathing suits, sweaters, tops, suits, and skirts (dressy and casual) at 25% to 75% off. TANNER CLOTHES, DONCASTER, and XIA are but a few of the brands worth waiting in line for. 14 stores. Headquarters: P.O. Box 1139, Rutherfordton, NC 28139.

Coats and Outerwear

Londontown Factory Outlet Store: You might have deduced, Watson, that this is the official outlet for the famous LONDON FOG apparel. Indeed it is, and fine-quality clothing is sold in these outlets, with smashing buys in rainwear and outerwear—light or heavy—including leather jackets. Sizes range from 4 to 26½ (women); 36 to

54 (men); 4 to 14 (girls); and 4 to 20 (boys). Prices are generally 50% below what you would expect. 19 stores. Headquarters: Londontown Blvd., Eldersburg, MD 21784.

Maternity

Dan Howard Maternity Outlet (also Maternity Clothing Factory): Dan's the man for the woman-in-waiting. These outlets specialize in high-quality fashionable maternity clothing at factory-direct prices (20% to 50% below retail). Each outlet carries 2,500 to 4,000 items: lingerie, casuals, dressy dresses, sportswear (coordinated or mixed), and even professional clothing suitable for female executives. 70 stores. Headquarters: 710 W. Jackson Blvd., Chicago, IL 60606.

Maternity Wearhouse (also Maternity Mart): During the best nine months of your life, you can be most fashionable and save money at the same time. These maternity shops carry a full line of maternity apparel, such as slacks, tops, dresses, sportswear, and lingerie, with brands including M.H. FINE, MA MERE, PUCCINI, GREAT TIMES, and JEANETTE, all at prices 15% to 20% below regular retail. 102 stores. Headquarters: 1219 Vine St., Philadelphia, PA 19107.

Bed and Bath

Fifth Avenue Bed & Bath Outlet: You take the IND "D" train and we'll take the IRT "6" to great savings on top-of-the-line bedding, bath, and kitchen items. This chain is the off-price partner of Bathtique, a NY-based chain of 85 bed and bath stores. Most prices are 20% off retail with larger discounts on closeouts and special purchases. Brands: MARTEX, FIELDCREST, CANNON, and more. Bath accessories are superior. 84 stores. Headquarters: 247 N. Goodman St., Rochester, NY 14607-1195.

Home Front: The Home Front is where all the action is: man (or woman) your stations and prepare to battle for better bargains. (And then, after it's over, go home, take a bath, and go to bed.) These outlets stock the ammunition: all types of linens (velour towels, designer percale sheet sets, quilted bedspreads, pillows, blankets, comforters), as well as dinnerware sets, cutlery, stoneware, and decorative accessories. Discounts of 20% to 50% (some up to 80%) on BURLINGTON, CANNON, WAMSUTTA, J.P. STEVENS, FIELDCREST, MIKASA, and more. 26 stores. Headquarters: 1745 Hayden, Carrollton, TX 75006.

Linens 'n Things: Probably the best of the bed and bath off-price outlets, the chain is owned (along with Marshalls) by the Melville Corporation. Famous-brand and designer sheets, bedspreads, towels, blankets, comforters, tablecloths, shower curtains, scatter rugs, toss pillows, and endless other home furnishings are available at 20% to 30% below what you would see in a department store. Brands: BURLINGTON, BILL BLASS, UTICA, MARTEX, DAN RIVER, and many, many more. 99 stores. Headquarters: 7 Becker Farm Road, Roseland, NJ 07068.

Stroud's Linen Warehouse: Stroud's draws the crowds because they've got the best money can buy for a lot less money: take a walk through their large name-brand inventory and you'll want to redecorate your bedrooms, baths, and kitchen. Why not, at up to 60% off? Besides linens, they also carry tablecloths, towels, shower curtains, and bedding bearing the names of MARTEX, FIELDCREST, SPRINGMAID, WAMSUTTA, CANNON, ROYAL FAMILY, DAN RIVER, CROSCILL, UTICA, and VERA. 22 stores. Headquarters: 11000 E. Rush St., Suite 21, South El Monte, CA 91733.

Three D Bed & Bath: Break out the 3D glasses from your 1950s trunk and head for the show. These outlets feature 30% to 60% discounts and present such stars as J.P. STEVENS, LAURA ASHLEY, AUDREY, BURLINGTON, CANNON, FIELDCREST, and WAMSUTTA. Top-quality merchandise includes sheets, comforters, bedspreads, towels, housewares, curtains, and bathroom accessories. 45 stores. Headquarters: 17120 Magnolia St., Fountain Valley, CA 92708.

Boating Supply

E & B Marine Supply, Inc.: This is the place to sail to for great deals on boating supplies and nautical clothing. Save 20% to 60% and more on marine marvels such as depth sounders, marine radios, electronic navigational aids, boat furniture, water skis, etc. They also carry fair and foul weather clothing, boat shoes, nautical ties, inflatable boats, teak galleyware, clocks, and barometers; everything a would-be sailor needs. Their most popular item, the All Weather Suit listed for $380, but E & B offered it for only $139.88. Nineteen convenient East Coast discount stores all stocked up with their catalog items (see Boating Supplies) and more. Headquarters: 980 Gladys Court, P.O. Box 747, Edison, NJ 08818.

Goldbergs' Marine: This company has been afloat for over 40 years. They offer savings of at least 20% off retail on pleasure boating equipment and nautical clothing (see Boating Supplies for their catalog details). With discount stores, one in New York City and one in Philadelphia, there's a boatload of savings to be found in their prices. Headquarters: 202 Market St., Philadelphia, PA 19106.

Books

Crown Books: Read any good books lately? If you answer yes, you probably know how expensive books have become the last few years, and you'd surely like to save 40% on the *New York Times'* best sellers in hardback and 25% on their best sellers in paperback. Thousands of titles are available at Crown, so read to your heart's content (and make your mind happy at the same time). 175 stores. Headquarters: 3300 75th Ave., Landover, MD 20785.

Publisher's Book Outlet: Extra! Extra! Read all about it! Discounts of up to 70% can be found at these outlets and that's something to write home about. A sea of subjects, tidal waves of titles, a veritable warehouse of hard-working authors (some in print, some remaindered, some unsure). Everybody from Aristophanes (and Art Buchwald) to Zola (and Zeno of Elea). More than 25 stores. Headquarters: 211 W. Young High Pike, Knoxville, TN 37901.

Department Stores

Ashley's Outlet Store, Inc.: Ashley's off-price outlets are the private labeler for Sears, J.C. Penney's, and similar department chains known for quality merchandise sold at good prices, although Ashley's prices are better at 20% to 60% less. A favorite with budget-bent consumers, these outlets sell a wide range of home items and family clothing. Labels include RALPH LAUREN/POLO, POLLY FLINDERS, LEE, LEVI'S, and WRANGLER. 125 stores. Headquarters: P.O. Box 7351, St. Louis, MO 63177.

Filene's Basement: The big-mama of the bargain basement bonanzas, Filene's is a landmark in the off-price clothing industry. The cavernous showrooms contain designer wear and sportswear for the family and many fine items for the home. Top labels: NEIMAN-MARCUS, BONWIT TELLER, SAKS FIFTH AVENUE, TALBOTT'S, I. MAGNIN, SAKOWITZ, BROOKS BROTHERS, BERGDORF GOODMAN. Filene's innovative automatic markdown program assures continual bargains through turnovers: price tags start at about 50% below usual retail and are cut by 25% (12th day); 50% (18th day); and 75% (24th day); then, if not sold (30th day), the items are donated to charity. 14 stores. Headquarters: 70 Inner Belt Road, Somerville, MA 02143.

Front Row: Owned by U.S. Shoe Corporation, these chains are off-price department stores selling fashionable men's, women's, and children's apparel and shoes. Known as the home of true minimum prices, Front Row's customer never has to wait for a sale. True minimum pricing means the lowest possible prices everyday so that your total wardrobe bill will always be less than at a department store. Front Row carries all top-quality, current, in-season, brand-name clothing. No seconds or irregulars. 11 stores. Headquarters: Atlanta Specialty Retailing, 5850 Peachtree Industrial Blvd., Norcross, GA 30071.

Marshalls: This off-price chain has marshalled the budget crowd since 1956, and has been "heading 'em up and moving 'em out" with great success. "Brand names for less" is their motto and they've positioned themselves as "the family retail store for the economy-minded shopper who's looking for brand-name quality merchandise." Need we say more? Discounts of 20% to 50% on a large selection of menswear, junior and misses fashions, lingerie, accessories, women's larger sizes, sportswear, children's wear, footwear, and domestics. Labels include ROUND THE CLOCK, UNDERALLS, ADOLFO, BURLINGTON, BERKSHIRE, JORDACHE, LEVI'S, ZENA, and SASSON. 261 stores. Headquarters: 83 Commerce Way, Industriplex 128, Woburn, MA 01888.

Mervyn's: Promotional department store chain based in Hayward, California, with 173 stores in 12 states, a subsidiary of Dayton-Hudson Company. Selection includes name-brand family apparel and some domestics and housewares. Headquarters: 25001 Industrial Blvd., Hayward, CA 94545, (415) 785-8800.

Ross: Ross says "Dress for Less," which is best, because shoppers don't have to pay "department store prices," even if they're shopping at Ross. Check out the labels: IZOD, CHRISTIAN DIOR, EVAN-PICONE, RALPH LAUREN, JONES NEW YORK, JOHN WEITZ, MUNSING-WEAR, JORDACHE, and a whole bunch more. First-quality, current-season, past-season . . . whatever the tags say, they represent 20% to 60% savings. Full lines of apparel for men, women, and children, as well as anything else one might wear or use in the home. 147 stores. Headquarters: 8333 Central Ave., Newark, CA 94560.

Solo (also Solo Serve): You won't be alone when you go to Solo (Serve) because savvy shoppers seem to know where the prices are low. Apparel brands (at 10% to 70% discounts) include ARROW, MAN-HATTAN, GANT, KENNINGTON, POLO (for men); ACT I, DIANE VON FURSTENBERG, VILLAGER, COLLAGE (for women); BILLY THE KID, HEALTH-TEX, PLAYSTUFF, LE TIGRE, GUMDROPS (for kids). Name-brand cosmetics (10% to 25% discounts) include LANVIN, POLO, HALSTON, NINA RICCI, GUCCI, MAX FACTOR, REVLON. Shoes, at 40% to 60% off, from BERNARDO, INNOCENCE, BANDOLINO'S, I. MILLER, ESPADRILLES. 12 stores. Headquarters: 7000 San Pedro, San Antonio, TX 78212.

Stein Mart: Gertrude would like these off-price stores and so would her cost-conscious friends. First-quality clothing and accessories for men and women, along with decorator home furnishings, are discounted 15% to 60%. There are some rosy deals in CHRISTIAN DIOR, TOWN & COUNTRY, RALPH LAUREN, PIERRE CARDIN, EVAN-PICONE, CHARLOTTE FORD, VALENTINO, HANES, SERGIO TACCHINA, TODD, CALVIN KLEIN. Women's and men's shoe departments offer great specials and linens are top-of-the-line and priced right. 13 stores. Headquarters: P.O. Box 1298, 219 Washington Ave., Greenville, MS 38701.

T.J. Maxx: Viva Maxx! Owned by Zayre Corporation, T.J. Maxx is one of the undisputed leaders among off-price chains. Maximum success is due to minimum prices (20% to 60% off) for brand-name fashion merchandise. Big selections of apparel for everyone, from classic business suits, popular sportswear, trendy coordinates, and accessories. Turnover is so rapid that each store receives an average of 10,000 new items a week. Giftware and domestics round out the clothing inventory. Shoe and jewelry departments in some stores. 225 stores. Headquarters: P.O. Box 500, 1 Mercer Road, Natick, MA 01760.

Winston's: Winston's wins bargain buyers' loyalty with their liberal store policies (returns for cash and credit, for example) and their 20% to 50% discounts on an array of items. Big brands include: JONES NEW YORK, LIZ CLAIBORNE, ANNE KLEIN, GLORIA VANDERBILT (for women); BOTANY 500, ARROW, MANHATTAN, STANLEY BLACKER, PURITAN, MEMBERS ONLY (for men); HEALTH-TEX, BILLY THE KID, CARTER (not Billy), PIERRE CARDIN (for children). Shoes include STRIDE RITE, BUSTER BROWN, JOHNSTON & MURPHY, FREEMAN FLOR-SHEIM, CANDIES, BANDOLINO, GAROLINI. Designer fragrances at 15% to 20% off from SHALIMAR, ARAMIS, YVES ST. LAURENT, POLO,

OPIUM, WHITE SHOULDERS. 21 stores. Headquarters: 21 W. 38th St., New York, NY 10018.

Fabrics and Yarns

Aunt Mary's Yarns Needlework Crafts: They carry over 500 colors of yarns, and have the best selection of acrylics, blends, and 100% wools in all price and quality ranges. Aunt Mary's also have open stock and kits for cross stitch, needlepoint, crewel, and plastic canvas; plus canvas, frames, rug backing, craft books, knitting needles, and macrame supplies. 15% off the suggested retail price every day on yarn, stitchery, and craft books. All needles and books are also 15% off the suggested retail price every day. 45 stores. Headquarters: P.O. Box 178, Rochelle, IL 61068.

Calico Corners: Shopping at Calico Corners will make you smile (or is it grin?) like a Cheshire cat, but it won't disappear like Alice's did in Wonderland. You can figure that someone in this business since 1948 knows their stuff: 30% to 60% discounts on prices for high-quality designer fabrics suitable for draperies, slipcovers, upholstery, bedspreads—everything except apparel fabrics. Their management has also managed to make customers happy with their attentive sales policies. 60 stores. Headquarters: Drawer 670, Wilmington, DE 19899.

Cutting Corners (also Interior Fabrics): Cut your decorating costs without sewing yourself into a high-priced corner. WAMSUTTA, COHAMA, LA FRANCE, and BURLINGTON are but a few of the points of interest on this savers' streets, and you can get there 50% faster. Lots of personal service adds to the pleasure of shopping in these outlets. Seven stores. Headquarters: 13270 Midway Road, Dallas, TX 75234.

Food, Spirits, and Tobacco

Fred Sanders, Inc.: Fred's mother must have been *some kinda cook* 'cause he got the sweet tooth bad, like, gag me with a spoonful of his chocolate (32 types), hard candies, toppings, ice cream, and baked goodies—all at 30% to 40% below what one would pay for similar-tasting sweets. No pan dulce here, just the hard stuff. All of their old-fashioned candy shops use only the finest ingredients; no artificial contents or preservatives. 38 stores (all in Detroit area). Headquarters: 100 Oakman, Detroit, MI 48203.

JR Tobacco: Groucho would probably like to live there; J.R. Ewing would probably make an offer to buy it for Southfork; and Milton Berle, George Burns, Bill Cosby, Al Hirt, Doc Severinson, Mario Puzo, and other cigar-chompers buy their stogies there. Discounts at this famous, world's largest cigar store run 30% to 60% for JR's private brands and all others. (*Connoisseur* magazine chose JR's Ultimate and Special Coronas as the two best cigars in the world.) Seven stores. Headquarters: 11 E. 45th St., New York, NY 10017.

Pepperidge Farm Thrift Stores: Here's the scene: a cold winter day, the wind slapping against the icy windows, snow settling on the evergreens. It's noon. What's on your mind? Soup, hot soup . . . and bread, good bread. Well, because Campbell's owns Pepperidge, like peas in a pod, they can not only warm your body, but heat up the savings with 30% to 60% discounts on their numerous products. So get out the sled, harness the dogs, and head for the Pepper-ridge. 60 Mill Plain Road, Danbury, CT 06810.

Gifts and Decorations

American Stationers: Get on an Amtrak and stop off at American Station-ers for 25% to 30% off on moderate to top-of-the-line stationery-related paper products, gifts, wrapping, cards, and office supplies. 20 stores. Headquarters: 104 Longale Road, Greensboro, NC 27409.

Cape Craftsman: These craftsmen have carved out a niche in the Early American woodenware market with their CAPE CRAFT PINE products consisting of kitchen items (holders for all sorts of things), bookends, magazine and luggage racks, candle holders, and more made from ponderosa pine. Also: brass accessories from China, Taiwan, and Hong Kong; porcelain figurines; prints; glassware; lamps. 39 stores. Headquarters: P.O. Box 517, Elizabethtown, NC 28337.

For Peanuts: "Nuts are given to us, but we must crack them ourselves," the old saying goes. These stores have nothing to do with nuts, but they've cracked the high-prices with their 50% (and more) discounts on first-quality closeout items acquired from companies such as HALLMARK and CURRENT. Greeting cards, gift wrap, stationery, party supplies, candles, and other gifts at wholesale and below-wholesale prices. 12 stores. Headquarters: 2407 Preston St., Ennis, TX 75119.

Irish Crystal Company: Founded by a Catholic priest in Ireland in 1970, this shining company has moved into the off-price market with merchandise usually associated with very high prices. (They've made special pieces for Pope John Paul II, the Prince of Wales and Lady Di, Bette Davis, and Ruth Gordon.) Their Irish-made, mouth-blown, hand-drawn, and hand-polished crystal is flawless and rated "superior quality" by international standards. 26 stores. Headquarters: 1655 Thousand Oaks Blvd., Thousand Oaks, CA 91360.

Party Warehouse (also Cedarhurst Papers): The Party Warehouse's low prices and engaging array of merchandise are worth celebrating. Dance down the aisles of Cowboy souvenirs or have the party experts (not the Cowboys, the Warehouse) make you some one-of-a-kind items, such as, perhaps, menus on the back of bounced checks. You'll save at least 20% on designer paper goods (PAPER ART, AMSCAN) and other big-ticket names: UNIQUE (from CABBAGE PATCH), MR T., A TEAM, HE MAN, and PLAYBOY BUNNY. (Boy, *that* would be a party!) You name it, they got it—or can get it—or make it. Seven stores (more on the way). Headquarters: 13619 Inwood Road, Dallas, TX 75234.

Red River Pottery: Gather down at the river for some hot bargains and make a "kiln" when you check out their pottery, artificial flowers, baskets, wicker, brass accessories, picture frames, Christmas trees and trimmings, and even furniture. Brands: ANCHOR-HOCKING, LIBBEY, J.P. STEVENS, and J.G. DURAND. Low prices, good quality, especially on RED RIVER works. Nine stores. Headquarters: P.O. Box 1967, Marshall, TX 75670.

Tuesday Morning: You may wonder (like we did) about the name of this chain. Here's the scoop: They don't operate on an ongoing basis but open four times a year during peak gift-buying seasons after accumulating sufficient merchandise for sales, which are announced in local newspapers, thereby creating mayhem and discount madness. At 50% to 80% discounts, no wonder why. Brands, not publicized, are the same as those in top department stores, with big values in housewares, tabletop items, gifts, linens, domestics. 71 stores. Headquarters: 14621 Inwood Road, Dallas, TX 75234.

World Bazaar: We all know that the world is bizarre, but these outlet stores are packed full of wicker and rattan furniture among other international items from the world's busy marketplaces. Select products purchased just for their stores come from surplus and overruns usually carried by their 250 regular retail stores. Eight stores. Headquarters: 2110 Lawrence St., Drawer 4, Atlanta, GA 30364.

Handbags and Accessories

Bruce Alan Bags Etc.: In a plasticized world where the "real thing" is fading from the shopper's grasp, Bruce Alan has bagged some great bargains. Into leather like you wouldn't believe: wallets, handbags, belts, luggage, accessories, and executive gift items at savings up to 75%. Brands: LIZ CLAIBORNE, LONDON FOG, OLEG CASSINI, AMERICAN TOURISTER, AMELIA EARHART, SASSON KNAPSACKS, SAMSONITE, ETIENNE AIGNER, STONE MOUNTAIN, ROLFS, BUXTON. 12 stores. Headquarters: 21-15 Rosalie St., Fair Lawn, NJ 07410.

Hardware and Building Supplies

The Home Depot: This national chain has stores coast to coast throughout the Sunbelt. Originators of the do-it-yourself warehouse, their warehouses are anywhere from 60 to 140 thousand square feet with a stock of 25 to 30 thousand items. All the top brand names are here at savings of 10% to 50% below retail. You'll love their personal, knowledgeable service and their 100% guarantee at any of their 60 stores. Headquarters: 6300 Powers Ferry Road, Atlanta, GA 30339.

Health and Beauty

Drug Emporium: "Every day is sale day!" is Drug Emporium's slogan, but they don't mean there's always *something* on sale, they mean *everything's* priced as low as it can go. They keep their margin low and there is no quantity limit even on the large selection of designer cosmetics and perfumes (including ELIZABETH ARDEN). Prices on health and beauty aids average 30% off; 50% off on sunglasses; 40% off on greeting cards; 20% to 40% off on prescription drugs. In business since 1977. 58 stores. Headquarters: 7792 Olentangy River Road, Suite D, Worthington, OH 43085.

F & M Distributors: F & M is a friendly merchant who wants to help you hang onto your hard-earned dollar and this is why shoppers will drive great distances to buy at these stores. Cosmetics, health, beauty, and cleaning aids are complemented by a selection of many other items that people always need. Everything is the best brand available, and all at discounts of 20 to 50% off. F & M shoppers always leave with more than they came for and the more they buy, the more they save. No limits, all manufacturers coupons are accepted, dealers welcome. Headquarters: 25800 Sherwood, Warren, MI 48091.

Odd Lot Trading: Revco, the new partner of Odd Lot Trading Company, has combined its expertise in low-price marketing strategies with this seller of manufacturers' overruns, closeouts, and discontinued name-brand products. National brands are discounted 25% to 75% and they carry everything from tools to towels, and an odd lot more. 53 stores. Headquarters: 1925 Enterprise Parkway, Twinsburg, OH 44087.

Phar-Mor: Opened its first store in 1982, will have 36 stores (approximately 35,000 square feet each) by the end of 1986 and 40 more at the end of 1987 in six states: Ohio, Pennsylvania, Virginia, Florida, South Carolina, and Georgia. Fastest growing chain of deep-discount drug stores in the United States. They buy only on deal so there are discounts up to 50% on a wide range of products including health and beauty aids, cosmetics, greeting cards, snacks, and auto supplies. Headquarters: P.O. Box 1588, 375 Victoria Road, Youngstown, OH 44510, (216) 792-3811.

Hobbies and Crafts

Michaels: Michael knows how to have a good time: creating a silk flower arrangement, constructing a model airplane, painting a picture, or framing a portrait. Try this out: take the family into Michael's and give everyone 20 minutes to find something. We're betting that each family member will find something to stir the creative fires (the stuff that keeps our hands and mind busy, remember?). Good discounts for good 'ole fun, with free framing service when you buy their frames (which works out to about a 25% savings off retail). 11 stores. Headquarters: P.O. Box 612566, Dallas, TX 75261-2566.

Housewares

Corning Designs Factory Outlet: There's nothing corning about these outlets because anyone who is world-renowned for their Steuben lead crystal is no fly-by-night company. (You can see the artisans molding, shaping, polishing, cutting, and engraving at the factory store in Corning, New York.) Corning's labels include (at discounts too) CORNING DESIGNS, CORNING WARE, CORELLE,

CULINARIA, LE CLAIR, and PYREX. Seven stores. Headquarters: 85 Liberty Village, Flemington, NJ 08822.

Fitz & Floyd Factory Outlet: Nobody's taken the fizz out of off-price housewares shopping, not even Floyd. One of the hottest china and fashion tabletop companies around today (the creators of the "mix-and-match" dinnerware concept), they offer striking designer houseware with price tags that won't shock you. Inventory includes special purchases, discontinued patterns, mix and match accessories, whimsical items, and the uniquely imaginative line of Fitz & Floyd giftware. Everything in the store is priced initially at 40% to 60% off with some pieces marked down as much as 70% off retail. Eight stores. Headquarters: 2055-C Luna Road, Carrollton, TX 75006.

Grand Finale: A division of the Horchow Collection, these outlets are the last word in fine furnishings and elegant accessories, as well as kitchenwares, linens, jewelry, and executive desk items. The low prices are rewarding: 25% to 50% off. Designers' names are not always given in the catalog, but we've found exceptional bargains on such items as a 20-piece set of ironstone by WEDGWOOD and a designed/stamped BACCARAT crystal perfume bottle. Headquarters: P.O. Box 34257, Farmers Branch, TX 75234.

Housewares Plus Inc.: Since most houses may have a kid or two around, at least some of the time, the PLUS side of these outlets is FISHER-PRICE toys, along with the 30% or more discounts on PLAYSKOOL, ANCHOR-HOCKING, EKCO, MIRRO, GUND, ONEIDA, LITTON, NELSON MCCOY, ALADDIN, OLD DUTCH, WHEATON, THERMOSERV, BRINN, AMERICAN HERITAGE, and RUSS BERRIE. 10 stores. Headquarters: P.O. Box 658, Reading, PA 19603.

Kitchen Collection: Chillicothe, Ohio-based 14-unit factory outlet chain is unique among outlet chains in that it is not owned by manufacturer. Although it was previously owned by Wear-Ever Aluminum, it spun off as a separate company and still is the exclusive factory outlet for WEAR-EVER cookware and PROCTOR-SILEX appliances. Headquarters: 71-87 E. Water St., Chillicothe, Ohio 45601, (614) 773-9150.

Mikasa Factory Outlet (also Dinnerware Plus, Table Top Fashions, China Glass and Gifts): *Mi casa, su casa.* The fine products sold in these outlets would fit well in anyone's home. Mikasa is ware the action is: dinnerware, stemware, giftware, flatware, cookware, along with crystal, china, table linens, baskets, and wicker items.

Most of the stock is first-quality and is discounted 30% to 60%. Patterns range from delicate florals to bold, colorful contemporary. 20 stores. Headquarters: 20633 S. Fordyce Ave., Carson, CA 90749, (213) 537-2060.

Pfaltzgraff Pfactory Store: The oldest manufacturer of pottery in the United States, their outlets carry irregulars from their popular hand-crafted stoneware at 40% to 60% discounts. In addition to their own lines, they sell closeouts of famous-name cookware and seconds from leading flatware manufacturers at the same level of savings. Seven stores. Headquarters: P.O. Box 2766, York, PA 17405-2766.

Revere Ware Courtesy Stores: These courteous manufacturers have been revered for 55 years, and they sell items that, for one reason or another, are factory seconds, but first in line in price at 50% discounts. Many styles, shapes, and sizes are available, all, of course, by REVERE WARE. 11 stores. Headquarters: P.O. Box 250, Clinton, IL 61727.

Wallpapers To Go: Go for it! You'll get wall-eyed looking at the 1,200 patterns of wallpaper sold in these outlets with savings of 10% to 40% on selected styles and patterns, including grasscloth, vinyls, flocks, and more. 87 stores. Headquarters: 3131 Corporate Place, Hayward, CA 94545.

Optical

Royal Optical: Over 440 nationwide retail outlets offering some of the best prices and service on single visual lenses, bifocals, trifocals, and progressive power lenses in brand name and designer eyeglass frames. Gradients, tints, all the extras are available. Headquarters: 2760 Irving Blvd., Dallas, TX 75207, (217) 638-1397.

Records

Hastings Records & Books: Make haste and get thee to Hastings Records & Books for some bopping and some hopping at some pop-u-lar prices, like, dig their discounts of 10% (bestseller books) to 25% (most records). Cassette tapes cover the moods from blues, rock, big band, jazz, and classical. 25 stores. Headquarters: 421 E. 34th St., Amarillo, TX 79103.

Sound Warehouse (also Peaches, and Buttons): Hear! Hear! The warehouse will now come to order, so break out the turntables. Top records, tapes, compact discs, videocassettes, and movies are available in a tremendous variety. Sound Warehouse is into making some noise with their promotions and if you check out their constant promotions (and card specials), you'll have something to sing about. 36 stores. Headquarters: P.O. Box 75879, Oklahoma City, OK 73147.

Strawberries Records & Tapes: Jam with your favorite jazz group; wail the cowpoke blues with Waylon; do the cha-cha or have some Fleetwood Mac. These outlets carry imports, closeouts, overstocks, private labels, and slow movers (but no losers). Everything in the stores is discounted, from pop and rock, to classical and contemporary. Special orders for hard-to-find platters. 38 stores. Headquarters: 40 California Ave., Framingham, MA 01701.

Tower Records (also Tower Video): The second-largest video and record company in the world, these chains tower over the little, high-priced retail stores. (You know, paying way too much for an album can really give you the blues.) Locations from New York City to Japan have special sales that are advertised in two-page spreads, so keep your eyes and ears open. More than 40 stores. Headquarters: 12711 Ventura Blvd., Studio City, CA 91004.

Shoes and Boots

Athletic Shoe Factory: You don't have to jump hurdles to get some 15% to 40% discounts on nationally known brands such as NIKE, ADIDAS, NEW BALANCE, PUMA, CONVERSE, SAUCONY, and TRETORN, or the private label, HI-TECH. Stores cater to middle-class men and women. 79 stores. Headquarters: 46 E. 4th Ave., San Mateo, CA 94401.

B & F Shoes: Take a stroll down to B & F for a new pair of first-quality shoes. Select your favorite style and color while being selective about the price you pay. Men and women can both save on walkouts by TOPSIDERS, GAROLINI, CORELLI, BEENE BAG, BASS, and FLORSHEIM, 20% to 50% less than regular retail. Handbags are also a good buy. 64 stores. Headquarters: Wohl Shoe Corp., 8350 Maryland Ave., P.O. Box 202, St. Louis, MO 63166.

Banister Shoe Outlet (also Freeman, French Shriner, Banister, Mushroom, and Manufacturers Shoe Warehouse): An official outlet for one of the world's largest shoe manufacturers of quality men's, women's dress, casual, and athletic shoes. Over 40 famous brands are available. Names like . . . RED CROSS, SELBY, JOYCE, BANDOLINO, PAPPAGALLO, MUSHROOMS, FREEMAN, FRENCH SHRINER, and many more. Discounts range from 30% to 50%. Famous brand handbags and other accessories in stock. 65 stores. Headquarters: 1 Freeman Lane, Beloit, WI 53511.

Barett Shoes: "Barett has everything a mall shoe store has except high prices" is their motto and they work hard to live up to that! They've got 189 stores in 18 states. And if that's not enough, their designer and famous name-brand women's footwear is $13.88, $16.88, or $19.88. Call their toll-free number (800) 334-5017 for the location nearest you. Headquarters: P.O. Box 34000, Charlotte, NC 28261.

Bass Shoe Factory Outlet: They don't sell shoes made from bass-skins, but you can fish for some true discount catches at these outlets. Try on their shoes, boots, ski boots, and loafers. They carry seconds and closeouts for both men and women, plus boots, clogs, and athletic shoes by other well-known manufacturers. Savings are 25% to 35%. 49 stores. Headquarters: 360 U.S. Route 1, Falmouth Office Park, Falmouth, ME 04105.

Bonafide Shoe Factory Outlet: These bargain shoe outlets are the real thing, from dress and casual to athletic. Brands include AMERICAN GENTLEMEN, AUDITIONS, CONTEMPO, POLLY PRESTON, BANDOLINO, 9 WEST, CANDIES, and JOHNSTON & MURPHY. Usual discount is 20% to 60% with similar savings on tennis shoes and handbags. 24 stores. Headquarters: P.O. Box 2009, Lynchburg, VA 24506.

Carr's: Carr's is linked into some of the *crème de la crème* shoe stores in the country. End-of-the-season merchandise is regrouped and shipped from some of the best retail stores to Carr's off-price stores and repriced at 33% to 70% off. Don't walk, run. Brands: CHARLES JOURDAN, STUART WEITZMAN, AMALFI, BANDOLINO, PAPPAGALLO, NINA, J. RENEE, and LIZ CLAIBORNE, . . . more than 30,000 shoes! 10 stores. Headquarters: 950 N.E. Loop 410, San Antonio, TX 78209.

Commonwealth Factory Outlets (also The Branded Shoe Outlet, Hanover Shoes Factory Outlet): Commonwealth has some uncommon bargains (40% to 60% off) for men's and women's medium-to-better quality shoes. Labels include HANOVER, BOSTONIAN, CLARKS

OF ENGLAND, ANDRE MARSEILLE, STETSON, CONVERSE, JOHNSTON &
MURPHY, BASS, HUSH PUPPIES, and NIKE. 34 stores. Headquarters:
118 Carlisle St., Hanover, PA 17331.

Connco Shoes: Nationally advertised athletic, dress, and casual
shoes for the whole family are sold in these chains, and their 20% to
50% discounts are no con job. Their big inventory of big name-brands
includes DEXTER, BASS, CHEROKEE, NICKELS, SELBY, NIKE, ADIDAS,
FREEMAN, FLORSHEIM, NUNN BUSH, SPERRY, CHILD LIFE, WESTIES,
and REEBOK. Also casual sportswear. 19 stores. Headquarters: 7500
Hudson Blvd., Lake Elmo, MN 55042.

Dexter Shoe Factory Outlet: Grab a cab and tell the driver to step
on it. Get to a Dexter's outlet, walk in, tell them the *Underground
Shopper* sent you, and take a load off your feet. Look around. This
manufacturer is known for its quality products. Prices are right-on!
And their Bargainland departments offer factory damaged shoes for
those on a shoestring budget. 21 stores. Headquarters: Railroad
Ave., Dexter, ME 04930.

Dunham Footwear Factory Outlets: "Great Footwear for the Great
Outdoors" is the slogan here, so don't go looking for ballet slippers.
We're talking shoes that were meant for walking. Founded in 1885,
they didn't get famous by not knowing where they were going. Climb
a mountain or climb into the family jalopy and head for the party
with a serious shoe: DUNHAM, CONVERSE, KANGAROO, SOFT SPOTS,
WESTIES, and more, at discounts up to 40%. 30 stores throughout
New England. P.O. Box 813, Brattleboro, VT 05301.

El Bee Shoes: El Bee (short for Elder-Beerman, the department
store chain that owns the outlets) takes the sting out of buying shoes.
Name-brands buzz: NUNN BUSH, STRATFORD, BRITISH WALKER,
JOYCE, 9 WEST, SOCIALITE, BASS, TROTTER, SUGARFOOT, ANDREW
GELLER, CAPEZIO, CARESSA. Discounts usually 25%, but frequent
sales of two-for-one, which would be at least 50% savings. 110 stores.
Headquarters: 153 E. Helena St., Dayton, OH 45404.

**Famous Brand Shoes (also E.J.'s Famous Brand Shoes, Nusrala
Name Brand Shoes):** Anyone who claims this chain's name has got
to be well-known just for the company it keeps: ANNE KLEIN, AIR
STEP, JOYCE, GAROLINI, PAPPAGALLO, OLD MAINE TROTTERS,
ANDREW GELLER, SAN ANTONIO SHOES, BALLY, JOHNSTON & MURPHY,
NUNN BUSH, and CLARKS. Men's and women's shoes and accessories

cut by 30% to 70%, from exotic skin evening pumps to beach sandals.
20 stores. Headquarters: 8620 Olive St. Road, St. Louis, MO 63132.

Famous Footwear: In over 230 stores throughout the United States,
Famous Footwear offers over 20,000 pairs in each store of first-qual-
ity, brand-name shoes at everyday savings of 10% to 50%. Famous
Footwear's men's, women's, children's, and athletic departments fea-
ture brand-name shoes like BASS, MUSHROOMS, JACQUELINE, CAN-
DIES, TEMPOS, CHEROKEE, NUNN BUSH, WEYENBERG, FRENCH
SHRINER, BOSTONIAN, REEBOK, NIKE, AVIA, ADIDAS, PUMA, KAN-
GAROO, and TIGER to name a few. Headquarters: 208 East Olin Ave.,
Madison, WI 53708.

5 & 10 Shoe Store: These folks won't nickel-and-dime you, but their
no-frills self-service outlets make for some 20% to 60% discounts on
shoes for the whole family. They stock a good selection of nationally
advertised brands like VIVIANA, AMY, ANDREA, CANDIES, BASS, COR-
ELLI, VISIONS, HIPPOPOTAMUS, 9 WEST, FOOTWORKS, NICKELS, CON-
NIE, KANGAROO, BUSTER BROWN, WILDCATS, SUGAR FOOT, PRE-50,
NIKE, BAMA, BRENTMOOR, CONTINENTAL, LEVI, GENTLEMEN, and
REGAL. 30 stores. Headquarters: P.O. Box 202, St. Louis, MO 63166.

Frugal Frank's Shoes: The frugal way to name-brand shoes, 27
Frugal Frank's stores nationwide offer a broad spectrum of name-
brand footwear at competitive prices. Fashion dress shoes for
women, casual styles for men, rough and tumble footwear for children, athletic shoes for everyone. Frugal Frank's has just the right
shoes at just the right prices for most every occasion and activity.
Many of the best-known brands, such as NUNN BUSH, REEBOK, and
9 WEST, are included in its extensive inventory. Headquarters: 233
Broadway, New York, NY 10279.

Frye Factory Outlets: Frye is to boots as bacon is to eggs. Discounts
of up to 50% can be found—and more—with first-quality goods as
well as slight irregulars. Handbags, men's and women's boots, hand-
sewns, and some leather accessories. Locations: Wilkes-Barre, PA;
North Conway, NH; Freeport, ME; and Marlborough, MA. Headquarters: 84 Chestnut St., Marlborough, MA 01752.

General Shoe Factory to You: These outlets are owned by Genesco,
Inc., the manufacturer of JARMAN, AFTER HOURS, HARDY'S, and
JOHNSTON & MURPHY shoes, plus other lines, such as NORTH STAR,
PUMA, WRANGLER, ADIDAS, LAREDO BOOTS, and KANGAROO.

Discounts from 20% to 35%. 18 stores. Headquarters: P.O. Box 1090, Nashville, TN 37202.

Gussini Shoes: Not just another shoe store, but another $13.88 shoe store, where there's just one price for every pair of shoes they sell, so you don't have to ask the price. Unbranded and branded shoes are in the racks, including DOMINIQUE, JOCELYNE, FRED WEST, and ROMORINI. 140 stores. 6940-A San Tomas Road, Elkridge, MD 21227.

Little Red Shoe House: There's a lesson to be learned at the Shoe House . . . don't pay full retail for WOLVERINE shoes. Owned by Wolverine World Wide (Hush Puppies), this manufacturer's outlet is the spot for casual shoes, as well as socks and handbags. Wolf up discounts from 25% to 30%. 112 stores. Headquarters: 9341 Courtland Drive, Rockford, MI 49341.

Lottie's Discount Shoes (also Dottie's, Maxine's, and in Stein Mart Department Stores): Lottie and her sisters Dottie and Maxine probably traded shoes on Friday and Saturday nights. But now Lottie's got a lotta BRITISH WALKER, EVAN PICONE, ANNE KLEIN, SELBY, BANDOLINI, and WESTIES. Discounts are beween 30% and 60% and their red tag sales cut deep into prices. Lottie's stores are in eight states. Headquarters: 712 E. H. Crump Blvd., P.O. Box 94, Memphis, TN 38101.

Quoddy Crafted Footwear: QUODDY and BROOKS are the labels made by this company, which has been in the family footwear business for 100 years. Comparable quality merchandise would probably be 20% to 50% more at a conventional retail store. Innovators in the industry (they popularized moccasin construction), they have some kinda sale called "Annual Moonlight Madness Semi-Annual Sale." Call for reservations. 40 stores. Headquarters: 1515 Washington St., Braintree, MA 02184.

Shoe Manufacturer's Outlet (also Nice Shoes): Wohl Shoe Company owns these outlets and they shoe know their stuff. One of the largest manufacturers in the U.S.A., they carry only famous brands of first-quality, current-season merchandise at 20% to 70% discounts, such as NATURALIZER, BASS, MAINE WOODS, TIMBERLAND, FRYE, BOSTONIAN, JOHNSTON & MURPHY, CLARKS, and AMERICAN GLAMOUR. 17 stores. Headquarters: 11 Rowan St., Norwalk, CT 06855.

Shoe Stop: Stop! Take one step at a time: first the shoes, then the savings. Men's, women's, and children's casual, dress-up, and athletic shoes at 10% to 40% discounts. FOOT BEATS are the store's private label, but you'll see ADIDAS slip in, as well as NIKE and CONVERSE and CALICO KID. 77 stores. Headquarters: 2525 Military Ave., West Los Angeles, CA 90064.

Shoe Times: The shoe must go on! And on and on. The outlets for the popular Shoe Town discount chain, they carry first-quality footwear and accessories (usually for women only) at 20% to 60% discounts. While the cast may be famous, they don't like to brag in public. Seven Shoe Times/200 Shoe Towns. Headquarters: 994 Riverview Drive, Totowa, NJ 07512.

SneaKee Feet: You don't have to go in the back door or disguise yourself to get to SneaKee Feet's savings. The arch-enemy of high-priced footwear, they sell NEW BALANCE, NIKE, ADIDAS, PUMA, CONVERSE, TIGER, and FILA running shoes, as well as HANG TEN, OCEAN PACIFIC, and BILL ROGERS sportswear. 12 stores. Headquarters: 5545 N.W. 35th, Fort Lauderdale, FL 33309.

Sporting Goods

The Finish Line: The race to the Finish Line is one where everyone is a winner because the low prices are the reward: 20% to 30% average discounts. Competing for attention are NIKE, ADIDAS, TRETORN, PUMA, NEW BALANCE, ETONIC, CONVERSE, SAUCONY, FREEDOM TRAINERS, and more. Items carried include workout suits, shorts, tank tops, shirts, footwear, and accessories. Mostly first-quality and current; some "blemished" products with only cosmetic imperfections. 15 stores. Headquarters: 7150 E. Washington, Indianapolis, IN 46219.

Oshman's Warehouse Outlet Stores: Son of Oshman's Sporting Goods (the full-price chain), these outlets stock the same merchandise at less seasonal times, so wait for the killing on prices: 33% to 75% discounts! Top brands: ADIDAS, BROOKS, CONVERSE, JANTZEN, HAGGAR, WRANGLER, LEE, LEVI'S, CHIC, GIVENCHY, SASSON, LORD JEFF—this is a sporting goods store? SHAKESPEARE, SHIMANO, BROWNING, FENWICK—sure it's not a literary agency? MCGREGOR, WILSON, RAWLINGS, SPALDING, DUNLOP, DAVIS—sure it's not a law firm? Six stores. Headquarters: P.O. Box 18234, Houston, TX 77223.

Second Serve: If at first you don't succeed (in finding savings), try, try again (this time at Second Serve). These outlets offer smashing discounts of 25% to 75% on ADIDAS, WILSON, RSVP, and COURT CASU- ALS clothing for men; and BELLWEATHER, LILY'S OF BEVERLY HILLS, and WILSON for women. Also: TAIL, TOP SPEED, PRINCE, CONVERSE, LOOM TOGS, WEST 1, LE COQ SPORTIF, TRETORN, and ETONIC. 37 stores. Headquarters: 1214 N.E. 8th Ave., Fort Lauderdale, FL 33304.

TVs and Appliances

Highland Superstores: Highland offers high discounts for the shop- per who has been looking high and low for a great buy on TVs, radios, tape recorders, video equipment, and major appliances. Top brands: SONY, RCA, ZENITH, PANASONIC, SANYO, MAYTAG, WHIRLPOOL, SHARP, LITTON, AMANA, FRIGIDAIRE, NORGE, EXCELLENCE, and HOTPOINT. The real low-down is that prices reflect a 20% to 25% drop below usual retail, and they offer a written guarantee that if you find a better price elsewhere during the life of the product, they will refund 125% of the difference. 34 stores. Headquarters: 21405 Trolly Drive, Taylor, MI 48180.

Tech HiFi: High-tech and high fidelity don't necessarily mean you've got to pay high prices. This company discounts TVs, video recorders, stereos, telephones, and related accessories 25% to 60%. Brands include JVC, PIONEER, MARANTZ, AKAI, JENSEN, and many more. The company was begun in the mid-1960s by six students at MIT; and in 1984 they took their growing business into the off-price chain market where they have made some noise. 66 stores. Head- quarters: 48 Teed Drive, Randolph, MA 02368.

Toys

Toys & Gifts Outlet: You don't have to be a kid to enjoy the toys, gifts, and other items at discounts (10% to 50%) that make shopping fun and games. Major brands include KUSAN, MATTEL, KENNER, PLAYSKOOL, LEGO, AMF, TOMY, FISHER-PRICE, MILTON BRADLEY, HASBRO, and PARKER BROTHERS. Toys are first-quality, closeouts, and discontinued items. Toys for tots are particularly good buys. 25 stores. Headquarters: P.O. Box 7189, Orlando, FL 32854.

Toys 'R' Us: This giant chain is for little kids, but big kids disguised as moms and dads can get a real kick out of the low-priced toys, generally stacked from floor to ceiling in huge stores. As far as selection goes, you can't beat Toys 'R' Us, for they have thousands of things to keep the idle hands occupied. Also, they have a good electronics section and some infant goods and furniture. 169 stores. Headquarters: 395 W. Passaic St., Rochelle Park, NJ 07662.

SALES-BY-MAIL

It's as easy as one-two-three to get special catalogs from the "Big Four" major catalog/retail stores—J.C. Penney, Sears, Montgomery Ward, and Spiegel. In addition to their regular books, they all put out sales and special-edition catalogs that are smaller, but you have to know how to get them. Each company has different rules on who receives these catalogs and you have to remember there are always expiration dates on items offered. Here are the rules:

J.C. PENNEY: You must place at least a $30 order from any regular catalog every six months from the same address.

SEARS: You must place a catalog order of $25 or more every three months. Extra copies of sales catalogs are available at their retail stores in the catalog department.

MONTGOMERY WARD: You must place three catalog orders every six months to receive the Christmas book, two Big Books, and all the sale catalogs.

SPIEGEL, Box 6340, Chicago, IL 60680: You must place two orders of $25 each within six months to receive their Christmas and summer sale catalogs.

CONSUMER "TOLL FREE" NUMBERS

A surprising number of major manufacturers have toll-free lines for consumers. These 800 lines are set up to answer consumers' questions about company products, but sometimes you can use them to get an answer to a general question, request a refund, or register a complaint. One suggestion for finding out whether a company has a toll-free hot line number is to look on the side panel of a company product to see if an 800 number is there. Another option is to call 800 information, (800) 555-1212, to ask whether a particular company has an 800 number; to do this you'll need to know the company's name exactly as listed. Some useful numbers we've found:

• Procter & Gamble has two toll-free numbers. One, (800) 543-1745, or (800) 582-0345 for Ohio residents, is for questions regarding bar soap and household cleaners. Another number, (800) 543-7270, or (800) 582-1891 for Ohio residents, is for beauty and health care products.

• General Electric has an Answer Center, (800) 626-2000, which cleared up instructions we received with a GE battery recharger and control settings on a GE refrigerator. We didn't get frozen out when we called this 24-hour hot line, either. When we called the Whirlpool Cool Line, a telephone troubleshooter listened patiently to an ailing Whirlpool dryer. Calling him at (800) 253-1301 (Monday through Friday, 8 A.M. to 9:30 P.M. EST) saved calling a serviceman and that, in turn, saved a lot of static.

• Cheeseborough Ponds gave us some good advice that helped us avert a bad case of the frizzies. Their hair and cosmetic question line operates Monday through Friday, 8:30 A.M. to 4:30 P.M. EST; the number is (800) 243-5320.

• Clairol also has a toll-free number, (800) 223-5800. This number is set up to help rescue do-it-yourself color jobs and permanents that get out of control.

• Scott Lawn Care has their own number, (800) 543-TURF, for prescriptions for ailing lawns, gardens, trees, and shrubs.

• Polaroid's (800)-225-1384 hot line will clear up cloudy pictures you might have with their cameras.

• And finally, if you're stumbling through the day bleary-eyed and weary from attending to baby's 3 A.M. room service requests, you might get (daytime) relief by listening to one of Beech Nut Baby Food's most popular recordings, "Sleeping Through The Night." Another on their "most requested" list of solid gold hits is "Solid Foods." These and other top recordings can be requested from 9 A.M. to 4 P.M. EST at (800) 523-6633. The recordings are geared to kids, newborn to 2 years old.

COMPANY INDEX

A

AAA All Factory Vacuums, Floor
Care, & Ceiling Fans, 60
AAA Camera Exchange, 96
AARP (American Association of
Retired Persons), 200
ABC Photo Service, 96
ABC Vacuum Warehouse, 60
A. Benjamin & Co., 120
A Brass Bed Shoppe, 211
A.B. Schou, 120
Ace Fireworks, 335
Ace Leather Products, 232
Ace Pecan Co., 185
A Cook's Wares, 271
Adam's Warehouse, 469
Adco Company, 289
Adds Telemarketing, 428
Ad-Libs Astronomics, 96
Aerocomp Inc., 136
A. Goto, 69
A.I. Friedman, 78
A.L.A.S. Accordion-O-Rama, 326
Albany Woolen Mills, 153
Albert S. Smyth Co., Inc., 121
Alexander Butcher Block and
Supply Corp., 271
Alexander Sales Associates, Inc.,
142
Alexander Wallpaper, 453

All American Fabrics, 153
All Electronics Corporation, 136
Allen's Shell-A-Rama, 238
Alliance Capital Reserves, 286
Allied Business Machine Systems,
345
Allyn Air Seat Co., 393
Al's Luggage, 233
American Archives, 121
American Auto Brokers, 110
American Baby Magazine, 200
American Discount Wallcoverings,
453
American Foundation for the
Blind, 200
American Health Service, Inc., 318
American Heart Association, 201
American Paint Horse Assn., 201
American Stationers, 484
American Stationery Co., Inc.,
The, 345
American Youth Hostels, Inc., 440
America's Best, 420
America's Hobby Center, Inc., 256
America's Pharmacy Service, Inc.,
318
Amishman, The, 185
Amity Hallmark Ltd., 345
Anders, 470
Andre Perrault, 379
Anka Co., 420

Annex Furniture Galleries, 211
Annex Outlet Ltd., 413
Ann Michele Originals, 471
Announcements By Willard Scott,
    201
Antique Imports Unlimited, 69
Apparel America, 471
Archie McPhee & Company, 335
Arctic Glass & Millwork Company,
    246
Arise Futon Mattress Co., 211
Arizona Champagne Sauces, 186
Arthur M. Rein, 46
Artie's, 472
Arts By Alexander's, 212
A. Rubinstein and Son, 35
Ashley's Outlet Store, Inc., 480
ATC Satelco, 428
Athens Mill Factory Outlet, 468
Athletic Shoe Factory, 490
A to Z Luggage, 232
Audio Advisor, Inc., 413
Audrey's Hideaway, 472
Aunt Mary's Yarns Needlework
    Crafts, 483
Austad's, 393
Auto Safety Hotline, 202
AVP (Animal Veterinary Products,
    Inc.), 359
A.W. Gotten, 385

B

Babouris Handicrafts, 21, 256
Bachmaier & Klemmer, 212
Bag N Bootery, 465
Bailey's, Inc., 246
Banana Republic, 238
B & F Shoes, 490
B & H Foto Electronics, 97
B & I Furniture Co., 346
Banister, 490
Banister Shoe Outlet, 490
Banker's Note, The, 472
Banque Ankerfina SA, 287
Bare Necessities, 467
Barett Shoes, 491
Barnes & Barnes, 213

Barry Manufacturing Company,
    470
Barth's, 168
Bartley Collection, The, 300
Bart's Water Ski Center, Inc., 394
Base Exchange, The, 421
Bass Pro Shops, 394
Bass Shoe Factory Outlet, 491
Batikat, 289
Beautiful Beginnings, 142
Beautiful Visions, 143
Beauty Boutique, 143
Beauty By Spector, 143
Bee Lee Co., 154
Beitman Co., Inc., 239
Belle Tire Distributors, Inc., 110
Bell's Guide, 202
Bell Yarn/Wonoco Yarn, 256
Bemidji Woolen Mills, 21
Ben Morris Jewelry Co., 122
Beno's, 463
Bent Tree Travel, 440
Berman Leathercraft, 257
Ber Sel Handbags, 233
Best Bros. Paint & Wallpaper
    Outlet, 454
Best Choice, The, 385
Best Products Co., 118
Bettingers Luggage, 233
Bevers, The, 247
Bike Nashbar, 395
Bike Vermont, Inc., 441
Bio-Control, 365
Bits & Pieces:, 335
B.J. Alan, 336
Blackwelder's, 213
Blair, 421
Blind Spot, The, 454
Blue Bell Factory Outlet, 463
Bluestone Perennials Inc., 365
Blum's, 386
BMI, 290
Bonafide Shoe Factory Outlet, 491
Bondy Export Corp., 61
Boot Town, 386
Boulle, Inc., 290
Bowden Wholesale Co., 247
Bowhunters Discount Warehouse,
    395

Boycan's Craft and Art Supplies, 257
Boyles Furniture Sales, 214
Branded Shoe Outlet, The, 491
Brand Name Fashion, 466
Brenda Allen, 472
Brewmaster, 300
Bristol County, 465
Britex-By-Mail, 154
Brookfield Nursery & Tree Plantation, 366
Brown & Co., 281
Bruce Alan Bags Etc., 486
Bruce Medical Supply, 319
Buffalo Batt & Felt Corp., 155
Burlington Coat Factory, 464
Burro, 301
Business Envelope Manufacturers, 346
Butterbrooke Farm, 367
Butterflies & Rainbows, Inc., 291
Buttons, 490
Buy Direct, Inc., 347

C

Cabela's, 396
Cache Valley Dairy Association, 186
Calico Corners, 483
California Cargo, 168, 386
California Sound, 413
Cal-Rich Ltd., 144
Cambridge Camera Exchange, Inc., 97
Cambridge Wools, Ltd., 155
Camelot Enterprises, 248
Cameo, Inc., 84
Campmor, 396
Campus Travel Service, 441
Cane & Basket Supply Co., 301
Cape Craftsman, 484
Capital Cycle Corp., 111
Caprilands Herb Farm, 367
Cap Tree Factory Store, 472
Career Guild, 46
Carlsen Import Shoes, 387, 396
Carole Block Ltd., 234
Carolina Mills Factory Outlet, 155

Carolyn's, 471
Carriage Trade Creations, 337
Carr's, 387, 491
Carry On Luggage, 234
Carter's Children's Wear Factory Outlet, 462
Carvin, 326
Catherine, 144
Caviarteria, 187
Cedarhurst Papers, 485
Central Michigan Tractor and Parts, 368
Chadwick's of Boston, Ltd., 47
Champion Retail, 476
Charles Loeb, 187
Charles Schwab & Co., Inc., 281
Cheeselovers International, 188
Cheeses of All Nations, 188
Chef's Catalog, The, 272
Chernin's Shoes, 388
Cherry Auto Parts, 111
Cherry Hill Furniture, Carpet & Interiors, 214
Cherry Tree Toys, Inc., 257, 302, 436
Children's Outlet, The, 462
Children's Place, The, 462
Chinacraft of London, 122
China Glass and Gifts, 488
China Matchers, The, 122
China Warehouse, The, 123
Chock Catalog Corp., 22
Chocolate Soup, 462
Clark's Corvair Parts, Inc., 112
Clearbrook Woolen Shop, 156
Clinton Cycle & Salvage, Inc., 112
Clothcrafters, 272
Clothes Hound, The, 466
ClothesTime, 473
Clothes to You, 473
Clothesworks, 473
Clothing Clearance Centers, 470
Clothing Warehouse, The, 466
Clothkits, 22, 302, 436
Clotilde, 258
Club Costa, 442
Cluett Factory Stores, 464
Coat Rack/Clothes Line, 465
Collinsworth, 273
Colonel Bill Newsom's, 189

Colonial Woodcraft, 302
Columbus Clay Company, 258
Colwell Business Products, 347
C.O.M.B., 61
Comfortably Yours™, 239
Commercial Office Products, 348
Commonwealth Factory Outlets,
    491
Company Store™, The, 84
Competition, The, 472
Comp-U-Card, 62
Computer Plus, 137
Connco Shoes, 492
Conney Safety Products, 319
Constantine's, 303
Consumer Education Research
    Center, 240
Consumer Information Catalog,
    202
Consumers Guide to Home Repair
    Grants & Loans, 240
Continental Assn. of Funeral &
    Memorial Societies, 319
Continental Lawn Mower Mfg.
    Co., 248
Corner House, 473
Corning Designs Factory Outlet,
    487
Cosmetique, 145
Cotton Dreams, 18
Council on International
    Educational Exchange (CIEE),
    442
Country Handcrafts Magazine,
    259
Country Hills Greenhouse, 368
Countryside Herb Farm, 368
Coupon Broker, The, 443
Craftsman Wood Service Co., 259
Craftways Corporation, 259
Creative Health Products, 169, 320
Creative House, 235
CRI Composers Recordings Inc.,
    379
Cross Creek, 260
Crown Books, 480
Crown Cultured Pearl Corp., 291
Crutchfield, 414
CSC Marketing, Inc., 415
Cultural Guild, The, 380

C.U. Restoration Supplies, 249
Current, 337
Custom Coat Company, Inc., 23
Custom Golf Clubs, Inc., 397
Custom Windows & Walls, 455
Cutting Corners, 483
Cycle Goods Corp., 397

D

Dairy Association Company, Inc.,
    369
Damart, 35
Damon Factory Outlet, 36
D & A Merchandise Co., 23
Dan Howard Maternity Outlet, 478
Danley's, 98
Danskin Factory Outlet, 468
Dazian, Inc., 338
Deak International, Inc., 203
Deepak's Rokjemperl Products,
    260
Deerskin Place, The, 36
Defender Industries, 91
Delta Hosiery Outlet, 468
Designer Depot, 464
Deva Cottage Industry, 24
Dexter Shoe Factory Outlet, 492
Dial-A-Brand, 62
Dick Blick Company, 78
Dimensions in Fashion, 473
Dinn Bros., 398
Dinnerware Plus, 488
Dinosaur Catalog, 436
Discount Brokerage Corp., 281
Discovery in Fashions, 473
D. MacGillivray & Coy, 156
Dollsville Dolls and Bearsville
    Bears, 437
Dorsett Distributing Co., 37
Dottie's, 494
Double-Time Jazz Records, 380
Dover Publications, Inc., 203
Down Generation/Sylvia & Sons,
    24
Dress Barn, 474
Dreyfus Liquid Assets & Dreyfus
    Group, 286
Drug Emporium, 486

Duk Kwong Optical Center, 320
Dunham Footwear Factory
  Outlets, 492
Dutch Gardens, 369

E

E & B Marine Supply, 91, 479
East Woods Press, The, 443
EBA Wholesale, 63
Echo Products, Inc., 359
E.C. Kraus, 303
Edinburgh Woollen Mill, Ltd., 25
Effective Learning Systems, Inc.,
  169
Eisner Bros., 398
E.J.'s Famous Brand Shoes, 492
El Bee Shoes, 492
Eldridge Textile Co., 84
Electropedic Adjustable Beds, 85
Elek-Tek, 137
Elkes Carpet Outlet, 108
Elkin Travel Inc./Cruises Only!,
  444
Emperor Clock Co., 304
Empire Diamond Corp., 292
Entertainment Publications,
  444
ESC Envelope Sales Co., 348
Essential Products Co., Inc., 145
Euro-Tire Inc., 113
Evan-Picone Factory Store, 466
Evergreen Bed & Breakfast Club,
  The, 445
Executive Photo and Supply Corp.,
  99
Explosafe Gasoline Cans, 113
Ezra Cohen Corp., 85

F

Fabulous Julie's, 462
Factory Direct Table Pad Co., Inc.,
  215
Factory Store, The, 86
Factory Wholesalers, 37
Fair & Square, 338, 437
Famous Brand Shoes, 492
Famous Footwear, 493

Famous Smoke Shop, 432
F & M Distributors, 486
F & M Sports Outlet, 399
Fantasy Collection, The, 292
Fashionation, 464
Fashion Barn, 474
Fashion Gal, 464
Fashion Gallery, 474
Fashion Mine, 464
Fashion Works, 474
Fidelity Brokerage Service, Inc.,
  282
Fidelity Daily Income, 286
Fidelity Products Co., 349
Fifth Avenue Bed & Bath Outlet,
  478
Filene's Basement, 480
Finals, 20
Finals, The, 25, 170
Financial Programs, 286
Fine & Klein, 235, 388
Finish Line, The, 495
Fitz & Floyd Factory Outlet, 488
5 & 10 Shoe Store, 493
Fivenson Food Equipment, Inc.,
  273
Flemington Fashion Outlet, 474
Flickinger's Nursery, 370
Focus Electronics, 99
Folks on Buck Hill, 399
Ford's Freighter Guide, 445
Foreign Commerce Bank, 287
Formfit Outlet, 468
For Peanuts, 484
Fortunoff, 124
47th St. Photo, 100
Four Seasons Greenhouses, 304
Fox River Naturals, 170
Frank Eastern Co., 349
Frank Mittermeier Inc., 79
Fran's Basket House, 215
Frans Roozen, 370
Freddy, 146
Fred Sanders, Inc., 483
Fred's Plant Farm, 370
Fred's String Warehouse, 327
Fred Stoker & Sons, 432
Freeda Vitamins®, 171
Freedman Seating Company, 114

Freeman, 490
Freeport Music, 327
French Shriner, 490
Friar's House, The, 70
F.R. Knitting Mills, Inc., 47
Front Row, 481
Front Row Photos, 339
Frostline Kits, 304
Frugal Frank's Shoes, 493
Frye Factory Outlets, 493
Functional Clothing, Ltd., 400
Furniture Barn of Forest City, Inc.,
    216
Furnitureland South, Inc., 216

G

Gallery Graphics, Inc., 70
G & G Projections, 38
Garden Camera, 100
Gelber's Mens Store, 38
General Shoe Factory to You, 493
Gentlemen's Wearhouse & Ladies
    Factory Outlet, 465
George Channing Enterprises/
    Incredible Arts, 71
Gered, 124
Gerry Sharp, Trunk Doctor, 305
Gettinger Feather Corp., 305
Gilliom Manufacturing Inc., 249
Ginger Schlote, 261
Glass House Works Catalog, 241
Glorybee Box, Inc., 261
Go Cart, 306
Gohn Bros., 48
Goldberg's Marine, 92, 479
Goldman & Cohen, 48
Gold 'n' Stones, 293
Golf and Tennis World, 400
Golf Day Products, Inc., 306
Golf Haus, 401
Goodfellow Catalog of Wonderful
    Things, The, 262
Good 'n' Lucky Promotions, 339
Good Shepherd's Store, 71
Gossard Outlet, 468
Grace Tea Company, Ltd., 189
Grand Finale, 274, 488
Greater New York Trading Co., 125

Great Factory Store, The, 474
Great Lakes Sportswear, 401
Great Tracers, 79
Green Pepper, The, 306
Green River Trading Co., 72, 307
Grieger's, Inc., 262
Grillot, 146
Guide to the Guides (Europe), 446
Gurney's Seed & Nursery Co., 371
Gussini Shoes, 494

H

Handart Embroideries, 274
Hanover Shoes Factory Outlet, 491
Harmonia Mundi—USA, 380
Harmony Supply Inc., 455
Harris Levy, Inc., 86
Harry Rothman, Inc., 39
Harry Zarin Co., 157
Harvard Trouser Company, 26
Haspel Factory Outlet, 466
Hastings Records & Books, 489
Hathaway Factory Outlet, 465
Hayim Pinhas, 433
H. DeCovnick & Son, 307
Healthtrax International, 171
Heathkit Electronic Center, 308
Hendricks Furniture, Inc., 217
Heritage Clock Co., 308
Herrschners Inc., 309
Hickory Hill Nursery, 371
Hicks USA, 236
Highland Superstores, 496
High Meadow Farm, 172
Hill Brothers, 388
Hill's Court, 402
Hirsch Photo, 101
Hit or Miss, 475
Hobby Shack, 263
Hobby Surplus Sales, 263
Hoffman Hatchery, Inc., 372
Holabird Sports Discounters, 402
Holcraft Co., 264
Hollywood Bread, 203
Hollywood Fancy Feather Co., 309
Holzman & Stephanie Perfumes
    Inc., 147
H.O.M.E. Craft Catalog, The, 264

Home Depot, The, 486
Home Fabric Mills, Inc., 157
Home Front, 478
Hoovey's Book Service, 72
House Distributors, 381
House of International
    Fragrances, 147
House of Leather, 465
House of Onyx, 293
Housewares Plus Inc., 488
Howron Sportswear, 26
Hudson Glass Co. Inc., 310
Hudson Vitamins, 172
Hunter Audio-Photo Ltd., 63
Huntington Clothiers, 39
Hurrah!, 475

I

Icemart, The, 49
Ideal Cheese Shop, 190
Ident-Ify Label Corp., 310
Imoco Inc., 275
Inlook Outlet, 475
Intercoastal Textile Corp., 158
Interior Fabrics, 483
Interiors By Sanz, 456
International Import Company,
    294
International Solgo, Inc., 64
Intertwine Yarn & Fiber Supply,
    158
Into the Wind, 340
Irish Cottage Industries, 49
Irish Crystal Company, 485
I. Tuschman & Sons, Inc., 27

J

Jaffe Bros., 190
James Bliss Marine Co., Inc., 92
James Roy Inc., 217
J & R Music World, 415
Jay's Yarns, 159
Jazz Aids, 328
J.C. Whitney & Co., 114
Jean's Silversmiths, 125
J.E. Miller Nurseries, Inc., 372

Jerryco, Inc., 422
Jerry's Artrama, Inc., 80
Jersey Camera, 101
Jess Miller Publishing Co., 446
Jilor Discounts, 350
Jo Harper, 474
John Mabry Menswear, 40
Johnson & Johnson, 204
Johnson Smith Co., 340
Jolene Children's Factory Outlet,
    462
Jos. A. Bank Clothiers, 40, 465
JR Tobacco, 484
J-R Tobacco Co., 433
J. Schachter Corp., 87
Juggling Arts, The, 241
Just Justin Take Out Boots, 389
Just Labels, 465
J.W. Bray, 389
J.W. Chunn Perfumes, 148

K

Karzundpartz, 115
Kennedy, Cabot & Co., 282
Kennedy's of Ardara, 49
Kennel Vet Corporation, The, 360
Kids Mart, 462
Kids Port, U.S.A., 463
Kids 'R' Us, 463
King's Chandelier Co., 218
King Size Company, The, 41
Kippen Group, The, 126
Kirkham's Outdoor Products, 402
Kitchen Bazaar, 275
Kitchen Collection, 488
Knight's, 159
Kolb-Lena Cheese Company, 190
KSA Jojoba, 148
Kuempel Chime Clock Works, 310
Kuppenheimer Factory Stores, 470

L

Ladies Factory Outlet, 476
Lady Annabelle, 50
L'Ambiance Furniture, 218

Lamp Warehouse/NY Ceiling Fan Center, 219
Lamrite's, 265
L & D Press, 351
L & H Vitamins, 174
Landmark Specialties, Inc., 350
Land's End, 20, 27
Lane Bryant, 50
Langtry Ltd. Shirt Co., 472
La Pinata, 341
Las Vegas Discount Golf and Tennis, 403
Laurence Corner, 341
Lee-McClain Co., 41
Left Hand Center, 242
L'Eggs Showcase of Savings, 50, 173
Le Gourmand, 191
Leichtung "Handys", 249
Leotards By Leticia, 173
Letter Box, 342
LHL Enterprises, 265
Lillian Vernon, 276
Lincoln House, 342
Linda's Hosiery Outlet, Inc., 51
Linens 'n Things, 479
Lingerie for Less, 321
Lionel Enterprises, 175
Little Red Shoe House, 494
L.J.'s Clothes Barn, 474
L.L. Bean, 174
Locator's, Incorporated, 126
Loehmann's, 475
Loft Designer Sportswear, The, 51
Loftin-Black Furniture Co., 219
Lombard's Sporting Goods, 403
Londontown Factory Outlet Store, 477
Long Distance Roses, 373
L'Oreal Guideline, 204
Lottie's Discount Shoes, 494
Luger Boats, 311
LVT Price Quote Hotline, 65
Lyben Computer Systems, Inc., 138
Lyle Cartridges, 416
Lynn Dairy Fresh from the Heart of the Dairy State, 191

M

Mail Order Plastics, Inc., 250
Mail Runner's Shop, The, 175
Majestic Drug Co., Inc., 321
Mak Inc., 276
Mallory's, 219
M & E Marine Supply Co., 93
Mandolin Bros., 328
Manganaro Foods, 192
Manhattan Factory Outlet, 466
Manufacturers Shoe Warehouse, 490
Manufacturer's Supply, 115
March of Dimes Birth Defects Foundation, 204
Marcus & Co., 294
Mardiron Optics, 102
Marshalls, 481
Mary Jo's Cloth Store, Inc., 160
Marymac Industries Inc., 138
Mass. Army and Navy Store, 422
Master Fashions, 42
Master Mechanic Mfg. Co., 250
Maternity Clothing Factory, 478
Maternity Mart, 478
Maternity Wearhouse, 478
Maxine's, 494
Mayfield Co. Inc., 52
May Hosiery Mills Factory Outlet, 468
McAlisters, Inc., 416
MCI Telecommunications Corp., 428
McKilligan Industrial and Supply Corp., 250
Mega Food, 176
Meisel Hardware Specialties, 266
Melnikoff's Department Store, 28
Mendel Weiss, 52, 322
Men's Wearhouse, The, 470
Mervyn's, 481
Messina Glass & China Co., 127
Mexican Chile Supply, 192
Mexican Kitchen, The, 193
Michael C. Fina, 127
Michaels, 487
Michel Swiss, 149
Mikasa Factory Outlet, 488
Milan Laboratory, 311

Miles Homes, 312
Mill Outlet, 466
Miscellaneous Man, 73
Modern Products Inc., 205
Mogish String Company, 329
Monsanto Engineered Products, 277
Moravian Sugar Crisp Co., Inc., 193
Morton Salt Co., 205
Moss Brown & Company, Inc., 176
Moss Street Menswear, 465
Mothers Work, 53
Ms., Miss, and Mrs., 53
Munsingwear Factory Outlet, 468
Muriel Siebert & Co., Inc., 283
Murray's Pottery, Inc., 73
Murrow Furniture Galleries, 220
Museum Editions New York, Ltd., 74
Mushroom, 490
Music in the Mail, 381

N

Natan Borlam Co., Inc., 18
National Business Furniture, Inc., 351
National Contact Lens Center, The, 322
National Music Supply, 329
National Wholesale Co., Inc., 54
Nationwide Auto Brokers, 115
Nat Schwartz Co., Inc., 127
NBO (National Brands Outlet), 470
NEBS, 352
Nelson's, 390
NEMC, 330
Nepal Craft Emporium, 74
Newark Dressmaker Supply, 160
New Bedford Seafood Council, 205
New England Divers Inc., 404
New England Frameworks, 266
Newport Sportswear, 466
New York Central Supply Co., 80
Nice Shoes, 494
Nite Furniture Co., 220
Non-Electric Heritage Catalog, The, 242

North Carolina Furniture Showrooms, 221
Northern Wholesale Veterinary Supply, 360
Noweta Gardens, 373
Nurhan Cevahir, 434
Nusrala Name Brand Shoes, 492
Nutrition Headquarters, 177

O

O'Connor's Yankee Peddler Warehouse Sale, 54
Odd Lot Trading, 487
Office of Metric Programs, 206
Olde Discount Stockbrokers, 283
Olden Camera, 102
Old Mill, 475
Olga Factory Surplus, 469
Olympic Sales, 352
Omaha Vaccine Company, 361
O.M. Scott & Sons Company, The, 208
Opportunities for Learning, Inc., 242
Orchard Street Bootery, 390
Oshman's Warehouse Outlet Stores, 495
Outlet, The, 466
Ovest Securities, Inc., 283
Oxford Sportswear Outlet, 476

P

Pagano Gloves, Inc., 28
Paint & Pattern, 456
Palm Beach Mill Outlet, 466
Pan American Electronics, Inc., 139
Paprikas Weiss Importer, 194, 243
Paradise Products, 343
Paragon Medical Products, 322
Paris Bread Pans, 277
Party Warehouse, 485
Patterns Unlimited, 128
Peaches, 490
Pearl Brothers Typewriters, 353
Pearl Paint, 81
Penn Leather & Coat Co., 465

Penn Square, 286
Penny Wise Warehouse Stores, 87
Pennzoil Company, 206
Pepperidge Farm Thrift Stores, 484
Permanent Portfolio Funds, 286
Petco Animal Supplies, 361
Pfaltzgraff Pfactory Outlet, 278, 489
Phar-Mor, 487
Phone Control Systems, 139
Pine Cone, The, 65
Plastic Bagmart, 278
Player's Music, U.S.A., 330
Plexi-Craft Quality Products, 221
PL Premium Leather By Hanover, 391
Plus Sizes, 476
P.M.I., 331
Polly Flinders Factory Stores, 463
Polyart Products Co., 81
Pony Creek Nursery, 373
Post Horn, 476
Potter's Shop, The, 267
Prentiss Court Ground Covers, 374
Presidential Greetings Office, 206
Priba Furniture, 222
Prince Fashion Outlet, 471
Prince Fashions Ltd., 29
Pro Shop World of Golf, 404
Publisher's Book Outlet, 480
Pyramid Products, 312

Q

Quality Furniture Market of Lenoir, Inc., 222
Quick & Reilly, Inc., 284
Quill® Corporation, 353
Quilts Unlimited, 88
Quoddy Crafted Footwear, 494

R

Radio Shack, 206
Rafael, 89
Rainbow Gardens, 374

Rainbow Hot Tubs and Spa Inc., 177
Rama Jewelry Ltd., 294
Ram Furniture Gallery, Inc., The, 223
Rammagerdin of Reykjavik, 29
Rayco Tennis Products, 405
Raymond Sultan & Sons, Ltd., 54
R.B. Mason Company, 251
Reading Clothing Outlet, 465
Reading Menswear Outlet, 465
Reborn Maternity, 55
Record Hunter, The, 382
Red Flannel Factory, 30, 469
Red River Pottery, 485
Reed Tackle, 405
Reich Poultry Farms, Inc., 375
REI Co-Op, 406
Reject China Shop, 128
R/E Kane Enterprises, 295
Relocation Research, 446
Rennie Ellen, 295
Renovator's Supply—5503, 252
Replacements, Ltd., 129
Revere Ware Courtesy Stores, 489
Rhythm Band, Inc., 331
Ric Clark, 323
Rice Council of America, 207
Richard Yerxa Jewelry and Silver, 129
Right Place, The, 464
Rite-Way Hearing Aid Co., 323
Road Runner Sports, 391, 406
Robin Importers, 130
Robinson's Wallcoverings, 457
Roby's Intimates, 55, 177
Rochester 100, Inc., 354
Rococo Records Ltd., 382
Rogers & Rosenthal, 130
Rolane Factory Outlet, 466
Rollerwall, Inc., 312
Roman Meal Company, 207
Romni Wools and Fibres, 161
Ronnie Draperies, 457
Rose & Co. Investment Brokers, Inc., 284
Rose Furniture Co., 223
Rose Records, 382
Ross, 481
Ross-Simons of Warwick, 131

Royal Gardens, 375
Royal, Grimm and Davis, Inc., 284
Royal Optical, 489
Royal Silk, 56
RSL, 56
RSP Distributing Company, 423
Rubin & Green Interior Design
    Studio, 89
Ruvel, 423

S

Safe Equipment Co, Inc., 252
St. Croix Kits, 313
Saint Laurie Ltd., 42
Samarth Gem Stones, 296
Sam Ash Music Corp., 332
Sampson & Delilah, 178
S & K Famous Brands, 471
Sandman, 224
S & S Discount Service, 67
S & S Sound City, 417
San Francisco Herb Co., 194
S.A.V.E., 195
Saverite Photo & Electronics, 103
Saxkjaers, 131
SBS Skyline, 429
Schapira Coffee Company, 195
Scudder Fund Distributing, Inc.,
    286
Second Serve, 496
Service Merchandise Catalog
    Showrooms, 118
7th Heaven, 18
Sewin' In Vermont, 66
SGF, 132
Shama Imports, Inc., 161
Shannon Mail Order, 132
Shapes Activewear Outlet, 469
Shar Products Company, 332
Shaw Furniture Galleries, 224
Shibui Wallcoverings, 458
Ship 'n Shore, 476
Shoe Manufacturer's Outlet, 494
Shoe Stop, 495
Shoe Times, 495
Shotgun News, The, 407
Show Off, 464, 473
Signal Mill Factory Outlet, 468

Silver Wallcovering, Inc., 458
Simpson & Vail, Inc., 195
Sizes Unlimited, 476
Skate Stop, 407
Slipcovers of America, 225
Smallholding Supplies, 376
Smart Size, 476
Smith & Hawken, 376
SneaKee Feet, 495
Sobol House, 225
Soccer International, Inc., 407
Sock Shop, 30
Socks 'N Such, 469
Solar Cine Products, Inc., 103
Solo, 482
Solo Serve, 482
Something Special, 473
S-100 Inc., 354
Sonshine Crafts, 67
Sound Reproduction, Inc., 417
Sound Warehouse, 490
Source for Everything Jewish,
    The, 243
Southpaw Shoppe, The, 244
Spencer Gifts, Inc., 343
Spiratone, 104
Splendor in the Glass, 267
Sportique, 473
Sports Hut, 408
Sportswear Mart, 476
Squadron Mail Order, 268
Stand-Buys Ltd., 447
Stanley M. Mirsky, 43
Star Professional Pharmaceuticals,
    Inc., 178
Star Route Hammocks, 226
Stationery House Inc., The, 355
Stavros Kouyoumoutzakis, 162
Stecher's, 132
Stein Mart, 482
Stein Mart Department Stores,
    494
Stephen Faller (exports) Ltd., 133
Stephensons Warmlite Equipment,
    408
Stereo Discounters Electronic
    World, 418
Sterling & China, Ltd., 133
Stock Room, The, 466
Strand Surplus Senter, 31

Strawberries Records & Tapes, 490
Stroud's Linen Warehouse, 479
Stu-Art Supplies, 82
Stuckey Bros. Furniture Co., Inc., 226
Stur-Dee Health Products, 179
Stuyvesant Bicycle, 409
Sugarbush Farm, 196
Sultan's Delight Inc., 196
Sunburst Biorganics, 179
Super Strength Systems, 180
Surplus Center, The, 424
Susan of Newport, 268
Sussex Clothes Ltd., 43
Suzanne's, 477
Sweetwater Hosiery Mills, 57
Swiss Konnection, The, 57, 296
Sybervision Systems, 180
Syms, 467

T

Table Top Fashions, 488
Taffy's-By-Mail, 181
Talbott Factory Outlet, 467
Tanglepoint Travel, Inc., 448
TBC, 409
Tech HiFi, 496
Telemart, 140
Telepro Golf Shop, 410
Tele-Tire, 116
Tempo, 464
Testfabrics Inc., 162
Texas Greenhouse Co., 313
Texas Rose Coffee & Tea, 197
Texas Securities, 285
Thai Silks, 163
T.H. Mandy, 477
Three D Bed & Beth, 479
Thrifty Prints, Inc., 355
Tibetan Refugee Self-Help Centre, 75
T.J. Maxx, 482
T.M. Chan & Co., 104
Tomahawk Live Trap Co., 362
Tool Importers Warehouse Sale, 253

Tower Records, 490
Tower Video, 490
Toy Balloon Corporation, 437
Toymaker Supply Co., The, 314, 438
Toys & Gifts Outlet, 496
Toys 'R' Us, 496
Trampolking Sporting Goods, 181
Travel Auto Bag Co., 236
Travel Companion Exchange, Inc., 448
Triblend Mills, 163
Tri-Steel Structures, Inc., 314
Trophyland USA, Inc., 410
T. Rowe Price, 286
Tuesday Morning, 485
Tuli-Latus Perfumes Ltd., 149
Turner-Tolson, Inc., 227
Turn-O-Carve Tool Co., 315
Typex Business Machines Inc., 355

U

Ueberseebank AG Zurich, 287
Uncle Dan's Ltd., 424
United Pharmacal Co., Inc., 362
Universal Suppliers, 425
Urban Ventures, Inc., 448
U.S. Department of Education, 208
U.S. General Tool and Hardware, 253
U.S. Optics, 244
US Sprint Communications, 429
U.S. Transmissions Systems, 430
Utex Trading Enterprises, 164
Utility Craft, Inc., 227
Utrecht Art & Drafting Supply, 82

V

Vacations to Go, 449
Valray International, Inc., 150
Vanderbilt Factory Outlet, 472
Vanderbilt Fashions, 472
Vanguard Group, 286
Van Heusen Factory Store, 467
Vanity Fair (also S.A. Peck & Co.), 297

Van Moppes Diamonds, 297
Van Pler & Tissany, 298
Varner Warehouse Sales Inc., 228
Veteran Leather Co., 269
Vickie-Bee Perfumes, 150
Vienna Health Products, 182
Viking Clock Division, 315
Virginia Alan Ltd., 477
Vitamin Specialties Co., 182
V. Juul Christensen & Son, 58

W

Waco Thrift Store Inc., 31
Wallcovering Information Bureau
    Inc., 208
Wallpaper Now, 459
Wallpapers To Go, 489
Wall Street Camera Exchange, 105
Walter Drake Silver Exchange, 134
Warehouse Carpets, 108
Wayside Interiors, 228
Way Station Fabric Shop, 164
Way Station, The, 477
Wear-Guard Corporation, 32
Webster Warehouse Outlet, 471
Weiss and Mahoney, 425
Wells Interiors, Inc., 459
Western Natural Products, 183
Western S & G, 140
West Marine Products, 93
Weston Bowl Mill, 278
Westside Camera Inc., 105
Wholesale Veterinary Supply, Inc.,
    The, 363
Wide World of Sporting Goods, 411
Wilbur Chocolate Candy Outlet,
    197
Wilderness Log Homes, 315
Windfall Mailing Lists, 356

Winona Knits, 467
Winston's, 482
W.J. Hagerty & Sons, 209
Wolff Office Equipment, 356
Women's Sports Foundation, 209
Wonder Craft, 165
Wood-Armfield Furniture, 229
Woodwind/The Brasswind, The,
    333
Woolrich Store, The, 165
Workmen's Garment Co., 32
Works of Max Levine, 75
World Abrasive Co., 254
World Bazaar, 485
World of Beauty, 151
Worldwide Discount Travel Club,
    449
W.S. Robertson Outfitters Ltd.,
    33, 58
Wurtsboro Wholesale Antiques, 76
Wynnewood Pharmacy, 151

Y

Yachtmail Co., Ltd., 94
Yankee Ingenuity, 279
Yarn Barn, 165
Years to Your Health, 183
Young Idea Ltd., The, 19
Young's Furniture and Rug Co.,
    229
Y's Way, The, 450

Z

Zabar's, 198
Zamart for Kids, 230, 438
Zamart Inc., 166
Zarbin and Associates, Inc., 230
Zeeman Manufacturing, 470
Zipp-Penn Inc., 254

CATEGORY INDEX

HARD GOODS

Appliances
Best Products Co., 118
Bondy Export Corp., 61
C.O.M.B., 61
Comp-U-Card, 62
Dial-A-Brand, 62
EBA Wholesale, 63
Focus Electronics, 99
International Solgo, Inc., 64
Jersey Camera, 101
LVT Price Quote Hotline, 65
Non-Electric Heritage Catalog, The, 242
Saverite Photo & Electronics, 103
S & S Sound City, 417
Service Merchandise Catalog Showrooms, 118

Art and Collectibles
A. Goto, 69
Antique Imports Unlimited, 69
Friar's House, The, 70
Gallery Graphics, Inc., 70
George Channing Enterprises/ Incredible Arts, 71
Good Shepherd's Store, 71
Hoovey's Book Service, 72
Miscellaneous Man, 73
Murray's Pottery, Inc., 73
Museum Editions New York, Ltd., 74
Nepal Craft Emporium, 74
Stephen Faller (exports) Ltd., 133
Tibetan Refugee Self-Help Centre, 75
Universal Suppliers, 425

Art Supplies
A.I. Friedman, 78
Dick Blick Company, 78
Frank Mittermeier Inc., 79
Great Tracers, 79
Jerry's Artrama, Inc., 80
McKilligan Industrial and Supply Corp., 250
New York Central Supply Co., 80
Pearl Paint, 81
Polyart Products Co., 81
Stu-Art Supplies, Inc., 82
Utrecht Art & Drafting Supply, 82

Beds—Regular and Futon
Arise Futon Mattress Co., 211
Barnes & Barnes, 213
Blackwelder's, 213
Electropedic Adjustable Beds, 85
Furnitureland South, Inc., 216
Hendricks Furniture, Inc., 217
James Roy Inc., 217
Murrow Furniture Galleries, 220
Nite Furniture Co., 220
North Carolina Furniture Showrooms, 221

Priba Furniture, 222
Rose Furniture Co., 223
Shaw Furniture Galleries, 224
Sobol House, 225
Utility Craft, Inc., 227
Varner Warehouse Sales Inc., 228
Wayside Interiors, 228
Wood-Armfield Furniture, 229
Zarbin and Associates, Inc., 230

Beds—Brass

A Brass Bed Shoppe, 211
Barnes & Barnes, 213
Blackwelder's, 213
Penny Wise Warehouse Stores, 87
Shaw Furniture Galleries, 224

Bedding and Bath

Cameo, Inc., 84
Company Store™, The, 84
Eldridge Textile Co., 84
Ezra Cohen Corp., 85
Factory Store, The, 86
Harris Levy, Inc., 86
J. Schacter Corp., 87
Quilts Unlimited, 88
Rafael, 89
Rainbow Hot Tubs and Spa Inc.,
    177
Rubin & Green Interior Design
    Studio, 89
SGF, 132

Boating Supplies

Defender Industries, 91
E & B Marine Supply, 91, 479
Goldberg's Marine, 92, 479
James Bliss Marine Co., Inc., 92
Luger Boats, 311
M & E Marine Supply Co., 93
Yachtmail Co., Ltd., 94

**Cameras, Opticals, and
Photographic Supplies**

AAA Camera Exchange, 96
ABC Photo Service, 96
Ad-Libs Astronomics, 96
B & H Foto Electronics, 97
Best Products Co., 118
Bondy Export Corp., 61
Cambridge Camera Exchange,
    Inc., 97

Danley's, 98
Executive Photo and Supply Corp.,
    99
Focus Electronics, Inc., 99
47th St. Photo, 100
Garden Camera, 100
Hirsch Photo, 101
Hunter Audio-Photo Ltd., 63
International Solgo, Inc., 64
Jersey Camera, 101
Mardiron Optics, 102
Olden Camera, 102
Saverite Photo & Electronics, 103
Service Merchandise Catalog
    Showrooms, 118
Solar Cine Products, Inc., 103
Spiratone, 104
T.M. Chan & Co., 104
Universal Suppliers, 425
Wall Street Camera Exchange, 105
Westside Camera Inc., 105

Carpets and Rugs

Arts by Alexander's, 211
Cherry Hill Furniture, Carpet &
    Interiors, 214
Elkes Carpet Outlet, 108
Furnitureland South, Inc., 216
Murrow Furniture Galleries, 220
Nite Furniture Co., 220
Paint & Pattern, 456
Priba Furniture, 222
Quality Furniture Market of
    Lenoir, Inc., 222
Warehouse Carpets, 108
Young's Furniture and Rug Co.,
    229

Cars and Parts

American Auto Brokers, 110
Belle Tire Distributors, Inc., 110
Burro, 301
Cherry Auto Parts, 111
Clark's Corvair Parts, Inc., 112
Euro-Tire Inc., 113
Explosafe Gasoline Cans, 113
Freedman Seating Company, 114
Go Cart, 306
J.C. Whitney & Co., 114
Karsundpartz, 115
Manufacturer's Supply, 115
Nationwide Auto Brokers, 115
Tele-Tire, 116

China

A. Benjamin & Co., 120
Albert S. Smyth Co., Inc., 121
Ben Morris Jewelry Co., 122
Chinacraft of London, 122
China Matchers, The, 122
China Warehouse, The, 123
Fortunoff, 124
Gered, 124
Greater New York Trading Co., 125
Kippen Group, The, 126
Kitchen Collection, 488
Locator's, Incorporated, 126
Messina Glass & China Co., 127
Michael C. Fina, 127
Nat Schwartz Co., Inc., 127
Patterns Unlimited, 128
Reject China Shop, 128
Replacements, Ltd., 129
Robin Importers, 130

Clocks

Bachmaier & Klemmer, 212
Emperor Clock Co., 304
H. DeCovnick & Son, 307
Heritage Clock Co., 308
Kuempel Chime Clock Works, 310
Viking Clock Division, 315

Computers

Aerocomp Inc., 136
All Electronics Corporation, 136
Best Products Co., 118
Comp-U-Card, 62
Computer Plus, 137
Crutchfield, 414
Elek-Tek, 137
Executive Photo and Supply Corp., 99
Focus Electronics, Inc., 99
47th St. Photo, 100
Heathkit Electronic Center, 308
J & R Music World, 415
Landmark Specialties, Inc., 350
Lyben Computer Systems, Inc., 138
Marymac Industries Inc., 138
Olden Camera, 102
Olympic Sales, 352
Pan American Electronics, Inc., 139
S-100, Inc., 354
Telemart, 140

Western S&G, 140

Cosmetics and Beauty Aids

Alexander Sales Associates, Inc., 142
Beautiful Beginnings, 142
Beautiful Visions, 143
Beauty Boutique, 143
Beauty By Spector, 143
Blair, 421
Cal-Rich Ltd., 144
Catherine, 144
Cosmetique, 145
Essential Products Co., Inc., 145
Freddy, 146
Grillot, 146
Holzman & Stephanie Perfumes Inc., 147
House of International Fragrances, 147
J.W. Chunn Perfumes, 148
KSA Jojoba, 148
Michel Swiss, 149
Phar-Mor, 487
Tuli-Latus Perfumes Ltd., 149
Valray International, Inc., 150
Vickie-Bee Perfumes, 150
World of Beauty, 151
Wynnewood Pharmacy, 151

Crystal

A. Benjamin & Co., 120
A.B. Schou, 120
Albert S. Smyth Co., Inc., 121
Ben Morris Jewelry Co., 122
Chinacraft of London, 122
China Warehouse, The, 123
Irish Crystal Company, 485
Kippen Group, The, 126
Locator's, Incorporated, 126
Messina Glass & China Co., 127
Michael C. Fina, 127
Patterns Unlimited, 128
Robin Importers, 130
Ross-Simons of Warwick, 131
Saxkjaers, 131
SGF, 132
Shannon Mail Order, 132
Stephen Faller (exports) Ltd., 133

Electronics

All Electronics Corporation, 136

Allied Business Machine Systems, 345
Best Products Co., 118
Bondy Export Corp., 61
Commercial Office Products, 348
Comp-U-Card, 62
Computer Plus, 137
Crutchfield, 414
Elek-Tek, 137
Executive Photo and Supply Corp., 99
47th St. Photo, 100
Heathkit Electronic Center, 308
International Solgo, Inc., 64
J & R Music World, 415
Jerryco, Inc., 422
Jersey Camera, 101
Jilor Discounts, 350
LVT Price Quote Hotline, 65
McKilligan Industrial and Supply Corp., 250
Olden Camera, 102
Olympic Sales, 352
Pan American Electronics, Inc., 139
Phone Control Systems, 139
S & S Sound City, 417
Saverite Photo & Electronics, 103
Service Merchandise Catalog Showrooms, 118
Typex Business Machines Inc., 355

Fabric (Apparel) and Yarns
Albany Woolen Mill, 153
All American Fabrics, 153
Bee Lee Co., 154
Bemidji Woolen Mills, 21
Britex-By-Mail, 154
Buffalo Batt & Felt Corp., 155
Cambridge Wools, Ltd., 155
Carolina Mills Factory Outlet, 155
Clearbrook Woolen Shop, 156
D. MacGillivray & Coy, 156
Gohn Bros., 48
Harry Zarin Co., 157
Home Fabric Mills, Inc., 157
Intercoastal Textile Corp., 158
Intertwine Yarn & Fiber Supply, 158
Jay's Yarns, 159
Knight's, 159
Mary Jo's Cloth Store, Inc., 160
Newark Dressmaker Supply, 160
Romni Wools and Fibres, 161

Stavros Kouyoumoutzakis, 162
Testfabrics Inc., 162
Thai Silks, 163
Triblend Mills, 163
Utex Trading Enterprises, 164
Way Station Fabric Stop, 164
Wonder Craft, 165
Woolrich Store, The, 165
Yarn Barn, 165
Zamart Inc., 166

Fabric—Upholstery
Barnes & Barnes, 213
Nite Furniture Co., 220
Paint & Pattern, 456
Priba Furniture, 222
Shama Imports, Inc., 161
Utility Craft, Inc., 227

Financial Matters
Alliance Capital Reserves, 286
Banque Ankerfina SA, 287
Brown & Co., 281
Charles Schwab & Co., Inc., 281
Discount Brokerage Corp., 281
Dreyfus Liquid Assets & Dreyfus Group, 286
Fidelity Brokerage Service, Inc., 282
Fidelity Daily Income, 286
Financial Programs, 286
Foreign Commerce Bank, 287
Kennedy, Cabot & Co., 282
Muriel Siebert & Co., Inc., 283
Olde Discount Stockbrokers, 283
Ovest Securities, Inc., 283
Penn Square, 286
Permanent Portfolio Funds, 286
Quick & Reilly, Inc., 284
Rose & Co. Investment Brokers, Inc., 284
Royal, Grimm and Davis, Inc., 284
Scudder Fund Distributing, Inc., 286
Texas Securities, 285
T. Rowe Price, 286
Ueberseebank AG Zurich, 287
Vanguard Group, 286

Fireworks
Ace Fireworks, 335
B.J. Alan, 336

Food

Ace Pecan Co., 185
Amishman, The, 185
Arizona Champagne Sauces, 186
Brewmaster, 300
Cache Valley Dairy Assn., 186
Caviarteria, 187
Charles Loeb, 187
Cheeselovers International, 188
Cheeses of All Nations, 188
Colonel Bill Newsom's, 189
E.C. Kraus, 303
Grace Tea Company, Ltd., 189
Ideal Cheese Shop, 190
Jaffe Bros., 190
Kolb-Lena Cheese Company, 190
Le Gourmand, 191
Lynn Dairy, 191
Manganaro Foods, 192
Mexican Chile Supply, 192
Mexican Kitchen, The, 193
Milan Laboratory, 311
Moravian Sugar Crisp Co., Inc., 193
Paprikas Weiss Importer, 194, 243
San Francisco Herb Co., 194
S.A.V.E., 195
Schapira Coffee Company, 195
Simpson & Vail, Inc., 195
Sugarbush Farm, 196
Sultan's Delight, Inc., 196
Texas Rose Coffee & Tea, 197
Wilbur Chocolate Candy Outlet, 197
Zabar's, 198

Furniture and Lamps

A Brass Bed Shoppe, 211
Annex Furniture Galleries, 211
Arise Futon Mattress Co., 211
Arts By Alexander's, 212
Barnes & Barnes, 213
Bartley Collections, The, 300
Blackwelder's, 213
Boyles Furniture Sales, 214
Cherry Hill Furniture, Carpet & Interiors, 214
Colonial Woodcraft, 302
Electropedic Adjustable Beds, 85
Emperor Clock Co., 304
Factory Direct Table Pad Co., Inc., 215
Fran's Basket House, 215

Furniture Barn of Forest City, Inc., 216
Hendricks Furniture, Inc., 217
Hudson Glass Co., Inc., 310
James Roy Inc., 217
King's Chandelier Co., 218
Kuempel Chime Clock Works, 310
L'Ambiance Furniture, 218
Lamp Warehouse/NY Ceiling Fan Center, 219
Loftin-Black Furniture Co., 219
Mallory's, 219
Murrow Furniture Galleries, 220
Nite Furniture Co., 220
North Carolina Furniture Showrooms, 221
Penny Wise Warehouse Stores, 87
Plexi-Craft Quality Products, 221
Priba Furniture, 222
Quality Furniture Market of Lenoir, Inc., 222
Ram Furniture Gallery, Inc., The, 223
Rose Furniture Co., 223
Sandman, 224
Shaw Furniture Galleries, 224
Slipcovers of America, 225
Sobol House, 225
Star Route Hammocks, 226
Stuckey Bros. Furniture Co., Inc., 226
Turner-Tolson, Inc., 227
Utility Craft, Inc., 227
Varner Warehouse Sales Inc., 228
Wayside Interiors, 228
Wood-Armfield Furniture, 229
Young's Furniture and Rug Co., 229
Zamart for Kids, 230, 438
Zarbin and Assoc., Inc., 230

Gifts and Stationery

Allen's Shell-A-Rama, 238
American Stationery Co., Inc., 345
Comfortably Yours™, 239
Current, 337
Good Shepherd's Store, 71
Handart Embroideries, 274
Letter Box, 342
Lillian Vernon, 276
Lincoln House, 342
Long Distance Roses, 373
O'Connor's Yankee Peddler Warehouse Sale, 54

Shannon Mail Order, 132
Spencer Gifts, Inc., 343
Stationery House Inc., The, 355

Government Publications
Consumer Education Research
    Center, 240
Consumer Information Catalog,
    202
Consumers Guide to Home Repair
    Grants & Loans, 240
Office of Metric Programs, 206
U.S. Department of Education,
    208

Handbags and Luggage
Ace Leather Products, 232
Al's Luggage, 233
A to Z Luggage, 232
Ber Sel Handbags, 233
Bettingers Luggage, 233
Carole Block Ltd., 234
Carry On Luggage, 234
Creative House, 235
Deerskin Place, The, 36
Fine & Klein, 235, 388
Gerry Sharp, Trunk Doctor, 305
Hicks USA, 236
Travel Auto Bag Co., 236

Hardware and Tools
Arctic Glass & Millwork Company,
    246
Bailey's, Inc., 246
Bevers, The, 247
Bowden Wholesale Co., 247
Camelot Enterprises, 248
Central Michigan Tractor and
    Parts, 368
Continental Lawn Mower
    Manufacturing Co., 248
C.U. Restoration Supplies, 249
Gilliom Manufacturing Inc., 249
Leichtung "Handys," 249
Manufacturer's Supply, 115
Master Mechanic Manufacturing
    Co., 250
McKilligan Industrial and Supply
    Corp., 250
R.B. Mason Company, 251
Renovator's Supply—5503, 252
Safe Equipment Co., Inc., 252

Tool Importers Warehouse Sale,
    253
Turn-O-Carve Tool Co., 315
U.S. General Tool & Hardware,
    253
World Abrasive Co., 254
Zip-Penn Inc., 254

Hobbies and Crafts
America's Hobby Center, Inc., 256
Babouris Handicrafts, 21, 256
Bell Yarn/Wonoco Yarn, 256
Berman Leathercraft, 257
Boycan's Craft & Art Supply, 257
Cane and Basket Supply Co., 301
Cherry Tree Toys, Inc., 257, 302,
    436
Clotilde, 258
Columbus Clay Company, 258
Country Handcrafts Magazine,
    259
Craftsman Wood, 259
Craftways Corporation, 259
Cross Creek, 260
Deepak's Rokjemperl Products,
    260
Ginger Schlote, 261
Glorybee Bee Box, Inc., 261
Goodfellow Catalog of Wonderful
    Things, The, 262
Grieger's, Inc., 262
Hobby Shack, 263
Hobby Surplus Sales, 263
Holcraft Co., 264
H.O.M.E. Craft Catalog, The, 264
Lamrite's, 265
LHL Enterprises, 265
McKilligan Industrial and Supply
    Corp., 250
Meisel Hardware Specialties, 266
New England Frameworks, 266
Potter's Shop, The, 267
Sonshine Crafts, 267
Splendor in the Glass, 267
Squadron Mail Order, 268
Susan of Newport, 268
Veteran Leather Co., 269

Homes
Green River Trading Co., 72, 307
Miles Homes, 312
Tri-Steel Structures, Inc., 314
Wilderness Log Homes, 315

Housewares

A Cook's Wares, 271
Alexander Butcher Block and
    Supply Co., 271
Chef's Catalog, The, 272
Clothcrafters, 272
Collinsworth, 273
Fivenson Food Equipment, Inc.,
    273
Grand Finale, 274, 488
Handart Embroideries, 274
Imoco Inc., 275
Kitchen Bazaar, 275
Kitchen Collection, 488
Lillian Vernon, 276
Lionel Enterprises, 175
MAK Inc., 276
Monsanto Engineered Products,
    277
Paprikas Weiss Importer, 194, 243
Paris Bread Pans, 277
Pfaltzgraff Pfactory Outlet, 278,
    489
Plastic Bag Mart, 278
Weston Bowl Mill, 278

Jewelry

ADCO Company, 289
Anka Co., 420
Batikat, 289
Ben Morris Jewelry Co., 122
Best Products Co., 118
B.M.I., 290
Boulle, Inc., 290
Butterflies & Rainbow, Inc., 291
Crown Cultured Pearl Corp., 291
Empire Diamond Corp., 292
Gold N Stones, 293
House of Onyx, 293
International Import Company,
    294
Marcus & Co., 294
Rama Jewelry Ltd., 294
R/E Kane Enterprises, 295
Rennie Ellen, 295
Richard Yerxa Jewelry & Silver,
    129
Samarth Gem Stones, 296
Service Merchandise Catalog
    Showrooms, 118
SGF, 132
Swiss Konnection, The, 57, 296
Vanity Fair, 297
Van Moppes Diamonds, 297

Van Pler & Tissany, 298

Kits

Bartley Collection, The, 300
Brewmaster, 300
Burro, 301
Cane and Basket Supply Co., 301
Cherry Tree Toys, Inc., 257, 302,
    436
Clothkits, 22, 302, 436
Colonial Woodcraft, 280
Constantine's, 303
E.C. Kraus, 303
Emperor Clock Co., 304
Four Seasons Greenhouses, 304
Frostline Kits, 304
Gerry Sharp, Trunk Doctor, 305
Gettinger Feather Corp., 305
Go Cart, 306
Golf Day Products, Inc., 306
Green Pepper, The, 306
Green River Trading Co., 72, 307
H. DeCovnick & Son, 307
Heathkit Electronic Center, 308
Heritage Clock Co., 308
Herrschners Inc., 309
Hollywood Fancy Feather Co., 309
Hudson Glass Co., Inc., 310
Ident-Ify Label Corp., 310
Kuempel Chime Clock Works, 310
Luger Boats, 311
Milan Laboratory, 311
Miles Homes, 312
Pyramid Products, 312
Rollerwall, Inc., 312
St. Croix Kits, 313
Texas Greenhouse Co., 313
Toymaker Supply, Co., The, 314,
    438
Tri-Steel Structures, Inc., 314
Turn-O-Carve Tool Co., 315
Viking Clock Division, 315
Wilderness Log Homes, 315

Medical Products

American Health Service, Inc., 318
Bruce Medical Supply, 319
Comfortably Yours,™ 239
Conney Safety Products, 319
Creative Health Products, 169, 320
Duk Kwong Optical Center, 320
Lingerie For Less, 321
Majestic Drug Co., Inc., 321
National Contact Lens Center, 322

Paragon Medical Products, 322
Ric Clark, 323
Rite-Way Hearing Aid Co., 323
Royal Optical, 489
U.S. Optics, 244
Vitamin Specialities Co., 182

Motorcycles
Capital Cycle Corp., 111
Clinton Cycle & Salvage, Inc., 112
Karzundpartz, 115

Musical Instruments
A.L.A.S. Accordion-O-Rama, 326
Carvin, 326
Fred's String Warehouse, 327
Freeport Music, 327
Jazz Aids, 328
Mandolin Bros., 328
Mogish String Company, 329
National Music Supply, 329
NEMC, 330
Player's Music, U.S.A., 330
P.M.I., 331
Rhythm Band, Inc., 331
Sam Ash Music Corp., 332
Shar Products Company, 332
Woodwind, The/The Brasswind,
    333

Natural Foods
Fox River Naturals, 170
High Meadow Farm, 172

Novelties
Ace Fireworks, 335
Archie McPhee & Company, 335
Bits & Pieces: The Great
    International Puzzle Collection,
    335
B.J. Alan, 336
Carriage Trade Creations, 337
Dazian, Inc., 338
Fair & Square, 338, 437
Front Row Photos, 339
Good 'N' Lucky Promotions, 339
Into the Wind, 340
Johnson Smith Co., 340
Juggling Arts, The, 241
La Pinata, 341
Laurence Corner, 341
Left Hand Center, 242

Paradise Products, 343
Southpaw Shoppe, The, 244
Spencer Gifts, Inc., 343

**Office Equipment, Supplies,
and Services**
Allied Business Machine Systems,
    345
American Stationery Co., Inc.,
    The, 345
Amity Hallmark Ltd., 345
B & I Furniture Co., 346
Best Products Co., 118
Business Envelope Manufacturers,
    346
Buy Direct, Inc., 347
Colwell Business Products, 347
Commercial Office Products, 348
ESC Envelope Sales Co., 348
Fidelity Products Co., 349
47th St. Photo, 100
Frank Eastern Co., 349
Jilor Discounts, 350
L & D Press, 351
Landmark Specialties, Inc., 350
National Business Furniture, Inc.,
    351
NEBS, 352
Olden Camera, 102
Olympic Sales, 352
Pearl Brothers Typewriters, 353
Quill® Corporation, 353
Rochester 100, Inc., 354
Service Merchandise Catalog
    Showrooms, 118
Stationery House Inc., The, 355
Thrifty Prints, Inc., 355
Typex Business Machines Inc., 355
Windfall Mailing Lists, 356
Wolff Office Equipment, 356

**Plants, Flowers,
Gardens, and Farming**
Bio-Control, 365
Bluestone Perennials, Inc., 365
Brookfield Nursery & Tree
    Plantation, 366
Butterbrooke Farm, 367
Caprilands Herb Farm, 367
Central Michigan Tractor and
    Parts, 368
Continental Lawn Mower
    Manufacturing Co., 248

· Country Hills Greenhouse, 368
Countryside Herb Farm, 368
Dairy Association Company, Inc.,
    369
Dutch Gardens, 369
Flickinger's Nursery, 370
Four Seasons Greenhouse, 304
Frans Roozen, 370
Fred's Plant Farm, 370
Glass House Works Catalog, 241
Gurney's Seed & Nursery Co., 371
Hickory Hill Nursery, 371
Hoffman Hatchery, Inc., 372
J.E. Miller Nurseries, Inc., 372
Long Distance Roses, 373
Noweta Gardens, 373
Pony Creek Nursery, 373
Prentiss Court Ground Covers, 374
Rainbow Gardens, 374
Reich Poultry Farms, Inc., 375
Royal Gardens, 375
Smallholding Supplies, 376
Smith & Hawken, 376
Texas Greenhouse Co., 313

Records, Tapes, and Videos

Andre Perrault, 379
CRI Composers Recordings, Inc.,
    379
Cultural Guild, The, 380
Double Time Jazz Records, 380
Effective Learning Systems, 169
Harmonia Mundi—USA, 380
House Distributors, 381
Record Hunter, The, 382
Rococco Records Ltd., 382
Rose Records, 382
SyberVision Systems, 180

Sewing Machines

S & S Discount Service, 67
Sewin' in Vermont, 66

Silver

A. Benjamin & Co., 120
American Archives, 121
Ben Morris Jewelry Co., 122
China Warehouse, The, 123
Greater New York Trading Co., 125
Jean's Silversmiths, 125
Locator's, Incorporated, 126
Michael C. Fina, 127
Patterns Unlimited, 128
Richard Yerxa Jewelry and Silver,
    129
Rogers & Rosenthal, 130
SGF, 132
Stecher's, 132
Sterling & China, Ltd., 133
Walter Drake Silver Exchange, 134

**Sporting Goods—
Camping and Outdoors**

Bass Pro Shops, 394
Bowhunters Discount Warehouse,
    395
Cabela's, 396
Campmor, 396
Folks on Buck Hill, 399
Frostline Kits, 304
Functional Clothing, Ltd., 400
Great Lakes Sportswear, 401
Green Pepper, The, 306
Kirkham's Outdoor Products, 402
New England Divers Inc., 404
Reed Tackle, 405
REI Co-op, 406
Shotgun News, The, 407
Sports Hut, 408
Stephensons Warmlite Equipment,
    408
Strand Surplus Senter, 31
Uncle Dan's Ltd., 424
Weiss and Mahoney, 425

Sporting Goods—General

Allyn Air Seat Co., 393
Austad's, 393
Bart's Water Ski Center, 394
Best Products Co., 118
Bike Nashbar, 395
California Cargo, 168, 386
Carlsen Import Shoes, 387, 396
Custom Golf Clubs, Inc., 397
Cycle Goods Corp., 397
Eisner Bros., 398
F & M Sports Outlet, 399
Finals, The, 25, 170
Golf and Tennis World, 400
Golf Day Products, Inc., 306
Golf Haus, 401
Healthtrax International, 171
Hill's Court, 402
Holabird Sports Discounters, 402
Las Vegas Discount Golf &
    Tennnis, 403

Lombard's Sporting Goods, 403
Mail Runners Shop, The, 175
Moss Brown & Company, Inc., 176
Pro Shop World of Golf, 404
Rayco Tennis Products, 405
Road Runner Sports, 391, 406
Service Merchandise Catalog
    Showrooms, 118
Skate Stop, 407
Soccer International, Inc., 407
Stuyvesant Bicycle, 409
Super Strength Systems, 180
TBC, 410
Telepro Golf Shop, 410
Trampolking Sporting Goods, 181
Vienna Health Products, 182
Wide World of Sporting Goods, 411

Stereo and Video

Annex Outlet Ltd., 413
Audio Advisor, Inc., 413
Best Products Co., 118
California Sound, 413
Comp-U-Card, 62
Crutchfield, 414
CSC Marketing, Inc., 415
Dial-A-Brand, 62
EBA Wholesale, 63
Focus Electronics, 99
47th St. Photo, 100
Heathkit Electronic Center, 308
Hunter Audio-Photo Ltd., 63
International Solgo, Inc., 64
J & R Music World, 415
Jersey Camera, 101
LVT Price Quote Hotline, 64
Lyle Cartridges, 416
McAlisters, Inc., 416
Olden Cemera, 102
S & S Sound City, 417
Saverite Photo & Electronics, 103
Service Merchandise Catalog
    Showrooms, 118
Sound Reproduction, Inc., 417
Universal Suppliers, 425

Surplus and Volume

America's Best, 420
Anka Co., 420
Base Exchange, The, 421
Blair, 421
Jerryco, Inc., 422
Laurence Corner, 341

Mass. Army and Navy Store, 422
RSP Distributing Co., 423
Ruvel, 423
Strand Surplus Senter, 31
Surplus Center, The, 424
Uncle Dan's Ltd., 424
Weiss and Mahoney, 425

Telephone Services

ADDS Telemarketing, 428
MCI Telecommunications Corp.,
    428
SBS Skyline, 429
US Sprint Communications, 429
U.S. Transmissions Systems, 430

Tobacco

Famous Smoke Shop, 432
Fred Stoker and Sons, 432
Hayim Pinhas, 433
J-R Tobacco Co., 484
Nurhan Cevahir, 434

Toys

Cherry Tree Toys, Inc., 257, 302,
    436
Clothkits, 22, 302, 436
Dinosaur Catalog, 436
Dollsville Dolls and Bearsville
    Bears, 437
Fair & Square, 338, 437
Toy Balloon Corp., 437
Toymaker Supply Co., The, 314,
    438
Zamart for Kids, 230, 438

Travel

American Youth Hostels, Inc., 440
Bent Tree Travel, 440
Bike Vermont, Inc., 441
Council on International
    Educational Exchange (CIEE),
    442
Coupon Broker, The, 443
East Woods Press, The, 443
Elkin Travel Inc./Cruises Only!,
    444
Entertainment Publications, 444
Evergreen Bed & Breakfast Club,
    The, 445
Ford's Freighter Guide, 445
Guide to the Guides (Europe), 446

Jess Miller Publishing Co., 446
Relocation Research, 446
Stand-Buys Ltd., 447
Tanglepoint Travel, Inc., 448
Travel Companion Exchange, Inc.,
    448
Urban Ventures, Inc., 448
Worldwide Discount Travel Club,
    449
Y's Way, The, 450

Trophies
Dinn Bros., 398
Trophyland USA, Inc., 410

Vacuums
AAA All Factory Vacuum, Floor
    Care & Ceiling Fans, 60
ABC Vacuum Warehouse, 60
LVT Price Quote Hotline, 64
Pine Cone, The, 65

Veterinary Supplies and Animals
AVP (Animal Veterinary Products,
    Inc.), 359
Echo Products, 359
Hoffman Hatchery, 372
Kennel Vet Corporation, The, 360
Northern Wholesale Veterinary
    Supply, 360
Omaha Vaccine Company, 361
Petco Animal Supplies, 361
Reich Poultry Farms, 375
Tomahawk Live Trap Co., 362
United Pharmacal Co., Inc., 362
Wholesale Veterinary Supply, Inc.,
    The, 363

**Vitamins and
Pharmaceutical Products**
America's Pharmacy Service, Inc.,
    318
Barth's, 168
Freeda Vitamins,® 171
Hudson Vitamins, 172
L & H Vitamins, 174
Mega Food, 176
Nutrition Headquarters, 177
Star Professional Pharmaceuticals,
    Inc., 178
Stur-Dee Health Products, 179
Sunburst Biorganics, 179

Vitamin Specialities, 182
Western Natural Products, 183
Years to Your Health, 183

Wallcoverings
Alexander Wallpaper, 453
American Discount Wallcoverings,
    453
Arts by Alexander's, 211
Best Bros. Paint & Wallpaper
    Outlet, 454
Harmony Supply Inc., 455
Interiors by Sanz, 456
Nite Furniture, 220
Paint & Pattern, 456
Priba Furniture, 222
Robinson's Wallcoverings, 457
Rollerwall, Inc., 312
Shibui Wallcoverings, 458
Silver Wallcoverings, Inc., 458
Wallpaper Now, 459
Wells Interiors, Inc., 459

Watches
Best Products Co., 118
47th St. Photo, 100
Hunter Audio-Photo Ltd., 63
International Solgo, Inc., 64
Marcus & Co., 294
Ross-Simons of Warwick, 131
Service Merchandise Catalog
    Showrooms, 118
T.M. Chan & Co., 104
Universal Suppliers, 425

Window Shades
Blind Spot, The, 454
Paint & Pattern, 456
Priba Furniture, 222
Ronnie Draperies, 457

WEARABLES
Accessories
Beitman Co., Inc., 239
Deerskin Place, The, 36
Fine & Klein, 235, 388
Utex Trading Enterprises, 164

Children's Apparel
Cotton Dreams, 18
Natan Borlam Co., Inc., 18
7th Heaven, 18
Young Idea Ltd., The, 19
Zamart for Kids, 230, 438

Family Apparel
Apparel America, 471
Clothkits, 22, 302, 436
Deva Cottage Industry, 24
Eisner Bros., 398
Gohn Bros., 48
Great Lakes Sportswear, 401
Howron Sportswear, 26
I. Tuschman & Sons, Inc., 27
Land's End, 20, 27
Laurence Corner, 341
L.L. Bean, 174
Melnikoff's Department Store, 28
Pagano Gloves, 28
Prince Fashions Ltd., 471
Rammagerdin of Reykjavik, 29
Red Flannel Factory, 30, 469
Sock Shop, 30
Strand Surplus Senter, 31
V. Juul Christensen & Son, 58
Waco Thrift Store Inc., 31
Wear-Guard Corporation, 32
Workmen's Garment Co., 32
W.S. Robertson (Outfitters) Ltd.,
    33, 58

**Lingerie, Hosiery, and
Underwear**
Chock Catalog Corp., 22
Damart, 35
D & A Merchandise Co., Inc., 23
Gohn Bros., 48
Goldman & Cohen, 48
Howron Sportswear, 26
I. Tuschman & Sons, Inc., 27
Lady Annabelle, 50
L'Eggs Showcase of Savings, 50,
    173
Leotards by Leticia, 173
Linda's Hosiery Outlet, Inc., 51
Mayfield Co. Inc., 52
Mendel Weiss Inc., 52, 322
National Wholesale Co., Inc., 54
Raymond Sultan & Sons, Ltd., 54
Roby's Intimates, 55, 177
Royal Silk, 56

Red Flannel Factory, The, 30, 469
RSL, 56
Sweetwater Hosiery Mills, 57
Taffy's-By-Mail, 181

Maternity Wear
Dan Howard Maternity Outlet, 478
Mothers Work, 53
Reborn Maternity, 55

Menswear
A. Rubinstein and Son, 35
Banana Republic, 238
Damon Factory Outlet, 36
Dorsett Distributing Co., 37
Factory Wholesalers, 37
G & G Projections, 38
Gelber's Men's Store, 38
Harry Rothman, Inc., 73
Harvard Trouser Company, 26
Huntington Clothiers, 39
John Mabry Menswear, 40
Jos. A. Bank Clothiers, 40, 465
King Size Company, The, 41
Lee-McClain Co., Inc., 41
Master Fashions, 42
Royal Silk, 56
Saint Laurie Ltd., 42
Stanley M. Mirsky, 43
Sussex Clothes Ltd., 43

Shoes
A.W. Gotten, 385
Barett Shoes, 491
Blum's, 386
Best Choice, The, 385
Boot Town, 386
California Cargo, 168, 386
Carlsen Import Shoes, 387, 397
Carr's, 387, 491
Chernin's Shoes, 388
Dorsett Distributing Co., 37
Fine & Klein, 235, 388
Hill Brothers, 388
Just Justin Take Out Boots, 389
J.W. Bray, 389
Mail Runners Shop, The, 175
Nelson's, 390
Orchard Street Bootery, 390
PL Premium Leather by Hanover,
    391
Road Runner Sports, 391, 406
RSL, 56

Taffy's-By-Mail, 181

Sweaters and Outerwear
Arthur M. Rein, 46
Babouris Handicrafts, 21, 256
Bemidji Woolen Mills, 21
Clothkits, 22, 302, 436
Custom Coat Co., Inc., 23
Deerskin Place, The, 36
Down Generation/Sylvia & Sons, 24
Edinburgh Woollen Mill, Ltd., 25
F.R. Knitting Mills, Inc., 47
Frostline Kits, 304
Green Pepper, The, 306
Harvard Trouser Company, 26
Icemart, The, 49
Irish Cottage Industries, 49
Kennedy's of Ardara, 49
Ms., Miss, and Mrs., 53
Prince Fashions Ltd., 29
Rammagerdin of Reyjavik, 29
Royal Silk, 56
RSL, 56
Swiss Konnection, The, 57, 296

V. Juul Christensen & Son, 58
Workmen's Garment Co., 32
W.S. Robertson (Outfitters) Ltd., 33, 58

Women's Apparel
Arthur M. Rein, 46
Career Guild, 46
Chadwick's of Boston, Ltd., 47
Dan Howard Maternity Outlets, 478
Lane Bryant, 50
Loft Designer Sportswear, The, 51
Mothers Work, 53
Ms., Miss, and Mrs., 53
O'Connor's Yankee Peddler Warehouse Sale, 54
Reborn Maternity, 55
Royal Silk, 56
RSL, 56
Saint Laurie, Ltd., 42
Sampson and Delilah, 178
Swiss Konnection, The, 57, 296
Taffy's-By-Mail, 181
W.S. Robertson (Outfitters) Ltd., 33, 58

READER'S FEEDBACK

1. Overall, I thought the book was _____ excellent _____ good _____ fair _____ poor.
2. I would like to see more listings in the following categories:

   a. _____ d. _____

   b. _____ e. _____

   c. _____ f. _____

   I would also like to see discount mail-order sources for the following lines or labels _____

3. I _____ (liked) _____ (didn't like) the way the book was organized.
4. I have bought merchandise from the following stores listed in your book and would rate them as (excellent, good, fair, poor):

   a. _____ rating _____ response time _____

   b. _____ rating _____ response time _____

   c. _____ rating _____ response time _____

5. I have had a problem with _____ . (Please describe.)

   _____ .

6. I have had an interesting, funny, unusual experience dealing with one of the listings. (Describe.) _____

   _____ .

7. Some good overseas bargain stores are _____

_____ .

8. I think the most important categories are: _____

_____ .

9. Your book saved me $_____ on a purchase of $_____

bought from _____ .

10. I will recommend *The Underground Shopper* to my friends.

Yes _____   No _____

IT'S CHIC TO BE CHEAP (and fun to be an *Underground Shopper*)! Help spread the word about discount mail-order shopping. Share your finds with our staff so we can include them in our next edition. We need your leads!

Thanks.

You need to check out: _____

_____

_____

Your name _____

Address _____

City, State _____ Zip _____

Phone (include your area code) _____

Mail your responses to: Feedback
                        The Shopper
                        P.O. Box 277
                        Argyle, TX 76226-0277